Book Division, The Hearst Corporation
New York, N.Y. 10019

Popular Mechanics Book of Bikes and Bicycling

By Dick Teresi

Book Division, The Hearst Corporation,
New York, N.Y. 10019

© 1975, The Hearst Corporation
All rights reserved.
No part of the text or illustrations in this work may be
used without written permission by The Hearst Corporation.

Many of the technical drawings that are reproduced here are the property of Xyzyx Information Corporation, and originally appeared in their two copyrighted books, *Derailleur Bicycle Repair* and *Coaster & 3-Speed Bicycle Repair*. These books thoroughly cover the major repairs that can be made to various types of bikes, and are small enough to be packed into any biker's touring kit. They are available from Xyzyx Information Corporation, 2116 Vanowen St., Canoga Park, Calif. 91303.

Neither The Hearst Corporation nor Xyzyx Information Corporation can assume any responsibility for the misuse of any of the line drawings or photographs showing the maintenance and repair of bicycles.

This book couldn't have been completed without the help of Henry Wolk, Helen Scott and especially Hostile Woman, her band of library marauders and 2200 notecards. Special thanks goes to Jackie Simes, Thomas Avenia and Lou Maltese for letting me pick their brains. Thanks also to Alvin Fernald, who took all the heat, and Carlo, Simon and Jimmy D. who got us off to England in time. No thanks goes to the guy who ran me over the curb down on Wall Street last summer.

Printed in The United States of America
ISBN 0-910990-56-5

Contents

Introduction

ONCE I PLAYED on a baseball team where the coach had three rules: You had to stand close to the plate when batting (or else you couldn't hit the outside pitch, he said). You had to hold the bat as close to horizontal as possible (to give you a level swing, he said). And you were never ever allowed to move your lead foot toward third base when swinging (the coach never explained why not). Well, we won more games than we lost and we figured maybe Coach knew what he was doing.

Then one day the coach took us to a big league game. This new guy came to bat. The coach snickered. The new guy stood a mile away from the plate. He held the bat straight up and down. And when he swung at the first pitch his foot ended up pointing directly at the third baseman. On the other hand, the ball ended up in the right-centerfield bleachers.

"Beginner's luck," muttered the coach.

Well, that rookie was Roberto Clemente, who ended up hitting over .300 almost every year he played. And ain't that the way it always goes? Most of us follow the rules, and then some guy comes along, sneers, and makes us all look silly. So much for advice.

This is a book full of advice. Lots of it. I honestly feel that most of it will help you through the tasks of buying and repairing a bicycle, and will make touring, camping, racing or just plain riding more fun. But there are times when you'll say to yourself, "Oh hell, I just don't want to do it *that way!*"

So do it your way.

Despite the millions of cyclists now on the road, riding a bike is still an individualistic thing. I hope you will find some guidance here, but remember that after you're through with all the business about frames and wheels, nuts and bolts, brands and models, what's really important is that you ride your bike *in your own way . . . and that you have fun.*

Speaking of brands, it's impossible, really, to give advice on what to buy without mentioning specific companies and making judgments, implied or otherwise, on their products. There are many good bike products which are not illustrated or mentioned here, which is not to put them down—there just wasn't room. Also understand that the mere fact a bike, a bike bag or a derailleur is pictured here does not mean *Popular Mechanics* endorses it.

Mostly I've tried to present the facts and alternatives as I see them. And whether you follow my advice or not, I wish you good pedaling.

D.T.

Chapter 1

Section 1: Your bike and how to buy it

Buying your bike

Beware. Shopping for your bike can be fun, but if you don't know what you're doing you can make some horrendous mistakes. This chapter points out a few of the pitfalls, explodes the 10-speed myth, tells what makes a good bike good, laments the demise of the three-speed, and discusses foreign vs. domestic models.

I CAN'T THINK of many things more fun to buy than a bike. Lots of good ones are available, they're all pretty cheap (compared to cars and other less interesting vehicles) and they last a long time—maybe forever if you choose wisely. But in today's complex bike world, finding the right bike is a little more complicated than it was when you were a kid—when all you had to choose was the red one or the green one.

There are so many thousand bikes to consider that you should know a few things before dumping your wad into the pocket of the nearest bike seller. Added to this is the fact that the bike world is full of myths, misconceptions, bad advice and downright lies.

Let's try to sort through the mass of details and myths with as little pain as possible, so you can venture out into the bicycle marketplace armed with enough facts to come home riding the set of wheels that's best for you. Take comfort in the fact that as a potential bike buyer you probably already have more common sense than other consumers even if you know very little about bikes. Most bike buyers at least ask one obvious question: "Are you sure it's not too big for me?" It's too bad we can't say the same about car buyers.

But there's much more to know; the first is what the market is like today.

Punching them out like cookies

THE INCREDIBLE VARIETY of bikes you can choose from spells good news and bad news: good because this means a lot of great models, bad because it also means a lot of lemons. Whenever I stroll through one of the less discriminating shops so common today, I get the feeling that some manufacturers must be great fans of P. T.

Barnum, who uttered the immortal words, "Never give a sucker an even break." I'm not saying that every bike manufacturer is trying to cheat the public. Let's just say that serving the consumer places a poor second to making a buck in some manufacturers' hierarchy of values.

And this attitude, at the time of a bike boom, can create pitfalls for the consumer. To illustrate, let's take a look at some figures supplied by the Bicycle Institute of America. In 1960 the number of bikes sold in the U.S. (including imports) totaled 3.7 million. Ten years later in 1970 that number had jumped to 6.9 million. In other words, in one decade sales had almost doubled. Although this was a sizeable increase, it came steadily over a ten-year span. Bike companies had ample time to adjust production to meet the demand.

Then all hell broke loose.

For some crazy reason, Americans started returning to two wheels by the zillions. *By 1972 bikes were outselling cars!* Immediately, politicians warned of a dangerous moral decay sweeping the land. Preachers spoke out from the pulpit about the spiritual cancer corrupting their 10-speed-happy congregations. Car-wash managers threw up their arms in despair and bicycle-book writers began unloading their wares on an unsuspecting public.

But no one could turn back. The bike boom was here.

The problem was that it came so fast that the bike companies couldn't keep up with the demand. Orders far outclassed production in 1971; and in the car-surpassing landmark year of '72 the companies started catching up—they built and sold over 13 million bicycles. That means that in just two years, from 1970 to 1972, *sales just about doubled,* a percentage increase equal to the growth rate of the entire previous decade.

Neat hanging display in this shop shows off several makes and models.

Norwegian attaches derailleur cables to frames at the Jonas Oegland plant. Here's one maker that expanded without sacrificing quality.

Production continues to boom. Sales now hit close to the 15-million mark every year. And while that's a good sign, it can also mean big trouble for the buyer.

Most companies were caught with their chainguards down when the boom hit. Many have expanded their production facilities to cope with the demand, but many haven't. So how are they whipping out twice as many bikes per year as they did in 1970? Unfortunately, the secret is that they use the same factories they always used and just push the bikes through at twice the speed.

Some firms stamp bikes out like cookies, and as a result there are some slipshod machines on the market. Recently I browsed through one of the most prestigious bike shops in a major city. I saw a row of bikes from a well-known European builder that shocked me. These were bikes priced at $170 and up, and they were full of amateurish flaws that you might have expected on $60 cheapo models in years past. The component parts—brakes, shifters and such—were just as good as always. The frame tubing had not deteriorated. *It was the way everything was put together* that didn't live up to the manufacturer's earlier standards. This was especially evident around the lugs, the little sleeves that join the tubes at the joints in the frame. The brazing job looked like it had been done by a third-grade finger-painting class. It was so sloppy I could actually slip a fingernail between the spearpoint of the lug and the tubing, a flaw you shouldn't have to tolerate in a bike costing nearly $200.

I also noticed that the newest line of bikes of a popular imported brand featured cheaper chainwheels and spoke protectors than appeared on the same line a year earlier. The only feature that the manufacturer saw fit to improve was the price tag, which was higher by about $20.

The brazing job looked like it had been done by a third-grade finger-painting class. Check every bike for workmanship

An employee in a West Coast bike shop informs me that in the past year many moderately priced 10-speeds (in the $120 to $150 range) have been coming through with slightly bent forks—a condition the untrained buyer might not notice. In years before the boom, the employee says, major flaws in these brands were rarely found.

One importer has even been so crude (or honest) as to openly declare that it is impractical to sell bikes that are built to last more than two years. Unfortunately, his statement implies that the bicycle business has discovered the wonders of planned obsolescence.

Now, this is not to accuse the bike industry of programming flaws into its products. But the lesson is clear. Even if its intentions are good, no company can bash out twice as many bikes per year without a decline in quality unless it doubles factory facilities and workers (assuming craftsmen with the appropriate skills can be found). Bike companies have not expanded their facilities to the same extent that

One newcomer to the bike field is Alfieri Maserati, famed maker of racing cars. He knows what he's doing, too! Far right, stores that sell only bikes are usually the best places to shop.

they've upped production—and it shows. Compounding the problem is the fact that every little business (and some big ones, too) that has a machine shop has started pumping cheapo bikes into the market to rake in some extra coin.

So arm yourself with a few facts (and some opinions) before wandering out into the cold, cruel world of bicycles. The first thing to consider is . . .

Where to buy

BIKE SHOPS are obviously the best places. Not very surprising or original advice, you may say, but some people do make the mistake of buying at discount houses, department stores, gardening supply stores, even drugstores.

Bicycles are shipped to retailers unassembled in crates. How well they are put together at the store determines to a great extent how good a bike you get. Generally, discount houses, department stores and the like include bicycles in their toy departments—which indicates how seriously they regard bikes. Usually the assembly of bicycles is left to employees in the toy section or some other sort of general employee, not a competent bike mechanic. In many cases, the stores don't take care of their bikes. I've seen models with broken spokes, snapped cables, dented tubes and other problems.

In such stores you're liable to get a badly-put-together and possibly a damaged bike. Even should you luck out and get a perfectly assembled machine, don't ever bother taking it back to the discount joint for repairs because there's no repairman in existence. Also, drugstores and other non-bike retailers who go into bike selling as a sideline rarely carry spare parts. This means you will have to find a real

bike shop which carries the same brand when you need parts.

I recommend buying from a discount or other store *only if you have considerable experience working with bikes and can put one together by yourself*. Often in such stores you *can* save a few bucks, especially during the winter. I once saw a 22-pound, $300 Japanese bike with sew-up tires on sale in December for $150. The store obviously had no regard for its worth as it was sitting in a corner literally covered with dust. I'd guess they had ordered a few of these expensive bikes by mistake and got stuck with them; cyclists shopping for competition-grade bikes won't look for them in discount houses. So if you know bikes and are a bit of a mechanic, you might check out the discount shops for that occasional rare deal (regular bike shops will never discount a top-grade bike very much).

Genuine bicycle shops are usually better bets, although by no means are they guaranteed gateways to paradise. But they usually employ mechanics who can assemble your bike and can fix it when it falls apart (or at least make a good stab at it). They can help fit you to the right bike, attach the accessories you want and stand behind the machine's warranty. Some may even include a service contract with the purchase.

Sorting out bike types

MOST BIKE SHOPPERS already know the general difference between one-speeds, three-speeds and 10-speeds, but there are a few misconceptions flying around, especially about 10-speeds, so let's run through the types in a hurry.

A good shop to avoid is one that piles rental bikes atop each other. Buy here, and your new bike may be in lousy condition.

Left, if you know what you're doing you can search the discount houses for that occasional rare deal. This top-of-the-line Itoh was offered on sale in the toy department of a discount store for $150. Normally it would sell for at least $100 more. Most bike stores will not discount good makes very much. Right, recognize it? Here's the old coaster-brake bike that most of us prowled around on when we were kids. It still makes a good rough-road or beach bike, but it's too heavy for very long trips.

We're talking only about *adult* bikes here and we'll classify them into four groups: the one-speed coaster-brake (sometimes known as the good old "American" bike); internal-hub-geared bikes (better known as three-speeds); derailleur bikes (10-speeds and others); and fixed-wheels (track bikes).

• *Coaster-brake bikes.* This is the bike most of us grew up on. It is heavy, usually runs on balloon tires, and you brake it by slamming the pedals backwards. We kids always called it an "American" bike as opposed to the kind of bicycle everyone aspired to, which was the "English racer," more properly known as the . . .

• *Three-speed.* We'll use the term three-speed to refer to all bikes which have more than one gear and in which the gear-shifting mechanism is contained inside the rear hub. These are properly called internal-hub-geared bikes, or gearhubs, but three-speed is easier to say. This group also includes two- and five-speed bikes.

The hub shifter changes gears in a manner too complicated to explain here (or anywhere), but it's normally activated via a cable with controls on the handlebars—either a lever or a twist grip. Braking is accomplished usually through hand brakes, though some use the old coaster brake.

This kind of bike is still known to many of us as the English racer simply because the most common brands sold in the U.S. years ago were English-made. We called them racers because compared to the 50-pound American clunkers they seemed like racing bikes. Kids today who want to go fast sneer at the poor old three-speed. What they dream about are . . .

• *Derailleur bikes.* These are today's glamour machines, better known as 10-speeds. But actually, bikes which use a derailleur to shift gears include five-speeds, six-speeds, 12-speeds and 15-speeds as well. To the untrained eye these bikes look all the same, and are commonly lumped under the label 10-speed. We'll go along with this mistake since it's easier.

A five-speed has one chainwheel up front and a rear cluster of five sprockets. A derailleur (a French word meaning "to derail") lifts and/ or pushes the chain from one gear to another. (Derailleur is properly pronounced dee-RAY-yer, but no one will know what you're talking about if you say it that way; dee-RAIL-ler is good enough.)

A 10-speed has two chainwheels in addition to the five gears in the rear. A front derailleur, simpler in design than the rear derailleur, flips the chain back and forth as desired. These two gears in conjunction with the rear five give you 10 speeds ($2 \times 5 = 10$, right?).

A rarer bird is a six-speed bike which uses a rear cluster of six gears, a design sometimes incorporated into bikes raced in cyclo-cross competition (a race in which cyclists pedal not over roads but cross-country over hills, fields, creeks and other niceties).

A 12-speed obviously employs the same six-cog rear design along with a double chainwheel. Fifteen-speeds are identical to 10-speeds except they have a triple chainwheel. There are also three-speed derailleur bicycles and even 20-speeds (four chainwheels), but these birds are rare, rare, rare.

By far the most popular is the 10-speed. And this is where the confusion sets in. Technically, a 10-speed bike is nothing more than what its name implies—a bicycle with 10 gears. But most people envision something much more when they hear the phrase 10-speed. They see down-turned handlebars, hand brakes, a skinny saddle, skinny tires, no fenders and a lightweight frame. While most 10-speeds and other derailleur bikes fit this description, there's no law that says a 10-speed can't have flat handlebars, a big springy seat, fenders, etc.

• *Fixed-wheels.* These are often called track bikes because they're normally raced on a track. They have but one gear, but don't confuse them with the one-speed, coaster-brake bike. That one gear is fixed to the rear wheel; they have no freewheel, cannot coast and have no brakes. You just say "Whoa" to your legs when you want to slow down, like you did when you were riding a tricycle.

Saving money by watching out for traps

THE MAIN WAY people waste money on bicycles is by buying the wrong kind. Choosing the right *type* may be the most vital decision you will face. You may already have decided what you need. But do

*Here's a traditional 3-speed, girl's model: 1) Speed selector—
a twist grip changes gears; on some bikes selector is a lever.
2) Speed selector cable. 3) Tire. 4) Wheel. 5) Front hub. 6) Bottom
bracket. 7) Inset shows coaster brake. 8) Crank and chainwheel.
9) Pedal. 10) Chain. 11) 3-speed hub. 12) Speed selector indicator.*

yourself a favor and postpone your purchase until you look over the
next few pages on bike types. The kind of bike you currently think
you need may be dead wrong for you. Make a mistake like this and
you haven't just wasted 15 or 20 bucks, you've thrown away the
whole price of the bike.

Be forewarned that in the next few pages you are going to look at
the dark side of the bicycle world, at least at first. This is not meant
to turn you off, but to help you avoid some common traps that can
suck up your money.

Exploding the 10-speed myth

THE BICYCLE WORLD is a world of myths and there is no more carefully perpetrated myth than that of the 10-speed's superiority. For the average consumer, making a choice among the types of bikes available is simple because there is no choice; he wants a 10-speed. This is based on the firm conviction that the 10-speed is the best-made, fastest and meanest machine on the market.

Well it ain't necessarily so. To equate the 10-speed with quality in today's market would be a serious mistake, although at one time it did make some sense. Years ago, before the great bicycle explosion, 10-speeds were ridden only by serious cycling enthusiasts—and the 10-speeds they rode were of high quality (though not necessarily expensive). You didn't see many junky derailleur bikes because there was no market for them—most people didn't even know what a derailleur was. Cyclists who knew about 10-speeds wanted good ones; hence 10-speeds were synonymous with quality.

When the bike boom hit and people started craving something more sophisticated than they were already riding, expert cyclists recommended the 10-speed, and this advice was propagated through magazine, book and newspaper articles. At that time the advice was sincere and even practical, as the junk merchants had not yet arrived on the scene.

Here are the parts of what might be called the classic 10-speed with down-turned bars, skinny saddle, racy frame angles and no chainguard or fender. What really make it a 10-speed, however, are its front and rear derailleurs, two chainwheels and the five-gear cluster in the rear.

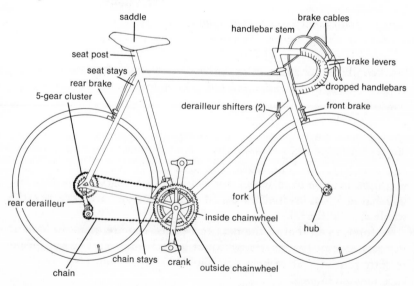

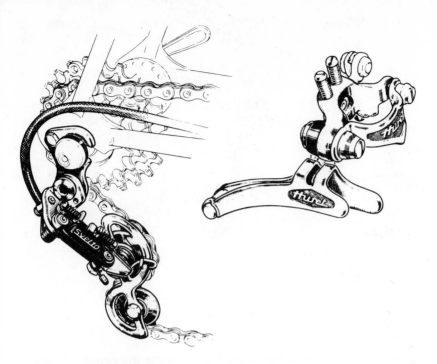

Three-speeds and 10-speeds are differentiated by their shifters.
A 10-speed needs two shifters, one front and one rear. The Huret
Svelto, top left, is a common rear derailleur frequently found on
medium-priced 10-speeds. Its job is to derail the chain among the
five gears. The Huret front changer, top right, pushes the
chain from one chainwheel to another. This combination gives you
more gears through a wider range than offered by the Sachs Torpedo
shown directly above. It is a 3-speed hub shifter. Its big
advantage is that it is self-contained, and therefore much less
vulnerable to dirt and damage than derailleurs.

A woman should have a bike comparable to a man's if they plan to cycle together. Otherwise couple-cycling can become a nightmare.

Don't get ripped off by the 10-speed myth. Despite what 12-years-olds think, every 10-speed is not 3⅓ times better than every 3-speed. And don't get fooled by model names. For instance, the maker of the 10-speed, bottom right, calls his bike a "lightweight" and cites its safety. Manufacturer of the 3-speed, top right, says his bike is built on a "standard" frame, and makes no special safety claims. Yet the "lightweight" tips the scales at a whopping 45 pounds; the standard-weight 3-speed is nine pounds lighter! As for saftey, the 3-speed sports front drum brakes, a type with an extremely positive action that won't fail in the rain like caliper brakes. The 10-speed features "safety" brake levers which may not be safe at all since they don't always give full stopping pressure. Also, take a look at those shift levers on the 10-speed—right up there on the top tube. Imagine what they would do to you in a fall! Your voice might instantly switch to soprano. Because of the whole mystique that has grown up around 10-speeds, this one commands the same price as the 3-speed despite its shortcomings. And here's the kicker: The 3-speed includes a chromed luggage carrier, internal wiring for generator lights, and an assembly tool at no extra cost.

Today the 10-speed=quality equation just doesn't cut it. Bike makers are exploiting the 10-speed myth and are merchandising derailleur bikes down our throats. As one bike company executive (who personally rejects the myth) put it: "People think a 10-speed is three and a third times better than a three-speed." This allows manufacturers to charge more for 10-speeds and sometimes limits profits on three-speeds. The result is a good mark-up on some very sloppily-made 10-speeds while some good three-speeds bring a smaller return. For instance, the same executive explained that two bikes built with similar frames and other components—only one made into a three-speed and the other into a 10-speed—might vary in production cost by

only a few dollars. Yet in a retail shop the 10-speed would fetch up to $20 more than the gearhub bike.

Get one thing straight: while 10-speeds on the average are made better than three-speeds, it is definitely possible to build a three-speed (or even a one-speed) that is faster, quicker and safer-handling than a 10-speed. A bike's quality depends, not on how many gears it has, but on the tubing used for the frame, the frame's construction, the wheels, tires, brakes, handlebars and other components.

I've seen some 10-speeds that I wouldn't send my worst enemy out on. One summer a New York magazine carried an article on a Red Chinese 10-speed that it described as a "Best Bet." The price was $59.95. I rushed to the store to examine this marvel and found out why it was so cheap. I could barely lift the iron monster. It looked like it had been made out of old water-pipe fittings. Yet the store (not a bike shop but a Chinese gift shop) was full of people like myself who had been suckered in by the magazine story. Unfortunately, many of them were actually placing orders for these little overweight beauties.

This is not to condemn 10-speeds at all. Most people, in fact, after reading this chapter will still opt for a derailleur bike. Yet this warning about the 10-speed myth is meant for them as well as for the cyclist who would be better suited by a three-speed. The warning is two-pronged:

1. Don't buy a 10-speed if a three-speed will do.

2. If you decide you need a 10-speed, take care; 10 speeds are no guarantee of quality.

The sorrowful demise of the three-speed

THE THREE-SPEED has fallen on hard times. This sounds like a contradiction, I know, after the above warning about the 10-speed hoax. But it's true. Here's the explanation:

People who seek quality above a certain level today are *forced* to buy a 10-speed.

The problem is that three-speeds are available in a smaller range of quality than 10-speeds. Three-speeds cost anywhere from about $50 to $100. Ten-speeds also start at about $50 but range upward toward infinity. Competition-grade models commonly cost around $500 and special-order bikes with titanium frames and special components can cost $1000 and more.

You'll find a similar difference in weight ranges. The clunkiest three-speeds tip the scales at 50 pounds, but only improve as you fork out more money to a low of 30 pounds. Some low-quality 10-speeds, believe it or not, also start in that same 50-pound range, but you can get derailleur bikes as light as 18 or 19 pounds. (I'm talking now about production models, not bikes made with ultra-thin tubes for breaking speed records.)

As you can see, 10-speeds range from drippy poor to ridiculously high quality. Three-speeds, on the other hand, start at that same

There are several 3-speeds parked here—evidence that they are making a comeback. They are a sensible alternative to the auto for short hops around town, and can help work off calories after lunch.

drippy poor, but range upward only to bikes of moderate-to-good quality. At one time you could buy three-speeds made with high-quality materials and components—lightweight tubing, super-strong hubs, slick-spinning rims, etc. For instance, the English Carlton, Raleigh Clubman and Record Ace three-speed bicycles were built with frames made from the same lightweight tubing used in professional 10-speed racers. They were also fitted with aluminum alloy components.

But these bicycles unfortunately have vanished from the American scene. The bicycle industry has pushed the 10-speed craze so hard and so effectively over the past few years that the three-speed's image has fallen sharply, though it remains *the* bicycle in Europe. To keep pace with the falling image, the bike companies have cut the specially made models from their three-speed lines, probably because they can't put appropriate prices on them. Most uninformed consumers would say, "Pay *that* much for a three-speed? Why, I can get a decent 10-speed for that kind of money!"

19

The upshot of all this is that the cyclist who wants a fine bicycle weighing under 30 pounds, but who prefers a hub-shifting model, is clean out of luck. Cyclists who already own such machines are holding on to them like they are bottles of vintage wines.

If you go looking for an ultra-lightweight three-speed, you will evoke one of two reactions: 1) Sympathetic and knowledgeable dealers will tell you such a bike is available—but only in Europe; 2) Callow youths will look at you in disbelief, as if you were a madman.

Now, let's get on with the more pleasant business of examining the good points of all four basic types of bikes, so you can find the best bike *for you*.

So then, what's the right bike?

FOR ADULTS who plan to do any *serious* cycling, the main choice is between three-speeds and 10-speeds. Coaster-brake and track bikes are okay, but their appeal is limited.

The coaster-braker will faithfully serve the guy who plans to make runs back and forth to the liquor store over fairly flat terrain. It's generally heavy but sturdy with gigantic balloon tires. While it won't take you more than a few miles with any speed, comfort or grace, its heaviness does lend it a certain indestructibleness. And the pachyderm-like tires don't puncture easily. Let's say you live on a farm in Minnesota and need a bike for banging over dirt roads. Or you live on the seacoast and you need a beach bike. The old American one-speed will do you well. It's also good for hazardous (to the bike) stunts. For instance, years ago a bunch of us kids used to ride our bikes down a hill and off the end of a dock into the lake. The object was to see who could splash farthest out. You wouldn't want to do that with your new $500 racer. It kind of dampens the lubrication. (It also hurts the human body, in certain spots, sometimes.)

The old one-speed coaster-brake bike can serve you well in certain situations

Track bikes are not for most people either. They're specialized machines that a few cyclists go crazy over, but you have to be a track racer or a real aficionado. See the chapter on these bikes if you're interested.

Hub shifter or derailleur—the most crucial choice

THAT BRINGS US down to the two biggies: three-speeds and 10-speeds. Choosing between them takes some serious thinking. As I implied earlier, more people pick the 10-speed, and later wish they had gotten the three-speed, than vice versa.

A major bike company recently conducted a study in which it found that the kind of bike most likely to be left unridden in the garage was the 10-speed. No wonder. It's not that a 10-speed is by any means inferior, but it is more difficult to operate and requires more maintenance.

Nevertheless, a lot of well-meaning husbands drag their wives to the bike shop and proudly buy two of these multi-levered wonders. All these couples really want to do is go cycling in the park a couple of times a week, or maybe cycle back and forth to the store. They have no intention of cycling cross-country. So they wind up with a bike that takes more care in shifting and adjustment than they want to give it. Instead of enjoying their ride they worry about when that chain is going to start kicking up as it grinds through an out-of-whack derailleur. The bikes which would be valuable to dedicated cyclists end up useless in the garage.

Generally, three-speeds are heavier than derailleur bikes, but serve perfectly for round-the-town jaunts or even for day-to-day commuting. Two or three gears are plenty for short trips, and while a gearhub bike's weight makes it slower than the average 10-speed, and while it won't handle the variety of terrain with the ease of a derailleur bike, it does offer several advantages:

1. *Protected gear shifter.* With the gear-shifting mechanism safely tucked inside the hub, there is less chance of it getting mortally wounded or excessively dirty. A derailleur is highly vulnerable as it sticks right out there in the open. Drop the bike on its right side, and you've had it.

Three-speeds have several advantages and are fine for round-town jaunts or even commuting

2. *Precise shifting.* You shift by clicking a lever, handlebar grip or whatever to a precise and set point. You can't miss hitting the gear right on the nose, and you always know by looking at your selector what gear you're in. A derailleur has no precise shift points marked on its levers. You shift by feel, and often beginners get the chain hung up between gears where it makes an awful noise as the bike shudders to a stop.

3. *Easier shifter maintenance.* Actually, there's not much you *can* do to a three-speed. You can oil a hub shifter and correct any problems in the gear selector, cable and the connection at the hub (called an indicator). But that's about it. The mechanism itself is fairly trouble-free. (By the way, it is actually a far more sophisticated device than a derailleur.)

4. *Cheaper.* As mentioned earlier, buyers expect to pay appreciably more for a 10-speed than a three-speed. So the manufacturer charges more.

One final note to three-speeders: Don't let salesmen, "experts" or your 15-year-old son talk you out of getting a three-speed if you sincerely believe that's what you want. Often a salesman will urge you to "move up" to a 10-speed. There's no reason to "move up" 30 or 40 bucks to get something you'll be unhappy with. Another danger is status envy. In today's cycling world, the 10-speed is considered the mount of "serious" bicyclists. This implies that three-speed riders are un-serious and trivial. Don't be swayed by this. I've met several experienced cyclists who have stuck with their three-speeds and who travel thousands of miles per year on them. And I've known rich people who wheel out their $500 Italian 10-speeds once a week for a

New buyers generally think that all derailleur
bikes look radically different from 3-speeds: down-
turned handlebars, skinny seat and all. These two
Fujis, 3-speed at the top, derailleur 5-speed
below, prove that this idea can be wrong. The two
bikes are identical except for their shifting
mechanisms. So if you want the wider-range versa-
tility of derailleur shifting, but don't want to
give up around-town amenities (flat bars, fenders,
etc.) be assured that there are plenty of bikes
to fill your needs. Incidentally, Fuji charges
about $5 more for the 5-speed than the 3-speed,
a fair price difference for two close-to-equal
bikes. Beware of the manufacturer who soaks you
for a derailleur bike that's no better than
a 3-speed.

short but conspicuous trip through the neighborhood. They spend more time talking about their bikes than riding them. Who then, would you call the serious cyclists? In my opinion, a cyclist's seriousness should be determined by how much time he spends on his bike, not how much money he spends on it.

What about the 10-speed?

BEFORE YOU 10-speed freaks wring my neck, I'd better explain that there's a definite place for these bikes. Ten-speeds account for about 50 percent of bicycle sales and, in fact, more space will be devoted in this book to 10-speeds than to any other type, so if you are a derailleur enthusiast you can keep on reading.

Anyone who plans to cycle long distances (over 40 miles at a crack) or who must commute to work over widely varied terrain can benefit from the wide range of gears a 10-speed offers. It is *the* tourer's bicycle.

It is also the bicycle you must look into if you seek real cycling excellence—a bike that is fast, light and responsive to the motions of your body. (The track bicycle also meets these standards, but requires too much riding practice for most people.) As discussed earlier, not all 10-speeds meet high standards, but you *can* find extremely high quality in the 10-speed market, quality you won't find among three-speeds and coaster-brake bikes at the present time.

The 10-speed bikes I have bought over the years I have purchased because they possessed the precision riding qualities I was looking for in any bike, not because they had 10-speeds. But the magic number 10 is a major selling point for many people.

Well, it really *is* a lot of fun, bopping that derailleur around through twice as many gears as you can shift in a $10,000 sports car. Besides being fun, that wide range of gearing is a real godsend at the end of a day of touring when your legs and lungs are giving out, the wind is kicking up and the closest shelter is at least 10 miles away.

The 10-speed is also good, surprisingly enough, for folks who have decided after years of inactivity to get back in physical shape. The natural tendency of health buffs is to buy the cheaper one-speed or three-speed because they want the bike "just for exercise." This could be a mistake. Let's say a 45-year-old man who has done nothing but shuffle papers at his desk since he left high school climbs onto his good old American one-speed and starts pedaling around the block. Everything's fine until he hits that first little hill on Third Street and finds that pedaling a 50-pound clunker is harder than it seemed at age 13. His heart also finds it difficult, and in its own inimitable way it may tell him so.

This is an extreme case, of course, but it can happen. A five- or 10-speed lightweight derailleur bicycle with extremely low gears will serve the exerciser a lot better. When you're first starting out you need those low gears to get back in the swing of things. And when you get healthier, you still have plenty of higher gears to move into so that the bike doesn't get phased out by your new-found fitness. Moving up through the gears also gives you an idea of how you're improving.

Besides, why not buy a lively, lightweight bike for exercise alone? After all, most people find that getting back in shape is a painful, discouraging task. Give yourself a break and make exercise as pleasurable as possible.

How cheap can I get a 10-speed?

YOU CAN BUY one *real* cheap, but don't.

The most popular price range, as this is written, is $120 to $170. If you're not willing to shell out $120 or more, go after a three-speed or a used 10-speed instead. To be sure, there are *some* acceptable 10-speeds costing under $120, but they are exceptions, and an inexperienced buyer will have trouble recognizing them.

How can I justify spending, say, $80 for a three-speed while condemning putting out the identical amount for a 10-speed? Easy. If $80 is your limit (to pick an arbitrary figure), you will get a lot more for it if you spend it on a gearhub bike. First of all, the 10-speed has perverted the pricing of bicycles; in short, the average $80 three-speed is a better-made bike than the average $80 10-speed. In effect, 10-speed customers help subsidize your three-speed. Take advantage of it.

If your dollar limit is low, put it on a three-speed. In effect, the 10-speed customers are helping subsidize your bike

More important, 10-speeds of low quality tend to function so poorly (if at all) after a few months that you'll wish you had bought a tricycle instead. The derailleur is the reason. Cheap 10-speeds carry cheap derailleurs. And while an expensive derailleur is not the key to enjoyable 10-speeding, a cheap one makes cycling unbearable. It will yank your chain around in a cruel and unpredictable manner, shifting when you don't want it to. It may even push the chain entirely off the chainwheel. This makes cycling a nightmare and may even sour you on the sport if you're a novice. A shoddily-made frame and poorly assembled cranks and chainwheel will also foul up the shifting on a 10-speed.

These problems can also result in a safety hazard. I frequently see young kids riding along with their heads turned backward and downward while they look to see what's wrong with the derailleur. A crumby rear shifter means you spend more time looking backward than forward—and this is the best way ever discovered to get absolutely creamed.

Three-speed hub shifters, even inexpensive ones, function far more reliably over the years than inexpensive derailleurs. A less-than-perfect frame on a three-speed also has little effect on shifting and therefore is less crucial than a 10-speed frame. This makes the cheap three-speed a safer choice than the cheap 10-speed.

*Left, today's kids stick out their tongues at the trusty old
coaster-brake bike and the once-proud 3-speed. Now all they want
(some are mighty foolish) is a 10-speed. Right, Nishiki Olympic is
a fine example of an inexpensive, minimum—but good—10-speed.*

Drop handlebars are also critical. Chintzy handlebars on a 10-speed can ruin your cycling. Flat handlebars support little of the rider's weight, as he must sit upright and simply grab the bars by their end grips for steering and balance. Drop bars, on the other hand, are designed so you lean a good deal of your weight on them and pull up very hard to help yourself up the hills. Cheap bars can bend or even break under this strain—a dangerous proposition. The handlebars are not nearly as crucial on a three-speed.

These are the two main arguments against the cheap 10-speed: 1) If you have under $120 to play with, with careful shopping you'll get a far better three-speed for the same money; and 2) Inexpensive 10-speeds can be a headache to operate and also a safety hazard.

However, some people still get that 10-speed fever even though they don't have 10-speed money. Emotions don't always wither in the face of logic, so don't let this advice stand in your way if you feel you just have to have those 10 gears. Go get 'em—but be careful.

New types of bicycles on the horizon

THE SURFACE hasn't even been scratched yet when it comes to designing new kinds of bicycles. Scientists are experimenting with bikes you lie down on, bicycles you pedal by moving your feet up and down instead of in a circle, bikes you pedal with your hands, bikes with sails and outriggers, etc. But production models of these oddball designs probably are years away.

In the very near future, however, we should be seeing new variations on old designs. Because of the energy crisis, bike makers, with lust in their eyes, are going after the adult buyer. According to *American Bicyclist and Motorcyclist* magazine, an industry spokesman predicted: "I look for the lightweight coaster-brake bicycle in 27-inch size to be the one consumers will buy. It will cost less than the three-speed and will serve the purpose for the consumer—that is, short trips to the stores, bus or railroad stations and other quick runs."

Another bike executive foresees "Bikes . . . equipped with large baskets to hold milk, dry cleaning and other items." And some newspapers are even looking for a manufacturer to produce heavy-duty delivery bikes. They're common throughout Europe.

What this all points to is a greater variety of vehicles within the next few years with an emphasis on utility. This means you will be better able to purchase the bicycle that most closely fills your needs.

But until that day of great variety arrives, you will have to compromise when deciding on the bike that fits you best.

Here's the classic newsboy's special. The energy crunch spurred some newspapers to return to heavy-duty bikes as delivery vehicles. This particular model is made by Columbia. It's so rugged you can hang almost any weight on it, front or back.

These three Raleigh models illustrate the wide range of 10-speeds made for the average, nonracing rider. There are cheaper models you wouldn't want to mess with, and more expensive models that are aimed specifically at racers and wealthy tourists. But these are good, basic bikes. At top is the Record, just above is the Super Course, and below is the International. From top to bottom (at the time this was written), they sold for about $120, just under $200, and nearly $400. All look similar, and all are 10-speeds. The difference lies in the quality of their components. Their weights, top to bottom, are 32, 29 and 25 pounds. The varying weights are significant, but other distinctions are more subtle, and explain the differences in quality and cost.

Types aside, what makes a good bicycle good?

OKAY, YOU'VE DECIDED what type of bike you want, now how do you determine quality so you can get the best deal?

What makes a good bike good is, of course, a matter of opinion. But here are the author's criteria, listed in order of importance:

1. *The frame.* This is the heart of the bike and the part most ignored by prospective buyers. It is also the most difficult part of the bike for the consumer to assess. It has no moving parts, yet it determines how straight the bike will track, how fast it will go, how comfortable it will feel, even how smoothly it shifts.

2. *Wheels.* These are the action parts of the bike. How light, true to round and how smoothly they spin on their axles will determine to a great extent how fast and safely the bike will travel. Some riders feel wheels are equal in importance to the frame.

3. *Tires.* The wrong tires can increase rolling resistance by as much as 15 or 20 percent. And an inadequate tread design can mean spills in tight corners.

4. *Handlebars and stem* (on 10-speeds). Flat handlebars aren't that important, but drop bars bear much of the weight of the rider and their stiffness contributes to effective pedaling.

5. *Gear shifters.* Most riders rank shifters, especially derailleurs, as the number one consideration. Of course they're important, but ask a bike salesman immediately about a model's derailleur before you ask about anything else and he'll know he's got a novice that he can lead by the nose.

6. *Brakes.* Almost all of them will stop you adequately when new. How often they must be repaired makes the difference.

7. *Saddle.* Doesn't really contribute that much to the performance of the bike, but definitely affects the welfare of your rear end.

8. *Cranks, chainwheels, freewheel, pedals, chain, levers, cables and other parts.* It's always dangerous to list any parts far down toward the end as some people take it to mean they're unimportant. If any of these components fail they can ruin the bike, but in truth they must be ranked below other items on the list.

9. *Paint job, styling.* Paint and chrome don't help the bike function any better, just protect it from the elements.

10. *Bells, bags, baubles and other accessories.* Nice things (maybe) if they're thrown in for free. But they shouldn't figure in your choice of a bike.

Some cyclists may argue with the order of this checklist, and it is certainly debatable. It all depends on your own personal needs and preferences. People who have had a bad accident, for example, put a heavy emphasis on good brakes. Riders with hemmorhoids stress the importance of a comfortable saddle.

Seriously, though, some riders reverse the order of the first two points—frame and wheels—saying the latter contribute more to speed. And some riders move cranks higher up on the list. But one point I'm sure of: Even though you can quibble with the exact order of the list, the basic parts of the bike—frame and wheels—are far more important than the hang-on parts—gear shifters, brakes, etc. I say this because bike enthusiasts these days seem to be parts crazy—especially when it comes to derailleurs and brakes. "Wow, look at that beauty! A Fettucini derailleur and Crouton brakes. Far out." That's the kind of comment you hear around bike shops, as if shifters and brakes were the central focus of a bicycle.

Don't make this mistake. Most every kid nowadays knows a good shifter from a bad one. Derailleurs are now status symbols in the youth bike culture, much like carburetor brands used to be the basic criteria for car hotshots in the 1950s. By learning about the rest of the bicycle, you get a leg up on other bike buyers. How to judge frames, wheels and other parts is detailed in the chapter on 10-speeds, since these are the bikes most people are interested in. But the information can be applied to all other types as well.

The warranty question

MORE AND MORE companies are stressing warranties. Many warranties are quite extensive. Raleigh, for example, guarantees that its bikes are ". . . free of any defects in workmanship and materials under normal use . . ." The warranty provides for "repair or replacement of original parts which, in Raleigh's opinion, are defective in workmanship or material, and which are returned to the dealer from whom the bicycle was purchased or to any authorized Raleigh dealer." Raleigh specifies no time limit, just states that the warranty does not cover defects, damage or deterioration due to normal use, accidents, misuse, etc.

Warranties like this are about all you can ask from the manufacturer and are excellent when you buy a widely distributed brand such as the Raleigh, Schwinn, etc., so you can wheel your sick bike into any authorized dealer when making those cross-country trips.

Your best warranty is the dealer from whom you buy your set of wheels. After all, he's the guy that's got to fix your bike if anything goes wrong

More valuable, however, is a warranty, free-service contract or whatever, given you by the man or woman who sells you the bike. Since it is the shop which will be making the repairs anyway, the dealer's willingness to stand behind his bikes may be more important than the manufacturer's. One giant Peugeot dealer on the East Coast repairs, adjusts and even lubricates the bikes he sells for three years. Not many shops offer such a deal.

More important than either a manufacturer's warranty or a shop service contract, I've found, is the simple promise from a dealer that he will fix your bike if it breaks (through no fault of your own). Trite but true. If you can find a dealer with a good reputation for treating his customers right, he should prove more valuable to you than a written contract. Tom Avenia, for example, a dealer in New York's East Harlem, offers no written guarantee—but then you don't need one with him. He's his own guarantee. He knows one of his bikes when he sees it, and doesn't hassle you about fixing it.

What if a bicycle comes with no warranty? Here's where the problem comes in. Many experts would advise you to accept no bike without a warranty, but this is unrealistic. Many fine foreign models currently do not carry guarantees of any sort, and yet they are excellent bikes. I've ridden competition-grade bikes that carried no warranty, and they were about as much bicycle as anyone would want.

Suppose you've narrowed down the field to two bicycles—one good bike with a factory warranty and a slightly better one with no warranty. Choose the better bike. A warranty, after all, may be just a piece of paper. You can't ride it (unless you're a real weirdo). And when your cranks snap in half or your brakes fail while coasting down a fast hill, having a warranty contract in your pocket is of little comfort. Your best guarantee is buying the best bicycle you can afford.

Foreign vs. domestic bicycles

THIS IS A TOUCHY SUBJECT, especially in these days when the American balance of payments seems in constant trouble. Buying American in these troubled times, I guess, would be the patriotic thing to do. But political reasons aside, you can't really say that buying an American-made bike is a better decision than purchasing a foreign machine or vice versa. Sometimes, though, this issue is raised; you'll hear arguments on both sides of the fence, blaspheming both domestic and foreign models.

The first anti-foreign argument you'll hear is: "Don't buy one of them immigrant machines, you'll never get it fixed." The flaw in this logic is that many of the parts on American 10-speeds are either

Here's the end of the Columbia assembly line. Columbia and other BMA member companies ship bikes like this, with both wheels installed. Foreign makers ship bikes with the front wheel off.

European or Japanese-made. About the only thing American you'll find on an American 10-speed is the frame. And you don't often need service on the frame.

Foreign bicycles may also appear to be inferior since they don't meet safety standards set by the Bicycle Manufacturer's Association of America (BMA). Many American bikes carry the endorsement, "BMA Approved," or some similar expression. Foreign bikes will not meet these standards and carry no such endorsement.

The BMA, however, has made a strong bid to discredit the safety of foreign bicycles, and late in 1973 even made an attempt to persuade the Consumer Product Safety Commission to adopt standards so rigid that imports would be either barred or effectively discouraged from entering the United States.

Here's the story: The BMA put pressure on the Commission to write a provision into the federal standards that would require the front wheels of bicycles to be factory installed instead of being shipped disassembled and then installed by the dealer. Shipping bikes with the front wheel unattached is a way that foreign manufacturers reduce crate size by one third and keep their shipping costs down. Most American bike companies ship their bikes with both wheels installed.

The BMA told the Safety Commission that factory installation of the front wheel makes the bike safer, and by implication, that shipping the bike with the front wheel off is dangerous. Had foreign makers, who account for one third of the 15 million bikes sold each year in the U.S., been forced to ship their products in the American fashion, prices on imported bikes would have jumped several dollars.

Fortunately the Commission would have no part of the proposal. "The bike industry has pressed for the provision because it would freeze out imports," said Richard O. Simpson, the chairman of the Commission.

According to *Business Week*, the Commission turned down the proposal on three counts, stating that:

1. The BMA failed to prove its point with any technical data.

2. The Commission itself failed to find any correlation between bike injuries and the failure to factory-install front wheels.

3. Factory-installed wheels are often misaligned anyway so that the dealer (or rider) ends up re-doing the job.

As any rider knows, bike owners themselves often remove their wheels (I don't know how the BMA figures we should fix flat tires).

It should also be pointed out that the Schwinn Bicycle Co., not exactly what you'd call a fly-by-night slipshod manufacturer, does not belong to the BMA, and ships its bikes in the foreign fashion— with front wheels off.

The BMA at one time was proclaiming that its code exceeded the federal standards because this particular proposal was rejected by the Commission while member companies continued to meet the front-wheel standard. This implied that bikes not meeting BMA standards were not as safe. This would include imported bikes. It would also include Schwinns.

The message is simply that foreign-made bicycles are not necessarily any less safe than BMA-approved bikes. There are unsafe American bikes; there are unsafe imports. You can apply no blanket rule to either. Judge any bike on its own particular merits. If any dealer starts extolling his bikes simply because they're American or because they meet the BMA code, it may be a tip-off that he doesn't have much to sell. On the other hand, if some shop owner tries to impress you with the prestige of owning one of his French, Italian or Lithuanian bikes, saying that they still know how to make bikes "over there," I'd be wary of him also. A lot of crappy bikes land on our shores every day from "over there."

A kind word about people who work in bike stores

WHILE WE'VE TALKED a lot about all the horrors that can befall you in a bike store, let's put in a small kind word for the people who work in them. There are many who, mostly because they don't understand your personal needs, will tend to direct you toward the wrong bicycle. But most I've talked to take a real interest in their work and actually care about the products they sell and service. This makes them much more pleasant to deal with than, say, your local aluminum siding dealer.

One thing that may strike you when entering a shop is the youth of the employees. As a friend of mine once remarked, "All you see are blue jeans and acne." But don't be ready to put this youthfulness down, as younger employees are often attracted to their jobs because of their genuine interest in bicycles, not because they have to make a living selling two-wheelers.

This youthful enthusiasm can work to your advantage. Young salesmen often hold strong opinions about what kind of bike and what sort of equipment you should buy. And they can usually back up their opinions with excellent rationale. Sometimes they will hold ideas opposite to those expressed in this book. Well, no one has a monopoly on bicycle opinions. Listen to what they have to say, even if it goes against what you've learned, and make them back up their opinions with reasons. Fight with them to see if their arguments hold up. No one says you have to be dissuaded from your own preference (like being pushed from a three-speed to a 10-speed), but this type of friendly debate can keep you informed of new developments and perhaps lead you in a pleasant direction you otherwise would have ignored.

In short, don't go to a bike store with no idea of what you want; but even when you shop with a thorough knowledge of bicycles, keep an open mind.

Allow the learning process to continue even after you finish reading the following consumer-guide chapters.

Chapter 2

The 10-speed primer

Look for a good frame first. Then you're going to hear a lot of talk about high-flange, center-pull vs. side-pull and other component details. Some of it is nonsense, some isn't. Here's a guide to help you through the flak.

FINDING A GOOD 10-speed takes more than finding a bike with the right stuff on it. First you have to figure out what the right stuff is for you.

At times, you may hear "features" being pushed on bicycles that just aren't features at all. Mystiques have grown up around certain types of frames, about certain types of components, that just don't make sense. Everyone halfway into bicycles seems to hold some half-baked theory about what's best and what everyone else should buy.

To illustrate, let's look at a newspaper advertisement for a 10-speed bike run by a large department store. Among the bike's so-called selling points, the ad listed:
* racer handlebars
* high-flange hubs
* no-fender racer style
* center-pull brakes
* spoke protector

The above features are commonly touted on low-priced 10-speeds. Running through them quickly, let's see if they're really features or not:

1. **Racer handlebars.** Most likely this is an out-and-out lie. What they really mean is that the bicycle has down-turned handlebars in the style that racers use. This is no deal, however. Cheap down-turned handlebars are no harder to make than cheap flat handlebars. Most likely the advertised bars will be the flimsy type that no racer would touch.

2. **High-flange hubs.** The flange of a hub is the lip that has holes for the spokes. Of late, high flanges, which stick out an inch or more from the hub, have gained popularity over low flanges, which stick out maybe ⅜ inch. Despite their popularity and the fact that some people

think they "look nice," high-flange hubs hold little advantage for the average cyclist. They stiffen the wheel, and for that reason are almost always used on track bicycles or on racing bikes designed for short races over smooth surfaces. Low-flange hubs allow for longer spokes which in turn absorb road shock, thus saving wear and tear on your body and on the wheels. Eddie Merckx, the Belgium racing star, won the 1972 Tour de France riding a bicycle with *low-flange* hubs.

3. **No fenders.** This is the one that really gets me. Imagine—they want you to be impressed with something you don't get! Granted, racers don't use fenders, but there's no reason to lay out more money for what the bike company didn't build. And in fact, many well-made bikes do sport fenders. They serve a purpose on wet roads.

4. **Center-pull brakes.** Many cyclists believe center-pull brakes are superior to side-pulls and that you should pay more for the center-pulls. This is a gross oversimplication. Getting back to Eddie Merckx's bike, it also had side-pull brakes. No, Eddie was not trying to save a few bucks with cheaper brakes. The very best brakes made are side-pulls.

5. **Spoke protector.** This is a plastic or metal disc on the right side of the rear wheel which keeps the derailleur and chain from getting tangled in the spokes. This is necessary on any bike with an inexact derailleur—one which might travel too far inwards. Most 10-speeds have such inexact derailleurs, so a spoke protector is necessary. But it's not something you should pay extra for. What the bike maker is really advertising is that his derailleurs are somewhat imprecise. It's like the barber who brags that he gives away free bandages with every shave.

It's not only buyers who are cheated by these phony features. The fact that consumers are fooled by this stuff drives shop owners crazy as well. As one dealer said, every customer who's read anything about bicycles thinks he's an expert. Some know-it-all will come into the

Some novices believe side-pull brakes are no good. So how do you explain this beautiful Campi Record model, the choice of racers?

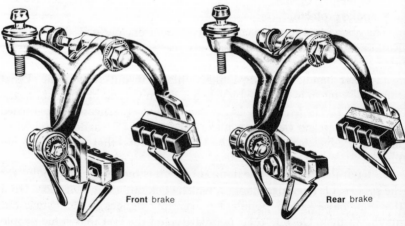

Front brake   Rear brake

shop and point out a $100 pair of Campagnolo brakes and inform his son that they are no good because they are side-pulls, not center-pulls. Or he'll reject a beautiful Legnano touring model because it has (yech!) fenders, of all things. Because of these misconceptions, decent bike dealers are often accused of trying to cheat prospective customers by "palming off" low-flange hubs on them, or for committing other imagined injustices. Many retailers have given up, and now sell people the stuff they've been led to believe is best, though it may in fact be all wrong for them.

Ten misconceptions about 10-speed bicycles

WE'RE GOING to take a thorough look at 10-speed bikes, starting with the frame and going through all the important components. But first, here are what I believe to be the ten most egregious misconceptions being bandied about at the present time. Some have already been touched on; some will be elaborated on shortly. But all of the following statements are believed to be the absolute truth by many novice cyclists. And all ten statements help steer thousands, and maybe millions, of buyers every year toward the *wrong* bicycle:

1. The most important thing about a bike is its weight: lightness equals quality; heaviness equals shoddiness.
2. A frame built with lugs is *always* better than a lugless frame.
3. Three-piece cottered cranks are *always* better than one-piece cranks.
4. Center-pull brakes are *always* better than side-pull brakes.
5. High-flange hubs are better than low-flange hubs.
6. Reynolds 531 tubing is the ultimate bicycle-frame tubing—all others are second-rate.
7. No fenders on a bike is a sign of class.
8. The best bikes have the highest gear ratios.

Would you believe a Brazilian bike? The Caloi Racer is made in South America but features mainly Japanese components.

9. When plunking the spokes on a wheel with your fingers, all the spokes should make the identical sound or the wheel is not properly trued.

10. A padded saddle is more comfortable than an unpadded saddle.

Now to explain what really is important, let's begin with the part that should be your main concern. . . .

What makes a good frame?

The frame is the most basic part of the bicycle; it determines how your bicycle rides and how it feels

THE FRAME IS the heart of the bicycle. Some say the frame *is* the bicycle. And with reason. It's the part the manufacturer puts his name on, the only one you can be sure he made himself.

The frame consists basically of eight tubes (see diagram): a short head tube, the three main tubes (seat, top and down), two seat stays and two chain stays. Usually the front fork is considered part of the frame also, but technically the frame is just those eight pieces, plus a bottom bracket, the assembly that holds the crank axle and joins the down tube, seat tube and chain stays at the bottom of the bicycle.

Your frame determines pretty much how your bicycle rides and feels. Ideally, a frame should be light and rigid but with enough flexibility to save your body from being worn out from road shock on a long ride.

Here are the parts of the frame that are referred to in the text.
It consists of eight tubes plus the front fork and bottom bracket.

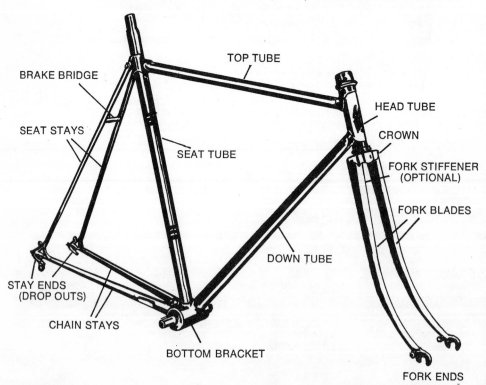

Cazenave Prestige is light in weight for a bike under $150—26 pounds for a 21-inch model, 27 pounds for a 23-incher. The frame is built with seamless tubing. It is hand-brazed with steel lugs.

Why it should be relatively light is obvious. Less weight to pedal. You'll be especially appreciative of a light frame when you hit that first hill. These days, many bike buyers choose bikes in the $120 to $200 range and for that much money they should be getting bikes that weigh from 27 to 33 pounds. A bike much heavier than 33 pounds represents a poor investment. Cheaper 10-speeds may tip the scales at up to 40 or 50 pounds, and aren't much fun. These bikes are made with weaker, seamed steel tubes. Because the basic material is weak, the maker uses more of it so the bike will hold together.

Should you desire a bike under 27 pounds, you'll have to pay out a lot more. As the weight goes down, the price goes up—and the increase in money is no way proportional to the weight decrease. For instance, a Peugeot UO8 weighs 29½ pounds, and costs about $150. The professional Peugeot, the PX10, weighs around 22½ pounds, costs $300. In other words, for the 25 percent reduction in weight, you get socked with a 100-percent jump in price.

As the weight goes down, the price goes up; when you try to break under the 22-pound limit you really have to shell out money

And when you try to break under that 22-pound limit, you really have to shell out money. Twenty-two to 24-pound bikes run in the neighborhood of $300 to $500. To strip off ounces here and there to get the bike down to 20 pounds requires a maker who will lighten the bike by drilling out chainwheels, brake levers, drop-outs and derailleurs, and by cutting out frame lugs. This will cost you an extra couple of hundred dollars or about $100 per pound. To go under 20 pounds you'll have to go with titanium parts or a titanium frame. This can boost the price to $800 or even $1000.

It's not worth it unless to race. Below 22 or 23 pounds, bicycles don't really get better, just lighter. Intricate drilling and cutting can add no quality, only save a road racer precious seconds. A 23-pound steel bicycle is about the best most cycle tourists ever require (and even a 23-pounder can be entered in a race should you ever feel the urge). Even if your budget keeps you in the $120 to $150 category, you will be able to pick up a 30-pound machine that will take you cross-country enjoyably.

By the way, don't believe the manufacturer's advertised weight. It is often false. Twenty-seven-pound bikes have a way of registering around 29 pounds when you put them on a scale. Often a builder will make several sizes of a model—say, from 19 to 25 inches—and he will advertise the weight of the smallest. There's no need to weigh a bike you're considering, but pick it up with your hands; this will actually give you a better idea of the bike than a scale. A well-balanced bicycle will feel lighter than a badly built bike of the same weight, proving that sheer numbers are not that important. (The weights mentioned above refer to the total bike weight, not just the weight of the frame. Components used also affect weight, but generally a builder will put light parts on light frames, heavy parts on heavy frames.)

Don't get hung up on weight alone

WHILE WEIGHT CERTAINLY makes a difference, don't make it your major criterion in judging a frame. This brings up a major misconception—that lighter always means better. *Rigidity* is actually more important. A highly flexible frame will waste more of your energy than a rigid frame.

Consider how much stress you put on your bike. Thrusting into those pedals flexes the frame side-to-side and up-and-down. That flexing wastes your energy. A stiff frame resists flexing, thus allowing more of your energy to be used for the serious business of propelling the bike forward, not sideways and up and down. A stiff frame will also corner better. A slushy frame will exhibit what is called "whip." If you're pedaling in a straight line and then take a hard right, the back half of a whippy frame will want to continue in a straight line. You can feel the rear end fighting you around a curve. Also, heading down a steep or long hill, a whippy frame will feel too cushy, less controllable and dangerous.

On rare occasions you may find a frame that is so rigid it feels amazingly safe, fast, maneuverable and responsive—but it transmits every bit of road shock to your arms, shoulders and rear end. How-

The least of your worries is getting a bike that's too stiff; most bikes are too soft. One exception is the Raleigh Professional Mark IV, which is aimed at racers and is too harsh for most tourists. But it's a fine—and expensive—bike sporting great equipment.

ever, you can pretty well eliminate the fear of getting such an overly rigid frame out of your mind unless you're buying a really high-priced machine. The problem with the vast majority of frames is that they're too whippy. Only track bicycles and an occasional short-course road-racing bike will be too stiff for most cyclists.

What makes some frames rigid and light, others heavy and whippy? Mostly it's the kind of tubes used and the way they're put together.

Sorting out steel tubes

THEY'RE MAKING bicycle tubes out of everything these days—plastic, aluminum, titanium—but the out-and-out favorite is steel. Cheap bikes are made with seamed tubing. This is nothing but a sheet of steel wrapped into a tube and then welded electrically where the two edges meet. Seamed tubing is straight gauge, meaning it is the same thickness its entire length. Do not buy a bike with seamed tubing except as a short-hop vehicle.

Better bicycles feature high-carbon tensile steel seamless tubing (no crease up the side) and may or may not be butted or double butted, as opposed to straight gauge. A butted tube is thicker at one end; a double-butted tube is thicker at both ends than it is in the middle. This makes infinite sense since tubes are subjected to the most stress at their tips where they join with other tubes. You can't tell whether a tube is butted or not just by looking at it since it is the inside diameter that varies—the outside is smooth, the same diameter all the way. Unless you're prepared to saw through the tubes in the middle of the bike shop, you'll have to take the manufacturer's word for it that his tubes are butted. In any case, high-carbon steel seamless tubing is the minimum tubing for an acceptable 10-speed.

The very best bicycles are made with chrome-molybdenum steel (chrome-moly) or manganese-molybdenum steel alloy tubing. In the latter category is the most famous of all bicycle tubing, Reynolds 531. This brings us to another mystique: that if you're looking for the very best bikes, you are getting something less than perfect if your bike isn't built with Reynolds. Well, Reynolds 531 is certainly *one* of the best and dozens of top frame builders will use nothing but Reynolds. Yet there are other brands of tubing that will serve well the cyclist looking for top quality. Among them are Columbus, Super Vitus, Falk and some of the Japanese chrome-moly tubes.

Let's look first at Reynolds 531 (pronounced five-three-one, not five-thirty-one) since it was the pioneer of high-quality bike material and is still the most popular among the high-priced set. The stuff is named after old Alfred Reynolds, originally a nailmaker in Birmingham, England, who invented the butting process way back in 1897. If you'll look at the drawing on page 40 you'll see how the tube varies in inside diameter. How Alfred figured out a way to get the tube to look like this is too technical to go into here, but the practicality of such a tube is obvious.

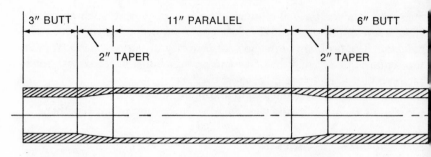

| 3" BUTT | 11" PARALLEL | 6" BUTT |
| 2" TAPER | | 2" TAPER |

Diagram shows X-ray view of butted tubes. The thinner wall saves weight, while the thicker wall, at the joints, adds strength.

The drawing shows a typical top tube of 21/24 gauge (21 gauge at the ends, 24 in the middle). The drawing is not drawn to scale, however. If in a fit of madness you decide to slice your top tube lengthwise to see how it looks inside, you won't be able to see the butt this easily; in fact, you won't even be able to feel it with you finger unless you have inherited the touch of Pablo Casals. A 21/24 tube varies from .022 inch in the middle to .032 inch at the ends. In other words, the difference is only one hundredth of an inch. Reynolds tubes vary from ultrathin to superultrathin, yet they will withstand pressures up to 90,000 pounds per square inch. They are used not only in bike frames, but in building aircraft and Jaguar motor cars.

Don't confuse Reynolds English steel with Reynolds American aluminum. A Reynolds frame bike refers to a steel frame, not an aluminum one.

Other fine tubes—deflating the Reynolds mystique

GOOD AS these tubes are, they are not the only good ones available. Unfortunately, cyclists often reject other brands because of the Reynolds mystique. Other brands are different and give the cyclist a different riding feel, but that doesn't mean they are inferior. One cycle shop, which caters to the racing set, sells only bikes made with 531. I asked the owner if this was because he was personally convinced it was the best material available. "No," he said, "but it's what everybody wants."

One make of tubing that's new on the cycle scene is called Super Vitus 971, a French tubing that's even a little lighter than Reynolds. It's also a little thicker. At this writing, only a few bike makers were using Super Vitus in their frames, but those we talked to raved about its strength and rigidity.

Another old standby is Columbus, an Italian brand that runs second in popularity to Reynolds. It is slightly thicker and heavier than Reynolds, so a frame made of Columbus is generally stiffer than a Reynolds frame and absorbs less of the rider's energy. Heavier riders,

Super Vitus 971 tubing is said to be even lighter than Reynolds 531. It is used on this Velo-Sport Super Frelon which weighs in at 21 pounds. The bike has double-butted 971 throughout.

Columbus double-butted tubing rates with Reynolds 531; it's heavier, but some racers prefer it for stiffness. Columbus is used throughout this Mirella 10-speed that costs more than $300.

track racers and racers who specialize in ferocious hill climbing often prefer the extra rigidity of Columbus tubes.

Some Japanese firms also make lightweight, high-strength butted steel tubing, and while metallurgical details are not readily available, the frames made with it (found on Japanese bikes generally) are a pleasure to ride. Still another tubing, lighter than Reynolds or Columbus, is called Super Fongius. And yet another good one is Falk.

The point to remember is that there are several fine brands of tubing for the connoisseur to consider. And while Reynolds 531 is always a safe bet, it's silly to reject a bike because it is not made of good old 531. If someone tries to sell you a bike made from Columbus or Super Vitus, don't accuse him of trying to gyp you.

By the way, these good tubes are not found only on super-expensive bikes. Some bikes in the under-$200 range even have Reynolds. However, such a bike (a Dawes is a good example) will use it only for the three main tubes, with cheaper stuff for the rest of the frame. Other makers will use Reynolds, but the straight-gauge kind, not double-butted. There are various combinations used, but anytime you see such names as Reynolds, Vitus, etc., you're looking at a decent frame. Any frame using Reynolds in any configuration will bear the Reynolds

There are several fine brands of tubing for the connoisseur, and they are not found only on the super-expensive bikes

green decal. To determine whether a frame is built with Columbus, Falk or any of the others, you'll have to ask for the manufacturer's specifications.

The art (or lack of it) used in joining steel tubes

EVEN WITH the best of tubes, you can end up with a lousy frame if the builder botches the job. And many of them do. Tubes are joined in one of two ways: welding or brazing. Brazing is generally considered superior to welding.

Cheaper frames are usually made by jamming the tubes together and welding them in place. The tubes are heated to extremely high temperatures and joined when molten. Heating weakens the strength of steel and therefore on welded frames you end up with a weak point just where you need it the least—right at the joints. Don't reject a bike outright just because it is welded, however. Some manufacturers, though admittedly only a few, do a decent job welding their lower-priced models by shoring up the weld joint with a bead or other reinforcement. Look for a raised area near the joint.

But in most cases better bicycles are *brazed* together. Brazing uses a metal alloy filler (brass or silver) to bind the tubes together. This can be done with or without lugs—those little sleeves the tubes fit into. The alloy brazing metal melts at a lower temperature than the tubes themselves—at about 1600°F. or even lower. When this much heat is applied, the brazing alloy becomes molten and seeps into the steel tubes, bonding them. While the steel tubes do get hot, they do not melt; therefore they lose less of their strength than they would if

Left, a Schwinn worker electroforges a production frame under high heat. Right, a craftswoman hand-brazes a Schwinn Paramount frame at much lower temperature, which produces a stronger frame.

welded. Reynolds 531, for example, drops from a tensile strength of 90,000 pounds per square inch to 80,0000 after brazing—still pretty strong stuff (albeit inadequate should the rider weigh over 80,000 pounds).

To lug or not to lug

LUGS, WHICH ARE MADE of steel, can strengthen the joint by adding extra metal and (more important) by distributing the stress over a larger area at the joint. Also, a frame made with lugs can be repaired. Damaged tubes can be removed from a lug and new ones re-inserted if they are silver brazed.

Some makers prefer brazing a frame without lugs, however. This brings up another widespread misconception: that lugged bicycles are always better than lugless bicycles. Actually, the skill of the frame builder and the quality of the brazing alloy are of the greatest importance. In general, lugs will provide a stronger bond, allow repair as mentioned above and look neater since they hide the actual joint between the tubes. But this is precisely where the problem occurs with lugged frames—you have no idea what the frame looks like underneath that lug. A lug can hide a multitude of sins: badly cut and poorly butted tubes and unevenly spread filler. So it's no guarantee.

The skill of the frame builder and the quality of the brazing alloy are of the greatest importance

Whether a frame is lugged or unlugged, the tubes should be cut and mitered to join each other precisely. According to Barry Harvey, a Canadian builder, "If the tubes are precision mitered, lugs are just window dressing." While this statement may be an exaggeration, it points out that the workmanship involved is more important than the material.

Also, many respected bike makers do build lugless frames. Holdsworthy Ltd. of England, for instance, has experimented with lugless bonding. Of course, Holdsworthy is a custom builder, but some mass producers also turn out good unlugged frames. The two giants, Schwinn and DBS, braze many of their medium-price frames together without the use of lugs as do Claude Butler and Lambert of England, to name only a few. As you can see, there are no hard-and-fast rules about frame construction. There are good bikes in both lugged and unlugged designs. And you can get burned both ways, too.

So what do you do? Judge each frame individually. You don't have the expertise of a metallurgist, but you can make a few spot checks. First, look for the smoothness of the finish around the joints, often a clue to the care that was taken. Look for cleanly filed lugs. The edges should not be ragged or rough to the touch. The finer the frame the smoother the transition from the lug to the tube. Run your fingernail around the edges of the lugs. Should your nail slip between lug and tube at any point, you have found a clumsy flaw. You should also find no filler material on the tubes. When checking out a welded or brazed-lugless frame, you can't expect the smoothness and beauty of a lugged design, yet the joint should be relatively smooth and even to the eye.

Don't reject anything short of perfection, because believe me you'll come home empty handed. You'll find file marks and even slightly buckled lugs on bikes costing upward of $500. The only frame I've ever seen that was virtually flawless was an Eisentraut (made by Albert Eisentraut of Oakland, America's top frame builder). A completed bike made on an Eisentraut frame would cost close to $700. But take a look at the frames on a variety of bikes—expensive, medium-priced and cheap—and you'll start to get an idea of what you can expect for the money you're willing to pay.

Another point: Bikes of the same brand and model may vary considerably (the old "lemon" theory holds just as true with bikes as with cars). Pick the best one for yourself.

The old "lemon" theory holds true: Bikes of the same brand and model can vary considerably

One final point on lugged frames: Beauty is a prime concern today in the bike world. The trend is to chrome the two front lugs, where the top tube meets the head tube and where the down tube meets the head tube, while the lugs at the joint of the top and seat tubes and the one at the bottom bracket are painted the same color as the rest of the bike.

A brazed frame generally is stronger than a welded frame, as brazing does not melt and thereby weaken the tubes. Brazed frames usually have lugs. One exception is this DBS Norge II, which is butt-brazed without lugs. The important thing is not the lugs, but whether the frame is brazed or welded.

You can't get much lighter than the Teledyne Titan Titanium frame. You order only the frame from Teledyne, specify the other parts yourself. Set up here with Japanese parts, it weighs about 18 pounds.

This is for decorative purposes only and has nothing to do with structural strength. Chromed lugs are no better than painted ones. Some makers also paint a fine line around the lug edge to differentiate the lug from the tube. And on special racing models, the lugs may be cut out, even with fancy patterns. Today there seems to be a fetish of little heart-shaped cut-outs in the center of the lugs; and of course these cut-outs are painted red. The purpose of all this is to save the racer a few fractions of an ounce and to look pretty (although this latter point is debatable unless you're really crazy about having sweet valentines all over your bike).

The titanium frame . . . bike of the future?

TITANIUM-FRAMED 10-speeds are already here. They're much lighter than steel bikes—by about three pounds—but whether they will replace steel bikes as the favorite mounts of racers and discriminating (and rich) tourists is to be seen.

The major builder of titanium frames today is an American company that specializes in making titanium tubing for aircraft and space vehicles—Teledyne Linair of Gardena, California. But to place the credit where it really belongs, the real father of the Teledyne titanium frame is Barry Harvey, an English-born racing champion (now a Canadian) who built his first titanium bike back in 1970 and then later joined up with Teledyne to mate his knowledge of frame design with the company's expertise in titanium.

The result is a frame called the Titan which weighs less than four pounds, compared to the six or seven pounds that the best and most expensive steel frames weigh. Harvey explains that while titanium boasts strength comparable to the best steel tubing, it also has a higher modulus of elasticity. This means it will absorb more road shock, good news for the rider's body. But this also means that titanium is less rigid than steel. So if you assembled titanium tubes into a frame with the same configuration as, say, a Columbus steel frame, you'd end up with a bike that was much too whippy. Harvey has compensated for this elasticity by radically breaking with tradition and making his tubes about ten percent larger in diameter than conventional steel tubes. He has also placed reinforcing liners inside the tubes at vital stress points.

Harvey and Teledyne have also designed the frame more in the style of a track bike than a road bike to compensate for titanium's elasticity. The seat tubes and head tubes are more erect than most bikes, with angles of about 74½ degrees from horizontal (as opposed to the 73-degree angles you now find on most steel bikes). The wheelbase is also shorter, much like a track bike, thanks to a tight rear triangle (formed by the seat and chain stays and the seat tube) and vertical rear drop-outs (drop-outs are the slots the axles fit into and are normally closer to the horizontal).

What results is a frame that features everything you'd want in a bike: ultralight weight for easy pedaling, elasticity for riding comfort and a track-bike-like configuration for maneuverability.

There's but one small hitch . . . the frame alone costs around $400. That's right, just one Teledyne frame will set you back more than a complete Peugeot PX10, a Fuji Finest, Zeus Competition, Paris Sport 1000 and several other steel bikes made with Reynolds or comparable tubing. You buy the Titan frame through a bike dealer and then specify to him what components you want hung on it. And after forking over $400 for a frame, it's unlikely you would want to skimp on the other parts. A fully outfitted 10-speed could therefore cost you around $700 or $800. Maybe more.

Is it worth it? Well, that's up to the rider. If you're a racer and you have the money, you'll want to experiment with the lighter frame. (By the way, at this writing American riders have won four gold and four silver medals in world track competition using Titan track frames.)

For the well-heeled tourist, it's a hairier problem. Certainly there's no lighter *serious* bike available. Teledyne does not sell complete bikes, only frames, but the company did assemble a sample 10-speed for demonstration purposes. Fitted mostly with Japanese equipment, the bike weighed in at a mere 18 pounds. I've ridden track bikes heavier than that. Its resilience over rough roads is a selling point for any tender-bottomed tourist. And if you're into such things as "pride of ownership," a titanium bike will certainly bring you plenty of that. You won't see many others like it on the block!

If you have the money, you may want to experiment on this new type of bicycle, especially if you're really hung up on weight. I'd recommend going the titanium route rather than buying a conventional steel frame that has been drilled out all over. Drilled-out bikes make sense for some racers, but what the touring cyclist ends up with is a bike that is considerably weakened for an inflated price. I'd put those extra bucks into titanium instead.

But most people, who aren't that crazy over saving pounds and who have saved for years to buy a topnotch bike, should go for a conventional steel frame at half price.

A final note on titanium frames: Don't look for any lugs. Titanium does not weaken when heated and therefore can be welded with no problem. No need for brazing or lugs. There is a titanium sleeve on the seat tube for extra strength, but this is not a brazed-on lug, simply a reinforcement. To track down a shop that sells titanium frames, write:

Teledyne Linair
Bicycle Division
651 W. Knox St.
Gardena, California 90248

The Teledyne frame, made of titanium, fitted mostly with Japanese equipment, weighed in at a measly 18 pounds

How serious is the plastic bike?

AT THIS TIME, not very. In the summer of '73, the Original Plastic Bike Company got a lot of publicity for its all-plastic (almost) bicycle. Prototypes were evidently built, photographed and stories on the bike were released to the press. Many publications, including *Popular Mechanics* and *Bicycling!* announced that a 17-pound bike costing under a $100 would soon be available. Unfortunately the bicycle, at this writing (a year later), still has not materialized. We were, in fact, promised a test bike which never was delivered.

The question remains: When and if this bicycle is available to the public, should you consider buying one? Well, since no one has yet ridden the bike, there can be no real judgment on its merit.

But the idea of an economy-priced, 17-pound bicycle is intriguing. This phantom bike features a plastic frame, but unlike conventional frames it is not composed of joined tubes. Rather, it has unibody construction—the whole frame is molded in one piece. Many of the parts are plastic, too: handlebars, hubs, freewheels, chainwheels, derailleur system, brakes, even the chain. This means you don't need to lubricate the bike.

The manufacturer *claims* its frame is stronger than steel and that its plastic hubs have been tested for 3000 continuous miles at an average speed of 25 mph. In fact, according to *Materials Engineering* magazine, the bike can stand up to a 400-pound person riding it at 30 mph and still have a 50 percent safety factor.

The problem with aluminum is that the joints are difficult to bind together, either by brazing or welding

In theory this all sounds nice, but how the bicycle will perform in actual road use is yet to be seen. If you need a bike just for short hops, it might be worth a gamble because of the low price; but for touring, stick to steel until the plastic bike has proven itself.

Aluminum and CFRP—more materials of the future

TOP-NOTCH COMPONENTS—cranks, hubs, derailleurs and the like—are now made with aluminum alloy, so why not frames? Well, there are some aluminum frames, but most makers don't see much hope for this material. While aluminum alloys are obviously much lighter than steel (that's why they're used for parts), the problem is that high-strength aluminum alloys are difficult to bind together at the joints, either by brazing or welding.

Nevertheless, at least two manufacturers have come out with aluminum models. The only production model is the Itoh SL-1, which is reasonably priced—under $170. Unfortunately, the alloy used is an extremely heavy one and the bike ends up weighing over 28 pounds! You can easily find a steel bike at that weight for the same or lower price.

Also there is a custom touring bike from Hi-E Engineering of Nashville, Tennessee, a maker of high-quality hubs and feeder-bottle carriers. Hi-E has developed an unorthodox way of joining aluminum tubes using special fittings and blind rivets. The result is a 10-speed weighing 17½ pounds. The tensile strength of the frame is only about half (40,000 psi) that of the highest-strength steel alloys, but it's certainly adequate for touring. Hi-E, at the time this is written, makes only custom bikes but plans to begin turning out production models shortly.

Another material of the future is CFRP, carbon fiber reinforced plastics. Fothergill & Harvey, a British firm, makes CFRP tubes and Carlton Cycles assembles them into frames. Carlton has come up with a CFRP track bike that weighs about ten pounds. Don't put off buying a bike until CFRP models hit the market, though. Materials Engineering estimates that a CFRP *frame alone* may cost $750.

You might also consider a stainless steel frame. Itoh offers a stainless bike, model SM-3, for under $200. Since stainless steel won't rust, it's not a bad idea if you plan to treat your bike badly, leaving it out in the rain, riding it underwater, etc.

Frame angles, forks, drop-outs and other frame stuff

UNLESS YOU'RE shopping in the $300+ category, you probably won't be concerned with frame angles—these are the angles the head and seat tubes are set from the horizontal. But just to give you an idea of what's what, an ordinary touring bike will have angles of 72 degrees; a racing bike and some advanced touring models feature angles of 73 degrees; 74-degree tubes are found mostly on short-course racing bikes and track machines; and bikes with tubes at 75 degrees are real killers.

Usually the seat and head tubes are parallel, but not always. Some racers wouldn't want 75 x 75 because the bike would be too uncomfortable, the ride too rough, but they would like the quick steering of such a bike. So they compromise—with a seat tube at 74 degrees and a head tube at 75. The specs of an expensive bike will list the frame

Odd stainless steel bike from Itoh is billed as "waterproof" for those who like to bike downriver. Bike is advertised at about 29 pounds, has Shimano Titlist derailleurs and a superwide range of gears.

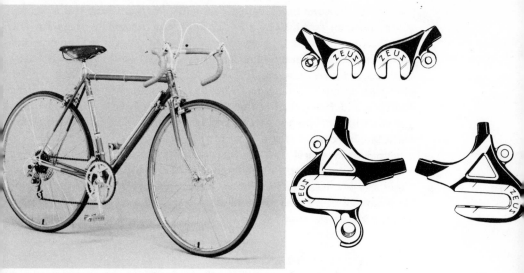

Fuji Road Racer S10-S is aimed at the tourist despite its racy title. A long wheelbase gives you a straight, smooth ride. Right, fork ends (drop-outs) are at the top, stay ends at bottom. Note that all four have eyelets for mounting carrying racks.

angles. Most bikes won't have this info readily posted, however. A good dealer or store mechanic may be able to estimate the angles for you just by eyeballing the frame (there is a method for computing the angles, but it's too bothersome for most people). In any case, I wouldn't mess with a frame with angles softer than 72 degrees.

Also take a quick look at the rear triangle formed by the chain and seat stays. The angles of these tubes will obviously vary greatly depending on the angle and length of the seat tube. Don't worry about the angles *per se,* but note how close the rear triangle brings the wheel to the seat tube, just as a rough gauge. A tight rear triangle will bring the rim (not the tire) within about 2½ inches or less of the tube. The closer the rim the shorter the wheelbase, which means quicker turns and possibly less whip. Some poorly designed frames have ridiculously loose triangles, resulting in a bike that's hard to turn and one that will flex annoyingly.

Forks are usually made by the bike manufacturer and are normally, but not always, made of the same material as the rest of the frame. What's important here is the rake, or the distance that the fork curves away from a straight line. This is easy enough to measure (extend a straightedge down the fork and measure the distance from it to the fork-end). Most forks rake out about two inches. This is about right for the average cyclist. The rake helps the bike track straight and absorbs road shock. If you want a bike which is quicker turning and more responsive, however, look for one with straighter fork blades. Be forewarned that a straighter fork requires a steady hand on the bars to keep it tracking straight.

Drop-outs, sometimes called fork-ends in front, are the four flat plates (two in front, two in back) with notches cut in them for the wheel axles. In front they are brazed, welded or otherwise connected to the fork blades, and in the rear they connect to the chainstays and seat stays. Good ones are forged into their shape; cheaper ones are stamped; crappy bikes sometimes have no real drop-outs—the fork blades are just squashed at the ends and notched out for the axle. Forget about these. Handy features to look for are eyelets in the drop-outs for attaching carrier racks.

Other stuff you'll find on the frame includes various fittings for mounting hand pumps, guiding the derailleur and brake cables, holding water bottles, etc. Sometimes the fittings are brazed on as part of the frame. Other times they will be screwed on. Brazing them on may weaken the frame slightly, but not enough to worry about.

Two basic rules for all frames

WHETHER YOU CHOOSE a frame made of steel, titanium, plastic or bamboo (don't laugh, it's been done), here are two checks you should make on a frame that have nothing to do with the material used.

Here's a simple test to measure for the right frame size: You need a clearance of about one inch between the top tube and your crotch

• 1. Make sure it's the right size. The size of a frame, stated in millimeters or inches, is determined by the length of the seat tube. Don't get this measurement mixed up with wheel diameter. Remember when you were a kid and aspired to a 26-incher, like every other kid? That was the size of the wheel. Today almost all 10-speeds have 27-inch wheels, but their frames vary in size from 19 to 25 inches.

The best way to measure yourself for a bike is the simplest. Straddle the bicycle, one leg on each side of the top tube, both feet flat on the ground. Do not sit on the saddle. You should have one half to one inch clearance between the top tube and your crotch. For obvious reasons. If you plan to buy a woman's-style bike with no top tube, fit yourself to a male bike to find your right size, then buy the appropriately-sized female model.

It's always better to buy a bike that's slightly too small (more than one inch clearance) than a bike that's too big (less than one-half inch clearance). You often will not be able to buy the precise size you need because some brands jump unevenly in frame size (i.e., 19, 21, 23 inches). Also, the kind of riding you intend to do should influence frame size. Plan mostly city riding? Choose a smaller frame for more clearance; you'll need it getting on and off a lot in traffic. Planning long, country tours? Take the bigger frame; the longer tubes will absorb more of the road punishment. But always get at least that half inch leeway.

You may have seen a rider height/frame size comparison chart in a shop or in some bike literature. Ignore such a chart. The simple old crotch-clearance test is best. The charts cannot possibly be accurate because people of the same height have different leg lengths. And bikes with the same size seat tubes may be different distances from the ground. How's that? Well, remember that seat tubes are set at different angles on different bikes; bikes with stiffer angles will have a top tube higher off the ground.

• 2. Make sure the frame is straight. Stand in front of the bike and sight along one edge of the head tube. The seat tube should line up perfectly with it. If these two tubes are aligned, the other two main tubes should also be okay. Eyeball the bottom bracket shell to make sure it sits at a right angle to the seat and down tubes.

Look for any dents or wrinkles in the finish. Not for the sake of looks, though. These flaws could mean that the frame has received a hard jar in shipping or handling and may be out of whack.

Eyeball the whole frame make sure the tubes are straight. Then look for dents or wrinkles in the finish

The absolute best way to check frame alignment is to ride the bike over wet pavement. When coasting in a straight line you should end up with one tire track—both wheels having traveled over the same path. However, this may be possible only with used bikes as most shops won't give you a test ride (nor will they supply a stretch of wet pavement).

Second best is eyeballing the bicycle from above to see if the wheels line up with each other. Or have a friend hold the bike up on its rear wheel while you check wheel alignment.

Here's another quick test: Revolve the cranks. Assuming the cranks themselves are not bent, the inside tips of both should come the same distance from the chain stays, seat tube and down tube. If they do not, *something* is wrong—either the stays, hanger shell, seat or down tube are out of whack, or the cranks are bent. Don't bother to figure out what's wrong. Don't take the bike.

Again, a bike may fail these tests, but that does not condemn all bikes of the same make and model. It's the old lemon theory again. If you find the bike appealing otherwise, ask to see another sample.

Sizing up components

ONCE YOU'VE SIZED UP a frame, you've pretty much sized up the manufacturer's workmanship. From now on you'll judge the quality of components he's bought from other manufacturers.

When it comes to bicycle components, you're going to be hearing one name over and over—a brand against which all other parts are judged. Campagnolo. This Italian company doesn't make every type of component, but those it does make are considered Number One: hubs, cranks, seat posts, brakes, chainwheels and derailleurs, among others.

There's quite a mystique that's grown up around Campagnolo. In fact, some kids even collect the *boxes* Campi parts come in. One bike dealer on the West Coast always makes two sales on Campi components: He sells the actual part to a cyclist and then sells the carton as a poster-type item.

Any brand that's built up that much of a mystique, you'd think, couldn't possibly be that good. But it is. After you check out dozens of other brands of gear, you'll find that Campagnolo always emerges as superior, or at least tied for Numero Uno with the competition. There are many misconceptions in the bike world, but Campagnolo quality isn't one of them.

As one importer said: "The only thing you can criticize Campi parts for is their price." And this is Campagnolo's big drawback. It's misleading to quote prices because they're out of date ten minutes after you write them down. But to give you an idea, as this is written, Campi side-pull brakes can run over $100 for the pair. Campi derailleurs run at least $55 for both front and rear. Right there you've spent $155 and you haven't even got a bike yet. Your only consolation is that Campi parts are a good investment. Your used parts three years from now will probably be worth much more than you paid for them.

Campi parts are terrific status symbols among young cyclists, but they do in fact perform beyond most other brands

And they probably won't be much the worse for wear. Campi parts are precision made and highly polished for smooth, low-friction performance and durability. Admittedly, part of their appeal is that they're aesthetically pleasing and are terrific status symbols among cyclists. But they also do in fact perform beyond most other brands and they do hold up over the years, even decades. They're not something you buy for your teen-aged kid who's not sure just how interested he is in cycling. They're for the cyclist who knows he's still going to be turning the cranks ten years from now.

The bike boom has caused fierce competition among parts makers, however, and several firms are challenging Campagnolo. Among them are some relatively new Japanese makers, so look for such names as Shimano, Sun Tour, Sugino, Hupelrider, Gran-Compe. Others are older European makers who always made relatively good stuff but who recently have been upgrading some of their parts, now that the market will bear the price of more expensive goods. You'll find such

Japanese components have made their mark, even in sometimes stuffy old Europe. This Motobecane L24, a traditionally fine French bike, sports a Sun Tour derailleur. Right, Schwinn bikes offer sturdiness, a reliable warranty, and a countrywide set-up of mechanics unequalled by other brands. But indeed they are expensive.

names as Huret, Zeus, Maillard, Simplex, Stronglight, T.A. and many others. Some companies make a broad range of components like Campagnolo. Among these is Shimano, whose Dura-Ace line includes parts that look amazingly like Campi parts. Others specialize in just one part, such as brakes (Mafac, for example). Still others may make a full line of parts, but have distinguished themselves in just one area. The best example is Cinelli, which makes all kinds of things but is the recognized champion of handlebars and stems in the Western world.

Components are most commonly made either of steel or aluminum alloy, the latter being more expensive and lighter. Aluminum generally means higher quality. Campagnolo is planning to come out with a full line of titanium parts. A bike with titanium components will weigh about a pound and a half less than a bike with aluminum components. Unfortunately, Campi will charge an extra 20 percent over their normal high prices for these special parts.

You don't need super parts to have fun cycling; in fact, the best of the gear may be wasted on you

But keep one thing in mind. You don't need these super parts to have a good bike or to have a fun time cycling. If you're not an extremely active cyclist, in fact, Campi gear may be wasted on you. Your Campi cranks will still be bright and sexy long after you reach that great cycle-path in the sky. Other brands are good, and considerably cheaper. Some reasonably-priced brands may even serve you better than the expensive Italian stuff. For instance, the Shimano Crane derailleur will shift the wide-range gears found on tourists' bikes better than the Campi shifter, which is designed for racing gears.

Following is a run-through of the major components. It's impossible to mention every name, so if you don't find a brand of hubs or handlebars that you're fond of, don't get sore; we're not implying that any name not listed here is no good. Knowing some brand names always helps, but you can learn a few general rules about components that will allow you to judge a part whether you've heard of a particular brand or not. Let's start with the action parts of the bike, the wheels.

Campagnolo not only works well—it's mighty pretty, too! Close-up of a Campi crank set, a front changer and pedals shows why so many cyclists lust after this particular brand of parts.

Round and round—choosing your wheels

THERE'S AN old saying: "An ounce on the wheel is worth two on the frame." Heavy wheels can slow a bike even more than a heavy frame. Tom Avenia, a veteran bike mechanic and former racer, says he's not convinced cutting the weight of a frame will improve speed. But, he adds, cutting wheel weight definitely will. That's why some racing coaches tell new people to put their money, if their funds are limited, into their wheels and to skimp on other parts.

Whether you agree with this or not—you may still justifiably place more importance on the frame—the ideal wheel is light, strong and, oddly enough, round. How closely a wheel approaches the ideal depends on the quality of the parts used and how they are attached to each other.

Wheels consist of three parts: rims, hubs and spokes. The bicycle wheel is a perfect example for Gestalt therapists, who believe that the whole is greater than the sum of its parts. Lay out a wheel's skinny spokes, flimsy rim and dinky hub and they don't look like much. An aluminum rim isn't even able to hold a round shape by itself. But put them together in the right way and you get a wheel that will support a 200-pound cyclist.

Hubs. Friction is your enemy here. Within the hub you have an axle spinning around inside ball bearings, which are contained in cups and held in place by cones. It's not easy to make good, round ball bearings or to make a precision hub. How well it's done determines to a great extent how smoothly your wheel will spin. So spin the front wheel on any bike. In fact, spin several front wheels on several models. You'll have no trouble seeing that some wheels spin more freely, longer, with less of a push from your fingers than others.

The standard bearing test is called the "three o'clock drop." This is where you position the wheel with the air valve at the three o'clock position. Now let loose of the wheel. The mere weight of the valve is supposed to make the wheel rotate at least a quarter of a revolution until the valve is at six o'clock. This is often a good test of a wheel, but oftentimes not. At times it only shows you that the manufacturer has equipped his bike with very heavy valves. You'll get a better idea of a wheel just testing it by feel. Some competition wheels are amazing, spinning several minutes from just a small push.

Also, while the wheel spins, put your ear close to the hub. Any noise means a poorly adjusted hub. Don't reject a bike solely on this basis, but insist that the hub be adjusted before buying.

Hubs are usually either steel or aluminum, the latter being more expensive. Hubs are either low-flange or high-flange, which brings us back to that controversy. If you cycle a lot over rough surfaces, low-flange are better for absorbing road shock. However, high-flange hubs are so popular you may not have a choice when buying a bike in the medium-price range ($120 to $200).

Maillard markets its hub parts under different names: Normandy and Atom. This is a Normandy hub with Atom quick-release.

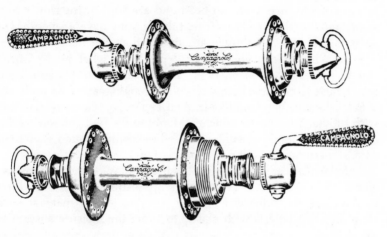

For rough roadways, low-flange hubs such as these Campagnolo models help dissipate the shock of bumps and cobblestones.

Some hubs are quick-release. The axle is hollow with a quick-release skewer that passes through to lock both sides to the drop-outs. You just pull a lever to release the wheel. Quick-release is a terrific feature, but admittedly a convenience, not a performance item (except for racers who must change wheels in a hurry). So if you're trying to cut costs, skip the quick-release. Carry a wrench or get a bike with the big wing-nuts you can unscrew by hand.

Other distinctions: Hubs all have holes in the flange to accept spokes, but the number of holes varies, 36 being the most common. This number of spokes probably will serve you well unless you're a very heavy camper, in which case you might want to go with a 40-spoke hub in the rear to help bear the load of stuffed panniers, a sleeping bag, tent, etc. (Of course, you'll need a 40-spoke rim as well). Most hubs have bearings packed in grease; more expensive ones use oil. If a hub is packed with fine oil, it will usually have a fitting in the middle so you can replenish the oil once a month.

The leading brand is still Campagnolo, though others are closing fast. Recently another firm tested every major hub made in the world to determine which was the strongest (its engineers wanted to copy someone else's design and they wanted to make sure they copied only the best!). They decided on Campi.

Two American firms, Phil Wood and Hi-E Engineering, also make hotshot hubs. Phil Wood makes a sealed-bearing hub you never need to overhaul.

Other good brands include Maillard (Normandy and Atom), Milremo, Cinelli, Shimano, Gnutti, Sanshin and Zeus.

Rims. There are two kinds: clinchers and tubulars. This refers to the kind of tire they will accept. Clincher rims, the more common, have a lip on both sides to hold the bead of clincher tires (the normal kind of tires, just like those on a car). Tubular rims need no such lip; tubular, or sew-up, tires have no bead and are held to the rim with glue, sticky tape or shellac. Therefore, tubular rims have a smooth, curved surface. They are also thinner and lighter than clinchers.

What kind of rim you choose depends on what kind of tire you choose (see the section on tires). But to tell the truth, you probably won't have a choice of rims if you're looking at bikes under $200. You'll take clinchers and like it. And expensive bikes invariably come with tubular rims, never clinchers. Only in the twilight zone is there a choice freely offered—usually with bikes costing around $200 to $300. And in these cases you'll pay about $10 or $20 extra for tubulars.

Tubular rims are invariably aluminum alloy. Clincher rims can be either alloy or steel. A few tubulars are also filled with wood inserts to reinforce the otherwise hollow rim. Some rim makers, such as Ukai, fill their wheels with plastic to avoid the moisure absorption of wood.

In clincher rims, the type of alloy generally indicates the quality. But mostly steel is what you're going to find at prices under $150. Rigida, among others, makes a good, relatively inexpensive steel rim. Other brands to look for, though not all are so cheap, include Mavic, Nisi, Super Champion, Ukai, Weinmann and Fiamme. All make both clincher and tubular rims.

Spokes. It's hard to get excited over spokes, and with good reason. For extra lightness get butted spokes—spokes that are thinner in the middle than at the ends. Unlike frame tubes you can spot butted spokes just by looking. Or run your fingers toward the end and you'll feel the butt. However, don't reject a bike just because it has straight-gauge spokes. In fact, spokes used on track wheels are straight gauge —their diameter is as thick as the butt end on butted road spokes, which means they consist of more metal. Stainless steel is a good spoke material. Robergel is one high-class brand.

The wheel as a whole. More important than all these parts is how they're put together. Granted, a maker who uses Campi hubs, Nisi rims and Robergel spokes is likely to lace a meaner wheel than a maker using inferior components. But at the lower end of the scale, some manufacturers get some pretty good wheels out of mediocre parts.

You're likely to run into three terms when shopping for wheels: laced, three-cross and true. Spokes on a laced wheel will touch one

More important than the wheel parts is how they are put together; mediocre parts can produce a mighty fine wheel

other spoke where they cross. In theory a laced wheel is stronger because road shock travels up a spoke and through the junction and is absorbed by a second spoke as well. Don't fret about this, though. It's a debatable point. I've seen some good bikes with unlaced wheels (not all Cinelli front wheels are laced, for instance).

Three-cross, four-cross, etc. refers to how many other spokes a spoke crosses from the hub to the rim, though it will not actually *touch* all of them. Track bikes sport four-cross wheels because they offer high strength, but you wouldn't want more than three-cross for the road. Custom-made wheels are sometimes tied and soldered. This means the spokes are tied at the point they touch each other and then soldered to make a firmer junction.

More important than all these details is the wheel's trueness. In other words, is it round? Don't look at it from the side; you'd need quite an eye to test it that way. Instead, spin the wheel and watch the rim as it passes the brake shoes. Watch one edge at a time. It should remain the same distance from the brake as the wheel spins. Ignore the tire. It could be seated improperly and its tread can mislead you.

Is the wheel round? Watch one edge at a time; it should remain the same distance from the brake as the wheel spins

This brings up another misconception: that you should check a wheel's trueness by plunking the spokes. I call this the "Harpo Marx Method" of trueness testing. If true, goes this old saw, each spoke should tinkle the same tone. First, a bicycle wheel makes a lousy musical instrument, unless you want to hook it to an amplifier and start a rock band. Second, it just doesn't work on the rear wheel. Because of the large cluster of gears on the right side, rear wheels must be *dished* in order to center the wheel between the stays. This can be done in one of two ways: The better way is to use shorter spokes on the right side. If you look straight down at the wheel, you should see the spokes angle farther to the hub flange on the left side. A short cut used by some makers is to tighten the right-side spokes more than the left side. But whether the right-side spokes are shorter or just tighter, they're going to sound a different pitch than the left side.

The spoke-plunking method theoretically works on the front wheel, but unless you have the deft touch and accurate ear of a professional harpist, rely on your eye. Spin the wheel, check the rim against the brake shoes.

Tires fill out the wheel. But they are so important a whole chapter is devoted to them later. This is not to imply they are more important than the rest of the wheel—but unlike the wheel, you will most likely be replacing them in the future, so you can ignore poor tires on an otherwise acceptable bike.

All sorts of curves—handlebars

FLAT OR DROPPED? That's your first question. Handlebars affect more than the hands. They determine how you sit on the bike. Flat bars are convenient around town. You don't have to hunch over, and you can see traffic a little better. However, for longer rides, go for the traditional 10-speed drop. Here's why:

Drop bars are more comfortable once you get used to them. For one thing, you must bend over to use them, cutting down wind resistance. Secondly, drop bars divide your body weight more evenly between the handlebars and seat. In other words, they take a load off your rear end. This can be a real godsend if you have hemorrhoids or similar problems. Believe me, I speak from experience. When a rough surface comes up you can easily lift your seat off the saddle. Not only does the bent position save on your posterior, it saves your backbone as well. When cycling in a straight-up position, road shock travels up the seat tube, into your rear and straight through the spine. You'll find your lower back hurting after several hours.

Drop bars are best, once you get used to them. They make good use of your arms and back

Also, drop bars make better use of your body. Leaning over, you can use the strength in your arms and back to offset the thrusts of your legs. Without your body firmly anchored in this manner, you can't pedal forcefully or effectively. Try pumping fast while sitting upright and you'll end up tilting side to side awkwardly.

If you're new to drop bars, your arms and shoulders may be sore at first, since they are bearing some of your body weight. But you should adapt to this quickly. You will also develop some muscles in the back of your neck because the bent position requires you to cock your head back to see ahead.

A final point for those skeptics who are convinced the bent-over position is clumsy and uncomfortable: Man was probably never meant to walk (or bicycle) in an upright manner. That's one of the main reasons we humans end up with backaches, come middle age. After all, look at the way apes walk. And when was the last time you saw a monkey in an orthopedic surgeon's office? Leaning over actually relaxes your back with the further advantage of allowing your chest to hang free for easier breathing.

There are an infinite number of variations of down-turned handlebars, but you will run into three main bends: Pista, Maes and Randonneur.

The Pista is the classic down-turned bar. The bar curves immediately away from the stem and usually ends up deeper below the stem than Maes or Randonneur bars. The Pista is designed for sprinting and you'll find it only on track bikes. Beautiful as it is, the tourist has no use for Pista bars because there's no flat area on the top for your hands, the position you use most on long trips. In fact, many track racers are now using Maes bars, especially in the longer events.

The Maes has a long flat top section and then curves downward and culminates in a straight, horizontal section that you can pull up on for speed work. The Randonneur is similar, except that it does not end in a straight flat section at the bottom of the curve. Instead it just angles mildly downward. Also, the top section is not strictly straight, but curves downward from the stem extension and then back up again. Both of these types are adequate for the tourist and it's unlikely you'd find a difference in performance between the two. With two exceptions: If you ever plan to race, the Maes bar gives you a better grip for sprints; and if you ever have suffered from numb hands, the Randonneur can ease this problem.

Handlebars come in either steel or alloy. Alloy is generally more expensive and usually indicates a better bike. The exception is the Pista track bar which will be made of steel because the racer exerts tremendous force on his bars and could conceivably bend an alloy model. A good set of track bars, such as Cinelli, will be chrome-plated steel and actual cost more than alloy road bars.

Some trusty handlebar brands are Pivo, Ava, Fiamme, Belleri, Philippe, GB and TTT. The recognized king of handlebar makers is Cinelli, with TTT a close second.

The second part of a handlebar set is the stem. This is the piece of metal that comes up out of the head tube and juts forward to hold the handlebar. The most important thing to check on the stem is its

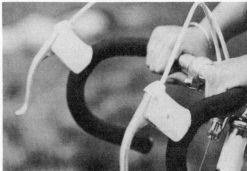

Left, Maes bar has a long top section, then curves abruptly and has a down section that's almost horizontal. Right, two nice, but unessential, features are padded lever housings and tape.

The forearm test for proper stem length is a good guide. With elbow on saddle tip, finger should reach rear edge of handlebar.

length. Surprisingly, bike makers don't always proportion the stem length to the size of the bike. You'll find 25-inch bikes with stems only 2½ inches long and 21-inch bikes with 4½-inch stems. And even if manufacturers displayed a little more logic in stem selection (long stems for big frames, short stems for small), you still wouldn't be guaranteed getting the proper stem length simply by buying the proper frame size because some very tall people have very short arms and vice versa.

To test for correct stem length, first set the saddle so it's about even with the top of the stem. Now place your elbow at the tip of the saddle and stretch your forearm straight forward. Your fingertips should reach the back edge of the handlebars at the end of the stem. If you can't reach it, the stem's too long and you'll have to stretch uncomfortably. Too short and you'll be cramped.

This forearm method is only a rough measurement. Better is a dealer who knows something about bicycling and will put you on the bike to see if everything is right for you. Unfortunately, not all dealers know what they're doing or want to be bothered with changing a stem. So use the quick forearm method if you've never been on a 10-speed before. Insist that the dealer give you the proper stem before you buy. Don't get talked out of this one.

Less important is the stem angle. Stems either stick straight out (horizontal) or angle downwards. Most experienced cyclists prefer a stem angle close to horizontal. Very steep angles are for sprinters only, and are usually found on track machines. Manufacturers rarely goof up this point, so just give it a quick look.

As far as brands go, your stem will usually be the same brand as the handlebars. One rough way to determine quality is by checking the type of expander used to hold the stem inside the headset. Normal stems have a normal protruding bolt. More expensive stems feature a recessed 7mm Allen nut.

Handlebar taping is entirely a matter of taste. The most elegant is narrow-woven cloth tape but some riders prefer the cheap plastic kind because it doesn't heat up your hands as much in summer. There's special padded tape for people with sensitive hands, but this stuff usually doesn't solve the problem—gloves are better. Whatever you get, make sure the ends of the bars are plugged. An un-plugged bar end can hurt you badly in an accident.

Those glamour components—derailleurs

I HATE TO TALK about these things because people get so hung up on them. So much so that they judge an entire bicycle simply by the brand name on its derailleur. Well, derailleurs are important; they're what make 10-speeds possible, and a crumby one can make cycling miserable. But derailleurs ain't the whole bike. Keep that in mind. Here's how they work:

First, the rear shifter, which switches the chain among the five or six cogs of the freewheel cluster, is the more important shifter on a 10-speed. The front derailleur (sometimes called a changer) switches the chain between the two (or three) chainwheels.

The rear derailleur is the key because it must do two things: it must derail the chain from one gear to another, and it must take up slack in the chain when derailling from big sprockets to small sprockets.

The derailleur derails the chain by applying pressure to the chain directly in front of the cluster. For instance, to switch the chain from the smallest rear sprocket (the furthermost outside gear) to the next larger sprocket, the derailleur pushes the chain slightly inwards toward the wheel. The chain is now deformed, out of alignment. Because the chain wants to follow the path of least resistance, it straightens itself out by spiraling out of the smallest gear and is caught on the teeth of the next sprocket.

The derailleur does not just bash the chain sideways with a rod or something, but applies its force through a jockey wheel. This is a wheel in a cage. The chain runs around the wheel and the derailleur pushes the whole cage sideways.

The shifting is not accomplished entirely by the derailleur. The shifter simply pushes the chain *sideways;* but the chain must also move *upwards* (or, more properly, *outwards*) to get from a small gear to a bigger one. Help is needed from the moving freewheel. As the derailleur pushes the chain sideways and it catches on the first teeth of the larger sprocket, the moving gear pulls the chain up and around until it is firmly seated. This is why you must be pedaling to shift a derailleur bike.

Simplex plastic-bodied derailleur abounds on bikes in the $100 to $200 category. It works very nicely, too, but may deteriorate after a while. Depending upon your financial standing, you can either replace it immediately or keep it until it screws up, then get another.

The best way to understand the shifting process is to hang the bike from the ceiling, turn the cranks and watch what happens as you shift. If you have a good derailleur, spin the cranks at a brisk pace, and move the shift lever evenly. You should see both motions (the sideways force of the derailleur and the outward force of the spinning freewheel) combine to move the chain in a smooth spiral.

After looking at it, it's really not all that complicated, is it? In fact, you could shift just by pushing the chain sideways with your fingers as long as the cluster was spinning. Of course, it's awkward to do this sitting on the bike.

The pantograph makes it all possible

All major derailleurs work in the same way; they simply deform a parallelogram into a "slantier" one

SO WE USE A DERAILLEUR. All major shifters work off the same mechanism, called a pantograph, which is based on the principle of the "deformable" parallelogram. If you'll remember from your high school geometry, parallelograms are the only figures which can change shape and still remain parallelograms. A rectangle, for instance, is a parallelogram whose sides are at right angles to each other. When you "deform" a rectangle by changing these angles, it is no longer a rectangle, but it remains a parallelogram because its opposing sides are still parallel to each other.

This principle is the basis of the pantograph—a machine most commonly employed by mechanical artists to copy drawings on a smaller or larger scale. The pantograph design is also incorporated into derailleurs. A derailleur's pantograph deforms into "slantier" parallelograms to shift the chain onto the larger sprockets. You change the shape of the derailleur via a cable which runs across the diagonal of its parallelogram. Shorten the diagonal and you lean the derailleur into the chain, shifting it to larger sprockets. This is what you're doing when you pull the shift lever *down* (which actually pulls the cable *up*). You're shortening the cable, thus shortening the diagonal, leaning the shifter inward. All derailleurs work basically in this manner, and understanding the theory behind your shifter will help you fix it when it goes on the fritz.

Bringing it back home again

WHAT WE'VE SEEN so far is how the chain climbs "uphill" from smaller to bigger sprockets (or higher to lower gears). This is the hard part. The derailleur re-forms into its original shape and brings the chain back downhill through the use of a spring. You allow the spring to bring the derailleur back down the cluster by pushing the shift lever upwards, thus letting out some cable. So don't think of shifting as pulling and pushing the cable. Think of it as pulling and *releasing*.

Because of the spring, the pantograph's natural tendency is to remain in its original high-gear shape. This is why you end up with only high gear when your cable breaks. Also, if the wingnuts on your shift levers are not tight enough, the derailleur will pull the chain back down the cluster. Theoretically, you could build a rear derailleur that worked just the opposite, with a spring that pulled the cage inward; then you would have to use hand pressure to shift it to the smaller outer sprockets. But since it takes more energy to bop the chain into the bigger cogs, this is best accomplished by hand action rather than relying on a spring.

Keeping the chain taut

ON ANY 10-SPEED, you need enough chain to handle the biggest gear combination (which is not the same as the *highest* gear combination). By this, I mean the chain must be long enough to go around the larger chainwheel in front, through the derailleur cage, around the largest rear sprocket and back to the chainwheel. The combination requiring the least amount of chain would be the small chainwheel and the smallest rear gear. The difference between the two combinations can be inches of chain. The derailleur must therefore take up the slack in the smaller combinations, otherwise you'd have extra chain slopping around which could catch on other sprockets, thus haphazardly shifting gears on you. Could be rather embarrassing.

The derailleur must have some way to take up the slack in the chain, which can amount to inches of metal

Therefore, right below the jockey wheel in the derailleur cage, you'll find a tensioner wheel. It looks exactly like the jockey wheel, but its function is to take up slack. The cage is spring-loaded and applies clockwise force. As you shift into smaller sprockets, the tensioner

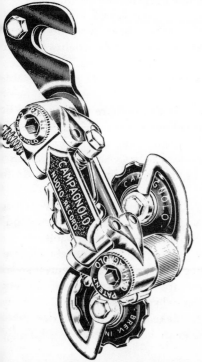

Campagnolo Nuovo Record is considered the finest of all derailleurs. It uses traditional swinging parallelogram design that makes for quick shifting between small, close-ratio sprockets, making it perfect for racing. However, some of the long-caged Japanese derailleurs handle big touring sprockets better.

63

wheel moves backward, clockwise. Conversely, the spring is weak enough so that it will let out chain when shifting to larger sprockets.

The wider the range of gears on a bicycle, the more slack must be taken up. Some shifters also use the jockey wheel to help in this task by allowing it to revolve around a pivot. As the tensioner wheel springs backward to take up slack, the jockey swings forward to help out (both, of course, are moving clockwise). Some derailleurs employ even a third slack-take-upper, the body of the derailleur itself, which can be spring-loaded at the top so it will revolve backward.

Often you will run across the term *derailleur capacity*, which will be expressed in numbers such as 13-30 (representing the number of teeth on the smallest and largest rear cogs it will handle). This range is partly determined by how long the cage is, but also by the derailleur's slack-gathering ability. Also remember that the rear derailleur is working even when you're just shifting the front changer, taking in and letting out chain. So chainwheel capacity is also listed for any rear derailleur, with figures such as 36-56. In a pinch, you can get along without the front, but not the rear. That's why the following discussion of derailleur selection is limited to the rear shifter.

The weak link on your bike

TO BE HONEST, I can't get all that excited over derailleurs, so the language here may be less than glowing. As described above, the derailleur is an ingenious device and must accomplish several tasks. But that's only theory. In practice, the whole thing breaks down.

In my opinion, there are only six or seven "good" models. They shift where and when you want them to, need little adjustment and don't break (too often). The vast majority of derailleurs fall into the "horrible" category. In between are a few I'd call "passable." Most bikes in the $120 to $200 category at best will have passable shifters. Some have horrible ones.

Virtually all derailleurs are either horrible or passable; make a shop change a bad shifter for you

This is said, not to discourage you, but to prepare you—and to be realistic. Forget about those pretty advertisements with the people who flash nice smiles while they ride their cheap bikes. Go out with any cycling group and you'll find several riders swearing at derailleurs that shift unexpectedly, refuse to budge the chain into low gear or throw it off the chainwheel.

Bike salesmen rank derailleurs as good, very good or excellent. And you can thank all the problems above to either "good" or "very good" derailleurs. That's why I prefer the terms horrible and passable.

To avoid horrible derailleurs, don't reject a bike entirely just because of its shifter—make the shop change the derailleur instead. Most shops will do this for the difference in price of the shifters (and maybe labor). This will cost you anywhere from $5 to $20 on the average. If the shop is unwilling to make the switch, go elsewhere. You want to do business with a shop geared to service.

Your alternative is to keep the original derailleur and give it a chance. Discard it for a new one as soon as it gives you trouble. You're not wasting a whole lot here—most cheap derailleurs cost under $10.

Despite this badmouthing, don't get scared off 10-speeds if you have use for a lot of gears. I only warn you because your friendly bike dealer will tell you what a wonderful mechanism your derailleur is. Then you go out and have trouble and you think to yourself: "Boy what a dummy I am. I can't get this wonderful, flawless mechanism to work." Well, you're not the dummy. It's your derailleur.

> Don't blame yourself for trouble. You're not the one at fault; it's that wonderful, flawless derailleur

Getting down to brands

YOU'LL BE pleased to know that the Campi Nuovo Record, the *cremé de la cremé* of derailleurs (and most expensive at about $40) is probably not the rear shifter for you. Unless you race. Low gears, which are what tourists (and out of shape people) need, can be better handled by cheaper models. We're going to look at six different brands of derailleurs, none of them American. We'll look at Simplex (French), Huret (French), Shimano (Japanese), Sun Tour (Japanese), Campagnolo (Italian) and Zeus (Spanish):

Simplex. This French company makes three models easily available in the U.S.: the Prestige, Criterium and the Super L.J. The Prestige abounds on bikes between $100 and $200. You'll recognize it by its plastic body, reinforced with steel. The name Simplex is another clue. The Prestige shifts nicely when new, gets worse with age. Its plastic parts may break down under heavy use. But for its under-$10 price it works as well as you could expect it to. It's not a bad choice if you expect to do only light cycling. If you plan a lot of long trips, though, pay the extra bread and hang on a better shifter—either that or shift very gently.

The Criterium is a little better model, but is also plastic and subject to the same problems as the Prestige.

Top of the line is the Super L.J., which is similar in design to the other two models but is made from aluminum alloy. This is definitely a good derailleur, but costly—only a few bucks less than Campagnolo. But it's also close to Campi in quality.

Huret. Also French, Huret makes several models, but the four most common in America are the Allvit, Svelto, Luxe and Jubilee. The Allvit is the counterpart of the Simplex Prestige. Replace it if you're planning long trips. The Allvit may last a little longer than the Simplex, being made of steel, not plastic, but is much harder shifting. In essence, the Simplex gives you nice shifting that may not last very long, while the Allvit provides long-lasting but hard shifting. For this reason, if you're going to replace the Allvit, do it right away. With the Simplex Prestige there is some logic in using it for a while to take advantage of its initial smoothness before replacing it.

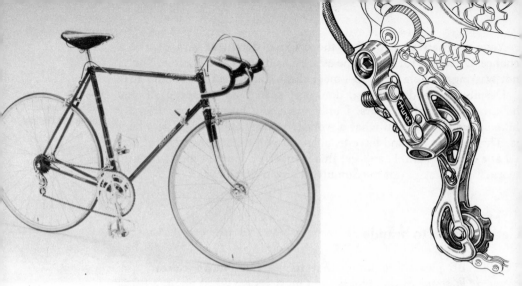

Raleigh Competition Mark III sports a Huret Jubilee derailleur, right, which is found on bikes just one bare notch below the professional level. Bike also has Reynolds 531 tubing.

A better bet than the Allvit is Huret's Svelto. The Svelto is still clumsier than the Simplex, but I prefer its all-metal construction for longer life. If your bike comes with a Svelto, give it a chance—it's a passable derailleur. Watch out, though. One Svelto model has a black plastic body; don't accept this one; stick with the metal. Better yet is the Luxe, which will handle lower gears than the Svelto or Allvit. It's made of steel also, but protected with chrome outside.

Top of the Huret line is the Jubilee, a beautiful alloy model that rivals the finest Campagnolo in workmanship—and price. Front and rear Jubilees will set you back about $50 if bought separately. Because of its price, and because it can handle only moderately low gears, the Jubilee is better left to the competition cyclist. Tourists may be better and more economically served by one of the better Shimanos or Sun Tours.

Shimano. This giant Japanese firm seems to be taking over the world's component business, at least as far as numbers are concerned. This company makes an incredible number of rear derailleurs, including: Lark-W, Lark-SS, Skylark, Lark STO, Eagle SS, Eagle GS, Eagle STO, Eagle GTO, GT-100, Tourney, Tourney GS, Titlest, Titlest GS, Crane and Crane GS.

All shifters up through the Tourney models are slight gradations in low-range derailleurs. The Titlest shifters are medium-range with the Cranes at the top of the line. GS after the model name generally means the derailleur handles a wider range of gears for touring (other brands use the initials GT).

The lower quality Shimanos are found on a variety of cheap 10-speeds and 5-speeds, though sometimes the bike maker puts his own name on the derailleur. Most common are the Lark and Eagle models. Both are roughly finished, made of steel and quite heavy. These lower

Shimanos are not known for their high quality. Trade up if you can to Shimano's newest model, the Titlest, a passable derailleur.

Better yet is Shimano's top model, the aluminum-alloy Crane. It comes in two configurations: the Crane and Crane GS, the latter being a wide-range touring derailleur. (Note: Touring derailleurs can be distinguished from racing shifters by their long arms extending downward. A chain must be deflected in front of a sprocket to be derailed into that sprocket; therefore, the bigger the sprockets, the longer the derailleur arm must be.)

I'd rank the Crane GS as the wisest choice for the tourist, better than even the slicker shifting Sun Tour V and Campagnolo Nuovo Record. It's slower and rougher than both, but holds up better than the Sun Tour and handles bigger rear sprockets than the Campi—it will take gears with over 30 teeth. Its main competition for the touring market is the Campi Gran Turismo, which is admittedly a slicker and even stronger mechanism. I still recommend the Crane GS, however, because it is more widely available and lighter. Let's say you're going to buy a $180 touring bike; it's likely to come with a Simplex Prestige derailleur. For $20 more (tops) you can switch to the Crane GS. The regular Crane model (non-GS) is a better bet for normal gearing (sprockets no bigger than 28 teeth).

Sun Tour (Maeda). All Sun Tours are passable. Sun Tour uses an ingenious design: The jockey wheel does not deflect the chain at a right angle to the plane of the cluster. Rather, the pantograph moves the cage at an angle, following the contour of the cluster—a sensible idea. (The Shimano Crane also features this design.)

Sun Tour's bottom-line derailleur, the GT, is reasonably priced, a

f you have a cheap and troublesome derailleur, consider the Shimano Crane as a replacement; it's relatively inexpensive. Right, Sun Tour derailleur derails the chain in a downward slant.

passable derailleur to switch to for little extra money if your bike comes with one of the cheaper Shimanos, Simplexes or Hurets. The Sun Tour V, V-GT and V-Lux are the expensive models—all very fast and smooth. The V-GT handles the wider ranges for tourists. The V is for normal gears; the V-Lux is the super racing model. All three of these derailleurs shift smooth as butter, smoother than the Campagnolo even. They may have one fault—they may break quicker than the Campi or good Shimanos. So if you plan to race, I'd stick to a more rugged brand even though some racers are now shifting with Sun Tour. If you don't ride that hard, though, and don't jam your derailleur into low gears under high pressure, any of the Sun Tours will give you pleasurable 10-speeding at reasonable prices. Even the V and V-GT models are less than half the cost of a Campi Nuovo Record.

One nice feature: Sun Tour shift levers have a ratchet action that further smoothes derailing, especially when shifting down under heavy load.

Campagnolo. This Italian company started it all and they still make the best. And still the most expensive. Luckily there are other brands that will serve you today (this wasn't true a decade ago). If you do have the money, however, and use close-ratio gears, I'd recommend spending it on a Campi because it will last and last and will probably appreciate in value as Campagnolo keeps escalating its prices. Think of it as an investment.

Only one Campi derailleur is suspect, the Valentino. This is a strong and sturdy derailleur, but a pain to work—it's difficult to shift into the lower gears. Many cyclists, however, like the Valentino for its durability. I'd rate it as passable.

The Gran Turismo is Campi's touring shifter. It weighs close to a pound (compared to the Nuovo Record's 8.5 ounces) and is practically indestructible. The maker says it will handle low gears with as many as 36 teeth on bikes with a smaller chainwheel as small as 36 teeth. What this means is that you can get a gear with a 1:1 ratio (36 x 36), which is about as low as you can ask (see the details of gearing and gear ratios on the following pages). The Gran Turismo is the perfect derailleur for 15-speed bikes (those with three chainwheels), but you won't see it on many stock bikes sold in this country.

The Nuovo Record is the ultimate derailleur; however it complains on gears that have up to 28 teeth

The Nuovo Record is the ultimate derailleur—most popular among racers. It's light, fast, durable, beautifully machined, beautifully finished. You really can't fault it for anything. However, it's not meant for extremely low gears. It's advertised to handle cogs up to 30 teeth, but I wouldn't try it. One bike equipment distributor (Big Wheel of Boulder, Colorado) more sensibly recommends it for bikes with a maximum low gear of 26 teeth. I've used it on gears up to 28 teeth and it handled these okay, but complained a little about it. You're also wasting the Campi if your gears are not narrowly spaced. The gears a racer uses differ slightly from each other. A racing cluster typically comprises gears of 14, 16, 18, 20 and 22 teeth, or even the extreme:

14, 15, 16, 17, 18! A more normal cluster might go: 14, 17, 20, 24, 28. The closer gears of the racer require a more precise shifter than the wide gears, and that's what the Nuovo Record is for. (A Simplex Prestige, for example, would have trouble finding gears on a racing cluster and would end up skipping sprockets frequently.) So if you've got or are getting a bike with wide gears, settle for a good Shimano or Sun Tour, and save money. Racers should get the Campi if they possibly can.

Zeus components may not be well known in this country, but they are fine, less-expensive versions of Campi shifters

Zeus. Zeus components, made in Abadiano, Spain, are not well-known in this country, except by racers. Basically, Zeus shifters are cheaper versions of Campagnolo—not as light, not as precise, but a reasonable alternative for those on a budget. The Criterium 69 is similar to the Nuovo Record and is used by many European racers. The cheaper Alfa 72 looks a lot like the Campi Valentino. An in-between model is the Alfa Junior.

Rounding up rear derailleurs

IN REVIEW, HERE ARE the derailleurs most commonly available that are good or at least passable:

Passable general-purpose models: Huret Svelto (steel model), Campagnolo Valentino, Shimano Titlest, Sun Tour GT. Of these, the Sun Tour GT probably shifts smoothest and is reasonably priced.

Good all-purpose or racing derailleurs: Simplex Super L.J., Huret Jubilee, Shimano Crane, Sun Tour V and V-Lux, Zeus Criterium 69 and Campagnolo Nuovo Record.

Passable touring derailleurs: Huret Luxe.

Good wide-range touring derailleurs: Sun Tour V-GT, Campagnolo Gran Turismo, Shimano Crane GS.

Left, Campagnolo Valentino isn't nearly as good as the Nuovo Record, but it's a strong and durable product. Right, typical front changer, as shown by this Huret Jubilee, is simpler in design than rear.

Derailleur manufacturers are constantly introducing new models and altering old ones so that the names are constantly changing. But the new products are often similar to the old and their names usually retain an old root so that you shouldn't have much difficulty in recognizing them (for instance, the Campi Nuovo Record is simply an update of the old Campi Record).

A bit of advice: Don't get trade-up happy. It makes infinite sense to strip a plastic Simplex off a $200 bike made with Reynolds 531 main tubes and clamp on something like a Shimano Crane. All you're doing is putting a good derailleur on a good frame. But don't strip a Shimano Lark or something off an $80 junker, throw on a Nuovo Record and think you've made a good bike out of it. It probably won' shift right anyway, what with its mis-aligned frame, imperfect chainwheels and a cluster that wiggles (common problems on cheap bikes).

A few words about front derailleurs

The Sun Tour is different from other front changers; it doesn't make sense but it works

STOCK BIKES INVARIABLY come with a front derailleur of the same brand as the rear. The job of the front derailleur is simple—it must move the chain from one chainring to the other.

Not all front shifters are true derailleurs in that they do not work off the pantograph principle. Instead, some use a push rod to knock the chain back and forth. These front changers are generally less accurate. In this category are the cheapest Simplex (Prestige), the Campi Valentino and some of the Zeus models. Most others use a pantograph.

Mention should also be made of the Sun Tour, which is different from other front changers. Normally, you pull down on the left lever to deform the parallelogram, pushing the cage outward and shifting the chain from the smaller to the larger sprocket. Pushing the lever back up releases the cable and a spring returns the cage to down-shift the chain. In other words, the power of your hand does the up-shifting; the spring does the weaker down-shifting. The Sun Tour works just the opposite. The spring does the stronger up-shifting, pulling the cage outwards. This doesn't seem to make much sense, but it works fine. What this means, though, is that you move the lever down to down-shift, up to up-shift, the reverse of any other front changer.

When trading derailleurs on a bike, it's best just to trade the rear and keep the front to simplify matters. If you have chosen your gears well, you will be using the front only one-quarter as many times as the rear, so almost any on the market will do. Some will just do better.

Straightening out gears and gear values

THE GEARS ARE just as important as the shifter. The five-gear cluster in combination with the double chainwheel gives you ten speeds. Obviously, low gears are easier to pedal, but propel you fewer feet with each turn of the cranks than high gears.

To get an idea of what kind of gearing you're buying, you can compute each of the ten speeds using one of two methods: gear *ratios* or gear *values*. A gear ratio is the number you get dividing the number of teeth on one of the rear cogs into the number of teeth on one of the front chainwheels. For instance, when the chain is on a 45-tooth chainwheel up front and a 15-tooth cog in back, the ratio is 3:1, or simply three.

But most cyclists today talk about gear values instead. This is the gear ratio multiplied by the diameter of the wheel, which in the case of 10 speeds is almost always 27 inches. In equation form:

$$\frac{\text{Number of teeth on front sprocket}}{\text{Number of teeth on rear sprocket}} \times \substack{\text{wheel diameter} \\ \text{(27 inches)}} = \text{Gear Value}$$

The value we end up with, say 70 inches for example, represents the size the wheel would be if you were riding a direct drive bike with a 1:1 ratio.

Use gear values based on the 27-inch multiplication figure to compare gears; it's a universal language

This is not a particularly valuable thing to know by itself. But it gives you an easy way to compare gears—i.e., you can see that a 100-inch gear is twice as big as a 50-inch gear, and will take you twice as far with each turn of the cranks.

The gear value is not the distance covered with each crank revolution, as some people believe. To get that you must multiply the gear value by Pi (3.14). Even that won't give you the exact distance, however, since all gear values are slightly inaccurate in that the actual diameter of any 27-inch wheel is not 27 inches—you'd have to figure in the width of your particular tires, inflated, to get an accurate figure. But don't bother. Just use gear values based on the 27-inch multiplication figure as a convenient away of comparing gears. It's a universal language, so other bike people will know what you're talking about. To save the trouble of working out the equation for gear values, use the handy chart.

Remember that what a particular gear feels like to your legs depends on the bike. A 60-inch gear on a Masi custom will probably be easier to pedal than an 80-inch gear on a Murray 45-pound 10-speed.

For a complete and exclusive gear chart for bikes with 27-inch wheels, turn the page. The chart will help you select the best gear values for your own needs.

Number of Teeth						Rear Sprocket					
	12	13	14	15	16	17	18	19	20	21	22
28	63.0	58.1	54.0	50.4	47.2	44.4	42.0	39.7	37.8	36.0	34.3
29	65.2	60.2	55.9	52.2	48.9	46.0	43.5	41.2	39.1	37.2	35.5
30	67.5	62.3	57.7	54.0	50.6	47.6	45.0	42.6	40.5	38.5	36.8
31	69.7	64.3	59.7	55.8	52.3	49.2	46.5	44.0	41.8	39.8	38.0
32	72.0	66.4	61.7	57.6	54.0	50.8	48.0	45.4	43.2	41.1	39.2
33	74.2	68.5	63.6	59.4	55.6	52.4	49.5	46.8	44.5	42.4	40.5
34	76.5	70.6	65.5	61.2	57.3	54.0	51.0	48.3	45.9	43.7	41.7
35	78.8	71.9	67.5	63.0	59.0	55.5	62.8	49.2	47.2	45.0	42.9
36	81.0	74.7	69.4	64.8	60.7	57.1	54.0	51.1	48.6	46.2	44.1
37	83.2	76.8	71.3	66.6	62.4	58.1	55.5	52.5	50.0	47.5	45.8
38	85.5	78.9	73.2	68.3	64.1	60.3	57.0	54.0	51.3	48.8	46.6
39	87.7	81.0	75.2	70.2	65.8	61.9	58.5	55.4	52.6	50.1	47.9
40	90.0	83.0	77.1	72.0	67.5	63.5	60.0	56.8	54.0	51.4	49.1
41	92.2	85.1	79.0	73.8	69.1	65.1	61.5	58.2	55.3	52.7	50.3
42	94.5	87.2	81.0	75.6	70.8	66.7	63.0	59.6	56.7	54.0	51.5
43	96.7	89.3	82.9	77.4	72.5	68.2	64.4	61.1	58.1	55.2	52.8
44	99.0	91.3	84.9	78.3	74.3	69.9	66.0	62.5	59.4	56.6	54.0
45	101.2	93.4	86.7	81.0	76.0	71.5	67.5	64.0	60.8	57.9	55.2
46	103.5	95.5	88.7	82.8	77.6	73.1	69.0	65.4	62.1	59.1	56.5
47	105.7	97.6	90.6	84.6	79.3	74.6	70.5	66.8	63.4	60.4	57.6
48	108.0	99.6	92.6	86.4	81.0	76.2	72.0	68.2	64.8	61.7	58.5
49	110.2	101.7	94.5	88.2	82.7	77.8	73.5	69.6	66.2	63.0	60.1
50	112.5	103.8	96.4	90.0	84.4	79.4	75.0	71.0	67.5	64.3	61.4
51	114.7	105.3	98.4	91.8	86.1	81.0	76.5	72.5	68.8	65.6	62.6
52	117.0	108.0	100.3	93.6	87.8	82.6	78.0	73.9	70.2	66.9	63.8
53	119.1	110.0	102.2	95.4	89.4	84.1	79.5	75.3	71.5	68.1	65.0
54	121.5	112.1	104.1	97.2	91.1	85.8	81.0	76.7	72.9	69.4	66.2
55	123.7	114.2	106.0	99.0	92.8	87.3	82.5	78.1	74.2	70.7	67.5
56	126.0	116.3	108.0	100.8	94.5	88.9	84.0	79.0	75.6	72.0	68.7

Front Chainwheel (vertical label at left)

* Values for 33-tooth sprockets are not given as this is a highly unusual gear

Bad news—your 10-speed is really a 6-speed!

WHEN SELECTING A bike, you can compute all ten gears if you want, and you can use all ten if you want, but I'd recommend considering only six (at most, eight) since some of the gears are inefficient and hard on the chain. (An explanation will follow.) Also, using all ten gears calls for some silly shifting. Take a look at one popular 10-speed that has chain wheels of 40 and 50 teeth and a cluster of 14-17-20-24-28. Set up in a chart, here's what the gear values would look like (I've listed the cluster in reverse order to get a progression of gears from low to high):

Consider that you have only six—or at most eight—gears since some are inefficient and hard on the chain

	28	24	20	17	14
40	39	45	54	64	77
50	48	56	68	80	96

The first thing you'll notice is that there is near duplication: the 40 x 20 (a 54-inch gear value) is but two inches different from 50 x 24

23	24	25	26	27	28	29	30	31	32	34*
32.8	31.5	30.2	29.0	28.0	27.0	26.0	25.2	24.3	23.5	22.1
34.0	32.6	31.3	30.1	29.0	28.3	27.0	26.1	25.4	24.6	23.0
35.2	33.7	32.4	31.1	30.0	28.9	27.9	27.0	26.2	25.4	23.7
36.4	34.8	33.4	32.1	31.0	29.8	28.8	27.9	27.0	26.2	24.6
37.5	36.0	34.6	33.2	32.0	30.8	29.7	28.8	27.8	27.0	25.4
38.7	37.1	35.6	34.2	33.0	31.8	30.7	29.7	28.6	27.8	26.2
39.9	38.2	36.7	35.3	34.0	32.7	31.6	30.6	29.4	28.4	27.0
41.0	39.3	37.8	36.3	35.0	33.7	32.5	31.5	30.5	29.4	27.8
42.2	40.5	38.8	37.3	36.0	34.7	33.5	32.4	31.3	30.5	28.6
43.4	41.6	40.0	38.4	37.0	35.6	34.4	33.3	32.1	31.3	29.5
44.6	42.7	41.0	39.4	38.0	36.6	35.3	34.2	32.9	32.1	30.2
45.8	43.9	42.1	40.5	39.0	37.6	36.3	35.1	33.7	32.9	31.1
47.0	45.0	43.2	41.5	40.0	38.6	37.2	36.0	34.8	33.6	31.9
48.1	46.1	44.2	42.4	41.0	39.5	38.1	36.9	35.6	34.6	32.4
49.3	47.2	45.3	43.6	42.0	40.5	39.1	37.8	36.4	35.4	33.5
50.4	48.3	46.4	44.6	43.0	41.4	40.0	38.7	37.2	36.2	34.0
51.6	49.5	47.5	45.7	44.0	42.4	40.9	39.6	38.3	37.3	34.8
52.8	50.7	48.6	46.7	45.0	43.4	41.8	40.5	39.2	38.1	35.6
54.0	51.8	49.7	47.8	46.0	44.4	42.8	41.4	40.0	38.9	36.5
55.2	52.9	50.8	48.8	47.0	45.3	43.4	42.3	41.0	39.7	37.3
56.3	54.0	51.8	49.9	48.0	46.5	44.6	43.2	41.9	40.5	38.1
57.5	55.1	52.9	50.9	49.0	47.2	45.6	44.1	42.7	41.3	38.9
58.7	56.3	54.0	51.9	50.0	48.2	46.5	45.0	43.5	42.2	39.7
59.9	57.4	55.1	53.0	51.0	49.2	47.4	45.9	44.6	42.9	40.5
61.0	58.5	56.2	54.0	52.0	50.1	48.4	46.8	45.4	44.0	41.3
62.2	59.6	57.2	55.0	53.0	51.1	49.3	47.7	46.2	44.8	42.1
63.3	60.7	58.3	56.0	54.0	52.0	50.2	48.6	47.0	45.6	42.9
64.5	61.8	59.4	57.1	55.0	53.0	51.2	49.5	47.8	46.4	43.7
65.7	63.0	60.4	58.1	56.0	54.0	52.1	50.4	48.9	47.3	44.6

(56 inches). Also note that shifting up consecutively through all ten gears takes a lot of shifting. The lowest gear is 39. One shift on the rear derailleur takes you up to 45. But to get to the next highest gear (48) you must down-shift the rear and then up-shift the front changer. To get to "fourth gear" you must down-shift the front, then double shift the rear . . . and so on. How the gears progress and how you must shift varies from bike to bike, but most require these double and triple shifts.

Instead, you make a 6-speed out of your bike by using only the gears in the solid box:

	28	24	20	17	14
40	39	45	54	64	77
50	48	56	68	80	96

You can also use the two gears boxed off with dotted lines if you need them. But the six-gear box is best. This gives you a one-shift-at-a-time progression and still preserves your lowest and highest gears.

More important, it eliminates four troublesome gears. The gears outside the box above require the chain to bend at severe angles—either because the chain is on the outside chainwheel and must travel to the inside of the cluster or vice versa. Never use the two extreme gears (in this case, 50 x 28 and 40 x 14). In these positions the chain is bent so much going from outside to inside or vice versa that it can rub against the front derailleur cage, and usually will.

Even in the gears boxed off by dotted lines you are losing some responsiveness because of the deflected chain. The middle gear of the cluster is the one cog that can be easily used in combination with either chainwheel as it is centered directly between them. You should set your bike up so that these two combinations will be your main on-the-flat riding gears. Ideally, the higher gear should be your main gear with the bike empty; the lower your main gear with the bike loaded for touring.

Some readers will balk at the suggestion that they not use all the gears they paid for. But really, six or eight gears, well chosen, will get you over even the most varied terrain. And speaking of well-chosen gears, that brings us to our next question. . . .

What are the right gears for you?

YOU CAN'T TALK sensibly about gearing with most people, especially men. Good old-fashioned *macho* always comes into play.

Once at a bike show I was standing with a group of people examining a new line of racing machines. The top gear was a 52 x 13—a 108-inch gear value, a normal high racing gear. And I couldn't help overhearing a paunchy, middle-aged guy telling his wife how *he* needed a bike with much higher gears than those on the racing bike.

And an acquaintance of mine once complained to me that his new 10-speed was no good. The highest gear, he said, was too easy for him. So I took a look at his bike. It had a high gear of over 100 inches! Too easy?

The point is that a lot of riders are hung up on strength. They equate high gears with masculinity. They like to think of themselves as supermen and try to ride accordingly. The great French racer, Anquetil, reportedly used a gear in the low 90s for his final sprints. Many track racers also use gears in this neighborhood, and this is for putting out a maximum effort over a distance of only 200 meters. Yet you find countless out-of-shape men who claim their 100-inch high gears are not tough enough for them.

They probably do use those high gears, though. How do they do it? By turning the pedals very, very slowly. Racers and good tourists practice the opposite method. They learn to turn lower gears very, very fast. A road racer will want to average over 100 rpm (crank revolutions per minute). An experienced tourist can average 75 to 90 rpm.

So what gears are right for that 75 to 90 rpm cadence? Well, you must take into account that the gears you need vary from bike to bike, and also depend on your physical condition. But suppose you're considering a bike in the 28- to 30-pound range, and that you're in reasonably good shape (and you will be after a couple months of cycling). There are two crucial gears you must have. First, you'll want a good on-the-level riding gear. About 60 to 70 inches is a good main gear for most people starting out. Make sure that this main gear is one of the two middle gears on the bike—that is, either the third or fourth gear in a six-gear progression, using the middle cog on the freewheel cluster. This main gear can be considerably lower than 60 inches if you wish, but not higher (forget about your ego for the moment).

The other crucial gear is your lowest gear—the small chainwheel in conjunction with the largest rear cog. No low gear is too low. You will always hit hills that make you get off and walk the bike. But look for a low gear around 40 inches if you plan to ride the bike empty, never strapping on panniers or other gear. Luckily, most good bikes in the 30-pound, $150 to $200 range will give you a 38- or 39-inch gear or thereabouts. But watch out if you're buying expensive models suitable for racing. Often the lowest gear on these jobs (say a 49 x 22) is around 60 inches. Ouch! Get ready for leg cramps. Make your dealer change the gearing before you buy.

The prospective tourist will also have to alter his gears in many other cases. The 40-incher will be too high for most hills when you've got 20 or 25 pounds of gear tied on the bike. Shoot for close to 30 inches or even below that if you can get it. About 32 inches will serve most people adequately. A 36 x 30 is just one combination that will give you this gear value.

Okay, if your new bike offers these two crucial gears—a normal and a low—it is adequate. Now look for two more important (but not crucial) features. First, you might want a good high gear so you can take advantage of tail winds and the good side of hills. A 90-incher should do it. You won't be in this gear for long periods and if it's not high enough that's no big sweat since you can always coast. I have yet to see, by the way, a stock bike which did not have a high enough gear; most come with a 100-incher.

More important, try for a fairly *narrow* range of gears. This is unorthodox advice, so I feel obligated first to state the orthodox view on gearing. Most experts recommend just the opposite for touring cyclists, saying you should get a wide range. The rationale behind this is that racers traditionally use a narrow range of gears, covering only 40 inches or so. Let's look at a typical racing set-up:

	22	20	18	16	14
49	60	66	74	83	95
52	64	70	78	88	100

Again the six most useful gears are outlined. The differences between these gears are significant enough to be of value for handling different terrain, but close enough so that the rider can choose the exact gear to fit his pedaling cadence. If there are huge gaps between gears he may not be able to find the one perfect for the occasion and will have to change his pedaling rhythm. To get these close gears and still have a good high sprint gear for the final rush, he must sacrifice— so he gives up low gears. His good body allows him to do this.

So what about weaker riders with slower bikes? Well, the experts say you should retain the same high gears a racer uses, but to add some gears at the lower end. So you end up with gear values ranging from, say, 38 to 100. This is what is meant by a wide range of gears.

In my opinion, this arrangement can stand in the way of good cycling. The long-distance tourist, just like the racer, should develop a high, steady cadence—the difference being that lower gears will be used and also a slightly lower cadence. But the cadence should be *steady* nonetheless. So once again, a fairly narrow range of gears is called for—only lower on the scale. Like the racer, you must sacrifice something for close gears. So you give up those superhigh gears.

This brings us to yet another bicycle myth: a 10-speed isn't any good unless it has very high gears. And the bike industry follows this myth religiously. Here's the wide-range gearing set-up on one of the most popular touring bikes ever sold in the U.S.:

	28	23	19	16	14
36	35	42	51	61	69
52	50	61	74	88	100

Again the useful six-gear range is outlined (and notice that the two marginal gears—in dotted lines—are identical, both 61s). Note that this bike gives you a good low gear, 35, and progresses fine to 42, then 51. But it skips an incredible 23 inches from 51 to 74 right in the middle of what is most riders' main riding range! You'd have to use one of the four unrecommended combinations to get a decent middle gear.

Why is it set up this way? Mostly to maintain those silly high gears that most of us aren't strong enough to use effectively. The most popular chainwheel size seems to be the 52-teeth model. These are used on racing and touring bikes alike, but they just don't make sense on the latter. Yet that's what you're likely to find as your outside chainring (with an occasional 50-toother).

Getting back to the bike above, it gives you a top gear of 100 when actually the next one down, 88 is all you should need. You could better use another gear in the middle range. Keep in mind that Mike Neel, U.S. pursuit champion, won the national title using a gear of only 94 inches—and this on a 20-pound bike in a race that lasts but five minutes. So what do you need that 100-inch job for—pedaling down cliffs?

Knowing full well that I'll never talk many riders out of their leg-breaking high gears, let me suggest an alternative set-up. The particular bike diagrammed above has a good touring cluster; leave it

So what do you need a 100-inch gear for—pedaling down cliffs?

alone and just change that monster 52-tooth chainring to a 46:

	28	23	19	16	14
36	35	42	51	61	69
46	44	54	65	78	89

This arrangement decreases the range by 11 inches, but still gives you an adequate high gear of 89. It also gives you a good on-the-level gear of 65 and a 78 for when you're traveling light and really feeling energetic (previously you had an 88 in the same position—really more of a sprint or downhill gear). And it eliminates the duplication in the two marginal gears. Now you have a 54 and a 61 if you absolutely need them instead of two 61s.

Mind you, many bike store people will scream if you ask for a close gear arrangement like this; some because they just don't want to make alterations on the bike and some because they're ex-racers who have a real need for big gears. Always choose your gears according to your own needs, not the guy in the store.

Don't mind the guy's screams. Always choose gears according to your own needs, not the guy in the store

I don't cite the gearing above as what you should definitely have, but only to give you an idea of what is involved in deciding on sprocket sizes. You may even want closer gears than are listed above. While some experts would describe this range as too narrow, it still isn't as narrow as a racer's gearing which usually spans only 40 inches (as opposed to 54 above).

The best way to find the best gearing arrangement is to decide on the bike you want, then write down the number of the teeth in all seven cogs. Go home and sit down with the gear chart to see how you can modify the gears for your purposes. Play around with various combinations to see how you can most easily get what you need.

How to change bicycle gearing to suit yourself

ANY DEALER WORTH his Lubriplate will alter the cluster for you. Some charge extra but it's worth it. Usually the gears on a cluster are separate cogs that can be replaced individually. Sometimes, though, the cluster is all one piece and you'll have to order a whole new unit.

The other way the gearing can be changed is by replacing chainrings. For some reason, many cyclists don't think of this even though it's a much easier operation. Dealers who don't do a big parts business, however, may not want to trade chainrings with you for fear of getting stuck with an extra part. In that case you may want to buy a new chainring outright. Let's say the bike comes with a 52-tooth sprocket. You want a 46. Buy the 46er, make the dealer put it on the bike and keep the 52 for some day when you're strong enough for it. Chainwheels are available in sizes from 28 to 56 teeth, though you don't see too many below 30.

Freewheel cogs are now available as big as 34 teeth, but you shouldn't have to go that big as long as you keep those chainrings small (it's silly to stick a 34-tooth gear on a cluster in order to get a 33-inch gear value from a 42-tooth chainring when a 37 x 30 will give you the same value with less weight from those big sprockets). To make shifting easier, keep those rear gears to 30 teeth or less. Gears also go as small as 12 teeth, but stick with the standard 14 or higher—the 12s and 13s wear too fast.

Be critical when selecting cluster progression and you then can keep the gearing in pace as you get stronger (or weaker) simply by switching chainrings. Remember this one rule: A smooth progression of teeth size does not give you a smooth progression of gear values. For example, 14-17-20-23-26 will produce increasingly bigger jumps as you shift up (from 26 to 14). The earlier-examined uneven cluster of 14-16-19-23-28 is quite a good one. Turn back and study the gear value progression you get with this cluster and you'll understand.

Is there a chance you won't need to change the gearing? Yes, in two instances. Racing bikes with racing clusters are usually well designed for their purpose. It's always the medium-priced touring 10-speeds that are the problem. Strangely enough, some of the heaviest, slowest bikes have the highest gears. But if you're just going to use a bike for commuting or other short trips, you can get along with stock gearing.

Fit the derailleur to the gears

WHEN YOU CHANGE the gearing, you may be switching it out of the range of the stock derailleur, especially if you go bigger than a 28-tooth cog in the rear. The derailleur must be able to clear the bottom of the biggest cog. Lower gears also require more chain and therefore the derailleur must have adequate slack-taking-up capacity.

Derailleurs have advertised ranges, usually marked on their packing boxes, such as 13-26-36-53. The first two numbers are the minimum and maximum teeth the cluster may have; the last two numbers represent the minimum and maximum chainwheel sizes. Often, only the cluster capacity is advertised (i.e., 13-26), and this is the most crucial information. I'd suggest not trusting these advertised ranges fully, and keeping your largest cog two teeth below the maximum (to

Shimano 14-17-21-26-32 freewheel cluster. Note that 26- and 32-tooth gears have alternate teeth missing.

28 teeth for a 13-30 derailleur, etc.). Of course, some manufacturers are more truthful than others. Usually the lower the stated maximum, the more I'd trust it. Any derailleur marked GT (Grand Touring) is usually good for cogs of 30 or more teeth.

Remember that chain length will have to be adjusted whenever gearing is modified.

Choosing stopping power—brakes

WHEN WE TALK ABOUT BRAKES we're in myth territory again. In this case the myth goes: Center-pulls are good; side-pulls are bad.

The best brakes made are Campagnolo side-pulls. Universal also makes side-pulls that are superior to almost any center-pulls. Weinmann makes a good economically-priced side-pull and Shimano makes a brake almost identical to the Campi model.

Let's examine the difference between the two types: Side-pulls pull from the side; center-pulls pull from the center. Got that? More precisely, both types of caliper brakes have two arms which rotate in opposite directions, thus clamping the wheel rim between two brake pads. But side-pull arms both pivot around one point on the side while center-pull arms each rotate on their own separate pivot. On side-pulls the cable is connected to both arms on one side; on center-pulls the cable is not connected to the arms themselves but to a little carrier centered above and between them. A transverse, or crossover, cable transfers the pulling action to both arms.

Left, center-pull brakes require a carrier which pulls up a crossover cable. Right, side-pull brakes swing both arms around a single pivot. When you depress the lever, the cable pulls the lower arms up and forces the upper arms downward.

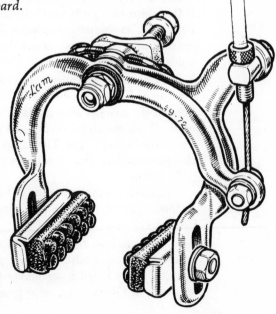

The reason side-pulls are badmouthed is because their design has two disadvantages:

• 1. On side-pull brakes, all the action is taking place around a single post and the complexity at this one pivot can create problems. The single post must handle two arms moving in opposite directions and also incorporates a spring to keep the arms open. This can mean a lot of friction and results in sticky brakes when something goes wrong. The center-pull eliminates a lot of problems with two pivots, each with its own spring. The post which serves as a pivot for both arms on a side-pull also holds the brake assembly to the bike's frame. To anchor the brake firmly, this bolt must be turned very tight, and if there are not good bearings isolating the two arms, turning the bolt tight may squeeze the arms together and cramp their movement. The center-pull eliminates this problem by using a separate bolt whose only job is to anchor the brake.

It's more difficult to get good side-pull than center-pull brakes, but the good side-pulls are considered the best of all

• 2. Also, with one cable compressing both arms, the force is often applied unevenly, sending one pad against the rim ahead of the other. The carrier on center-pull brakes and its crossover cable assure equal pull on both arms.

Okay, so it looks bad for side-pull brakes. Admittedly, it is more difficult to make a good side-pull than a good center-pull. But not impossible. And the good ones that are built are considered superior to the center-pulls. They are simpler, with fewer moving parts, and they save on weight (besides its extra pivots, cable and carrier, the center-pull needs a separate anchoring crossbar). More important, side-pulls, if made well, provide a more positive action because they use only one cable. Your effort on the levers is transferred directly to the brake arms.

But if they are not made precisely, side-pulls aren't worth having. If you want side-pulls, you'll be safe sticking to the brands mentioned: Universal, Weinmann, Shimano and Campagnolo. Otherwise stick to center-pulls. In this one aspect the old myth about side-pull inferiority holds some water.

Because of its simplicity, the side-pull design is attractive to third-rate manufacturers who have botched the job over the years and flooded the market with loads of crumby brakes. These side-pulls exhibit all the problems mentioned earlier and are the reason side-pulls have such a bad name. The range of brakes goes something like this: cheapies—side-pulls; medium-price—center-pulls; expensive—side-pulls again.

There are too many brands of brakes to mention them all, but added to those named above, a few widely popular makes are Mafac, Dia-Compe, GB and Zeus.

Features to look for: quick-release levers (makes it easier to remove wheel), with cable adjusters (so you can take up slack caused by cable stretch) and padded lever hoods (a nice place to rest your hands on long rides). Quick-releases in lever housings (as on some Weinmann brakes) generally work better and easier than those situated at the end of the cable housing right above the brake assembly itself.

The shorter the lever arm the greater the force you can apply to the rim. So go with shorter arms if you have the choice. If you are buying clincher rims and big tires, you will probably need the longer arms. If you are buying a track bike you will be forced to get short-armed models because of the minimal clearance under the crown and bridge. Good side-pulls will usually fill this need.

Look for a strong spring action. Most brake failures do not result from arms that fail to close, but from arms that fail to return. Often a stretched cable is at fault, but a good spring will help overcome this problem. One difference between Universal's cheaper center-pulls and their good ones is the size of the spring.

The rubber used in brake pads varies in hardness. Universals generally have hard pads, for example; Mafacs use very soft ones. The softer kind tend to grab a little better when new and give good stops, but they wear out a lot faster. It's a matter of preference, really. I've worn out Mafac pads in a couple of months, but it doesn't really matter since they're cheap and easy to replace.

Generally, there isn't much difference among brakes when it comes to stopping power. They all stop you smartly in dry weather. None of them work well in the rain (Mafac's soft pads are probably the best). The better brakes may stop you a little faster, but mainly their advantage is smoothness, longevity and special convenience features.

Comfort consideration—the saddle

NOW WE'RE GETTING into a sensitive area—mainly your hindquarters. It is with great reluctance that I place this item so far down the list in importance. But obviously most readers, especially younger riders, will not be much concerned with where they sit. Those of us who are of a softer nature need to pay more attention to selecting the proper saddle, however, since the wrong seat can end a ride prematurely.

First there's the question of padded or unpadded. Reasonably enough, most prospective cyclists believe padded saddles offer more comfort than the unpadded kind. However, saddles that attempt to take the sting out of the road using cushy padding or springs or both don't always work. Springs can make you bounce from side to side and soak up your pedaling action. And many cheap padded saddles are basically metal plates with some fluff and then a cover over the whole affair. After a while the weight of your body pushes the padding to either side and what you end up sitting on is the bare metal. Never buy one of these things unless they throw in a free tube of Preparation H.

If you want padding, make sure the seat has a plastic, not a metal, base and that the padding is very firmly packed. The best padded seat

It's a delicate question: Should you go with a padded or unpadded saddle?

available is the Unica, which has a plastic (nylon, actually) base, a thin layer of foam rubber and a covering of leather. But this seat is costly (about $20). Other saddles (cheaper ones) with this design will soon be appearing on the market and may be worth examining. The cyclist searching for a bike in the medium-price range, though, is best off with an unpadded chair.

Watch the shape. Those big touring seats can bind your skin; a skinny saddle gives you less to sit on, but is more comfortable

As for shape, the skinny "racing" saddle serves the tourist as well as the competitor. Racing saddles vary in shape, but what's important is that the front part is skinny to allow pedaling room for your thighs. Those big so-called touring seats can bind your skin and restrict your movement. The skinny saddle gives you less to sit on, sure, but will be more comfortable overall.

The third concern is material. Throwing out metal seats as unacceptable, we're left with three alternatives: plastic, leather and nylon/leather. Plastic often feels softer than leather—at first. The problem is that it won't break in. Leather is a safer bet. Most leather seats are harder at first, but will eventually reach a compromise with your rear end (a little persuasion from neat's foot oil and saddle soap will help). Trading your new bike's plastic seat for a leather one will normally cost you a few bucks more, but is worth it for most riders.

Nylon/leather seats consist of a nylon base covered with thin leather. They don't really break in, but they don't need to. They're fairly pliable to begin with. Unica has pioneered this type of saddle and it's now ahead of even the very best leather brands in popularity among racers. It is lighter than a leather saddle, and though expensive, is still cheaper than some all-leather professional models. The Brooks top-line leather saddle, for instance, costs over $25. An unpadded Unica nylon/leather saddle costs about $17. And you can get a Japanese version even cheaper. Where the nylon/leather seat gets beaten out by the pure leather models is in the area of breaking-in. While the Unica type saddle is comfortable enough, it will never conform to your individual contours the way all-leather does.

Left, a soft padded saddle built on a steel base with springs. Avoid this type, as springs waste energy. Right, a padded saddle on a leather or plastic base is a much better bet.

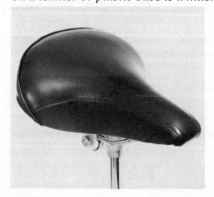 

For those on a budget, a medium-priced leather seat is the answer. There are a zillion brands, many of them adequate. You can compare softness on different saddles just by feeling. Two companies that make a wide range of good leather seats are Brooks and Ideale. Once you break in a good leather seat and are satisfied with it, keep it even if you change bikes.

Cranks and chainwheels

YOU HAVE THREE choices of cranks: cotterless, cottered and one-piece.

Cotterless cranks are best and are invariably made from aluminum alloy. Unlike cottered cranks, there is no cotter pin that goes through the cranks and into the axle. You will need a special cotterless crank tool to tighten these cranks (the tool varies from brand to brand). It is wise to tighten the cranks every 25 miles or so for the first couple of hundred miles to make sure they are properly seated. The new cotterless aluminum cranks are quite strong so you needn't worry about breaking them even if you are a strong pedaler. When they first became popular, many track racers stuck with the old steel design for added strength. Today even trackies are switching over to cotterless alloy. Cotterless cranks appear on bikes costing $250 or more.

Cottered steel cranks are common on medium-priced bikes. They're perfectly adequate for most riders. Bike-world myth has it that the third type of cranks, one-piece (sometimes called American cranks), are inferior to cottered cranks. The cranks and the axle are all one

Below, for a medium-priced bike, all-leather saddle is your best bet. It'll be hard at first, but will break in. Right, this is the Nervar cotterless crank with a double chainring. The crank arm and star-shaped extenders are all one piece. Changing chainrings is the easiest way to modify a bike's gearing.

piece. This design is often found on kids' bikes and is usually a little heavier than cottered. But that doesn't mean it's no good. If a crank breaks, the entire assembly must be replaced, but they don't break very often. And there is less to go wrong. The trouble with the cottered variety is that the damn pins can wear out of shape and fall out. And if you continue to ride the bike when this happens you can destroy the cranks.

To check cottered and cotterless cranks, grab the pedals and put the cranks in the horizontal position. Now move the pedals back and forth slightly to make sure the cranks are moving together and that neither is clunking around loosely on the axle, even moving a fraction of an inch without the other one. One-piece cranks, of course, are not subject to these problems.

Don't mix brands of chainwheels and cranks; they may not jibe

Good brands include Campagnolo, Stronglight, T.A. and Sugino; others include Shimano, Nervar and Zeus. Stronglight steel cottered cranks are quite common on medium-priced bicycles.

The most important thing to consider about chainwheels is their number of teeth, which we've already discussed. Otherwise, chainwheels are made by the same people who make cranks. I don't recommend mixing brands of chainwheels and cranks because they won't usually connect to each other.

You may want to use the chainwheels to check gear alignment. Get down low and sight through the space between the chainrings back toward the cluster. The middle sprocket in back should be centered between the two chainwheels. Make sure chainwheel teeth are not bent.

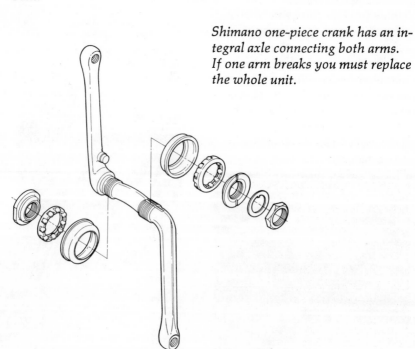

Shimano one-piece crank has an integral axle connecting both arms. If one arm breaks you must replace the whole unit.

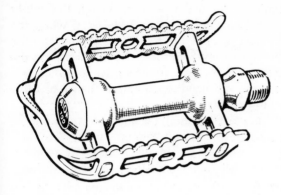

This Atom rattrap model is a good economy-range pedal. All a pedal has to do, after all, is revolve freely and supply a place to put your foot. But if you have money to burn, get the special Campi black models: Would you believe $40?

Pedals, chains, clusters, levers and other stuff

FOR 10-SPEEDS I would stick to rattrap (all-metal) *pedals.* Even if you're presently scared of toe clips, you may want to add them someday and they won't attach to the rubber kind of pedals. If you're not getting clips, also look for pedals with gripping teeth on both sides to help you maintain a firm foothold. Racing pedals that must be used with toe clips are smaller, have no teeth and have only one side that is used as a pedaling surface.

The best pedals have ball bearings. Usually you can judge the quality of a pedal just by looking at it

In general, pedals with ball bearings are better than those without. Spin the pedals to make sure they move freely. Campagnolo again makes the best, but Lyotard makes some reasonably priced models with a reduction in performance few can detect. Generally you can judge pedal material just by looking—some are thin and flimsy and can be bent, especially if you sideswipe something when walking the bike.

Chains are not something you choose a bike by, despite their importance. If everything else is right, trust that the manufacturer has not skimped on this item. Check for tightness, though. Hold the top of the chain tight with the chainwheel (by pushing down on the pedal with your hand) and see how far you can pull up on the chain. About ¼ to ½ inch is right. Don't do this test on the bottom section of chain because the spring action of the derailleur will let you deflect plenty of chain. Two good chain brands are Regina and Sedis.

The most important thing about *clusters* is the number of teeth in their cogs. Cyclo, Regina and Everest are top names, but there are other good ones too. Atom makes a lot of medium-price-range freewheel clusters and Shimano specializes in giant sprockets. Shimano's newest freewheel sports a 14-34 range with every other tooth missing on the two biggest gears to make shifting easier.

Some *shift levers* are better made than others, but I'd go with whatever comes with the derailleur you choose. It's not really worth it to go through the bother of installing Sun Tour levers to work your Simplex Super L.J. derailleur, for instance, even though this might be a nice arrangement. What you should check, however, is where the levers are mounted. The best place is the traditional position on the down tube. You can't be injured on them there. Second best is on the tips of the handlebars, but shifters here are expensive and require a longer cable taped up around the handlebars—more chance of cable problems and uncomfortable on the hands.

Unfortunately, a new popular position for shift levers is on the handlebar stem. I'm against them on two counts: 1) They are dangerous; you could impale yourself in a head-over-handlebars accident, and 2) you could turn the handlebars accidentally in the act of shifting.

Never accept a bicycle which has shift levers on the *top* tube, for obvious reasons.

Headset. The headset holds the fork in the head tube so it can be connected to the handlebar stem and you can steer the bike. Turn the handlebars and make sure the whole handlebar-fork assembly swivels smoothly (the headset is basically a complex group of bearings, races and nuts). It should not bind and you shouldn't hear any noises coming from the head tube.

Bottom bracket assembly. This holds the cranks in the frame, and includes an axle and two sets of bearings and cups so everything spins smoothly. To test the bottom bracket, lift the chain off the chainwheel and spin the cranks. They should spin smoothly, without binding, and once again you should hear no finky noises coming from the assembly.

Paint job, finish, styling. Obviously this is just a matter of taste. Chrome, however, does serve a function. Often the bottom six inches of the front fork blades and four inches of the rear stays are chromed to protect the bike against rocks or gravel. Some expensive bikes are chromed all over. This has the advantage of not chipping, plus it makes the bike a little easier to clean. And on a bright day you will blind everyone on the road. Then again, some racing bikes are not chromed at all, because chrome adds weight and a professional racer probably doesn't lose too much sleep over chips in his paint job.

Highly polished components such as derailleurs and chainwheels are also convenient because grease and dirt won't adhere to them as easily. Campagnolo (who else?) is the champion of parts polishers.

Reality vs. your dreams

THAT'S THE GAMUT of bike components, and you probably have already formed some preferences about what you want. However, you most likely won't be able to go out and find the precise parts you want on any one production bicycle. You'll have to compromise.

Be reasonable. You can't expect a bike store to replace every item on the bike. Remember that some parts are easier to change than others.

The safest position for shift levers is on the down tube. These are Sun Tour levers (on a Fuji) which feature a ratchet action for smoother shifting, especially when you're trying to get that chain on those big sprockets while pedaling hard up a hill.

Windsor Carrera, made in Mexico, sports handlebar-tip derailleur levers by Sun Tour. It also has sew-up tires, a covered nylon racing saddle, Dia-Compe brakes.

Let's say you find a bike you like except for one thing: You're not pleased with the rims. Either forget about it or find a different bike. Changing a rim means building a whole new wheel. This is not a reasonable proposition for a medium-priced bike. Either the salesman will tell you to take a walk or he'll agree to the switch for an extra $40 or $50.

Anything a dealer cannot re-sell easily is going to cost you—stuff like headsets, cranks, bottom brackets, handlebars, etc. Also, it just makes sense when buying a bike in the middle-price category to change as few things as possible to keep the cost down. Otherwise you'll be pushing yourself into a whole new price range without a commensurate rise in quality. Just the same, there are a few parts that you should insist on changing if you are at all dissatisfied with them:

1. *Gears.* If you don't have a low enough gear or a good normal riding gear or even the proper range of gears, why buy a 10-speed? You throw away your money if you don't get the gears you need.

2. *Derailleur.* When your shifter gets shiftless in Cheyenne you'll be sorry you didn't spend the money back in the shop.

3. *Handlebar stem.* It's no good if it's the wrong size.

4. *Saddle.* An easy operation for the dealer and a meaningful one for you if the alternative is riding on cruel plastic or metal.

Be forewarned that many dealers are reluctant to make these alterations, even at a price, as too many of them are simply interested in selling with no regard for service—especially those who up until last year were selling washing machines or ran beet-and-meatloaf em-

Here's a nice, but certainly unessential, feature—chrome on six inches of the fork blades to protect against flying gravel.

poriums. That's why it's worth it to go to a shop geared to a free exchange of equipment (if not free in price, at least free in spirit) even if that means traveling several miles out of your way.

How do you find such a place? One clue is advertising. Those which advertise component names (Campagnolo, Cinelli, Zeus, etc.) and/or custom frames (Masi, Eisentraut, Colnago, Bob Jackson, Ron Kitching, Holdsworth, etc.) are likely to offer finer service.

Getting lucky

OFTEN MANUFACTURERS will not list specific brands of components in their specifications, but simply state: steel derailleur, alloy handlebars, rattrap pedals, etc. This is especially true in moderately priced lines which are in high demand and for which the maker never knows if he can get enough parts. He may not be able to get enough Simplex Prestige derailleurs, for instance, and have to switch to Huret Allvits or Sveltos. Your goal is to make this work to your advantage. Gitanes, for instance, sometimes come with Sun Tour derailleurs, sometimes with Simplex. You may see them side by side in the store. Demand the Sun Tour equipped model. Gitanes also come with either the good Lyotard pedals or some other nondescript brand. Take the Lyotard. The price remains the same. If two different stores are selling Atalas, go to both places. The bikes may not be equal at all, though prices probably will be.

The mythical test ride

THIS WHOLE DISCUSSION of parts is totally silly, you may say, when the best way to choose a bicycle is to ride a bunch of them and pick the one you like best. No argument, in principle. But the cold truth is that you seldom are permitted a test ride. Sometimes you'll be allowed to pedal around the parking lot, but that's really not enough.

If you are allowed an extensive test ride, though, just ride the bike the way you intend to use it and:

1. See if you can ride it no-hands (test of a straight frame).

2. Lean the bike hard around corners to check for frame whip.

3. Try out the brakes coming down a good hill (not necessarily a panic stop, just see if you can control the bike safely).

4. Climb a hill pulling up hard on the handlebars (you'll be able to feel how much give there is in the headset and in the frame and handlebars—most bikes will creak a little bit, a really good one won't).

5. Shift liberally, but especially try down-shifting while climbing hills, the roughest test for a derailleur.

6. Find a downhill stretch of road and, starting at the top, see how far the bike will coast with absolutely no pedaling. Test other models on the same road for comparison.

While you probably will never have the chance to do these things before buying a new bike, you probably will before buying a used one.

A final word about price

BICYCLES REALLY ARE different, even though they may look the same. And a $200 model will be a lot more fun to ride than a $130 model. You can get a minimum bike for $120, but go higher if you can afford it. On the surface, the differences between a minimal bike and a good or even excellent one seem extremely subtle. But even the greenest cyclist will be able to feel these subtleties once he begins moving the bike down the road. And the encouragement of a slick-moving bike is often the impetus that transforms a person from a weekend pedaler to a hard-core 100-mile-per-day biker.

Remember also that with inflation the cost of a minimal bike will be rising—perhaps to $175 within the decade. Ten-speeds which today go for $150 cost only $110 three years ago. The cost of racing bikes and top-notch touring bikes has been escalating even faster. But for those of you interested in the very best despite the cost, read on.

Chapter 3

Bikes for the connoisseur

Racers will definitely want the advantage of a good bike, but tourists can have fun on a superbike, too. Get ready to mortgage the house and sell the kids, though.

FIFTEEN YEARS AGO you could buy the best bicycles in the universe for between $100 and $200. The prices of top-grade bicycles have outraced even normal inflation since then so that competition-grade production bicycles now *start* at close to $300 and go on up to $600. Go after a custom model and you could pay $800. (In fact, you can pay $1,000 or anything you want—but that's a rip-off that will be discussed later.)

Is any bike worth it?

Racers don't have to be convinced. But how about tourists?

Well, $800 is a bit extravagant perhaps, but almost any cyclist can indeed benefit from a high-priced bicycle—if he can afford it. The idea that the quality built into these bikes is too subtle for any except for the very experienced to detect is false. *Anybody* can tell the difference between a Raleigh Grand Prix (about $150), for example, and a Raleigh Professional Mark IV (about $500) just by riding them both.

Another argument against spending big money for a bike is that it's like buying a racing car—a non-racer can't possibly take advantage of the bike's speed. Well, that's nutty. There's no speed built into a bike, no engine, no source of power. One way of looking at it is that a racer's all-out effort on a competition bicycle pushes him along at 25 mph as opposed to maybe 20 mph on a lesser bicycle. But another way of looking at it is that a tourist who normally struggles to maintain 10 mph on his old 10-speed can get that same 10 mph from a better bike and not even work up a sweat.

There's another important advantage—especially when you're pedaling somewhere 2,000 miles from home: Good components on good bikes don't break or malfunction nearly as often. And I'm talking about more than just the derailleur. Fine workmanship in such fine points as cables, levers and cable fittings on the frame can make the difference between a joy ride and a trip full of headaches.

Anyone can tell the difference between a lousy bike, a good one, and a really superb one. You can even detect subtle differences in quality

Luis Ocana, foreground, winner of the 1973 Tour de France, rides a Motobecane Team Champion. Note very small rake to the fork.

Exactly what is a great bicycle?

TO GET AN IDEA of what league we're talking about, let's break down a competition or supertouring bike, part by part. We'll first look at the specifications of a typical can't-get-any-better bicycle as it comes from the factory in Europe:

Frame: Your ultimate bicycle will have either Reynolds 531 or Columbus tubing. However, tubes like Super Vitus and those made from titanium are showing up more and more. The frame will be silver-brazed—may or may not have lugs. Fork and stay ends will be Campagnolo, as will the headset and bottom bracket assembly.

Wheels: Campagnolo hubs, but rims could be any of a number of brands—Fiamme, Mavic, Nisi, Super Champion or Scheeren (rare). Spokes vary.

Handlebars and stem: Cinelli, though some go with TTT.

Crank and chainwheels: Campagnolo.

Derailleurs: Campagnolo.

Brakes: Campagnolo side-pull.

Pedals: Campagnolo Super Leggera (the black titanium kind).

Cluster: Regina, Cyclo or Everest.

Chain: Regino Oro (the gold-colored model).
Saddle: Unica nylon/leather or Brooks Professional all-leather.
Seat post: Campagnolo.

Okay. That's the usual combination of parts you'll see on any European maker's top model—basically it's Reynolds tubes, Cinelli bars with Campi all over the place. I don't say this is the ideal bike—there may be other combinations that would serve you better. But what's listed above is the standard against which other bikes are measured. Such a production bicycle will run at least $500. It would be hard to go wrong with this bike. But you can go cheaper with little drop-off in performance. We'll get to how you can skimp on this ideal later on. First let's look at . . .

The difference between custom and production bikes

SINCE THE BIKE BOOM, there seems to be some newspaper story at least once a month that mentions "crazy connoisseur cyclists and their custom-made Peugeots, Atalas, Motobecanes . . ." or something like that. Well, don't get misled. To most reporters, anything with a foreign name costing over $200 must be "custom." The companies mentioned make good bikes, to be sure, and they really run into money, but custom-made they ain't. What we're talking about mostly here is choosing a high-priced *production* bicycle.

According to Falcon Cycles, it takes 3½ hours to build just the frame for this Model 76. It has Reynolds 531 tubing, Cinelli handlebars and lots of Campagnolo parts including brakes (inset). This bike also is sold under other brand names.

What's the difference? Well, about $200 to $300 to start. Take that bike just described, the one with Reynolds, Campi, etc. You buy it off the floor ready-made and you pay $500. Order the frame separately to your own specifications from a famous builder, have wheels built to your order by another builder and then hand-pick the exact components you want, and you'll end up with a bill in the $700 to $800 neighborhood. You might end up with exactly the same parts as the production bicycle. It's not that custom frames and wheels cost $300 extra, though they do account for part of the price difference; it's buy-

Many manufacturers make their top model—their showpiece—a racer, with their best tourist model the next step down. That trend is illustrated by these two Fujis, the Fuji Racer (just below) and the Fuji Finest, at the bottom. The Racer costs about $150 more than the Finest, a tourer. Racer frame is completely handmade, while the Finest is a production model.

ing all those components essentially piece by piece that runs up the bill. The big bike maker buys stuff by the gross and gets a cut rate; you don't.

Obviously the thing to do is to find a ready-made bike that comes close to your ideal bike. And you probably will be able to find precisely what you want unless you are especially tall, short or have some anatomical aberration. You may want to switch parts somewhere on the bike—perhaps you want a Brooks rather than a Unica saddle, for example—but modifications like these will run only a few bucks here and there, certainly a lot cheaper than a custom job.

Touring bike or competition model?

IT'S DIFFICULT to separate racing bikes from touring bikes these days for two reasons: 1) They have similar components, and 2) Bike manufacturers have the ludicrous habit of sticking the words "Racer," "Champion," "Competition" and "Professional" into the titles of as many models as possible, whether they're racing bikes or not. "Professional what?" I sometimes ask.

So what's the difference? *Ideally* the distinction between a racing and a touring bike is not necessarily one of quality. It's a matter of design. A great touring model is just as hard to make as a great racer.

The most important difference is the frame, and here the manufacturer's specification sheet can be extremely useful because you can't always tell the difference between frames by looking. What you want to know are the frame angles. The racing frame is stiffer, with head and seat tubes at 73-, 74- or 75-degree angles. A touring bike will be set at 71½, 72 or 73 degrees. The tourer will have a greater fork rake—two inches or more as compared to 1½ to two for the racer. The touring bike may also be built with thinner steel in its tubes than its racing counterpart. (Surprise! Many touring bikes are therefore lighter than racing bikes—so don't think you got gypped if your racing bike is a fraction of a pound heavier than your neighbor's tourer.) Here you'll have to ask the dealer what the tube gauge is because it isn't usually listed on the spec sheet (remember, the higher the gauge number, the thinner the metal).

Gadzooks! Many touring bikes are actually lighter than many racing bikes. That doesn't mean a slightly heavier racer is a ripoff

The racing frame—upright, stiff tubes and minimal rake—gives the racer little energy absorption and quick handling. The softer frame of the tourist bicycle will straighten out harsh surfaces for less body fatigue.

More crucial is the wheelbase, which also may not be listed on the spec sheet. The specs may tell, however, whether the bike has a short (racing) or long (touring) wheelbase, which is good enough. The wheelbase on two bikes of identical size (same length seat tubes) and with identical frame angles can vary because of two factors: fork rake and, more important, chain-stay length. Chain stays vary between 16 and 18 inches long. Get a frame with stays around 16½ inches and with a fork rake of about 1⅝ inches and you'll have a bike with little frame whip that'll respond instantly to every steering or body motion and will take you quickly through tight corners.

As a tourist, you may find this undesirable. You may not want the bike to change direction every time you scratch your ear. A longer fork rake will help keep the bike moving in a straight line with little attention; and longer chain stays will increase the wheelbase to help

Schwinn is one manufacturer that doesn't believe the tourist model is less important than the racer. This P15 Paramount with optional fenders comes with a long wheelbase and long fork rake. It is different from, but in no way inferior to, P13 racer.

Note the very short wheelbase—only 39½ inches—of this DBS Norge IV. The bike has a Reynolds frame, Cinelli handlebars and lots of Campi equipment except for brakes, seat post.

ou carry heavier loads without making handling difficult. A longer wheelbase helps any vehicle maintain a straight run, and on a touring bicycle it has the added value of keeping luggage between the axles where it will have a minimal effect on steering. As you add more weight it's best to stretch out the fork rake and chain stays. Some bikes built for accommodating front and back panniers with a tent and sleeping bag strapped on top of a carrier have a rake of 2¾ inches and chain stays of 17½ inches. Such a bike will carry the load safely, but you pay for this with lack of responsiveness and a rather unexciting ride.

A longer wheelbase and a longer fork rake will help keep you traveling a straight line, but your bike may be as unresponsive as a cold woman

So what should you get? Well, racers will want a racing bike, and will have no use for a touring model.

Tourists, though, have a hairier decision to make. A touring bike may seem the obvious choice, but many times it's not. Many times a particular brand's best model is essentially a racer with a few modifications thrown in to pacify the tourist (like eyelets on the drop-outs for mounting a rack). The company's next model down will likely be much more of a touring bike in design, but will be hung with what you consider inferior components (and you promised yourself last time you'd never again buy another plastic Simplex). You really want a bike with the best parts available and there's no bike store around that sells a pure touring bicycle with the Campagnolo, Cinelli or whatever equipment you lust after. What do you do?

Examine your cycling needs. If you will use the bike *only* for touring under heavy load, then swallow your pride and go with the cheaper touring model. You'll need the gentle angles and long wheelbase.

But frankly there will be times when you'll want to throw off those panniers and go joy riding. In such cases, a touring frame just won't satisfy you. I'd go with the competition model if it's built on angles no steeper than 73 degrees. In fact, with today's resilient tubing, you can find touring bikes with these same 73-degree angles. There's no doubt that the touring frame is more stable under load, but it takes some of the fun out of cycling when you want to ride light. Get the

What you see here is what you pay for—the skill of a craftsman. He is filing the head lug of a Schwinn Paramount frame.

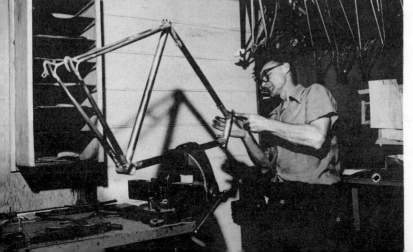

racing bicycle and have some fun. Assuming the wheelbase isn't ex
tremely short, you should be able to handle the bike under load i
you're a skillful and attentive rider. I've toured on bikes with chai
stays slightly under 17 inches and fork rakes of about 1¾ inches with
out noticeable problems. It requires judicious packing to balance th
bike side to side and fore and aft, but you should practice the art o
loading even with a tourist model.

Other differences between tourist and racing models include thing
already discussed: lower gearing vs. high gearing, maybe Randonneu
bars vs. Maes, fenders vs. no fenders. You can change a racing bike'
gearing easily and cheaply enough, and a Maes bar will serve mos
people for touring. Fenders can be added if you wish for a few bucks

Tourists are gaining, but not yet first class

IN THE PAST, those who wanted a high-quality touring bicycle i
this country had to go the ultraexpensive custom frame route or wer
forced to buy a competition bike and modify it, as described above
This was because foreign bike makers recognized that the only Ameri
cans in any number willing to spend money on a bike were racers, s
most exported models were aimed at them.

Most manufac-
turers, let's face it,
assign their very
best craftsmen to
their racing
models; the tourist
models get what's
left

Since the bike boom, people are a little freer with the bike dollar, s
European and Japanese makers are exporting more expensive tourin
models to the States. This gives the tourist more of a choice tha
previously, but the trend remains, as stated before, of making touris
models not quite up to par with racing models. A manufacturer tend
to put his best craftsmen to work on the racing frames, which are hi
showpieces; and he hangs better parts on those frames. His tourin
frames usually will be faster-made production jobs with lower qualit
parts. An unfortunate situation.

Ideally a good touring model should be just as good as a good race
—just different. Rene Herse, perhaps France's greatest builder, ha
practiced this theory for years—he prefers to use his art for tourists
not racers.

But he's an exception. So at present, if you want to tour and don'
want to pay top dollar, you're in great shape—good, but not great
touring bikes are easy to come by. But for tourists who want the ab
solute best, the racing bike, modified, is still the best bike. Unless yo
want to go custom.

Knowing where you can (and where you can't) skimp

OKAY, YOU'VE THOUGHT it over and decided that $500 is too ric
for your blood. Campagnolo parts are nice, but then so is eating, pay
ing the rent, etc. But you still want a bike that's out of the ordinary
something better than the standard $150 10-speed. Well, "economy'
luxury bikes are the answer because there are some items on a $50

model that can be replaced with cheaper brands, with little or no loss
of performance. If you're a racer, this means a bike that's just as fast,
just as maneuverable. For tourists, this means a bike just as easy to
pedal and just as stable. You may have to give up top-brand prestige,
convenience features and maybe trade-in super-long-life durability
for moderate durability. But the actual running performance of the
bicycle will be very close to the ideal. Let's go over the skimp list, spec
by spec:

Frame: Never skimp here. You'll want butted tubing, no matter
what brand. Granted, it's often difficult to tell whether a Columbus
frame was put together by Magnificent Marcello, the master of the
factory, or Clumsy Luigi, his apprentice. But if it's made with Reynolds
531, Super Vitus, Columbus or a Japanese equivalent, you'll still get
a topnotch frame. The frame is the heart of the bicycle. Put your
money here and you'll have a firm basis to build on later, when you
want to replace a cheaper crank set or whatever. But hang the best
parts in the world on a mediocre frame and you've still got a mediocre
bike.

Put your money in your frame, which is the heart of your bike. You can exchange the hung-on junk later, when your uncle dies

You may want to depart from the standard Campi headset and bottom bracket assembly, however. Stronglight, Shimano and other companies make competent, cheaper units.

Wheels: Try very hard not to skimp here. Get Campagnolo hubs if
you can. But if you must you can save a few bucks with Normandy
Competition hubs, which are close in quality. Campagnolo hubs are
packed in fine oil, the Normandy in grease. Tourists may prefer grease-
packed hubs for greater protection in the rain.

There's no use skimping on rims—all the good ones are close in
performance, close in price. Geography more than anything else will
determine which brand your bike has: French bikes will go with
Mavic, Super Champion; Italian bikes will have Fiamme, etc. Spokes
aren't a big deal. In fact, cheaper spokes which are straight-gauge are
usually stronger than their more expensive butted counterparts.

Handlebars and stem: Racers will want Cinelli or TTT, which are
close in quality and almost identical in price. GB bars are also found on
good bikes. This is one area where the tourist can skimp, but the
racer can't—the tourist won't be putting as much pressure on those
bars and stem, and can go with one of the many adequate brands
available. Some companies, such as Paris Sport, make their own house
brand of handlebars, making it unnecessary to call on Mr. Cinelli (or
Mr. TTT). This also keeps the price of the bike down.

Crank and chainwheels: Skimp. Campi is best, but you can get along
with cheaper, be you racer or tourist. Stronglight, T.A., Zeus, Shimano
or Sugino aren't as pretty, but they'll do the job.

Derailleurs: Skimp. Tourists will do better with Shimano or Sun
Tour anyway, because they handle those big clusters easier. Racers can
go with Zeus, the Huret Jubilee or Simplex Super L.J. Racers can also
use the Japanese brands, but because of their slant pantograph design,
a longer throw on the shift levers is required for each derailment. If

you're comfortable with such an arrangement, by all means go Japanese. But if you like short-throw shifting, stick with the conventional swing-parallelogram designs.

Brakes: Skimp, by all means. You don't need those outrageously priced Campi side-pulls. Shimano side-pulls cost only half as much, but that still makes them outrageous—three times more than most other brands. Go for Universal, Weinmann, Dia-Compe, even Mafac . . . anything that will stop the bike.

Pedals: Skimp. Lyotard and Mikashima are good alternatives to Campagnolo.

Cluster: No sense skimping here as this is a high-wear area. You won't save that much either. Get a good one. Zeus has a new lightweight model that's reasonably priced.

Chain: Get a good one, but you don't need the Regino Oro model, which is costly.

Seat post: Skimp. Anything that holds up the saddle and doesn't bend will work.

Saddle: Don't skimp. However, the cheapest Unica nylon/leather model is an excellent saddle and almost $10 cheaper than a comparable all-leather model.

If you're buying a French bike you might consider this aluminum Simplex Super LJ derailleur, a good alternative to Campi.

The Zeus freewheel cluster has six finely built gears, but it weighs only 250 grams—about 130 grams lighter than a Regina gear cluster. The two outer gears are one piece.

How much will all this save me?

PLENTY. As you probably noticed, the scheme above was to keep away from that old, costly Campagnolo except where necessary (hubs), while still ending up with the essentials—good frame, good wheels and a comfortable saddle. Many manufacturers make just such a model with a reduction in price of at least $100, sometimes up to $200.

Zeus, for instance, makes what it calls a Competition model for budding racers. It has a Reynolds 531 frame (but with Durifort forks) and Cinelli handlebars and stem. The rest of the bike is basically Zeus equipment and you end up with a price under $300. The Alfa derailleur is a little rough shifting and I'd prefer Campi or Normandy hubs, but it's still a basically excellent bicycle. Zeus's proclaimed aim is to sell a bike with an excellent frame and excellent handlebars, but with second-line hang-on parts that the rider can replace with finer components as he becomes more affluent. A good idea.

The most famous bicycle built along these same lines and in the same price range is the Peugeot PX-10. It also sports Reynolds 531 (including forks), but skimps the rest of the way. Unlike the Zeus, though, the Peugeot is a tourist bike. Peugeot has a well-financed racing team, and they push that image a lot, talking up the PX-10 as a racing bike. Budding racers beware. I have a feeling that all that racing advertising is for the tourist who has Walter Mitty dreams of racing only. The bike has been softened up in recent years, now has 72-degree angles and a full two-inch fork rake, making it good for touring but not ideal for racing. A Peugeot spokesman admitted to me that of the 25,000 PX-10s sold in America every year, few will ever see a serious race. It comes with a plastic Simplex which should be traded in for something better.

Zeus Competition might be called an "economy" expensive bike. It has good basics such as Reynolds tubes and Cinelli bars; rest of bike is less expensive stuff that can be replaced later.

I mention these two bikes because they are extreme examples—bikes with a basic high quality (though just barely) at a savings of over $200. One is a racing bike, the other a tourer. Then, of course, there are variations all along the line. The first thing a maker will do to cut a bicycle's price is go with something other than Campi brakes. That should be your first cut as well. From then on it's what is important to you. Just shoot for that good frame, good wheels.

Choosing nationalities

MOST HIGH-CLASS BIKES sold in the U.S. come from four countries: Italy, France, England and Japan. At present only one such bicycle is *made* in America—the Schwinn Paramount.

You can't generalize much about how each country builds its bikes (i.e. you can't say England makes better cycles than France, etc.). But there are some tendencies. Japanese bikes, for instance, carry Japanese parts, are built with Japanese tubes. You won't find Campagnolo cranks or Mavic rims on a Nishiki bicycle, for obvious reasons. The exchange of components among the European countries is much freer; some European makers even use Japanese parts.

An Italian or a French bike isn't necessarily more emotional than an American bike, but it's likely to have a bigger conglomeration of parts.

But European builders do tend to stick to home-grown parts when-ver possible to keep the price down. This is why it's sometimes wise o stick to Italian bikes if you want Campagnolo equipment. Let's say ou want a French bike for some reason; you'll save money by finding model hung with the best French parts (brands like Stronglight and Mavic as opposed to brands like Campagnolo and Fiamme). Or let's ay you have your heart set on Reynolds tubing; go with the English or French and stay away from Italian bikes, whose makers would rather work with Columbus.

Watch out for status rip-offs

What's happened to our sense of values? Some people are sorely tempted to buy a bike just because the price is set extremely high

A FEW MANUFACTURERS are taking advantage of the bicycle's new-found status by not trying to hold prices down at all; in fact, they seem to use outrageously high prices on their bikes as advertising come-ons to upper-middle-class types who equate price with quality.

The Maserati MT-2, for instance, costs over $250 more than similar all-Campi models. Is the frame that much better? Not in my opinion. Are Maserati's Campagnolo parts better than other brands' Campagnolo parts? Of course not. I cite the Maserati because it's received a lot of publicity, but there are other rip-off brands as well. To be fair, Maserati makes a whole line of bicycles and many of them are reasonably priced, but the MT-2 just isn't one of them. For that extra $250

French bikes with Cinelli bars and Campagnolo equipment normally cost more than comparable Italian models, but not this Follis 472. It costs $170 less than the Follis 572 (and less than most similar Italian bikes) because it uses mostly second-line parts except for the derailleur, which is Campagnolo.

you could go with a custom-built frame with parts of your own choice, right down to the drop-outs, spokes and seat post. A much better investment for your money.

The lesson is to shop around and compare bikes part by part to get an idea of the prevailing price. Most *production* bikes hung with identical parts will be close in price.

There are also some custom models available that cost $1200 and more. One such is the Condor which features elaborately designed lugs and chainwheels drilled out in fancy patterns. All this "beauty" might be fine if your tastes happen to run to the excesses of rococo art, but it doesn't make the bike run any better. Another disgusting development in recent months is an outfit that sells gold-plated Campagnolo parts.

Shooting the works—buying a custom bicycle

YOU REALLY WANT something special; a bike built just for you. Old Marcello sitting in the shop reading your instructions as he sticks your frame together. I wouldn't order a custom bike, however, unless you know what you're doing. Say you've done quite a bit of riding already and you know you need a frame with, say, 72 x 74 angles instead of the standard 73 x 73. Or you might want extra long stays for carrying a heavy load, but you want them a special thickness and reinforced to avoid whip. Or you're extra short or extra tall. Then a custom bike is for you.

Plus there's the advantage of hand-picking each component to be hung on the bike. You may not want Campagnolo throughout. Perhaps you prefer Phil Wood permanently-sealed hubs. Or you may want a Japanese shifter for your low touring gears. Maybe you want a Randonneur bar instead of the standard Maes. Or you might want something really unusual—like a hub brake on the front wheel (maybe you live in a rainy climate and are afraid of brake failure).

There are several ways of buying a custom bicycle. The classic method is to buy just the frame from a frame builder. Have the wheels put together by a wheel builder. Hand-pick the rest of the parts yourself. Then have the whole shebang brought together by a shop mechanic you trust. Obviously, the best way to go about this is to find a bicycle shop whose owners have formal connections with a frame maker whose services you want. There are many good frame builders. But among the best are Masi, Poghliaghi, Cinelli and Colnago of Italy; Hetchins, Holdsworth, Bob Jackson of England; Herse and Singer of France, to name just a few. In America, the only man to see is Albert Eisentraut of Oakland, California.

Most of these frame builders will also put an entire bike together for you. And this is a good idea if you're planning to pick the bike up in Europe for a vacation and want a full, working bike waiting for you. (This is not a good idea if you want an Eisentraut—who wants to spend a vacation in Oakland?) But most builders have their own pref-

Here's the bike for you: You choose every part that goes on it, and a genuine craftsman assembles the whole thing under your supervision

erences in parts and they may not coincide with yours. Of course, you're giving the orders, but they just may not feel comfortable working with certain components. Mention Shimano to a French builder and he may slap you across the face. However, the one-builder-one-bike method is more convenient and a little less costly.

Cheaper still is to order to your specifications a bicycle from the factory of a normal mass producer. Most of the better manufacturers offer this service: Schwinn, LeJeune, Frejus-Legnano, Libertas, Mercian, Paris Sport and many others. Remember that "cheaper" doesn't mean bargain prices. We're still talking about price tags over that of production bikes. In other words, $600 and up.

Most builders have their own distinct preferences. Mention Shimano to a French builder and he might slap you across the face

Where to buy

YOU CAN ORDER a custom bike on your own. Write the frame builder, order the parts through a mail-order house and bolt everything together yourself. Attempt this only if you're a skilled mechanic and understand bicycle construction thoroughly—and I mean *thoroughly.* Otherwise you may find that all those nice parts just don't work with each other. Cinelli interchangeable hubs, for instance, won't work on a standard frame.

Your best bet is to find a shop that does this kind of work. This gives you more leverage with the frame builder (some will not deal with

Get help if you order a custom frame. Here Jackie Simes, a great pro track racer, works out a frame design in his Nanuet, N.Y. shop.

*A Reynolds craftsman bends a fork blade to the specified rake—
a highly skilled job that still is done by hand.*

individuals) and makes it easier to get the parts you want. Besides, it's always good to have one establishment that's responsible for the bike as a whole, preferably someplace close to home. It's a drag to have to call up Mr. Masi (or Mr. Paris Sport) to complain that your new bike doesn't shift right.

If you're laying out hundreds of dollars you don't want to deal with a schlepp who writes up your order and rushes you out the door

Plus, knowledgeable as you think you are, it's good to draw on the advice of a professional when ordering a bike. He can help you choose a design and suggest parts that will fit your purposes, perhaps parts you don't even know exist (new stuff is invented all the time). You'll want help and advice in drawing up the specs for that dream bike.

I've had good luck dealing with shops run by racers or ex-racers. They usually understand equipment a little better than the pure businessman types. They're also usually more interested in bicycles and are willing to discuss your options with you. I mention this because when you're preparing to lay out hundreds of dollars, you want more than just some schlepp who writes it up on an order blank and rushes you out the door. Find a shop that will make the plain act of buying an occasion in itself.

Some fine points to look for

HERE ARE SOME DETAILS to look for, whether you're buying a production or custom model:

Frame: Look for Prugnat lugs. Look also for frame stiffeners if you're a racer, or if you're a tourist who wants a tight bike. Fork stiffeners are those two long triangles running down the insides of the fork blades. Also look for reinforcements around the rear brake bridge and the chain stays bridge. These are little diamond shapes where the bridge attaches to the tubes.

Another important frame consideration is hanger height, sometimes called *drop*. This refers to how far the bottom bracket drops beneath a line drawn through the axles. An easier way to think of it is how close to the ground the hanger (or bottom bracket) comes. A low hanger keeps you lower on the bike, and reduces wind resistance. But your pedals could hit the ground when cornering hard. A high hanger eliminates this problem, though it offers more rolling resistance. What to choose? Racers who plan to compete in criteriums with lots of twisty turns will need the high hanger. So will track sprinters who must maneuver up and down the oval. But if you can get away with it, take the low hanger. This is where tourists have an advantage over most racers, since they won't be leaning sideways into turns.

Another consideration is the brand of bottom bracket assembly you want in the hanger shell. Campagnolo is the standard, but the Phil Wood permanently sealed bottom bracket is a good one, too, and you don't have to overhaul it. Lately a lot of Eisentraut frames are coming through with the Phil Wood model. Another item you might consider is the Teledyne titanium spindle, which will save you a few ounces (the spindle is the axle that runs through the bottom bracket).

I also prefer a frame with brazed-on fittings for cables, especially the rear brake cable. Normally, the cable is contained in a housing that runs along the top of the top tube and is clamped in place. This long housing can make brake action sticky. Some builders therefore braze on two fittings *under* the tube, one at each end. No cable housing is needed between these two points, cutting down friction. However, you then must be careful about picking the bike up by that top tube or else you'll crimp the cable. A nice touch also is an Allen key seat pillar clamp.

Wheels: Campagnolo hubs are the standard, but you might want to try Phil Wood or Hi-E hubs, both exotic American products rarely found on production models. There are even more exotic models on the market, such as Cinelli's interchangeable hubs. These allow you to use the wheel on either the front or the back. The gear cluster is not attached to the rear wheel, but to the stay end. This way when you change a wheel you needn't shift the bike into high gear—only the wheel comes off, the cluster remains attached to the bike. This lets you take off in the same gear you were in when you stopped. The stays must be spread wider to accommodate this arrangement, however.

Unica saddle made of nylon and
leather is light, comfortable.
It also comes in padded, suede
and buffalo versions.

Ideale 90 leather saddle is
pretreated for softness—an
excellent saddle for the tourist. Note adjustable clip.

You might also give some thought to spoke design. You'll want
the usual 2-cross or 3-cross arrangement in the rear for extra strength.
But in the front you might want to try radial spoking (the simplest
design—the spokes go straight from the hub to the rim, no crossing).
Radial wheels are easy to build, easy to true and offer less air resistance than the other designs. They're not as strong but that's okay
up front unless you expect some rough terrain.

The ultimate in strength are tied-and-soldered wheels, and these are
special order only. What will a pair of tied-and-soldered custom wheels
cost you? About $100.

Pedals: Campi's black titanium models are considered the ultimate.
But if you plan to wear cleats they will wear out a little faster than the
regular aluminum alloy models. You might be better off with the
"cheaper" Campagnolo pedals.

Saddle: The two top choices today are Unica and Brooks. You may
not realize, though, that Unica comes in several different models. The
cheapest is uncovered nylon, which I wouldn't mess with. The
standard model is nylon with a leather top, more comfortable and what
you'll normally find. However, there are three other (more expensive)
models to consider: 1) nylon/leather with padding; 2) nylon/suede
with padding; and 3) the ultimate, nylon, padding and then a top layer
of buffalo leather. All of these saddles are light, comfortable and perfect for racing. But the buffalo is often hard to get. And the suede isn't
a good idea if you're antsy in the saddle and like to slide around a lot,
stand up in the pedals, etc., because it grips into your seat.

The Unica line of saddles is fine for the tourist as well, but if you
really want comfort, get an all-leather model. I'd recommend a brand
you don't often see. Brooks makes the leather saddle usually found on
expensive bikes, but it's extremely hard and will take a long time to

A suede saddle
isn't such a hot
idea if you're
antsy in the saddle
and like to slide
around a lot

break in. The Ideale 90 saddle is much softer. Unlike the Brooks, it is close to being broken in when new, having been pretreated. This is the most comfortable leather saddle I've ever ridden. Specify the Ideale 90 especially if you're planning to take delivery in Europe for a cycling vacation there, because you'll want a comfortable bike right from the start. Another convenient feature is its adjustable clip which lets you easily adjust the saddle tilt right on the seat post.

Cranks: If you have extra long or extra short legs, you may want cranks different than the standard 170mm. They come in 165, 167.5, 172.5, 175 and 180 sizes as well. Track bikes normally come with 165mm cranks. The shorter cranks give you a nice fast-spinning feel. The longer cranks provide more leverage for the hills. You may want to consider crank length in light of the frame you've chosen. If you have a low hanger, long crank arms might bring you dangerously close to the ground. And if you have a steep head tube angle and a short fork rake, your toe clips could hit the front wheel when cornering.

Pump: Silca makes a pump which needs no clip. Its top is contoured to fit against the top tube with prongs at the bottom that rest on the bottom bracket joint.

White tape and all—bikes only a racer should touch

MOST RACING BIKES can be enjoyed by tourists as well. There are a few exceptions. These are bikes with superstiff angles (like 74 x 75) and bikes that have been drilled out. You'll find some models which have holes all over the place—in the chainwheels, drop-outs, brake levers, lugs, even chain. This can add over $100 to the price. Only a racer would want this. Tourists will waste their money and get a weaker bike. In fact, racers on a budget should also stay away from these models as they won't last as long.

White tape won't make a racing bike go any faster, but you'll show up mighty fine in the photographs

Tourists should stay away from white handlebar tape. It gets dirty in a hurry. Racers, on the other hand, should always use white tape. It won't make the bike any faster, but you'll show up better in photographs.

Think twice about a 15-speed

WHEN WE TALKED about gearing in the previous chapter, I mentioned how tourists should ideally have gears at close intervals, like racers. But unlike racers, the tourist pays by giving up gears in the top end rather than the low end. What do you do if you want extremely low gears for going up mountains and extremely high gears for coming down the other side, and also want a close range of gears in the middle?

The answer is the 15-speed. With a triple chainring of 30-40-50, for example, and a standard rear cluster you should be able to handle any terrain in the universe, except for parts of Pluto. I don't think it's worth it. The reason is that the triple chainwheel causes a lot of problems—acute chain angles in many gear combinations (like from the largest front sprocket to one of the larger rear sprockets), a lot of slack to be taken up when the chain is on the smaller sprockets, and sloppy shifting among the three chainrings. The 15-speed doesn't give you 15 efficient gears—more like nine. With a judicious choice of gears you can get adequate gears out of your 10-speed. (You can imagine how ludicrous this statement sounds to old-timers who have spent all their lives on one-speeds.)

A final word about friends, guilt and money

SOME PEOPLE, even those who have the money, balk at spending between $300 and $800 on a bike. It does seem a shame to spend the same money on a bicycle that you'd pay for a used car. Prices have gone up, to put it mildly. In 1971 a certain Italian bicycle (Columbus tubing, lots of Campagnolo) sold for $250; in the summer of 1972 it went up to $350; by the fall of the same year it was $375; one year later it sold for $400; and in early 1974 you had to shell out $460. In other words, in three years the price almost doubled.

If you pay these prices, your non-biking friends will give you a rough time. You should be spending that kind of money on more adult items—such as pink flamingos for the lawn.

There's no doubt that prices are incredibly high, maybe too high for what you get—certainly compared to what you got a few years back. Even so, it makes sense to pay that $400, or whatever, to get the bike you want. This is especially true if you ride every week and spend your two- or three-week summer vacation in the saddle as well.

The main problem that gets between the cyclist and the bike he wants (and can afford) is good old-fashioned guilt—propagated by friends who can't possibly understand such a purchase. I weathered this abuse years ago, even when good bikes were much cheaper. People who thought nothing of owning two cars accused me of being extravagant. The idea foisted upon us bikers is that we're all decadent profligates because we put so much time and money into kid's stuff. Well it's something to think over . . . but not for long. If most Americans can justify spending $4,000 every three years for a large machine to carry them 12 miles to work, then you can justify $400 for a machine that will take you cross country, strengthen your heart and lungs—and will last you a lifetime to boot.

For an idea of what bicycle parts are available and how much they cost, send for one of the many catalogs available. Here are three good ones:

Big Wheel, Ltd., 340 Holly St., Denver, Colorado 80220. ($2.10)

Cycl-Ology, Wheel Goods Corporation, Dept. D., 14524 21st Avenue North, Minneapolis, Minnesota 55441. ($2.00)

Cyclo-Pedia, Department B, 311 N. Mitchell, Cadillac, Michigan 49601. ($3.00)

Chapter 4

The forsaken 3-speed

Just because many bike companies and cycle snobs don't take the 3-speed seriously doesn't mean you shouldn't. Buying a good one takes as good an eye as buying a 10-speed

THE 3-SPEED makes an ideal round-the-town or commuter bike. The hub shifter gives you just enough gear variance to make pedaling easy for short trips, and is generally more dependable and freer from injury or maintenance than a derailleur. You can chain your 3-speed to a post while you go to school or work and when you return will find a bike that shifts just as good as when you left it, even though some clumsy lummox may have tripped over it in the meantime. The guts of the shifting mechanism are contained inside that protective hub.

Also, the current bicycle scene with its glorification of the 10-speed has kept 3-speed prices at acceptable levels. But you have to be careful. Because the 3-speed has lost its sex appeal in recent years, some manufacturers have stopped taking them seriously and are slopping them together.

How does a good 3-speed differ from a good 10-speed?

IT DOESN'T, REALLY. Pick a 3-speed using the same criteria as you would for choosing a 10-speed as outlined in previous chapters. Look at frame tubing, frame construction, wheels, brakes, etc. Of course you won't be able to get the supercomponents you find on luxury 10-speeds—sew-up rims, Columbus tubing, cotterless cranks and all— but don't let yourself get stuck with junk either. Wheels should be true no matter what kind of hubs and rims they have. And a frame should be aligned no matter what the pedigree of its tubes. But besides following the same general advice that applies to the 10-speed buyer, there are a few special problem areas that crop up on 3-speeds:

Some 3-speeds are so heavy they probably were made from old anvils

- **Excessive weight.** 3-speeds are made from cheaper, heavier tubes than 10-speeds, which is okay I guess, since they charge a lot less for them. But some makers really get piggy and construct their 3-speeds from old anvils (or so it seems). Some of these babies hit 50 pounds. A commuter bike can stand a little more weight than a

Left, the 3-speed remains the most convenient round-the-town cycle, at a considerable savings over the 10-speed. Right, this 3-speed has a good lugged frame. Also try to get such things as a front hub assembly complete with locknuts and washers, and a headset with a keyed washer. Avoid rubber pedals.

10-speed so you can kick it around, but 50 pounds is ridiculous. You should be able to get one 37 pounds or under. And look for brazed joints if you can get them.

● **Shoddy headset.** This is the assembly that holds the fork in the head tube and lets you steer. A good headset has a big locknut at the top, then a keyed washer, and then an adjustable cup (sometimes there's also a brake-cable hanger—see the "Headset" section of the chapter on maintenance and repair). Cheap headsets omit the keyed washer. Without this washer your headset is more likely to come loose, and adjustment will require two giant wrenches which you may not own.

● **Rubber pedals.** Get rattrap (all-metal) pedals if you can; they don't wear out and you can attach toe clips to them, which you can't

Simplified photo shows the guts of a Sachs-Torpedo automatic 2-speed hub. This model also comes with a coaster brake.

Take-apart or fold-up bike is convenient for those with little space. This DBS Kombi has some nice touches: hub brake up front that won't fade in the rain, shopping basket and rattrap pedals.

o with the old rubber kind. Also look for pedals with ball bearings. hey rotate more smoothly, won't hang up.

● **Over-simplified hub assembly.** Any front hub needs ball races, earings which run around them, and cones to hold them in. A good ub will then have a locknut that can be tightened against the cone, nd a washer between them to prevent the cone from turning as you ghten the locknut. Some bike companies cut corners by eliminating ie washers. And some go so far as to eliminate the locknut too. In iat case the fork ends, which are narrowly spaced, serve as the lock-uts. This type is a pain; it means spreading the fork to pull the wheel ut or put it back in. Also, you'll probably have to re-adjust the cones verytime the wheel comes out of the bike. Try to find a bike with a omplete hub assembly.

● **Cheap side-pulls.** The best brakes made are side-pulls. But a heap center-pull is better than a cheap side-pull. Get a 3-speed /ith center-pulls and save yourself problems. Universal, Weinmann, ampi and Shimano make fine side-pulls, but you won't find these rands on 3-speeds.

hoosing a shifter and the right gears

ECIDING ON A BRAND of shifter shouldn't be your main concern. heck out the frame and wheels first. There's not much you can do to heck out a hub shifter because the mechanism is hidden from view. sk for a test ride. And when you're turned down, at least get the back ·heel off the ground and turn the cranks at the *same* rpm in all three ears (you must stop pedaling, of course, each time you shift). Does ie bike shift smoothly? And is the hub giving you three distinct gears? ou should feel the difference in pressure required on the pedals maintain a steady rpm. And the speed of the back wheel should vary.

Some standard brands of hub shifters are Sturmey-Archer, Shimano nd Sachs-Torpedo. This last brand is especially interesting because it

Ask for a test ride, and when you're turned down, make a few action tests right inside the shop

offers some departures in design from the standard 3-speed hub. One is a simple 2-speed which you shift, not with a lever, but by back-pedaling slightly. Another is an *automatic* 2-speed hub gear. When you hit about 10 mph it automatically shifts into second.

Gear values are rarely discussed when talking about 3-speeds, and I don't know why. People assume all 3-speeds give you the same three gears. It's true that most hub gears give you this arrangement: Normal, or second, gear is a direct drive; first, or low, gear is 25 percent lower and third, or high, gear is 33⅓ percent higher than normal gear.

However, just because the percentage differences between gears is identical on all 3-speeds, that direct drive on which the whole arrangement is based can vary widely. It all depends on how big or small those sprockets are, just like on a 10-speed. If you don't understand this point, read the section on gearing in the 10-speed chapter. Figure out a 3-speed's direct-drive gear value before you buy it (don't bother to calculate the high and low gears, as these are always going to be plus 33⅓ and minus 25 percent, respectively). I'd shoot for a normal gear value of about 60 to 70 inches, even lower if you live in a hilly neighborhood. (With a 60-inch normal gear you would have a 45-inch low-gear value and an 80-inch high gear.) Should the 3-speed you're considering have 27-inch wheels, you can use the gear value chart in the 10-speed chapter for figuring that normal gear. If it has 26- or 28-inch wheels (or anything else), use the old formula:

$$\frac{\text{number of teeth on chainwheel}}{\text{number of teeth on rear sprocket}} \times \frac{\text{wheel diameter}}{\text{(in inches)}} = \text{gear value}$$

What about the fold-up bike?

ONE POPULAR TYPE of gearhub bicycle today is the collapsible or fold-up bicycle. These bikes come with little 20-inch wheels and can be folded or taken apart in the middle. Most are a take-off on the English Moulton.

For some reason, the companies who make these things do a superb job in general. The Moulton is a great bike, but unavailable here, and so are the DBS Kombi Lux and the Raleigh model which can be had in the U.S. There are many others: Pony, Amica, Bugatti, among them. They aren't much good for touring as they're heavy (most go over 35 pounds) and the little wheels aren't all that stable. But they're a lot of fun for shopping trips and other short hops. I know a guy who mounted a Tupperware box on the rear carrier of his wife's little fold-up bike. He thought it would be handy for carrying a gallon of milk or a loaf of bread. Instead, she planted it with daisies. Made quite a refreshing sight. . . .

One caution: Despite their small size and foldability, the heavy weight of these bikes is a drawback for apartment dwellers who live above the first floor and don't have an elevator or a butler.

Chapter 5

The track bicycle–plain
but beautiful

Before you dismiss the fixed-wheel (or track) bicycle as a machine suitable only for maniacs who zip around the high-banked track of the Velodrome, take another look. Fixed-wheels are cheaper, lighter, faster and more maneuverable than their 10-speed counterparts. Here's the dope on how they're made, how to modify them for street use and how to ride them.

IN A WORLD that's fallen head over heels in love with the 10-speed, the fixed-wheel (or track) bicycle could be described as a plain, unsophisticated piece of equipment. And it is.

But that's only one way of looking at it. It can also be described as a refreshing study in no-nonsense performance. This kind of bike is called a fixed-wheel (or sometimes just a "fix") because it has but one rear sprocket, which is fixed permanently to the rear wheel. *There is no freewheel.* This means you cannot coast, and the pedals must continue to turn as long as the rear wheel is turning. The fixed-wheel is also called a track bike because its use in recent years has been primarily restricted to racing on a track.

And that's exactly where most bike salesmen think it should stay. They don't like to mess with the fix because it has no fancy shifter gizmos to brag about. And I must admit that a 3-, 5- or 10-speed model is best for most people. But I don't want to ignore those of you who may be seeking something more adventurous.

The fixed-wheel is nothing new, of course. It was here before the freewheel was invented, and there have always been a few riders who have stuck with this design. Today more and more cyclists are rediscovering the fixed-wheel and riding it over normal streets and roads with no intention of ever trying out their treads on a track.

Track bikes arrive from the factory with no brakes. They also differ from conventional road bikes in that they have shorter wheelbases, straighter forks and stiffer frames. A fix rides much rougher than a 10-speed but offers greater speed and control. The man or woman who

The track bike is basically a one-gear, stripped-down, go-for-hell machine. There are no brakes. To slow down, you do what you used to do on your tricycle—make your legs go slower.

prefers a track bike over a 10-speed is similar to the driver wh chooses a fast-cornering sports car over a cushy-riding luxury car.

The first thing you're going to notice as you look at track bikes i that they're sleek and uncomplicated. They have no derailleurs, n double chainwheels, no cables of any sort and none of the bridges o fittings needed to guide these cables.

It may look ugly at first, but in action it looks like an exotic dancer in the final moment of her act

This may bother you at first. Bike boom advertising of the '70s ha taught the public to judge a bike by how many sprockets, derailleurs levers and other gizmos are hung from its frame. A track bike look like an exotic dancer in the final moments of her act, in comparison t most bikes you see on the streets today.

But to the experienced eye, the track bike is a thing of beauty— clean and uncluttered. The fixed-wheel is the quintessential bicycle devoted to going forward and around corners very fast—and nothing else.

Why non-racers should consider a track bicycle

I CAN'T IN GOOD FAITH recommend a track bike for everyone. Be cause of the fixed gearing it can be dangerous. You cannot coast. You cannot shift gears. This means you have to be in good physical shape And track bikes are stiff and uncomfortable for some people, especiall on long trips.

But the claim of experts that track bikes are good only for racing i pure bunk. However, the track bike does require a rider who takes hi

cling seriously and is willing to put in some effort to learn how to
de it safely.

On the other hand, there are many good reasons for riding a fix,
en for those of you who have done little riding as yet. Here are six of
ose reasons:

- **Maneuverability.** Even the clumsiest cyclist can ride a track bike
ith his hands in his back pockets, steering around sharp curves with
ly hip movements while constantly pedaling. It's almost as if the
ke were an extension of your body. With hands back on the handle-
rs you can make a U-turn in about six feet. Try that with a 10-speed.

Think back to the last time you went to the circus. Remember the
robat who bicycled across the tight wire—sometimes blindfolded
d sometimes juggling or doing other tricks at the same time? The
nd of bike he used was a fix. Acrobats have appreciated the nimble-
ss of the track bike for years. You've also probably seen them
cycle backwards. The fixed gearing gives the bike reverse. (But I
ouldn't try this at first as it requires considerable balance; you have
 think backwards.)

- **Speed.** The combination of light weight (15 to 21 pounds), stiff
ame and fixed gearing gives the track bike superior speed—especially
ver short distances. But nobody says you have to ride it fast. You can

*ere's how fixed-wheel bikes are made to be ridden—at high speed
ound the track. "Fixes" have superior speed for short distances.*
bert F. George photo

*Schwinn Paramount track costs about $150 less than the Paramount
road bike. It weighs about 20 pounds and is not overly rigid, so
you can use it on the road if you know what you're doing.*

take advantage of the bike's speedy characteristics to ride at the same
speed as everybody else, only you'll be putting in far less effort for
the same results.

This ease of pedaling comes not only from the light weight, but also
from the lack of a rear derailleur. Just take a look at a 10-speed's
power train. The chain has to run through the shifter's two pulleys and
has extra slack in it to allow for smooth derailing. A fixed-wheel has
none of this nonsense to eat up your pedaling energy. No one's ever
done a scientific study on how much energy this extra friction wastes,
but I asked a random selection of racers, bike mechanics and bicycle
design engineers and they all estimate that the derailleur set-up eats up
as much as five to ten percent of your pedal power (with most of them
leaning toward the higher figure).

Perhaps more important than either light weight or the fixed gearing
is a track bike's stiff frame. A 10-speed's flexible frame absorbs a lot
of road shock to give you a more comfortable ride. But it also absorbs
some of your muscle power. A track bike is more efficient at converting
your leg thrusts to forward motion rather than soaking that power in
the tubes. We'll discuss why the track frame is stiffer later on.

• **Maintenance.** There's much less to go wrong. The derailleurs are
the first things to get screwed up on a bike, and track bikes don't have
any. Rear wheels are easier to get at to adjust or overhaul because

here's no freewheel to remove first. And there are no cables to snag, crimp, stretch or break.

I admit that a track bike's lack of shifting ability makes it less than ideal for very long trips over varied terrain. On the other hand, you'll never be stuck in the middle of Kansas with a wrecked derailleur. Another point: Because of a track bike's close tolerances and because there is but one chainwheel and one rear sprocket, power train alignment is always close to perfect. When replacing a rear wheel on a 10-speed (such as after repairing a blown tire), it's nearly impossible to get that power train lined up precisely for smooth shifting (what with five rear sprockets and two chainwheels).

• **Price.** Admittedly there is no such thing as a cheap track bike. Most track bikes are made for competition and therefore are almost always hand-made to the highest standard using high-quality tubing (the most common today being Reynolds 531 double-butted). Top-line fixed-wheels are priced in the $300 range. They rarely go higher than this. Of course, this is no bargain per se. On the other hand, for about $300 you get the best frame that the manufacturer can produce.

Now compare that price to what you'd have to pay for a top-of-the-line 10-speed. For instance, the difference between Raleigh's best 10-speed and their track bike is about $200. The difference between Schwinn's track Paramount and their 10-speed Paramount is about $150. The extra money goes into the extra components used on a 10-speed and for the various fittings needed to accommodate these parts. The frame itself, however, and sometimes even the rims are usually slightly inferior to those on a fixed-wheel. In effect, you're getting a basically superior bike at a savings of up to $200.

• **Safety.** This is a strange feature to mention, especially in light of

Most track bikes are made for racing and therefore are hand-made with loving care and the best of materials

LeJeune track bike is extremely light— about 15 pounds. For that reason it's easy to unload off a car rack.

Even some kids find the "fix" safe enough to ride. This lad raced his track bike in Central Park.

Pepsi-Cola photo

the fact that certain federal government busybodies have propose
regulations that would effectively ban track bikes from public road
because of their inability to coast. These regulations are not yet law
however. (See the end of this chapter for tips on converting your trac
bike for safer street use.) It's true that a track bike can be dangerou
for the novice, but unqualified slurs against the fix are usually the ut
terances of naive or publicity-seeking public officials, or propagand
from bike dealers or manufacturers who would rather sell the mor
lucrative (for them) 10-speed.

There has been one champion of the fixed-wheel in recent years
however; namely Tom Avenia, a New York bike dealer who has bee
quite vocal in his opinion that the fix is safer than the road bike. Ton
stresses the feeling of intimacy that track riders have with thei

You have a feeling
of oneness with
the bike, partially
because your feet
spin constantly
with the wheels

bicycles. "You feel like you're part of the bike," says Tom who, despit
the fact that he makes his living by selling mostly 10-speeds out of hi
East Harlem shop, rides a super-rigid track bike himself. That feelin
of oneness with the bike he talks about comes partially from the fac
your feet spin constantly with the back wheel, and partially from th
rigid frame that you steer almost entirely with body action. And tha
instant steering can save you from a collision or let you dodge a ba
pothole at the last second.

Avenia cites the old six-day bike races in Madison Square Garde
in which 30 men would be zooming around the track at one time. Onl
on fixed-wheels, says Tom, could that many men ride that fast in tha
small a space. With 10-speeds you'd have bike parts (and mayb
human parts) scattered all over the track before the race was over.

Avenia also makes the point that pedaling through heavy traffic o
a conventional bike requires constant braking to keep from hitting car
or pedestrians. You're always grabbing at those brake levers, an
should your hands be out of position (everybody has to scratch onc
in a while), braking is just that much slower. On a fix, there's no nee
to use your hand brake even if you have added one. With fixed gearin
you have absolute control over your speed. If traffic slows down ahea
of you, you just retard the pedals with your feet—no extra hand-to
brake motions are necessary.

You can also ride a track bike slower without losing your balance
saving you the bother of constantly dismounting and mounting agair
when caught in heavy traffic. In fact, an adept rider can sit on an ab
solutely motionless fix without toppling over.

• **Exercise.** The fixed gearing keeps you in better shape by keeping
you from getting lazy. It won't let you coast; it forces you to peda
constantly. Take a conventional bike on a mile ride and notice th
number of times you quit pedaling and just coast. The fix will eliminat
this inefficient habit, thus keeping you from losing momentum anc
helping you develop a smoother pedaling action. Also, constant pedal
ing keeps your muscles working so they don't have a chance to coo
off and become fatigued.

What gives the track bike its superior handling and speed?

OKAY, I'VE MADE A LOT of claims about the fix's speed and responsiveness. You're probably wondering what structural differences could possibly make the track bike so much more maneuverable than a road bike. Here's the story:

The track bike's responsiveness is due mainly to its short wheelbase, straight forks and rigid frame. Take a look at the rear wheel of almost any track bike and notice how far forward it is in relation to the seat tube. Note also how close the front wheel comes to the down tube. This is a result of the ultra-sharp angles of the seat and head tubes which give the track bike a more upright frame and a wheelbase inches shorter than a road model. This, of course, means quicker turning. Road bikes generally are built with frame angles of 72 or 73 degrees (90 degrees would be straight up and down). Track bikes feature 74- or 75-degree frames.

Now look at the front forks of any of the track bikes shown. Straight, aren't they? Take a look at a photo of a 10-speed. With your eye, draw an imaginary straight line down the fork past the point where it curves forward to the drop-outs. The distance from that straight line to the drop-outs is called the rake. A track bike's fork is raked also, but about ½ to ¾ inch less. The purpose of the rake is to absorb road shock, keeping much of the vibration from reaching your arms and shoulders. The rake also helps the front wheel move in a straight line.

Close-up shows LeJeune's straight fork and sprint-style, down-slanted handlebar stem that positions the bars lower.

Note the lugs, the connectors between the tubes. Track bikes are almost always lugged for greater strength.

But rake detracts from precise steering. So track bikes sacrifice the comfort of the big rake for quick steering.

Two factors explain the fix's stiffer frame. First, the frame tubes themselves are usually thicker. Columbus makes one type of track tube, for example, which is .004 inches thicker than its standard road bike tubing. Larger diameter seat and chain stays are also usually found on track bikes. Second, the frame is shored up even more by some craftsmen who use long-line lugs to join the tubes, especially at the bottom bracket and fork crown. Sometimes braces are also built into the seat-stay bridges. What you end up with is an ultra-stiff frame that should last you a lifetime. In fact, some track frames are actually heavier than the frames on some road bikes, despite the fact that the fix uses shorter tubes and stays. (Of course, total weight is less than the road bike because of the lack of derailleurs, etc.)

Other differences from road bikes include a track bike's sturdy fork ends. The fork ends are the flat plates at the end of the fork arms in front and at the intersection of the stays in the rear that have slots (drop-outs) for the wheel axles. Track fork ends have no eyelets for mounting accessories or derailleurs and are thicker to take the pressure of very firmly turned axle nuts. Track bikes never have quick-release wheels because in competition a racer may accelerate from a standstill to 30 mph in seconds. If you're buying a fixed-wheel for non-track use, however, there's no harm in installing a quick-release, especially on the front wheel.

Probably the most blatant quality of a track bike to a conventional cyclist is the direct-drive gearing. But also note that the power train is shorter than on a 10-speed. The chainwheel and rear sprocket are very

Power train is quite short thanks to the upright frame and the short chain stays. The particular combination shown here gives a gear value of about 93 inches—much too high for normal street use.

close together because of the upright frame and short chain stays. This short distance contributes (albeit slightly) to quicker acceleration. Some riders try to improve on this responsiveness by using a block chain. This is a stiffer chain that alternates solid block links with normal open links. This means only every other link will accept sprocket teeth so sprockets with widely spaced blunt teeth are used.

Handlebars usually drop deeper on a track bike in a Pista style and are sometimes made of steel rather than aluminum alloy (used on the highest quality road bikes). Chainwheels may also be steel to handle the stress of high-speed racing.

Finally, weight distribution is more even on a fix. Thanks to the absence of a rear derailleur and freewheel cluster, the total weight is almost equally divided between the front and rear halves. This allows you to throw the bike around with body thrusts without that heavy rear end holding you down.

Some personal comments from people who ride the fix

THERE YOU HAVE the technical qualities of the fixed-wheel, but the mechanical specifications don't paint the full picture. You have to go to the people who ride the fix for the flesh-and-blood story.

Lou Maltese of the Century Road Racing Association (a New York club) tells his younger racers, even those who plan to specialize in road events, to practice on a fixed-wheel bike. "Sometimes," he says, "one of my racers will come to me and complain that he's riding every day, but just can't seem to go any faster. The problem is that he's not putting anything into the ride. I tell him to take out his fix. You can't be lazy with a fix."

When the expert was asked which bike he'd choose just for fun, he promptly answered, "The fix."

Lou used to race back in the 1930's, at one time holding several speed records. When asked to choose between the fix and the 10-speed he is quick to say that the 10-speed is the only bike for long road races. But when I asked him what bike he would pick if he just wanted to ride for fun, he smiled and just as quickly answered, "The fix."

Road races are sometimes won by cyclists on fixed-wheels. I once watched Gerry Temple, one of Century's riders, beat out a field of 15 cyclists in a 42-mile race using an 88-inch gear. Gerry admits that in a tougher field quality riders on road bikes would lose him on the hills. But he says he rides a track anyway because it keeps him in better shape.

You will often see track bikes winning less important road races. Admittedly this is not a testimony to the superiority of the fixed-wheel as a road machine, but rather reflects the physical superiority of certain riders. Nevertheless, it proves that fixed-wheels are good for more than just track racing. You can read in many books that track bikes are no good for road or street use. Don't believe it.

But what about regular people, who never plan to race? Tom Dawes, a 30-year-old father of two, rides his track bike around upper Rock-

Recessed Allen nut in the stem is a convenience factor and also looks nice, but some cyclists criticize it as being weaker than the conventional bolt found on most bikes.

land County in New York State. "It's sometimes a big pain when I hit those hills," says Tom, "and I sometimes feel like trading it in for a 10-speed. But I can't. It's too much fun." This is basically the same response you get from anybody who rides the track. The bike suddenly transforms the clumsiest of us into instant acrobats.

Tom Avenia has convinced several of his customers to give the fixed-wheel a try instead of jumping on the 10-speed bandwagon. These are not just blood-and-guts riders either, says Avenia, but "timid souls." Says Tom, "Let a sixteen-year-old kid try a fixed-wheel and he's hooked. He'll fall in love with it." The same is true of us guys who are a lot older.

Who makes them and where you can buy them

OUTSIDE OF THE Schwinn Paramount, most track bikes are made in Europe: Raleigh, Atala, Gitane, LeJeune, Peugeot, Zeus, Frejus and many others make and sell the fixed-wheel. Some Japanese makers (such as Fuji) also make track bikes but have been slow to export them to the U.S.

Most dealers don't stock track bikes; however, most will order a "fix" for you if you put money on the line

You can usually order a track through any dealer who handles the 10-speeds of any of the brands named. The problem is that most dealers don't stock fixed-wheels. This is especially true in areas where there is no track racing—which means about 90 percent of the country. There are tracks on both the East and West coasts and a couple in Illinois and Wisconsin. So if you live in North Dakota your best bet is to write one of the distributors listed in the appendices for instructions on how to order a bike. Of course, any builder (such as Masi) who makes custom bikes will be happy to whip up a track model for you.

As I said earlier, cheap track bikes are hard to find. But one model to check out is the Gitane standard track which runs under $150.

Civilizing your track bike for road or street

UNLESS YOU'RE A RACER, I wouldn't recommend riding a stock track bike. Here are some suggested modifications—the first two are most important:

1. Brakes. There aren't any. So install a front-wheel caliper brake to aid the natural braking action afforded by the fixed gearing. You'll need it, especially at first.

2. Gearing. Choose the size of your rear sprocket with care. Most track bikes come with a chainwheel/rear sprocket ratio that gives the bike a gear value of around 90 inches. This is for people who want to hit speeds of 40 mph on a smooth track. This will not only wear you out, but make it very difficult to retard the pedals once you get going. If you want to prove your masculinity, a 90 or 100-inch gear is a good one. But if you want to have a good time on a bicycle, I'd recommend no higher than a 70- to 80-inch gear (or very roughly, a ratio between 2.5 and 3.0 to 1), maybe even a lower gear if you live in a hilly area or your legs aren't well built up yet. Do some experimenting, if you can, on a 10-speed first. Find the gear you use most. The gearing your track bike should have will be slightly higher since a track is easier to pedal.

When buying a fixed-wheel, remember that the stock gearing can be altered by changing either the chainwheel or rear sprocket. Obviously the latter is easier, cheaper. Check the number of teeth on the chainwheel, and using the gear value chart, find the rear sprocket size that will provide the gearing you want. For instance, a bike that comes with a 49-tooth chainwheel and 15-tooth rear sprocket has a gear value of 88.2 inches. Change the sprocket to an 18-tooth job and you'll have 73.5-inch gearing. Don't take any baloney from your dealer. If he can't or won't change the sprocket, don't buy the bike. This detail is more important on a track bike than a 10-speed because the gear you choose will be the only one you'll have to work with. Remember that changing the sprocket will also require lengthening the chain. When you get stronger you can switch to a smaller sprocket (or vice versa if you get weaker).

3. Pump. Track bikes don't come with pumps or fittings to hang them on. Imagine a racer standing in the middle of a track pumping up a tire after a blow-out while his competition laps him ten or twelve times. Wouldn't make sense. But for normal riding you'll want a pump and a bracket to hold it. The pump, of course, must be the type that fits Presta valves which are found on sew-up tires, the only tires used on track bikes. If you want to spend the money, you can have pump hangers brazed on. However, this is a needless expense. The bolt-on types are just as good and, should you ever decide to race, the brazed-on hangers could not be removed easily and might cut you in a crash.

4. Spare tire clip. These usually cost about $1.50 and screw on beneath the saddle. But an old toe strap will do just as well.

5. Order heavier tires. Fixed-wheels may come with tires as light as four ounces. Much too fragile. You might want to go as high as 14 ounces, depending on where you plan to ride. A good compromise between track and road tires is the D'Alessandro Imperforabile. These silks are stock on Atala's track bike and weigh 9¾ ounces.

6. Handlebars. The deep-curved Pista style bars are usually stock, though road-type handlebars are showing up more and more (see the LeJeune model on page 124). With your hands in the low power position on a Pista bar (such as on the Schwinn bike), you may find you must arch your back too much for comfort. A Maes or Randonneur bar may be more to your liking, providing more hand positions than the Pista.

7. Quick-release. You can safely install a quick-release hub on the front wheel. You could do it on the rear also, but a bolted-on rear wheel is not a bad idea even if you don't race because you can exert a lot of pressure on that back wheel should you lock it up hard making an emergency stop. Besides, once you get the hang of a track bike you'll probably find yourself making ferocious accelerations just for the fun of it. Carry a wrench for changing tires.

8. Install a freewheel. Don't get me wrong. I think fixed gearing is fine and even preferable if you can handle it. But the inability to coast and the danger of constantly turning cranks is unacceptable to some people. Adding a freewheel will solve this problem, and while it will sacrifice some of the responsiveness and control of the bike, you will still be left with a machine that is stronger, lighter, faster and more maneuverable than a 10-speed. And you won't have any derailleurs to mess with. Of course, you will need two hand brakes if you install a freewheel.

Note the sturdy lugs joining the tubes to the bottom bracket, and how little clearance there is between the rear wheel and the chain stays. Track-bike tires look smooth but have a sticky feel.

On a track bike the rear drop-outs open to the rear so the wheel won't pull out when some supersprinter puts on the pressure.

Learning to ride the fixed-wheel bicycle

IN THE HANDS AND LEGS of an expert, the fixed-wheel is one of the safest bicycles on the road. But because of its fixed gearing, a track bike can be murder when ridden by a novice. Here are some guidelines for beginners:

1. **Find a safe practice area.** It's crucial to find a road or paved surface with no traffic when you're first learning. The parking lots of large shopping centers on Sundays are a safe choice, though admittedly boring. If you prefer a deserted road (and can find one), choose one with no sizable hills. Pedaling uphill is no problem—it's zooming down steep hills with the cranks whirling madly that panics most novices.

Never take your first fixed-wheel ride in traffic!

2. **Tighten toe straps hard.** All track bikes come with toe clips and straps. The straps must always be pulled very tight so you can properly retard the pedals for slowing or stopping. Don't worry about getting trapped in the pedals. Unless you're wearing cleats, which I don't recommend, it's hard to pull the straps so tight you can't remove your feet when you come to a full stop or in an emergency.

3. **Mounting.** You mount a track bike almost like any other bike with toe clips. In fact, I wouldn't recommend mounting a track bike unless you've had experience mounting a freewheel bike with toe clips. Because there's one difference. With a freewheel-equipped bike, you straddle the frame, put one foot in a clip, push off, and while the bike is rolling you hold the pedals steady with the one inserted foot so you can insert the other. On a fixed-wheel bike you can't hold the pedals steady. Once the bike is rolling the pedals will keep turning and you have to be smooth enough to slip your foot in as the pedal revolves.

4. **Braking.** This is the toughie. And this is why I strongly suggest installing a front-wheel brake to help you out. However, let's first discuss stopping with the assumption that there are no brakes on your

Track bike gives lively, responsive ride on streets.

bike. Even if you have a brake, don't use it during the learning period. It will keep you from mastering the fixed gearing and could be dangerous; you could injure your legs if you hit the brake too hard while pumping the pedals hard.

Start out pedaling slowly (I probably don't have to tell you this unless you've had a lobotomy lately). Before you ever try braking, see how it feels to retard the pedals to slow the bike. Practice until you get it down to a smooth motion. If holding back on the pedals lifts your rear end off the saddle, you're doing it wrong. Most likely you're trying to do it all by pushing down on the trailing pedal. Use both feet evenly—pulling up on the leading pedal, pushing down on the trailing.

Now try some stops at slow speeds. All-out braking is the same basic motion as retarding the pedals, only this time hit those pedals violently to lock up the back wheel. Again, try to exert equal pressure with both feet. It's not a bad idea to use cheap tires when first learning since braking like this will really wear them down. It's a price you'll have to pay. As you practice more and more stops at higher speeds, check to see that the axle nuts remain tight. Braking puts a lot of pressure on the whole wheel assembly. It may also wear out the rear sprocket faster, but again I think the practice is well worth it. Once you feel confident in your ability to handle the fixed gearing, use the front brake if you have one, coordinating your hands and feet.

Experienced cyclists use other methods of stopping or slowing the fixed-wheel bike. Some retard the front wheel by rubbing it with a gloved hand. Some can put the bicycle into a controlled sideways skid, and I've talked to some riders who claim they can jump the bike slightly into the air, locking up the pedals while the rear wheel is off the ground. I don't suggest attempting any of these methods.

5. How to coast. You can't. Try relaxing down a steep hill and you'll be thrown over the handlebars. You have to keep your feet moving. This is actually good practice for developing a fast and steady cadence. Once you have confidence in your braking ability, try "fanning" your feet in the pedals down some fast hills. You're not really exerting any pressure—just keeping your feet in time with the wildly spinning cranks.

The fixed gear is good training even when you go back to your road bike. It promotes the tendency to pedal constantly which is the key to any type of efficient bicycling—road or track.

Chapter 6

Bicycles for women

Women who want to buy a bike might do best to skip this chapter altogether. So-called "men's" bikes usually are the best bets for women. Still, if you're really scared of that top tube . . .

FROM CASUAL OBSERVATION, I'd say that women learn how to ride a bike *properly* much faster than men do. I've often noticed couples cycling together, sometimes on identical bikes, sometimes with the woman on an inferior bike (never with the *man* on an inferior bike), and invariably the rider with the smoother pedaling motion will be the woman.

Here's why: The man, conditioned early in life into believing exercise must be painful, will be pedaling along in the usual ultra-masculine high gear. The woman, on the other hand, will be spinning the cranks in a gear her legs can easily handle. But to keep up with her partner, she will therefore be pedaling faster and more consistently.

The result is a man going: PEDAL!-(pant)-PEDAL!-(groan)-PEDAL!-coast-coast-coast. While the woman goes: pedal-pedal-pedal-pedal-pedal, etc. The woman's constant, smooth, brisk motion with no coasting gives her far greater balance, higher pedaling efficiency and better conditioned legs than her sometimes-pedaling, sometimes-coasting partner.

So much for the idea of a frailer sex. And so much for the companion idea that this mythical frailer sex needs an inferior bicycle—or the so-called "girl's" bike. All women who are serious about bicycling should consider buying a "man's" bike, not a girl's. Because the girl's models *aren't quite as good.*

The reason is the frame. The classic woman's bike has no top tube, but in its place a U-shaped tube that drops down from the head tube and connects to the seat tube a considerable distance beneath the seat post. Originally, the purpose of this was to permit the rider to wear a full skirt. But it has the side effect of weakening the frame.

There's a good reason for having the top tube where it belongs . . . up top. That way it makes a triangle with the down and seat tubes.

And a triangle is the strongest geometrical shape. Substitute a U shaped tube and you end up with sort of a deformed rectangle. just *has* to be weaker and places more weight toward the bottom c the bike, thus upsetting top balance.

So why give up strength and balance for the dubious privilege o wearing a full skirt? Who wears dresses anymore anyway? Frankly I don't think that's the real reason women prefer women's bikes thes days. Since the old full-skirt reason doesn't hold water anymore i light of modern fashion, women's bad feelings about convention; frames have to be blamed on *tubotopophobia*—fear of the top tub As one woman told me, "I feel claustrophobic on a man's bike."

Well, really, this is nothing but female chauvinism, stemming fror women's firm belief that they have more to lose from falling on th top tube than men do. This just isn't true, as any man will tell you And if you buy the right size frame for your body, regardless of you sex, you will be reasonably safe.

Still, I realize that logic doesn't always conquer old fears, especiall if you grew up on a girl's bike. If you can't see yourself perched ove a top tube, there are several women's models on the market that wi give you a good ride, even over long distances.

Best news has been the development and proliferation in recen years of the mixte (or unisex) frame. This bike has no top tube, bu it doesn't replace it with a U-tube either. Instead the mixte fram employs *two* tubes running in tandem from the top of the head tub all the way to the drop-outs in the rear where they are joined to th seat and chain stays. Along the way they are also attached to th seat tube. In this fashion, the tubes are forming triangles, albei longer and less rigid triangles than are formed on conventional men' bikes.

Choose this design over the U-type frame for a bit of extra strength Of course, it doesn't offer as much space for a dress, but then that' not really why you're getting a woman's bike.

After deciding on frame type (U-shape or mixte), judge the bik by the same criteria you would judge any 10-speed (or 3-speed o coaster-bike).

Are other parts on women's bikes lousy?

A COUPLE OF YEARS AGO, *Ms. Magazine* ran a letter by W. J McHugh, a Chicago engineer, who claimed that the women's bicycle he tested proved to be only half as fast as men's bikes, and tha men's bikes had seen more improvements over the years because s many more had been sold.

Now, while I hate to defend the bike companies, I think McHugl has gone a little too far. I agree that many women's bikes do no steer or handle as surely as a man's. But there's no proof that men' models go *twice* as fast as women's. In fact, it would be difficult t nd any two bikes that are at such extremes. The most important eterminants of speed are the tires and wheels; if these are equal on wo different bikes, the bikes will be close to each other in rolling esistance, regardless of the frame. The superiority of the man's rame lies in strength, steering and therefore safety, not so much in peed.

uji S10-SL is very similar to the S10-S men's model. Fuji solves he problem of a long, contorted brake cable by placing the brake >n a bridge between the two mixte tubes.

Another woman's frame style which is neither U-tubed nor mixte is he double-down-tube type of bike. The substitute top tube leaves in open space, but it's straight rather than curved.

You can easily tell whether a bike company is skimping on part for its ladies' models. Just apply the same rules and look for the same brands you would look for on a man's bike. A Normandy hub is a Normandy hub, whether it's on a man's or a woman's bike. There are no such things as women's hubs, women's derailleurs, women's cranks, etc.

You may find, however, that the rear brake doesn't close as smoothly as a man's, but this is not the fault of the brake. It's that frame again. Because of the absence of a top tube, the rear brake cable must be run down the substitute "woman's" tube, then up the seat tube, back down the over the seat stays to the brake. This long, bent cable can cause problems. Look for good, smooth bridges at the bend points—some makers even use pulley wheels, which is a nice idea.

Many manufacturers make a woman's version of their most popular man's bike—usually one in the $150 price range—and this will have exactly the same components as the man's configuration, with two common exceptions.

Take an example: The Paris Sport 500L Ladies 10-speed has the same Huret Svelto derailleur, Atom cluster and Weinmann brakes as the Paris Sport 500 men's 10-speed. However, instead of a racing saddle it has a sprung, padded saddle, and instead of a Maes handlebar it has flat bars.

Should you take what the manufacturer wants to give you? Well, it's up to you, but probably not. Look at those two items:

• **Saddle.** I'm against sprung saddles on women's bikes for the same reason I don't like them on men's: They waste your energy. Some of the power from your leg thrusts goes into bouncing you around on your seat.

As for padded or unpadded, skinny or wide, I'd suggest the same thing as for men—a skinny, unpadded, leather saddle in the medium-price range, nylon/leather if you want to spend more. However, I really can't claim expertise in this area, never having had a woman's anatomy. Some women insist that a woman's parts are more tender and vulnerable than a man's, and that a wider, padded saddle is called for. Well, okay, maybe they have a point. Get your wide, padded saddle if you want, but make sure it's well-packed and built on a plastic or leather, not a metal, base.

Also, don't wear pantyhose or any other tight, non-porous, non-absorbent clothing while you are cycling. Your skin needs to breathe, too, and you're going to be (yech!) sweating. Stick to cotton underwear with legs, rather than briefs.

• **Handlebars.** Here I stand firm. Plan only round-the-town trips? Keep the flat bars. Otherwise get the down-turned models. Don't give me any stuff about women not being able to bend over. (In truth, one female friend complained that leaning down over Maes bars exposed her too much when wearing low-cut clothing. So, big deal. Wear something else.)

Top, probably the ultimate in women's bikes is this Schwinn Paramount P-60. It has a double-down-tube frame made with Reynolds 531 throughout. A nice extra that comes with the bike is a small set of Compagnolo tools. Left, the author advises most female cyclists, including this happy one, to buy a man's bike because the frame is stronger. Below, if you have trouble lifting your bike around (no top tube to grab) you'll like the carrying handle on this DBS model. It pulls up for use, folds down when not in use. Five-speed weighs about 32 pounds.

Tips for geishas

THOSE WITH EXTRA small feet, take care that you buy the right size toe clips (which you definitely should have for longer trips). Clips come in three sizes: small, medium and large. Medium will fit all but a few riders. The large toe clips are for giants and for those who wear Bozo the Clown shoes; few men and fewer women need these. But the small size is a different matter. Some women have exceptionally small feet. If you wear smaller than, say, a size six shoe, stick your foot in that medium-size clip (invariably what the stock equipment will be) and try it for size before leaving the bike store. Insist on a smaller clip if you need it, or you'll be pedaling on your arch.

And, of course, buy the right size frame. Straddle a comparable men's frame to determine what you need: just like men, you need ½ to one inch clearance between top tube and crotch.

Some women tend to have weak hands, and find trouble working quick-release levers on wheels. Try out the quick-release gadget on a bike before buying. If you find it too tough to work easily, go with a conventional wheel and carry a wrench with you instead—this will give you a lot more leverage. It will also save you a few bucks, as quick-release hubs are more expensive. Of course, you can loosen up the quick-release a few turns to make it easier to snap closed—but this produces a dangerous wheel.

Another situation calling for a woman's bike

WHILE THE MAN'S STYLE bike is still the best deal all-around, you may want to stick with a women's frame if you plan to do mostly city cycling with a lot of getting on and off, or if you need a bike especially for winter riding in climates with lots of snow. Through ice and slush, the lower center of gravity of the woman's bike is actually a plus, and the absence of a top tube is convenient since you'll be grinding to a halt a lot. This goes for men as well as women.

A final word of advice

THE BIGGEST MISTAKE I see on the road today is couples riding unequal bikes. Here's some guy on a Reynolds 531 frame and sew-up tires, and his wife is pedaling a heavier bike with fat tires. It doesn't make for compatible cycling or touring.

Buy a bike that's equal in quality to the one your cycling partner rides.

Chapter 7

Two essential "accessories" –tires and locks

When it comes to rolling resistance, tires are the most important part of the bicycle. And when it comes to keeping your bike, get a lock you believe in unless you want a bad case of bike-thief nerves.

RECENTLY A TEAM of three engineers sought to determine what makes one bicycle roll faster than another. The team, headed by Prof. Chester Kyle of California State University (Long Beach) pitted a 30.5-pound Czechoslovakian Rapido against a 23.5-pound LeJeune in a coasting contest. The LeJeune, costing about $200 more, won— much to the relief of the LeJeune owners who had just sold their children into slavery to buy one. The LeJeune had sew-up tires; the Rapido had clinchers.

Then, to see what would happen, the three engineers, according to their report in *Bicycling!* (July, 1974), put the LeJeune wheels and tires on the Rapido. And what happened? The Rapido nearly equalled the rolling performance of the LeJeune. The team concluded that the only *measurable* difference in performance between a racing bike and an average clunker *on level ground* is caused by the higher-pressure sew-up tires.

Sure, this experiment tested the bikes while they were being coasted, not pedaled (pedaling would presumably bring other factors into play, such as frame rigidity, etc.), but it pointed out an important lesson to every cyclist: *NEVER SKIMP ON TIRES.* Whether you go the clincher or sew-up route, get the best tires you can afford if speed or pedaling ease is important to you. Now that doesn't mean you should reject a bicycle because you don't like its tires. Just replace them at the first opportunity.

As you must know by now, there are two kinds of tires: sew-ups and clinchers. Clinchers are standard tires; sew-ups (or tubulars) have their tubes sewn up inside them and are more expensive. They are thinner and offer less friction on the road. But their main attribute is the high pressures to which they can be inflated. Most high-pressure

Don't reject a bike because you don't like its tires. Just replace that lousy rubber at the first opportunity. Get the very best tires you can afford

135

clinchers can be inflated to a maximum of 70 or 75 pounds. That
rock-bottom minimum for sew-ups and the maximum may range up ⊦
140 pounds (for track racing). That's extreme, of course, but 10(
pound pressures can be safely used on most sew-ups. Obviously th⸱
makes the tire rounder, harder, easier rolling. Sew-ups, however, ar
thinner-skinned and more prone to flats and punctures.

Which do you choose?

Sew-up tires are
expensive, a pain
to patch, and a
pain to pump up
properly, but they
deliver an unbe-
lievably responsive
ride

YOU MAY NOT have a choice. Tubular rims and tires come only o⸱
fairly expensive bicycles—over $200. Clincher tires come on cheape
bikes. Once in a while you will find a bike in the twilight zone betwee⸱
the two that comes with either (usually with $15 or so added to th⸱
price for sew-ups).

Get sew-ups whenever you can unless you plan to limit your ridin⸱
to the city only. Sew-ups are a pain to patch, and a pain to pump t⸱
those high pressures, but they give you an unbelievably responsiv⸱
ride. Another advantage is that it's easy to carry several spare tire⸱
with you on a trip and fix the flats when you get home. Changin⸱
sew-up tires on the road is considerably faster than changing or patch⸱
ing clincher tubes. Even on short trips, attach a spare under your sad
dle with a toe strap or get a special tire clip (Vittoria and Zeus botł
make one). And if you want to avoid the hassles of repairing sew-up⸱
altogether, you can usually find a good bike shop that will fix them.

Stick with clinchers if you need only a utility vehicle and care only
about reliability, not riding feel. And of course you'll stick witl
clinchers if that's what came with your bike. Some riders who hav⸱
expensive bikes with sew-ups as original gear have clincher rims mad⸱
up especially for riding over rough surfaces. A nice idea, but expensiv⸱
and not necessary for most cyclists. You can ride sew-ups in the cit⸱
if you're careful about avoiding potholes and glass, and carry th⸱
correct pressure.

Selecting clinchers

WHILE SELECTING the right clincher tire isn't as critical as selecting
the proper sew-up, you can do a lot to improve your bike's ride by
finding the best clincher skins. With sew-ups you must worry abou⸱
getting a tire that's too light and vulnerable for your purpose. Clincher
cyclists are spared this worry; get the lightest clinchers available and
you'll still have a durable touring tire.

Get the best you can because the price difference isn't that much.
Many bike makers ridiculously shave costs by slapping on cheap tires.
This saves only a couple of bucks and degrades performance incredibly. For instance, one popular medium-price 10-speed comes with
tires which retail at about $4 apiece. Yet for only $1.50 more per tire
you can move up to really good Michelin or Hutchinson tires. Get the
dealer to trade up for the difference in price.

Always watch out for the maximum pressure, which should be printed on the side of the tire. A good high-pressure clincher should accept pressures up to 70 or 75 pounds. I wouldn't go with a tire requiring a lower pressure, as this is all important.

You can usually tell which clinchers are best, just by looking. Take a look at some Hutchinsons or Michelins and compare them to others in the shop. Cheap tires have deep, crudely formed treads, often with untrimmed fragments of rubber hanging on, and are much heavier to make up for poor workmanship and cheap material.

Don't worry about tread design. Most popular are the straight grooves, called a rib pattern. Some tires have a mixed tread of straight grooves and cross-hatching. The rib pattern is faster; the mixed pattern gives a little more hold to the road. Either is perfectly adequate.

Sorting out sew-ups

PICKING THE PROPER SEW-UP can be a real pleasure, since there is a model for almost every riding purpose. Paying for them, on the other hand, is less fun. They start at around $8 and go on up to $30. In weight they start at around 4½ ounces (suitable only for racing on smooth tracks) and go on up to over a pound. The really good tires have a silk fabric, but most are cotton.

Again, get the best you can afford. Good tires last longer; they're easier to repair and to work with, and are generally faster. Best, however, doesn't always mean most expensive or lightest, and here's where the problem lies. You want to get the lightest tire you can get away with for the roads you'll be riding. For tourists this means a tire no lighter than about ten ounces or else you're playing with fire (better stock up on patch kits). And when you talk about tires over ten ounces you're talking about cotton rather than silk tires. Silk tires are generally more resilient than cotton and therefore regain their shape faster after you hit a bump.

I've found only one silk heavy enough for long-distance touring—the Clement Campionato Del Mondo, a ten-ounce model. Racers also like these heavy silks for training rides as they're less likely to puncture than lighter racing tires (ten ounces is heavy for a silk). Unfortunately they cost around $25, but are extremely fast, responsive, and can be ridden at pressures to 115 pounds without too much worry.

With this one exception, tourists will be choosing among cotton tires. And there are so many models and so many prices it's impossible to pick any "bests." Instead, choose a sew-up by finding the weight you need. Don't forget, ten ounces is the minimum. This means on ideal, smooth roads. The worst roads should be handled by a sew-up a pound in weight or more. Probably you'll want something in the middle—about 13 or 14 ounces—to use as an all-purpose tire. Finding the exact weight and brand for your needs is usually a trial-and-error process. Don't worry about matching tires front and rear. While look-

Your goal should be to get the lightest tire you can get away with on the roads you are traveling. Most tourists are playing with fire if they go below ten ounces

137

ing for that perfect tire, put different tires on each rim. See how they compare. You may want to stick a tougher tire on the rear as that's where you'll be having most of your flats.

A feature to look for is a butyl tube. Sew-up tires lose a lot of air every day and therefore must constantly be pumped up. The butyl tube holds pressure a little better than a natural tube, though I think its ability to do this is overrated.

The general advice above is meant for tourists and other pleasure bikers. Racers have no use for general advice. You'll want silks, of course, but then you must match tire weight, tread design and inflation to each particular course. Depend on other riders in your club to guide you in tire selection.

Neither fish nor foul

Here's a far-out hybrid; shaped like a tubular tire, but it's mounted like a clincher, and has a tube

A HYBRID TIRE fairly new on the market is the Corsa Strada, distributed by Raleigh. It's built like a clincher tire, with a bead, and fits on clincher rims. It has a separate tube which can be patched like a clincher tube. But it is light in weight for a clincher (17 ounces complete with tube) and is shaped more like a tubular. It can be inflated very hard—to 90 pounds. However, it's difficult to mount on your clincher rim and may be hard to find. The Corsa Strada uses the new 1⅛-inch inner tubes (as opposed to the standard 1¼-inch tubes).

Another option is the new Japanese lightweight clincher tire which also uses the 1⅛-inch tube. It's heavier by an ounce and a half than the Corsa Strada, but easier to mount.

Blowing it up—inflation tips

WHEN INFLATING TIRES, follow this one rule: While overinflation is bad, underinflation is worse. *When in doubt, add some more air.* Underinflation, at best, will ruin your tubes and tires. At worst you could dent a rim when hitting a pothole because the squishy tire won't be able to absorb the blow. Underinflation also allows the tire to flex excessively which could squeeze the tube against the rim inside and cause a blowout. A soft tire will also be more vulnerable to glass, which can adhere to the tire and work itself through the tread. Overinflation, of course, can strain the tube and make blowouts more likely, but the primary tire sin among cyclists is underinflation.

Clincher tires should have their maximum pressure printed on the side. If not, ask before buying. Most run about 70 to 75 pounds (on good 10-speed bicycles). On clinchers I recommend always inflating to maximum pressures to take advantage of the better roll. The one exception to this is on extra hot days, when the heat will increase pressure beyond the limit. Keep it three to five pounds lighter on these days.

Get a gauge, or at least borrow one until you get the feel of your tire when it is properly inflated. While riding, look down at your tires. They should just *barely* bulge out toward the bottom.

Sew-up inflation is a little trickier. You don't have to worry about going over the maximum here because it usually ranges from 110 to 150 pounds. As for minimum, get at least 75 pounds in the front and 85 in the rear. This is for a light rider with no gear. Heavier riders and those with heavy panniers obviously must go higher. You can get a good idea just by eye—keep those tires from bulging when you're on the bike. Pressures around 100 pounds are perfectly safe on sew-ups. You might want to keep it ten pounds lower for rough terrain, but never go below that 75–85 minimum.

You don't have to worry about over-inflating a sew-up tire; the maximum ranges from 110 to 150 pounds

Racers may want to go considerably above the 100 pounds that a tourist would use. However, some racers recommend low touring-like pressures to avoid too much bouncing. Some stylists don't like to have their stride broken by those frictionless jumps through the air that accompany extremely hard tires.

Always use a gauge for sew-ups. It's hard to distinguish between 110 and 100 pounds just by poking the tire with your finger. Be sure you get the right kind of gauge—there are different models for clinchers and sew-ups because of their valves.

That other essential accessory—the pump

EVERY BIKE SHOULD HAVE a pump that can be clipped to the frame, though many bikes are sold without them. Buy a good pump and save yourself a lot of frustration. For clinchers, which have the standard Schraeder valve, I like the Bleumel pump for both price and performance.

Sidewalls that reflect the light were developed by Goodyear, almost certainly will be mandatory in the future.

139

When you inflate sew-up tires, clamp your thumb over the tire to hold pump head firmly in place, avoiding damage to valve.

A sew-up tire has a different kind of valve, called Presta. A regular pump won't work on it. Two kinds that will are the Silca and Zefal. Both are good portable pumps. To inflate sew-ups, you must unscrew the valve stem counterclockwise a few turns. Test to make sure the valve is open by punching the stem inwards to see if it lets out air. A Presta pump has no hose; it is fitted right over the valve and must be held firmly to avoid damaging the valve. Sew-ups are hard to pump up to proper pressure, so get ready to sweat. If you want to use a gas-station air hose, get yourself an adapter to screw over the Presta valve. Adapters cost about 25 cents.

Whether you're inflating clinchers or sew-ups with an air hose, shoot air into the tire in short spurts to avoid destroying the tire. Clinchers, of course, are more critical because they take less air.

If you want to go the luxury route, get a big T-handle pump in addition to your portable pump. It will save you plenty of sweat

Because sew-ups leak air so rapidly and because the high pressures they need are difficult to pump into the tire, I recommend getting a good T-handle, plunger-type pump in addition to your portable model. The Var pump is my favorite. It's huge, has a built-in gauge, and an adapter that lets it fit either sew-ups or clinchers. But it costs about $25 (available from big cycle supply houses—the addresses are listed at the end of the chapter "Bikes for the connoisseur"). Raleigh makes a cheaper plunger pump with gauge (about $10 less), but its adapter and hose assembly is less durable than the Var's and sometimes trouble-some. Frankly, these big pumps are nice, but definitely luxury items—you can get by with a good hand pump and plenty of sweat.

By the way, for those who used to ride sew-ups but switched to clinchers to avoid repair problems (or for those of you who have two sets of rims—clinchers and tubulars), you can get by with just your good Silca pump if you buy clincher tubes with Presta valves. Michelin makes such a tube, a pretty good one, and if you're traveling in Europe you'll never have trouble replacing it.

Taking care of your skins

JUST LET COMMON SENSE prevail. Don't ride over curbs, look out for glass and other harmful objects. Don't ever ride on underinflated tires.

Don't be an old lady about your wheels, though. I wouldn't devote my life to getting optimum mileage out of a set of tires. There are times when you hit rough roads. Don't get off and carry the bike. Ride like hell, just like you always do. Okay, so your tires will wear out faster. Big deal. Too much emphasis is placed today on taking care of equipment rather than on riding for fun. Also, don't go swerving around glass to avoid a puncture and get bounced by a truck instead. Ride through glass on busy roads, then stop and brush it off. Glass and other objects don't usually cause punctures on first contact, but wear themselves in as the wheel revolves. Another idea is to wear gloves with a tough palm so you can brush off stones and glass while riding.

Put first things first. When you hit rough roads, don't get off and carry your bike just to save your tires. Your bike is supposed to be carrying you

Don't leave sew-ups strapped under your seat for long periods of time. Unfold them at the end of every day to allow them to regain their shape. If you're lucky enough to go several months without having to use your spare (hah!), replace one of your regular tires with the spare for shape purposes.

A final note: Don't be leery of sew-ups just because they average more flats than clinchers. After a while you get the hang of how to ride on sew-ups (and learn what pressures to use on what roads) and the flats get farther and farther apart. One rider who just completed an 1800-mile journey reports he got by with just one flat. Not many clincher riders could do that well!

Paranoia time—locks

KEITH RICHARD, rhythm guitarist for the Rolling Stones, tells how a former piano player with the rock group used to play while standing up at the keyboard so he could see out the window to keep an eye on his bicycle.

It just goes to show that bike thieves affect all of us, even rock stars. It's no fun to worry about your bike every time you leave it somewhere. So unless you can afford to lose it, buy a lock that you have confidence in.

Adequate bike locks all seem to have three things in common: They're heavy, awkward and expensive. You can get by with a cable lock or a skimpy chain in Europe maybe, but other countries of the world are hopelessly backward when it comes to bike thieves. We seem to grow the real professionals right here in the U.S. You need some heavy-duty help to hang onto your mount.

To test the effectiveness of various locks, the Charles River Wheelmen (a Massachusetts branch of the League of American Wheelmen) subjected seven popular locks of various types to four popular bike-thief methods: prybar, smashing, boltcutters and shearcutters. The locks tested included chains, cables and two were the new U-shaped type of lock—the Kryptonite and the Citadel. Here are the results of that test:

141

Citadel is balanced to sit through the saddle frame, but it can swing back and forth, as shown here.

Product	Prybar	Smashing	Boltcutters	Shearcutters	Approximate Price
Citadel	not cut	not cut	not cut	not cut	$22
Kryptonite	not cut	not cut	not cut	cut 16 sec.	$17
⅜" Campbell Thru-Hardened Chain	not cut	not cut	cut 95 sec.	not cut	$18
⅜" Campbell Case-Hardened Chain	not cut	not cut	cut 2 sec.	not cut	$10
Spoiler Lock	not cut	not cut	cut 30 sec.	cut 1 sec.	$15
Campbell Cable	not cut	not cut	cut 12 sec.	cut 1 sec.	$4
Trelock	not cut	cut 60 sec.	cut 35 sec.	cut 3 sec.	$4

As you can see, the Citadel U-shaped lock came in first, not being cut by any method. The Kryptonite U-shaped lock and the Campbell thru-hardened chain seem tied for second, both having failed only one test. However, I'd give the Kryptonite the nod over the chain because it could not be cut by boltcutters, a method which accounts for 80 percent of all recorded bike thefts. Though this U-shaped lock can be foiled with shearcutters, according to the Wheelmen's tests, it's a pretty good bet since shearcutters are much less common than boltcutters—a thief does not like to carry the shearcutters because they are huge and also will not cut through chains, the most common bicycle locking device.

If you can't get one of the U-locks, note that the thru-hardened chain proved tougher to cut by over 90 seconds with boltcutters than the more popular case-hardened chain. Note also that the thru-hardened model along with the U-shaped devices all cost appreciably more than the other locks.

Here the Citadel is secured in the ideal position—around the seat tube and an immovable object.

Now, to be perfectly honest, this whole test was set up and financed by Bike Security Systems, which makes the Citadel lock, which makes the tests appear, at first glance, to be somewhat suspect. However, the Charles River Wheelmen conducted the tests themselves, and this is a group with cycling's best interests in mind. Also, the Citadel's main competitor, the Kryptonite, made a good showing which lends credibility to the test.

Another lock to look into is the Gara/Lok, which costs about $20 and guarantees your bike against loss from theft for one year. The I.O. Prague Corp., which makes the lock, will pay off only on the first $100, however, which isn't that much consolation if someone makes off with your new Colnago. Still, it's an impressive offer for most cyclists.

So which should you choose?

PRICE SEEMS TO BE a good indication of quality in locks. The ones that are rough to crack all cost in the $20 category. Whether you need that much protection is up to you. If you leave the bike unattended on the street in any major city, get the very best—one of the U-locks. At the bottom of the line are the cable locks which I consider good only for use abroad in less thief-ridden countries than ours or to serve as nuisance value only when leaving the bike for less than two minutes.

If you get a chain, be sure you get a padlock that's equal to it. Then make sure the chain is pulled tight around the bicycle so that the thief can't place it against the pavement and smash it.

Do all the obvious things as well: Take the front wheel off when possible and secure it with the locking device to the bike. Lock up the bike where it will be under observation, making it harder for the thief to work on it.

I've also noticed that most lock manufacturers give this advice: Always lock your bike to an *immovable* object. I always thought most people could figure this out themselves, but just in case you had notions of locking your bicycle to a beagle or a moving cab, forget it.

That other alternative—insurance

IF A BICYCLE is stolen from your home, it *should* be covered by your homeowner's insurance, but it will be subject to a $50 or $100 deductible in most cases. If stolen away from home, it may or may not be covered. You'll have to check with your agent, as this varies too widely to make a general rule, according to the Insurance Information Institute. I couldn't pin these people down, but my guess is that newer policies will not cover bikes swiped away from home unless a "bicycle floater" is written into the policy at extra cost. Inland Marine offers such a floater at $12.50 per $100 value for full coverage (no deductible).

But let's say you have no homeowner's insurance. Can you get bike insurance? The answer is yes, but it's awful expensive. Keene and Company (sometimes called Yosemite Insurance Company) is one outfit that will insure you, but it's just as expensive as Inland Marine: $12 per year for a $100 bike and $4 per year for each additional $50 value. In other words, in less than ten years you will have paid for your bike all over again. If you want, you can get application forms at many bike stores or write Keene at 999 N. Sepulveda Blvd., El Segundo, Calif. 90245.

My advice is to buy a good lock and be careful as hell with your bike. And maybe organize a committee for the advocacy of capital punishment for bike thieves (though, on second thought, anyone who likes bikes that much can't be all bad).

Chapter 8

Section 2: At your best on a bike

Cycling techniques: riding for skill and physical fitness

Incidental—but good—advice on how to make your wheels a part of you, or vice versa. It takes some time and practice, but the results will be far greater riding pleasure and genuine physical well-being.

WATCH A BICYCLE RACE, and you'll see all sorts of styles. Some guys are smooth as silk—upper bodies rigid as still-lifes with feet whirring the pedals in perfect circles. Others thrash about in the saddle and bang the pedals up and down like pistons. And there are countless variations in between.

No one cycling style can be considered right or wrong. Different methods work for different racers. The same goes for everyday riders and tourists. Eventually you will find your own riding style. But until you discover it, probably after hundreds of miles of riding, here are some fairly orthodox tips that have helped many cyclists.

Setting the saddle and handlebars

MOST BEGINNERS set their saddles too low. This forces the knees uncomfortably high and doesn't allow proper extension of the legs for full power. When the pedal is at the bottom of its stroke (with the crank aligned with the seat tube) your leg should be *almost* extended. The problem is defining what is meant by "almost." The easiest way to get the almost-extended position is to sit on the bike and move the pedal to the bottom of its stroke. At this point you should be able to rest your *heel* flat on the pedal with your leg fully extended. Raise that seat post until you can lock your knee. Now when you pedal normally, with the *ball* of your foot on the pedal, your leg will be slightly and properly bent.

Another method, unleashed on the world in 1967 by Vaughan Thomas in an article in *Bicycling!* magazine, requires you to adjust

Don't forget your seat post is adjustable. Get that saddle up and stretch out your legs

145

the saddle so its distance from the pedal is 109 percent of the length of your leg measured from the crotch to the floor. This gives you basically the same result as the heel method, albeit more scientifically, as Thomas arrived at his 109 percent figure by testing over 100 cyclists. Many seasoned cyclists scoff at this method as being pretentiously sophisticated. I'm inclined to agree with them. Besides, it tickles like hell to have someone measure your inseam.

Your saddle can also be moved forwards, backwards and tilted on its clip. Centered over the post is the position to try first, but you may want to move the seat slightly forward if you pedal quickly but lightly, or back a little if you make slower but more powerful plunges with your legs. The favored tilt position has the nose of the saddle pointed ever so slightly upwards.

Handlebar height is more a matter of personal taste and where you like your hands most of the time—on the tops or down on the hooks. But a rough rule of thumb is to keep the top of the bars at the same height or slightly lower than the saddle top. Experimentation is called for, but if you feel you must stretch too far to reach the bars, replace the stem with a shorter one immediately.

Learning to shift

SHIFTING 3-SPEEDS is no sweat. *A gearhub should be shifted only when coasting.* Stop pedaling and flick the lever, turn the twist grip, or whatever.

Ten-speeds are trickier. *You must be pedaling when you shift.* And never back-pedal while shifting or you can gum up the whole works.

You will doubtless have a little trouble when first shifting a 10-speed, so take the beast to a parking lot or other traffic-less area to try it out. When shifting, grab the whole lever in the palm of your hand to give you more control, rather than just using your fingertips. The levers have no stops or set positions for each gear. You pretty much shift by ear and feel. When you hear the chain clunk into that next gear you let go of the lever. When starting out, however, you'll probably either shift two or three gears at once by mistake or you might

Girls, far left, display two common mistakes in form: they're pedaling on their arches and their saddles are too low to allow proper leg extension. Male rider, near left, keeps his inside pedal up when leaning into a turn to avoid scraping the ground.

shift one and a half gears. In other words, the chain will be hung up between sprockets. You'll hear a lot of noise when this happens. If you continue to ride like this you'll waste your energy in excess friction and wear away your chain and sprocket teeth. Fiddle with the shift levers until the chain is firmly seated.

Most of the shifting is done with the right-side lever. This controls the rear derailleur. As you pull down you are shifting the chain onto the larger (lower-gear) sprockets. The left-side lever bops the chain between the chainwheels up front. Pulling down shifts the chain outward to the larger (higher-gear) chainwheel. (Sun Tour front derailleurs work just the opposite.)

You must often move the left-side lever *after* shifting the right-side lever. This is because a rear shift will alter the angle of the chain from chainwheel to freewheel. And this, in turn, will often make the chain rub against the front derailleur cage. In this situation, if you hear noise coming from up front, move the left lever ever so slightly to eliminate it. By shooting a quick glance straight down you can see whether the chain is centered in the cage.

To make shifting as easy on yourself and the bike as possible, spin the pedals briskly, evenly and with light pressure when moving those levers. Derailleurs most often come apart under heavy hill climbing when riders are forcing the pedals up and down with great, awkward, powerful strokes. It's harder to move the chain into those bigger (lower-gear) sprockets anyway, and shifting into them under strain is called jamming. Of course, you will have to jam at times and a good derailleur will stand up to the strain—but cheaper ones won't. So shift according to your equipment.

To avoid jamming, anticipate your shifts. When you see a hill coming at you, shift down before you start feeling the strain. And remember to shift back up again when you hit the top of the hill, no matter how tired you may feel. Often riders will go up a long, hard hill in their lowest gear, then relax when they get to the top and coast down the other side. Then, should a situation come up at the bottom requiring extra speed, they will spin uselessly until they have time to shift out of low gear.

Getting spooked by power-train noises

THEORETICALLY, you should be able to ride your 10-speed without making any noise outside of the sound of your tires against the pavement—or so the manufacturers tell us. But on all but the most expensive models you can fiddle with the shift levers until your fingers turn blue and you're not going to get rid of power-train noise. Don't get upset. Most likely the noise is due to inherent flaws in the bike, nothing you're doing wrong. Sometimes noises are not caused by mechanical problems at all—loose carrying racks, sandows, mud caught beneath fenders, etc. The lesson is clear: Stay cool, strange noises usually don't mean much. The worst thing you can do is constantly look backwards at your derailleur to see what's wrong.

Physical techniques—using your legs, and less obvious tips

MOST RIDERS waste energy. They sway side to side, "helping" their legs along with torso motion, or so they think. This doesn't really help; it just slows down your cadence. Keep your body rigid from the waist up. This doesn't mean your upper body isn't doing any work; you use your back, shoulder and arm muscles to anchor your torso steady so it can offset the strokes of your legs.

Pedaling motion. Once your torso is set, it's up to your legs to move the pedals around. Remember the obvious: pedaling is a circular motion. Most riders ignore this simple principle and make pedaling nothing more than alternate downward thrusts of the legs. Try to apply pressure to the pedals throughout the entire cycle. Move your feet in smooth circles rather than imitating a straight-line piston motion. Toe clips and straps (medium-size clips fit most people) will help you immensely in this task. Whether you have toe clips or not, pedal with the ball of your foot, not your arch. You get more force that way and you won't injure your arch.

Pulling up in the stirrups really lets you turn on the power. But few tourists master this technique

Pulling up. The main function of toe clips for most people is to help keep their feet in the correct position. However, they can do more than that for you. With the straps tight you can pull up with one foot as you push down with the other. This divides the effort between both your legs and also gives you a smoother pedaling action. Should you entertain visions of racing, you'll have to learn to do this consistently. Tourists and round-the-blockers can give it a try, too—you'll be amazed at how much more power you can apply to the cranks. However, pulling up in the stirrups is an unnatural motion for most people's leg muscles and will tire you in a hurry.

Cadence—twiddlers and plungers

CADENCE is the number of times you rotate the pedals every minute over a consistent period of time. Some experts are fond of saying that everyone has his own natural cadence. I find it hard to believe that, contained in the genetic code you received from your parents, is the speed you will twirl your bicycle pedals. It's mostly a matter of conditioning. Most cyclists pedal too slowly in too high a gear.

What's fast enough? I'd say 75 rpm is a good minimum. What's too fast? Don't worry about it. Having too fast a cadence is like having too much money—a rare problem. One pro champion estimates he keeps a cadence of 90 or 95 rpm when just pleasure riding. If you can get yours up to 85 or 90 you're a rare tourist.

If you're new to cycling, you'll be lucky if your cadence is anywhere near 60. Time yourself, but not just for one minute. Give yourself at least ten minutes and count the pedal revolutions. Then divide by ten (or whatever) for an average cadence. Low, isn't it? You're probably slow-pedaling to begin with and then you lose further strokes because of maybe a hill or two and, most important, those frequent times you just quit pedaling and coast.

So for most people, the solution to finding their "natural" cadence is not the answer because that cadence is most likely ridiculously slow —like about 40 rpm. The reason? Outside of being in poor physical condition, novice cyclists use gears that are much too high for them. Male cyclists seem to get joy out of grinding away in gears that would make track riders wince. (Women cyclists, in general, are not so scatterbrained.) So get that cadence up around 75. Do it by shifting way down. Forget about your masculinity. Get a chest wig instead. Go down to first gear if you have to, just get that cadence up.

That 75 rpm minimum mentioned earlier is admittedly approximate, but it's a good guideline. Slower cadences really don't allow you to develop an efficient, circular foot motion, and they don't keep your legs loose enough. After you reach this minimum you may decide it's a comfortable speed for you and simply pedal harder (using higher gears) as you gain strength. On the other hand, you may choose not to go into higher gears as you grow stronger, but instead seek higher and higher cadences.

The cyclist who chooses the first option—pounding slowly but with power—is called a *plunger*. The latter cyclist, who spins the cranks briskly and evenly but with light pressure, is a *twiddler*.

Now while both methods are legitimate, I must admit that I favor twiddling over plunging, especially for the long-distance tourist. Higher cadences mean smoother foot action and less wasted body motion. Plungers, while they may develop superior leg strength, usually waste a lot of energy through bouncing and body sway unless they have tremendous upper body strength to hold them steady.

The beat goes on—maintaining cadence

ONCE YOU FIND the cadence that's "you"—a certain revolutions-per-minute at a pedal pressure you find comfortable—you must maintain it or you've wasted your time. That means maintaining it over hills, down into valleys and into the wind. Your body should now be

Forget about your "natural" cadence. Let's face it, your beginning pace will be ridiculously slow. Develop high rpm

used to that hard-found cadence, so keep it if you want to maintain highest efficiency. This is where all those fancy gears you paid for come into play. There are exceptions. Obviously, you'll have to give up that nifty 85 rpm spin when you hit Mt. Everest or when riding into Hurricane Hilda. And those who are sticking with a track bike or one-speed can forget this advice entirely.

Riding the straight and narrow, and other skills

PEDALING TECHNIQUE is the roughest thing to master; by the time you've developed a steady cadence you'll be adept at actually *driving* the bike without having thought about it. But until then, here are some things to keep in mind:

Riding straight. You certainly don't want to weave out into the middle of the road. At times you may have to ride straight and steady next to a line of parked cars while the traffic streams by on your left. In these cases there's little room for error. Practice following painted lines in parking lots or a line along the side of a country road. The *worst* way to ride straight is to keep your eyes on the line immediately ahead of the bike and try to hold your front wheel on it. Notice that your front fork is raked forward a couple of inches. This helps the bike hold a straight line. Follow the same principle with your eyes. Watch the line at least 30 feet up the road, and you'll have better luck.

Braking. Don't forget you have a front brake. The rear brake lever is normally located on the right side and since most riders are right-handed they tend to rely on this brake. But for an emergency stop you'll need both. When riding along, most of your body weight is on the rear wheel so rear braking gives you better traction. But in a hard stop your weight will shift forward onto the handlebars giving you better traction up front. Learn to use that front brake.

Cornering. Slow down before you hit a tight corner—the kind you have to lean into. Braking while you and the bike are tilted sideways, especially braking the front wheel, can send the bike skidding out from under you. So get the machine down to the correct entry speed before you hit the curve. If you must brake, brake only on the rear during the turn. And don't try to shift while cornering. Keep in mind, too, that wherever you lean the bicycle severely, the inside pedal could hit the pavement, especially if your bike has a low hanger and long cranks. Practice keeping that inside pedal motionless and up during turns.

Get rid of the masculine mystique

HERE'S A MESSAGE just for the men, as it's a problem few women seem to have. I'm referring to the pressure many of us have received, playing in high school and other amateur sports, to push ourselves as severely as possible to prove our masculinity. Such as the misplaced pressure exerted by a university swimming coach, who hangs a simple one-word sign at the end of his practice pool. It reads: "PAIN." It also brings to mind my soccer coach back in Minnesota who made us practice bare-chested in 35-degree November weather. And the track coach I knew who wasn't satisfied unless his distance men vomited.

Well, if you have honed your ability to suffer to a razor's edge, it can serve you well should you decide to cycle competitively. But this "masculine" urge has no place in recreational cycling and touring. Remember, the object is to have fun, and it's hard to have fun with jolts of pain shooting up and down your legs.

Physical fitness—your body and the machine

WHEN GERMAN SCIENTISTS X-rayed the chests of more than 200 athletes and nonathletes several years ago, they made a remarkable discovery: Some types of athletes whose bodies rippled with muscles weren't in very good a shape. Wrestlers and high jumpers, for instance, had heart volumes no larger than nonathletes. Tennis players and sprint-distance swimmers didn't do a whole lot better, with heart volumes about ten percent larger. Those who did stand out, with hearts 20 and 30 percent larger, were rowers, cross-country skiers and long-distance runners and swimmers. And at the top of the heap were professional cyclists—their heart volumes averaged 40 percent above normal.

> The key to skillful cycling is smooth pedaling. To feel married to the bicycle you must pedal constantly and avoid coasting

That's the beauty of cycling—it works the most important muscle in the body, the heart, as well as developing your lungs and circulatory system. It is this internal development which will protect you in later life from heart attacks and other illnesses. Just as important, cycling develops general cardiovascular fitness which gives you energy and endurance useful in any other physical activity, be it hiking, running, football, tennis or whatever. How this "training effect" of the internal organs works to your benefit is explained in Kenneth Cooper's book *Aerobics* (published originally by M. Evans and Co.; paperback edition published by Bantam). Cooper, an Air Force doctor, has also devised an ingenious point system that helps cyclists (among others) get into shape and stay there. Cooper cites bicycling as one of the three most valuable exercises, along with endurance swimming and running.

Just be patient with your body. A well-known cycling organization proposes a program that supposedly whips *anyone* into shape in 30 days. You start out in awful shape, pedal five miles the first day, escalate that every week, and by the end of the month, according to the book, you're as fit as a Tour de France champion and are pedaling 50 miles a day with a fully loaded pack. Well, that might work for 16-year-olds, but you over-30-year-olds who haven't done much lately outside of a little golf or pub-crawling will need at least 10 to 15 weeks of gradual training before you're ready for 50-mile trips. (And by that I mean a 50-mile trip that leaves you feeling pleasantly tired at the end of the day, not one where you can taste the blood in your

Stephen Loutrel, an assistant professor at M.I.T., developed this rear fender strobe for safer night riding. The photographer time-exposed six strobe flashes as cyclist rode past.

mouth for the last 20 miles.) Everybody's different, so don't put yourself down because it takes you several months to get in shape rather than 30 days.

Cycling as weight control

CYCLING REALLY BURNS UP the calories. Unfortunately, those of us who get fat do so because we eat more than we need. If we need only 2000 calories a day, we'll eat 2500; and if we bicycle all day and need 5000 calories, glory be we'll eat 5500. I've taken 90-mile-per-day trips and somehow gained weight on them. I've also polished off several cheesecakes with that famous rationale: "I'll work them off tomorrow on the bike."

Cycling is not a total substitute for dieting for most of us slobs. But used in partnership with some sort of intake control, it's dynamite. Dr. Fred A. Brandt, M.D., writing in *Bicycling!* (March 1969) reported that riding on level ground at 9.4 mph burns up seven calories *per minute.* Just think, in a mere two-hour ride you'll burn up 840 calories.

Brandt also claims riding at 5.5 mph uses up five calories per minute; really pushing it, 13 mph, burns up 11 calories per minute. Let's say you take a nice leisurely ride, covering 55 miles in ten hours. That's 3000 extra calories burned up for the day. Since one pound equals approximately 3600 calories, after a week of cycling at this rate you'll have lost 5.8 pounds, providing you kept your food intake the same.

And for those who don't want to lose weight, but just want to use cycling as an excuse to eat a lot more, just remember that one portion of strawberry shortcake will require you to go out and ride for at least 49 minutes, according to the Blue Cross Association.

And this can be quite a trick with a gutful of wet strawberries and mushy cake.

Chapter 9

Section 3: Touring on a bike

So you want to bicycle long distances?

A tragic tale of an abortive odyssey, and how to avoid looking as dumb as our hero. Advice on what gear you need, how to ride, groups to ride with and a rundown on nifty bike packs and camping gear.

I'LL NEVER forget my first bicycle trip. I checked the weather forecast the night before and hit the sack at 10 o'clock so I could get an early start. But I was so excited I stared at the ceiling until four in the morning before finally falling asleep. I awoke unrested at eight o'clock and had to fight rush-hour traffic all the way out of the city.

Two hours later I realized I had made another mistake. I had cleverly checked out the weather for the area I was leaving, not the area I would be bicycling through. I started out on a beautiful autumn day in my hometown, and quickly rode into an unseasonal snow storm as I headed west. My ungloved hands nearly froze to the handlebars. Pedaling hard into a cold, heavy wind, I seemed to be sweating and shivering at the same time. I stopped at a restaurant for lunch; I was so tired and my fingers so numb that a full glass of milk slipped out of my hands.

Minutes later I discovered another mistake. After climbing a steep hill I found myself staring at a mountain range that went on and on and on. My free gas-station map had never told me about this. I had charted my course to follow the shortest possible route from my house to my planned destination, a youth hostel 75 miles away. Everything looked flat on the map. The world just wasn't built that way.

Refusing to backtrack, I found the only road leading out of the mountains and toward (sort of) the youth hostel. It was a three-lane truck highway with a debris-covered shoulder that I was forced to ride on. My rear tire soon blew and my day ended in a cheap trucker's motel where I repaired my bike and listened to the roar of semi-trailers. The next morning, waking up with a bad cold, milky pants and no more spare tire to rely on, I gave up the fight and dragged myself home.

If I avoided making any of the typical mistakes of bicycle touring on that trip, I can't imagine what they were. Even so, that trip was a lot of fun. But there's no reason to go through all that torture. The aim of this chapter is to help you minimize the agonies of two-wheel travel so you can concentrate on its joys. Here's what you're in for:

Bicycle touring—last bastion of the gypsy spirit

AFTER TASTING long-distance bicycle travel, you'll find a long car drive a dry and unsatisfying experience. On a bike you're not closed in by 4000 pounds of sheet metal. Bike touring throws open the smells and sounds of the landscape, not just the sights (seen through a dirty windshield). And, of course, there's the sensuous pleasure of actually pedaling the bike, and the feel of the wind on your face.

But added to this is the sense of independence—the adventurous spirit it takes to set out on a bicycle. You depend on the strength and endurance of your own body, not on engines and gas stations. With the exception of backpacking, bicycle touring is probably the last practical form of non-motorized cross-country travel. But unlike backpacking, it allows you to cover great distances—3000-mile coast-to-coast trips now are quite common. And many cyclists are discovering that the Lewis-and-Clark-like spirit of touring is almost as rewarding as the normal pleasures of bicycling itself.

But unlike backpacking, when you are cycle-touring you are tied

Bike touring permits you to explore little-known areas, yet to cover relatively long distances compared to backpacking. And you can do it alone—or with as many other guys and gals as you wish.

down to a machine and public roads. Because of this specialized machine and where you have to ride it, special problems arise and special plans must be made. Keep in mind that much of your trip will be governed by Murphy's Law (anything that can go wrong *will* go wrong).

Now let's take a look at the things you *can* control so your first bike trip doesn't become a carbon copy of mine.

Le Grande Tour (or tripping on the cheap)

PURE CYCLING FUN comes from riding with as little as possible hung on the bike. This calls for the Grand Tour. Instead of filling your panniers with cooking utensils and sleeping gear, you fill them with money . . . or credit cards. (I suggest stuffing large bills, such as 50s and 100s, in the left side of your saddle bags and small bills in the right.) The Grand Tourist takes only a few personal items, sleeps in motels and hotels, and eats in restaurants. This is nice because it keeps the bike light. Pedaling is easy, and living is comfortable.

Not everyone can afford this style of touring, however, and it's just as well. Those of you with little money can make it across the country, too, *if you buy the right camping gear and learn how to use it.* Some people with all the money in the world still prefer to go this route because camping allows them to go places where there are no civilized accommodations; it gives them a sense of independence; and because camping can be pleasurable in and of itself. In any case, the advice in this chapter applies to both you campers and Grand Tourers. Readers in the latter category may have no use for the sections on sleeping bags and tents, but I suggest you take a look just the same—perhaps you turned off camping years ago, and you're not aware of how lightweight and convenient some of the new gear is.

The most important item to take with you

UNDOUBTEDLY the most important stuff to take with you is money. This even goes for those of you who plan to cook your own meals and sleep under the stars. Bikes break down and need to get fixed. Torrential rainstorms can force you to take shelter in a motel. Clothes get ruined. Sleeping bags get eaten by bears. One of the biggest mistakes cyclists make (especially younger ones) is that they underestimate how much money they will need. Money is wonderful stuff . . . even for rugged outdoor types. Remember, after camping out for a week or more, you may want to take a room for one night just for a soft bed and a warm shower.

Credit cards, if you can get them, are convenient substitutes for the real stuff. There are two basic kinds that are of interest to the cyclist: 1) Bank cards, and 2) Travel and Entertainment (T&E) cards. Bank cards (such as Master Charge and BankAmericard) usually are free,

Bike touring takes you off the beaten path. You can explore forest paths that motorists and even snowmobilers can't negotiate.

will let you make extended payments, and are generally easier to get than T&E cards. Travel and Entertainment cards (such as Diner's Club, American Express and Carte Blanche) usually charge a yearly fee ($15 or more), make you pay in full every month and are aimed at the businessman. T&E companies also make you meet stricter credit requirements; card holders usually make over ten grand a year and have held the same job longer than anyone should really want to. Banks that issue Master Charge or BankAmericard are more liberal (though not much) with their cards.

For travel within U.S. boundaries, bank cards are by far the best bet. Besides being free, easier to get, and offering credit, they are more valuable to the cycle camper in that you can buy *things* with them. T&E cards are good for *services* (restaurants, hotels, etc.), but are worthless for buying that replacement Spatini derailleur you desperately need. That's the advantage of bank cards—you can charge services (car rentals, motel rooms, etc.) just as with T&E cards, but you can also buy stuff like bicycle parts and camping gear with them. Bank cards are also accepted at more run-of-the-mill businesses than T&E cards, which are aimed at higher-echelon travelers. This can be a blessing in disguise, as most cyclists are sweaty and dirty at the end of the day and don't want to deal with overly elegant establishments.

For European touring, T&E cards are superior because American bank cards aren't usually accepted over there. And of all the T&Es, American Express is the most widely honored abroad. There is one catch, however: American Express is not usually honored at those quaint, little places in Europe that you might be looking for; hotels and other establishments that take AE are often hokey, expensive tourist traps that might offend your sensitivity and your budget. Still, that AE card is a mighty good thing to have in an emergency.

Many credit cards today (both bank and T&E) are also good for obtaining loans on the road so that you can convert them to real cash if you're allergic to the plastic kind.

If you can't qualify for either major kind of credit card, try applying for a gasoline card (such as Shell, Exxon, Texaco) as they are often easier to get even if you don't own a car. While not as widely accepted as bank cards, they often will be of help in a pinch.

In any case, before you pedal off into the sunset, make sure you have enough money or a credit card to get you back home again should everything go wrong. Because sometimes it does.

Choosing a touring bike

IF YOU ALREADY own a bike and aren't willing to get a new one just for touring, don't worry. I'm not going to tell you your bike is no good for bike tripping. Really, any bike will do, but some do better than others. The *ideal* bike is an ultra-lightweight 10-speed built with double-butted titanium or manganese-molybdenum steel tubing and weighing between 17 and 22 pounds. Such a bike costs between $300 and $1000.

Touring on such a bike is a joy, but such a bike is certainly no necessity. A friend of mine recently pedaled from Memphis, Tennessee, to New York City and back on an old 37-pound Rudge three-speed. He loaded it down with overstuffed panniers, a heavy canvas tent and an old-style cotton sleeping bag that he strapped on his rear rack with twine. He covered all the gear with plastic dry-cleaning bags and frankly the whole setup looked like hell.

But he made it. And had a good time, too.

Perhaps you've heard the true-life account of Dervla Murphy, an Irish nurse who in 1963 bicycled from Ireland to India, and later wrote a book about her experiences (*Full Tilt: Ireland to India on a Bicycle*, E. P. Dutton & Company, Inc., 1965). Dervla chose a 36-pound bike with flat handlebars to make her 4500-mile journey.

Obviously, then, you don't need that $500 Italian bike to go touring. Both riders I mentioned—Dervla Murphy and my friend from Memphis —were in tremendous physical shape, of course. If you also are in good shape, a three-speed or even an American coaster-brake bike will do. Luckily bike touring is still one mode of travel that can be enjoyed by people with little money—not just middle-class or rich folk.

If you aren't in good shape, you'll have to make up for it with money. Buy yourself a lightweight multi-geared bike, or risk riding into the jaws of death by exhaustion.

In any case, a multi-geared bicycle of some sort is always preferable, whether it's a 2-, 3-, 5-, 6-, 10-, 12- or 15-speed (don't laugh, they're all available). The reasons are obvious: You can vary the pedaling force necessary to adapt to the terrain, varying loads of equipment and the wind. Being able to shift down is also a welcome quality toward the end of the day when your legs are tiring and you still have 10 miles to go to your destination.

The secret of enjoyable touring is more in your body and mind than in the bike

So, I refuse to write off any bicycle as a touring machine—especially if it's the only one you have or can afford. Don't let the 10-speed snobs put you down or discourage you if all you have is an ancient 40-pound clunker. The secret to enjoyable touring is more in your body and mind than in the bike.

However, there are a few machines that, if you have a choice, you should pass over, as they don't readily lend themselves to touring:

• **Folding bikes.** These are great for the city, but their tiny wheels and relatively heavy weight (about 38 pounds) make them hard to pedal. Their poor balance, which is inconsequential on short hops around the city, can be tiring and dangerous during long trips. In fact, I don't recommend any bike with smaller than standard wheels. Choose a model with 26-, 27- or 28-inch wheels.

This is usually a no-no. Folding bikes are great for short hops, but don't try to ride one from Houston to Duluth. Mighty tiring!

• **Track bicycles** (and the good old American coaster-brake bike). Only the adventurous and healthy should attempt to tour on a track bike because it could be dangerous, with its fixed gearing and no brakes. Also, there are no fittings to hang racks or other eqiupment on. A handlebar bag would be easy enough to install, but other gear would take special fittings. You could solve the track bike's inability to coast by installing a freewheel and then add two handbrakes for stopping power. However, you still would have but one gear to work with. This obviously is a great inconvenience when you hit hills or wind.

By the same reasoning you'd have to be unenthusiastic about the American coaster-brake bicycle as a touring machine. On the other hand, remember Dervla Murphy, the lady who cycled from Ireland to India? The first thing she did to prepare her bike for the trip was to rip off its derailleur. Less to go wrong was her reasoning, and that "unsophisticated" bike took her 4500 miles. Makes you think, doesn't it?

• **15-speed bikes.** Triple-chainwheel, 15-speed bikes are made especially for touring. Yet I wouldn't recommend them for much of anything. Hell, *ten* gears is more than you really need. A 15-speed gets its extra five gears from a third chainwheel that's considerably smaller than the other two (a typical combination is a crankset with 36-49-54-tooth sprockets). The extra 36-tooth sprocket is set three millimeters to the inside of the 49-tooth sprocket. As I explained in an earlier chapter, that extra 3mm means the chain must go through ridiculous contortions to reach from the big sprocket in front to the big sprocket in back (and from the smallest sprocket in front to the smallest sprocket in back). This makes for a lot of trouble: the chain often rubs the front shifter cage, slips off the outside chainwheel, and the extremes in chain tension make for inefficient pedaling. If you need extra low gears for mountain touring, I'd suggest instead a 10-speed with one very small chainwheel (32 to 36 teeth).

Who needs a 15-speed bike for touring? Hell, ten gears is more than you really need

The sticky problem of correct gearing

GEARING IS ALWAYS a sticky subject because it's totally a matter of individual preference and physical ability. Some racers can go cross-country with nothing lower than a 70-inch gear. You may want a 30-inch gear at times. And there are so many other variables. The bike, for instance. A 70-inch gear may be hard to pedal on a 40-pound El Cheapo bomb, while being a breeze on a Cinelli. And then there's the weight of the load you plan to carry. In any case, if you have yet to buy a bike, check the chapter on gearing first. If you already have a bike, keep these things in mind:

1. Let's say you have a 10-speed and you have used it only for non-touring purposes. If you must often shift into the lowest gear to get up hills, you'll be in trouble when you load on camping gear. Have that rear cluster changed to include some bigger sprockets to provide lower gears for hill climbs.

2. The same goes for three-speeders and coaster-brakers. You cannot change *how* the hub shifter on a three-speed shifts, but you may find a dealer who will install a larger rear (or smaller front) sprocket for you. This will make all three of your gears lower. The same goes for one-speeds. Of course, you might need to adjust or change the length of your chain when you install different sprockets.

A brief rundown on handlebars, saddles, fenders, and tires

IT'S A MINORITY VIEW, but I believe you should tour with the type of handlebars you have found comfortable in normal riding. Frankly, the drop bars (Maes or Randonneur) are more efficient once you get used to them. But if you're not used to dropped bars, stick with your flat bars for that first long ride.

Saddle. If you already have a bicycle and a seat you find comfortable, for heaven's sake (and the sake of your rear end) don't change now. A broken-in $2 job is worth far more to you than that super-expensive Mozzarella leather-and-plastic saddle from Italy. The biggest drawback in starting off a tour with a new bike is that its stiff saddle can wreck your rear end. It sometimes takes a few hundred miles of riding to break in a new leather or plastic-leather seat. Often there's no time to log that many miles before you take off on your big trip. So you can speed up the softening process by applying neat's foot oil or mink's oil.

Ron Testa, a photographer who took a 2300-mile bike trip through the South, accidentally discovered a new method of softening his saddle when a truck buzzed him during a heavy rainstorm. The side-draft from the truck drove him sideways and dumped him in a deep puddle. His bike was completely soaked and had to be overhauled. But one good thing came out of it. Testa says that soon after he resumed his ride, he discovered his formerly stiff saddle was soft and pliable, and fit his rear end like a glove. I wouldn't recommend that anyone go out and fall in a puddle, but the mania some cyclists have about protecting their saddles against the rain seems to be unfounded.

Fenders. No self-respecting, pimple-faced teen-age kid would have fenders in this day and age, but they do serve a purpose: they keep water and mud from flipping off your tires (especially the rear) and onto your back. You can always tell the fenderless cyclists at hostels and campgrounds by the black stripe down the backs of their shirts.

On the other hand, fenders are a pain to remove to get at flat tires and other problems, and usually add a couple of pounds or more to the bike. A good compromise is the half-fender that covers only part of the wheel, or the plastic kind that attaches and removes easily.

Tires. Whether you go with clinchers or sew-ups is often determined by what kind of bike you have, since each kind of tire requires its own distinct rim. If you're buying a brand of bike that gives you a choice (and this is rare) choose the sew-ups for touring and camping. With

You can always tell the fenderless cyclists at hostels by the black stripe running down their backs

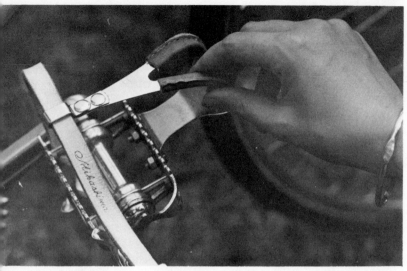

Even if all you
have in the way of
a bike is a one-
speed clunker,
don't be embar-
rassed to get a
feeder bottle

*Toe clips and straps may give your feet claustrophobia at first, but
they help on a long trip by keeping your feet in proper position with
the ball of the foot squarely on the pedal.*

less weight on the rim and less rubber on the road, sew-ups give a
livelier, faster and more-fun ride. Sew-ups do puncture easier, however, and are difficult to patch on the road. So take at least two extra
tires with you to avoid patching. If you tour with clinchers, you could
get away with packing just a patch kit, but take a couple of extra tubes
just for safekeeping—they're light.

A not-so-desperate plea for toeclips

TOECLIPS AND STRAPS are by no means a necessity but are recommended. You can attach the clips to any rattrap (all-metal) pedals and
they'll cost you only a few bucks. The clips (which usually come in
small, medium or large) will keep your feet in place on the pedals; it
sometimes gets tiring keeping the balls of your feet on the pedals for
hours at a time so there's a tendency to let your feet slip, and pedal on
your arches. The straps, pulled snugly, allow you to pull up on the
pedals as well as push down.

You may well be afraid of toeclips, especially if most of your riding
has been done in the city where you're constantly getting off and on
your bike, and must often stop quickly because of nutty drivers. But
when touring you will be cycling for miles at a time without having to
stop—which is a good time to get used to clips and straps, and to conquer the natural feeling of foot claustrophobia that many people
suffer.

Still, if the idea of being strapped to your own bike turns you off,
can't rightly blame you. There's a rumor that toe straps were invented by an old kamikazi pilot. So why not compromise? Use toeclips

alone, without the straps. You won't be able to pull up on the pedals, but the clips will keep your feet in place. And maybe that will make you comfortable enough to want to use the straps eventually.

Some very picky points—spokes and hubs

YOU PROBABLY have given little thought to how many spokes you want in your wheels. You'd have to be pretty whacked out to spend too many restless nights worrying about this detail. But those who are perfectionists might consider getting a bike with 40 spokes in the rear wheel rather than the usual 36. While you are cycle-camping over unfamiliar roads, you're likely to hit potholes, rocks and bad bumps that can give your rim a bad case of the wobbles, especially the rear-wheel rim which carries more of the rider's weight and the load of panniers. An extra four spokes shore up that vulnerable rim.

As for the spokes themselves, choose non-corrosive or rust-resistant ones, because you'll probably hit some rain sometime. Stainless steel spokes are the best (and look pretty).

High-flange hubs are all the rage these days because they look nice and because bicycle advertising has touted them as superior. But for rough roads, low-flange hubs are often better because they use longer spokes to reach the rim. This means there's a longer distance over which road shock can be dissipated.

But these options—low- or high-flange hubs, type and number of spokes—are usually only offered if you're custom-ordering a mighty expensive bike. Does your bike have 36 spokes of indeterminate material with high-flange hubs? Don't worry. These details are hardly critical.

Get a feeder bottle

FEEDER BOTTLES, plastic containers that sit in brackets clamped to the bike, are usually associated with fancy 10-speeds only. But even if all you have is a one-speed clunker, don't be embarrassed to get a bottle. It's essential that you satisfy your thirst constantly as you ride. Don't wait for hours, and then gulp down a gallon. Feeder bottles come in two basic types: those that fit into brackets screwed onto the handlebars, and those with brackets that can be clamped onto either the down or seat tube. The problem with the handlebar type is that it can interfere with a handlebar carrying bag. However, some handlebar carriers will hold two feeder bottles, a definite advantage.

Strip the bike down to basics

MAKE A HARD-NOSED evaluation of everything on your bicycle. Generators and headlights are nice frills for zipping around the neighborhood, but they add weight and the generator soaks up energy from

Be ruthless in stripping your bike down to the very essentials. Take off the kickstand, generator, lights, even the fenders. Don't pedal an ounce of extra weight

There's really no good way to carry a heavy chain (this guy's going to have a pain in the neck) so leave it behind on a long trip.

the wheel that could be used for carrying you down the road. A French arm-band light and reflector will help if you should be caught on the road after dark.

A kickstand is heavy. Take yours off. It only works on level, paved ground anyway. Lean your bike against a tree.

As I said earlier, fenders are useful for shielding you from splattering mud and water. If you don't mind·a dirty back, save a pound or more by leaving the fenders at home.

Bells, horns, speedometers and raccoon tails are definitely out.

To chain or not to chain

THIS IS A HAIRY QUESTION. I've done it both ways. It depends on how you feel about your bike and how paranoid you are about crooks. If you're staying away from cities, take a chance on leaving your lock and chain at home. The trouble with chains is that the more expensive a bike you own, the heavier the chain must be to protect it. That cancels out some of the advantage of having an expensive, light bike. Chains are also hard to pack. A chain won't always fit around the seat post if you keep sew-up tires tied there. And even if it does fit there, the lock often clunks against the frame. I once tried carrying a heavy chain around my neck to avoid this problem and ended up with a splitting headache. A suggested compromise is a cheap, light chain and lock that will serve for those short periods when you have to leave the bike to buy food or visit the john. There's no perfect answer.

Long-distance riding techniques

WHEN YOU'RE GOING long distances, say 40 miles or more per day for more than one day at a time, you have to adopt a different philosophy toward bicycling than the occasional day-tripper. This doesn't mean you should give up your natural cadence, or change that smooth, efficient pedaling motion you've developed riding around your neighborhood.

But in going long distances, keep two things in mind:

.1. It's not how many miles you cycle in one hour that's important; it's how many miles you have covered at the end of the day that counts.

2. The object of touring is to have fun, not to punish yourself.

I don't necessarily list these points in order of importance. And believe me, they do complement each other. If you waste yourself on any one short stretch, it turns your day into a drag. Your legs get heavy, you get fatigued and you cover fewer miles.

Road-touring is not like cycling to work. You're not dealing with short time limits. Rather, you have a full day at your disposal. Specifically, you have a stretch of about 16 hours to work with (allowing eight hours sleep) if you choose to ride some at night, and about 10 to 15 hours to work with (depending on the season) if you plan to ride only during daylight. Try to stretch out your riding over all the hours you have at your disposal. Hotshots pedal like hell and burn themselves out by noon. The most comfortable way to travel is to keep going as *long* as possible (really!), even though that may mean toning down your usual ferocious pace. For some strong, but short-distance, riders, this is difficult. Here are some tips:

Don't try to be a hotshot or you'll burn yourself out by noon. Pedal as long as you can, but tone down your usual hotshot pace

It's no crime to walk up hills

ONCE I WAS TOURING through upper New York State when I approached a steep hill. I wasn't feeling tired yet, but the temperature was about 90 degrees in the shade. I had 45 miles behind me and 25 miles yet to go to reach my destination for the night. So I got off the bike and started walking it up the hill. Halfway up I met a grizzled old cyclist, complete with racing helmet, who was walking his bicycle *down* the hill. "Get back on that bike, young fella," he growled at me. "You got to ride up those hills if you want those muscles to grow." He then told me he walked his bike down hills because he hated to coast. I told him politely that he could stick his freewheel up his sprocket, and continued walking up the hill.

The old man's prejudice against a walking cyclist is a common one. In fact, many of us have an obsession with conquering every steep hill without getting off the bike. It becomes a matter of personal honor. But it's a good trait to give up. A friend of mine regularly cycles between New York City and Cape Cod, a round trip of over 600 miles,

Tired? Don't be a martyr. Walk the bike until you feel rested. Walking gives your lungs and rear end a breather, keeps muscles warm.

in less than six days. The secret to his fast time, he says, is that he walks up all the big hills.

The reason behind this is that riding up big hills expends incredible amounts of energy while yielding a rather paltry forward distance in return. If you're a former Olympic marathon champ and have energy to burn, ride up every hill. But if you're like the rest of us, a good rule of thumb is that if a hill makes you huff and puff while giving you a speed of less than five miles per hour, get off. You can walk up at a speed of only two mph less. And while you may save up to half an hour's time pedaling up every big hill you meet, those hills will take their toll by making you end your day an hour or so earlier.

So where's the advantage in punishing yourself?

Some more ideas to save your poor bod

FIRST OF ALL, try to start your trips in early morning. At sunrise if you can. This is painful for most of us conditioned to a nine-to-five existence. But if you can do it, you'll avoid rush-hour traffic, which saps not only physical energy, but nervous energy as well. Starting your ride by dodging killer cars in heavy traffic is a good way to put yourself in a miserable mood, which can stay with you even when you finally hit those good roads. This advice is not so crucial for those who don't live in cities. You guys can sleep later.

Take frequent, short rest stops instead of infrequent, lengthy ones. Long rests allow the blood to desert your muscles, and they cool off. When you get back on the bike, pedaling feels tight, sluggish and painful just like when you started out in the morning. This is also another good reason for walking up hills if you feel tired. Walking the bike allows you to rest, while keeping your leg muscles warm and toned up.

You do your body a dirty trick if you live in air-conditioned comfort for months, then head cross-country on a bike under the August sun

Avoid air conditioning when cycle touring in the summer. This may sound like insanity; for many of us the summer is a perpetual search for air conditioning. But believe me you'll be doing your body a disservice by living and sleeping in an air-conditioned house during June and July and then setting off in August for a cross-country bike trip under the sun. The body has its own system for dealing with the heat of summer. The blood thins out, actually increasing in volume—thus creating its own natural cooling system. Air conditioning inhibits this natural adjustment of your body to summer weather. It fools your body into thinking it's still spring. Then when you go riding under the sun it can do you in.

How to avoid numb hands

A PROBLEM peculiar to long-distance bicycling is numbness and tingling in the hands. Toward the end of the second day of my first abortive trip, my hands became so numb I could change positions on the handlebars only with considerable effort. And when I got home my fingers were so stiff I couldn't even open the door.

Other riders have complained of electric-like shocks running through their fingers. The cause for these problems is that, when you grasp the handlebars, constant pressure is applied to the middle of the hands. This presses the nerves running to the fingers against the bones in the middle of the hand. Also, road shock transmitted to the hands from rough surfaces contributes to this effect. Not everyone is prone to this problem, but if you discover you belong to the numb-hands club, here's what to do:

1. Make sure you frequently change hand positions. If you have flat-style handlebars, it might be worth your while to switch to down-turned bars because they offer more hand positions. Randonneur bars are better for people with hand problems than the Maes bar. The Randonneur bar offers more hand positions and the final portions of the downturned ends are gently sloped rather than jutting out straight, parallel to the ground, like Maes bars. Keeping your hands on the parallel-to-the-ground portion of the Maes bar puts maximum pressure on that vulnerable palm portion of the hands.

Even in summer, wear gloves. They will protect your hands from numbness and blisters

No matter what kind of handlebars you have, change position every 10 minutes or so. Even with flat bars you can find at least a couple of different positions. This will let different parts of the hands absorb the gripping pressure and road shock.

2. Wear gloves. You can buy special bicycle gloves with padding in the palms or you can make your own by cutting off the fingers of an old pair of gloves and sticking in a piece of sponge or some other sort of padding. The idea of wearing gloves may seem silly, especially if you plan to tour in the summertime. But their main function is not to keep you warm, but to protect you from numbness, road shock and blisters. If you can't stand the idea of gloves, an alternative is to pad the handlebars.

3. Get a shorter handlebar stem. They come in lengths from about one-and-three-quarters to four inches. The longer the stem, the more of your body weight will be concentrated on your hands, and the greater the chance of numbness setting in. A shorter stem will put you in a more upright position, taking the load off your hands.

4. If all these steps fail to solve the problem, you may have to make radical changes to your bike or get a new bike entirely. A frame with less severe angles (i.e., seat and head tubes set at 72° rather than 73° or 74°) will make for a softer ride and eliminate vibration. If you have high-flange hubs, you might consider getting new wheels made with low-flange hubs. If you take all of the measures listed above and your hands still grow numb, I'd suggest you give up bicycling and buy a car. Too bad.

Are you a downhill runaway?

WITH A LOADED BICYCLE you have to ride differently. You'll know it as soon as you get on. You'll have to use lower gears and take it easier around sharp curves. But there's another difference you may not be aware of. With extra weight you gather extra momentum high-balling down steep hills. That means it takes longer to stop. So take it easy until you find the limits of your brakes.

Eating on two wheels

I ONCE COVERED 55 miles on two cans of warm beer, three devil dogs, six glazed doughnuts and an orange (for nutrition). This was dumb. On the road you lose a lot of moisture and salt and can burn up a big load of calories (about 400 an hour if you average nine mph). To replenish this burnt-up energy you can't depend on the usual three-meals-a-day routine (nor can you depend on road-side junk food as I did).

On long trips, eat several small meals so your system gets a continuous flow of fuel. You're going to need more food than normal while cycling, but you'll have to keep your meals small. Here's why: Let's say you ride like blazes for five hours and then decide to stop for a bite at McBurgers, that famous road-side eatery. You put away six cheeseburgers, four milkshakes and a pound of French fries. Now try getting back on the bike and pedaling hard. It won't work.

When you first get on your bike in the morning, pedaling is stiff and even a little painful. Right? After the blood starts flowing to the muscles, you start feeling good. Now if you stop and stack a big meal in your gut, all the blood has to rush back to your stomach to digest the food. Okay. Now get back on the bike. Your muscles are cold again, just like they were in the morning, and must share the blood supply with your overladen digestive system.

Avoid this problem by putting only small amounts in your stomach so you don't have to divert enormous amounts of blood away from the muscles. In fact, learn to eat as you ride. Take small sips of liquid from your feeder bottle as you ride. Water, sugared water or a sweetened mixture of ice tea and orange juice are all good beverages to carry. Stay away from alcoholic or carbonated beverages. Booze cuts down your alertness and reflexes, and all the sugar in soda pop tends to add to your thirst rather than lessening it. Oranges are always good to carry because they quench thirst and supply food at the same time. It's best to peel them and separate them into sections before throwing them in a handlebar bag so you can just pop a section into your mouth while riding. Beef jerky is a handy food that provides both protein and salt balance.

And the classic snack food of touring cyclists is called gorp—a combination of equal portions of salted nuts, dried fruit and chocolate M&Ms.

What does the well-dressed cyclist wear?

ANYTHING THAT'S COMFORTABLE really, as long as it doesn't flap around too much. Bell-bottom trousers and sport coats, for instance, can be a nuisance. Full-length dresses or tails are also out.

Seriously, most normal clothing that seems reasonable for cycling will do. I wouldn't bother buying special racing shorts or suits.

To combat cold weather, veteran cyclists recommend the many-light-layers school as opposed to the heavy-jacket school. Several layers of light clothing trap warming pockets of air, and as the temperature varies you can remove or add layers to keep conditions perfect for your body. Some riders recommend wearing a string shirt next to your body. This absorbs some body moisture while providing pockets of air.

A light nylon jacket in cooler weather will cut the wind and reduce evaporation from your body while adding little in weight. However, since nylon doesn't breathe, a windbreaker can sweat you up pretty badly on a long hard pull. Everyone in the hostel may be hostile.

In summer, a headband will keep both the sweat and your hair out of your eyes.

Cotton is probably the best material for bike clothing. It's light, absorbent and easy to clean (important on the road). While cotton drawers are standard gear for most men, some people find they develop especially sweaty or sensitive rear ends when riding. A pair of cut-off sweat pants may be the answer. This goes for women as well as men.

For those who feel victimized by their own saddles, chamois-lined pants will save aches and boils. I've even heard some cyclists recommend slipping a slice of beef or liver into the seat of the pants—but meat prices being what they are I'd look for a cheaper substitute.

If you normally need glasses, wear them. If not, shatterproof sunglasses are a good idea to protect your eyes from dirt, flying gravel kicked up by passing cars and that occasional wayward bug. At high speed a fleck of dirt can blind you temporarily.

A big deal is often made about the correct shoes. Several books and articles published recently warn the rider never to wear tennis shoes if his bike has metal pedals. Supposedly, the pedals will begin to cut into the feet after only a few hours. This is baloney, in my opinion. I've had a rough time finding any cyclist who admits to having this problem. Sneakers are light, washable and dry out quickly after being soaked in a downpour. In short, they're perfect for cycling. If you're worried about hurting your feet, get stiff-soled sneakers. Some sneakers made primarily for jogging (Puma makes a pair) also serve cyclists well, as their soles provide more protection than conventional sneakers. Regular leather shoes also work fine, but boots are heavy and sometimes too wide to fit in toeclips.

Special fancy bicycle shoes are, of course, perfect while you're on the bike. The steel plate used to reinforce the sole lets you put more pressure on the pedals. However, the steel reinforcement also means you can't walk in the shoes; you'll destroy both the shoes and your feet. So you'll have to carry a pair of real shoes with you, and change everytime you want to get off the bike. That means a lot of bother and extra weight in your pack.

For rainy weather there are special hooded ponchos that cover almost your entire body to keep you dry. But these are vulnerable to the fun-house effect: A strong wind can catch underneath the garment and swirl it up around you. A headwind tends to push the hood back off your head, and a tailwind can push it forward over your eyes.

Rain gear of some sort is necessary when touring in cold weather. But in summer you can get away with none—you can just relax and enjoy the rain hitting your body and then let the sun dry you out as you ride. If you hate water anywhere on your body except in your mouth, try rain gear that comes in the form of separate waterproof pants, jacket and hat. This is better than the poncho type. A compromise is a lightweight raincoat that clings to your body and won't catch the wind.

Here's a sample packing list for the long-distance U.S. or European tourist:

Here's what the well-dressed long-distance bike tourist will wear. Pack these duds in freezer bags

1 pair of shorts (in summer)
1 pair of sta-prest pants for men and women (or wrinkle-resistant dress)
2 pair of socks (wool or heavy cotton)
1 waterproof nylon windbreaker
1 sweater or sweatshirt
2 cotton undershirts
3 pairs of cotton underpants
1 waterproof hat
1 pair of shoes (preferably one pair that will serve for both pedaling and normal walking purposes)
1 plastic raincoat or other rain gear
1 string shirt (optional)
1 pair of bicycling gloves with padded palms (if prone to hand numbness)

Pack your clothes in clear freezer bags (or other plastic bags). That extra bit of waterproofing can be a godsend as my photographer friend who was dumped in a giant puddle by a passing truck learned the hard way. By the way, his cameras were ruined also. So if you're packing photo gear, give it all the protection you can.

Some other stuff you might want to pack

THE FOLLOWING is a basic guide for the first-time tripper. You will eventually devise your own list to suit your own peculiar needs, particular travel plans and jaded desires. Remember that what you take can be affected by how many other cyclists there are in the party. It's silly for everyone to bring his own sewing kit, tool kit and cooking gear if there are going to be three riders sticking together. Each guy (or girl) brings certain things that are shared. Divide responsibilities wherever you can, and you'll ride lighter.

Any liquids or lotions that come in glass containers will not last long on the road. Transfer them to plastic bottles.

Now, here's the list:

> Usual toilet articles (soap in plastic traveling dish, toothbrush in case, toothpaste, tube shaving cream, safety razor, and deodorant if you're the considerate type. Consider growing a beard if you're a man or going "natural" if you're a woman—that way you can avoid packing shaving gear)
>
> 1 dark towel (gets just as dirty as light towel but won't look so raunchy)
> 1 short length of nylon clothesline plus clothespins or safety pins (why do you think you're bringing so few clothes?)
> 1 plastic bottle of dishwashing/clotheswashing liquid
> 1 first-aid kit (a must)
> 1 roll toilet paper or bundle of Kleenex (especially if you're traveling in Europe, land of hostile toilet paper)
> 1 sewing kit (optional)
> 1 Swiss-Army-type knife (Camper model)
> 1 French arm-band light
> 1 flashlight (optional)
> 2 sandows (invaluable for zillions of strapping-on jobs)
> 1 tool kit (this will be covered in detail at the end of chapter)

Carrying the weight

FIRST, HERE'S WHAT NOT TO DO. Don't carry anything on your back. Now, I know people who get away with strapping on a backpack for short hauls. And I've seen cyclists who do it over long distances. If you want to try this, okay. But it makes more sense to let your bike carry the weight and free your body to provide the locomotion. A pack

Each biker brings certain things that are shared. If you divide responsibilities you'll travel considerably lighter

cuts into your shoulders, puts extra weight on your already tender seat and can block your rear vision. Worse yet, a loaded backpack raises your center of gravity. When you strap that extra weight high on your body you make it easier to spill when leaning into corners.

This is not a good practice. A backpack raises your center of gravity, making it easier for you to spill on a tight corner.

Left, this Swiss-made carrying rack, or a similar one, is a must for carrying panniers. Right, clamp fits into slot of AYH panniers.

To carry the load on your bike, you'll need a rear carrying rack. The most popular one today is the Swiss-made Pletscher. It weighs about a pound, has a large spring-loaded clamp which will grab onto a set of panniers, books or whatever. It is also drilled out in the rear to accept a reflector. There are other rear carriers available, however. The Touring Cyclist Shop of Boulder, Colorado, sells a carrier that is extra strong for campers who plan to tote a lot of weight. (Complete addresses of all equipment firms mentioned are listed at the end of this chapter.)

The most essential bikepack equipment to have is a good set of panniers to hang on your rear rack. Technically, panniers are wire baskets that hang on either side of the rear or front wheel. These contraptions are still available in some shops and you often see women using them to lug groceries home from the market in Europe. But these are considered archaic for the modern cycle tourist, and panniers have now come to mean any canvas or nylon saddle-bag-type packs that hang on either side of a rear carrier.

Other bikepacks include handlebar bags for the front, saddlebags that hang from the bicycle seat, and front panniers. The most comfortable combination to go with is just two packs: panniers in the rear and a handlebar bag up front. Even with panniers you still have the top of your rack to work with: tents, sleeping bags or other gear can be tied on with rope or sandows.

Left, Touring Cyclist Shop carrier is heavy duty (28 ounces) for toting big loads. Right Karrimor carrier is nylon-coated steel.

Avoid front panniers if you can. They make steering difficult. Bags that hang from the saddle aren't so hot either as they are difficult to secure and will often sway back and forth annoyingly as you ride. Also, if you are short, riding a short-framed bike with the seat post extended only slightly, there may not be enough room to hang a saddlebag without having it resting on the rear wheel.

Packing the bike

BEFORE GOING into the specifics about styles and brands of panniers, here are a few general tips on loading your bike. Whether you're going to rough it all the way and carry camping gear or plan to go hotel-hopping, there are three general rules:

- **Keep it light.** I'd say 30 pounds *maximum* is a good rule of thumb. When deciding what to take, another good rule is: When in doubt, leave it out.
- **Keep the load balanced.** Try to equalize the weight packed in each of your panniers. Otherwise you'll have to lean sideways to maintain control. A loaded bike is always going to be rear-heavy, even if you use a handlebar bag. This is unavoidable and shouldn't present too much of a problem unless you exceed the 30-pound limit.
- **Keep the weight low** and near the center of the bike. Most bike packs that you buy are designed to do this for you. Just don't pile gear too high on your rear rack, or so it overhangs the rear end.

Left, tour-outfitted Nishiki is well equipped for long trips, but lights and generator could be left off to save weight. Right, Cannondale panniers can be slid rearward for more pedal clearance.

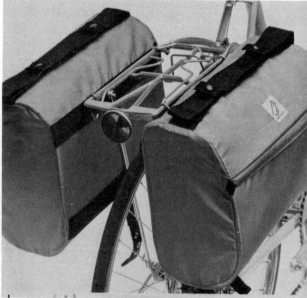

The nitty-gritty on panniers

LET'S GET DOWN TO DETAILS. When shopping for panniers, one thing to watch is that they don't hang down so far they interfere with the operation of the derailleur or extend so far forward that you'll bop them with your heels as you pedal.

Since panniers can cost as much as $50, your budget may not be able to handle such conveniences. A workable substitute is a pair of army surplus knapsacks or carrying bags approximately the size of the panniers you would need.

But assuming you can afford store-bought panniers, look for the following features: First, buy waterproof nylon bags. This is easy since most fall into this category. About the only major company left that makes the bulky, heavy canvas bags is Karrimore Products of England and they are now switching over to nylon. Look also for such refinements as reinforced fasteners, and such conveniences as outside pockets for small items, Velcro closures, and if they are going to double as your luggage, the ease with which they can be attached to and detached from the bike.

For the lightweight tourist who plans no camping, Bellwether has what it calls a small touring pack for about $20. It's a basic pannier arrangement with nylon zippers and Velcro closures on outside pockets. If you can't find it in bike stores or camping outfits, you can order it from L. L. Bean or Ski Hut (addresses at end of chapter). Bellwether also makes a line of bike packs called the "Professional."

Bellwether's Grand Touring Pack holds 2200 cubic inches of gear, sells for about $30, and is aimed at the camping cyclist. Right, the smaller touring pack holds 1200 cubic inches, costs about $20.

Costly and aimed at cyclists who travel extensively, they feature lots of Velcro closures and convert in seconds to backpacks.

For those who need more room, Touring Cyclist Shop of Boulder, Colorado, makes an ingenious set of panniers. They detach and attach to the bike easily, can be zipped together for carrying with an attached shoulder strap, and can even be attached to a pack frame for backpacking. These panniers are very roomy with 10 separate compartments, are very well made of heavy rip-stop, waterproof nylon with all zippered closures covered for weather protection, and . . . are very expensive—about $50.

You might also want to write for a catalog from the Gerry Company, which specializes in backpacking equipment but also sells very roomy panniers for about $30. You may find the Gerry bags at camping or backpacking equipment stores. Other large panniers to check out are made by Bellwether (called the Grand Touring model), Karrimore and Cannondale. And don't forget panniers and other equipment sold by American Youth Hostels (see the New York address for the catalog). Their bags lack conveniences, but are inexpensive and do the job.

> *These cyclepersons are demonstrating the versatility of Touring Cyclist panniers. Guy in foreground has them on his bike, gal carries very same panniers by a shoulder strap, and hiker (who knows what sex?) has them on a backpack.*

Left, Touring Cyclist panniers weigh 1 pound 3 ounces each, and each has three pockets attached to main bag. On top of the rack is the Daytripper, good for carrying loose items such as maps and a sweater. Right, they attach with bottom spring and top hook.

Soft handlebar pack from Bell-wether fits all carriers, holds overflow gear. It costs about $20.

Another model features Velcro closure on front pocket, comes with a shoulder strap.

Gerry pack fits either on the handlebars or behind the saddle.

Karrimor handlebar bag converts to shoulder bag.

Penny-conscious biker who sews can save with Holubar bikebag available in kit form for about $8.

This front bag support is widely available, fits easily over all handlebars, weighs 15 ounces.

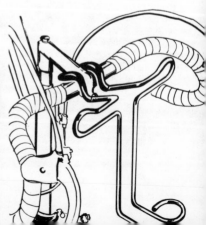

Hunting for handlebar bags

HANDLEBAR BAGS should meet the same standards as panniers—waterproof nylon-reinforced fasteners, ease of detachment, etc.—plus some others as well. First, make sure any bag you buy doesn't interfere with the brake cables and won't hang down on the wheel when fully packed. It's best to buy a metal support to hang the bag on. I once naively bought a Bellwether pack with no rack, packed it full of gear and didn't notice how much the bottom was sagging. Within two blocks the front wheel had worn a hole through the pack. Bellwether now provides racks with their bags.

For convenience the top of the bag should open away from you so you can get at things (specifically food) while you're riding. Other niceties include shoulder straps and a transparent map holder on the top.

These bags are good for carrying your small daily needs such as camera and film, sweater or jacket and other small items.

Bellwether makes two packs both of which can double as shoulder bags off the bike. One is a soft pack for under $10 and the other a little larger for about $5 more. Bellwether also makes a third pack, its "Professional" model, which runs close to $20 but features a map holder, support, and converts to a bona fide backpack. Gerry makes an interesting teardrop-style model for about $16 that holds about the same amount as the middle-priced Bellwether bag. And if you're really ambitious you can make your own handlebar pack with a kit from the Holubar Company. The kit costs about $8.

I won't go into saddle-type bags or front panniers here as I think they should be avoided if possible. However, if your tastes run toward these packs, see photos on page 181.

Camping equipment—sleeping bags

CYCLISTS SHOULD THANK their lucky stars for the backpacking craze. In recent years camp-gear manufacturers have developed lightweight equipment specifically for backpackers—sleeping bags and sleeping pads, tents, stoves, cooking equipment and dried foods. This gear suits cyclists perfectly, and backpacking stores should be the first stop for any prospective bicycle camper.

The first concern for any camper is his sleeping bag. Since most of your cycling will most likely be in the more temperate months, you can save both money and weight by avoiding bags made for cold weather. Your budget will dictate what you can spend, but the ideal to aim for is a nylon sleeping bag filled with anywhere from a pound and a half to a maximum of two pounds of down.

The reason is simply that of weight and efficiency. Pound for pound the nylon/down combination retains more body heat while allowing excess moisture to evaporate than the heavier, synthetic-filled cloth bags. The nylon/down bag dries quickly when wet, compresses to a surprisingly small size and, most important for insulation purposes, fluffs up more efficiently to provide that insulating layer of dead air that retains your body warmth. Total weight of such a bag is usually two or three pounds.

Assuming you can afford a down bag (they usually start about $40), look for other features such as a mummy shape. This is the most efficient shape for cool climates; it saves weight and retains heat. For warmer nights you might prefer the rectangular shape which lets you zip open the side and bottom for more ventilation. Rectangular bags also give you more leg room, while mummy bags make you feel well . . . mummified. If you're traveling with your husband or wife or a close friend, you might want to look for compatible bags that zip together for a cozy sleeping arrangement.

If you're lucky you can find an Army surplus down-filled mummy bag for a real savings, but given the popularity of Army surplus stores these days, this likelihood gets slimmer with every passing week. If you are tempted to save a few bucks by going with a cloth bag, give it a second thought if you can afford better. A cloth bag will certainly keep you warm enough on a summer night but weighs approximately five times what a good nylon/down bag runs. My old cloth bag weighs almost 10 pounds and would therefore allow me only 20 pounds of other gear to keep within the 30-pound commonsense weight limit. American Youth Hostels has some reasonably priced down-filled bags and L. L. Bean carries Fiberfill bags that are a good synthetic substitute for down. But if price is no object you should check the Holubar catalog for some of the best bags you can buy. With any sleeping gear, be sure you get a nylon stuff-bag to keep it in.

What to put between your sleeping bag and the ground

NOW THAT YOU HAVE a sleeping bag you'll need something to plop it on unless lying on cold, wet ground is your thing. At the very least you'll need a ground cloth to protect you from the damp. A sleeping mattress or pad will be comfier, however.

Given the choice, go for a sleeping pad for a number of reasons. First, there is the old bugaboo, weight. Even a lightweight backpacker's air mattress weighs close to two pounds, while a foam sleeping pad weighs a little over one pound. What's more, the sleeping pad insulates your body against ground chill more efficiently than an air mattress. Makers of air mattresses say that heat from your body warms the air in the mattress thus insulating you from the cold ground. Unfortunately, what usually happens is that the ground cools the mattress first. Another advantage of the pad is that it never goes flat and doesn't require any artificial respiration in reverse, which is what you must do to roll all the air out of an air mattress.

A three-quarter-length pad that cushions your shoulders and hips is fine—but add a waterproof covering if you don't want the pad to

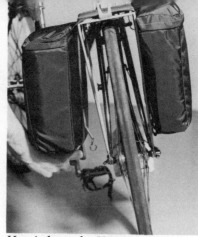

Handlebar bag support keeps the bag from riding on the wheel or interfering with brake cables.

Here's how the Karrimor front panniers spring-hook on and off the front carrier.

Cannondale's seat pack has quick-release latches.

You have direct access to pocket in Karrimor pannier while riding.

Stuff Sac from Karrimor can be carried on the rear rack, behind the saddle, or on the handlebars.

This neat saddle pack from Bellwether has zipper closure, weighs only 6 ounces, costs about $5.

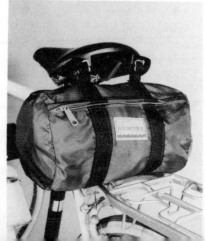

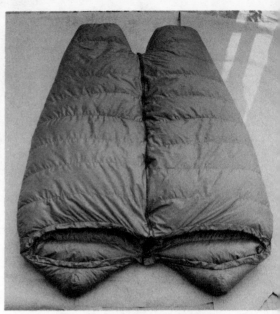

Left, goose-down Gerry mummy bag boasts an extra-large "foot" for additional kicking comfort! Right, L. L. Bean bags can be zippered together to form a double bed.

become a large sponge on wet ground. Ski Hut, Holubar and L. L Bean all sell a lightweight pad made of Ensolite that offers the sam advantages as a regular foam pad but doesn't need a waterproof cover ing. Its only drawback is that it is thinner and may not give as cush a feel as an air mattress or two-inch sleeping pad.

On the trail of the perfect touring tent

ONCE AGAIN the backpacking craze has come through for the tour ing tent shopper. It's now possible to get a sturdy, waterproof nylor tent, big enough for two and weighing only about 4½ pounds, for . little over $40. As with sleeping bags there are zillions of brands an as many different prices. They have variables too numerous to de scribe. However, here are a few key points to remember:

First of all, yes it's nylon again for the basic material. Mainly be cause of its light weight and strength. The cheaper nylon tents ar made of waterproof, plastic-coated nylon. If you buy one of these make sure it has netting at both ends for proper ventilation. Nylor tents keep out water efficiently, but also keep *in* the moisture of you breath and perspiration. This can make living in a nylon tent a humi and downright hot experience.

The better nylon tents are not coated; they "breathe," thus allowin moisture to escape, giving you a dry little tent. Unfortunately thes tents are *not* waterproof and require a second roof or wall to kee

ain and heavy condensation off your body. This means you can
nvest in some exotically priced tents.

An alternative is to buy something like the backpacker tents advertised in L. L. Bean's catalog, and then get a cheap plastic or
plastic-coated nylon sheet to cover the outside. This layered arrangement gives you good ventilation while keeping the rain off your head.

Another feature to consider is complete waterproof flooring. The
best design is waterproof nylon that continues part way up the wall of

*Above, L. L. Bean's backpacker tents are extremely lightweight, but
may require an extra top fly in hard rain. Below, Gerry's lodgepole
tent houses two, features doublewall construction.*

Super Tube Tent from Holubar costs about $25. It weighs less than 3 pounds, makes a one-man floored tent or a two-man floorless tent.

the tent, giving protection on the sides as well as the bottom. Also, look for doors and netting that close completely, with no bug leaks.

Size is another consideration. Get a tent big enough to hold all your gear once it's unpacked and spread out around you, with enough room left over to prepare a quick meal on a rainy day. Even the color can make a difference, especially during the hunting season. A bright orange or red tent is one way to insure you won't be mistaken for a sleeping moose by some idiot hunter. The same goes for clothing. Moving cyclists are favorite targets of deer hunters, so don't give these bloodthirsty characters any excuses. Don't wear brown! Try to get some orange or red garments on your body. Never wear antlers.

Take along at least one pole even for a tube tent. Those trees never seem to be the right distance apart

An alternative to spending a lot of money on a tent is to make one. Some companies such as Holubar sell their tents (and sleeping bags if you're that ambitious) in kit form with precut material, thread—the works. If you or someone you know is moderately handy with a sewing machine this can be a real cash-saver. Holubar, for example, sells a two-man tube-tent kit for about $25, with netting at extra cost.

Tube tents, whether in kit form or ready-made, are simply shelters that set up like open-end tents, and always appear in catalogs tentpole-less with the top strung on a rope between two trees. The guys who draw pictures in tent catalogs always find two trees the perfect distance from each other, but this situation is sometimes difficult to find in the real world. I'd advise bringing at least one pole.

Tents for hard noses—tarps

FOR THE REAL outdoor spartan who doesn't need all those fancy tents with rain flies, mosquito netting, waterproof floor and all that, tarps are single-piece shelters. They are cheap waterproof squares or rectangles that can be used instead of a tent. I know one guy who bicycled for six weeks with nothing but a plastic tarp and a couple of tent pegs. When he camped for the night he anchored one side of the tarp on the ground and tied the peak of his lean-to to his bicycle. How did it work? Fine, he told me—except for the rain and mosquitoes.

If you're determined to try it the primitive way, there are a number of ready-made tarps or tarp substitutes available to serve the purpose. Most camping suppliers carry waterproof nylon tarps with ties attached. Then there's a nifty item called a Versa Tarp made from reinforced plastic and equipped with an ingenious ball and clincher tie system called Versa Ties (logically enough) that lets you arrange the placement of your guy lines any way you want.

If you want to make your own out of raw material, you'll do best to look for a heavyweight nylon (three-ounce-weight or more) that is waterproof. Nylport, a coated nylon fabric, is one good example; you can buy it from Holubar equipped with grommets and ties for variable shelter configurations. On a really tight budget? Get a sheet of polyethylene and adapt it for a shelter with Tarp-Tys—strips of adhesive vinyl with grommets in them.

Odds and ends

NYLON CORD always comes in handy so carry about 30 feet or so. Tent poles come in aluminum sectional or telescopic models, but if you have the bread, get the nifty kind that collapse and have internal connecting elastic. The best tent pegs are the bright-colored plastic ones that are easy to see and don't bend when you bash them with a rock. And unlike the spindly skewer kind, they don't disappear into the ground forever.

Stoves for the road

CAMPING ALMOST ALWAYS means cooking for yourself. Again, thanks to the backpackers, a good selection of compact dependable stoves is available. There are two general types: one which uses liquid gas (white or leaded) or kerosene, and another that uses butane gas in a pressurized can.

In Europe you can't always count on getting white gas or kerosene for your stove. One that burns butane gas is a better bet

Less convenient of the two is the liquid-fueled stove because it can get a little messy and can be inconvenient in Europe where white gas and kerosene are not universally available. There is one model, however, that uses both leaded and white gas, so you can fuel up at any gas station. It's a little brass Swedish stove called Svea. One tankload does about a day's worth of cooking. For a little extra security get it with an aluminum fuel bottle (from L. L. Bean, Ski Hut, Holubar or almost anywhere) that holds about six days' worth of cooking fuel.

No matter how careful you are, liquids tend to spill, stain or leak—a hazardous risk if the liquid is flammable. That's why the butane stove is safer, neater (while requiring less paraphernalia) than the liquid-gas stove. The most common model is the American-made Gerry ministove that costs about $12 with one cartridge and weighs about 17 ounces (10 for the cartridge, 7 for the stove). The French-made Bleuet costs about the same and weighs about one pound more.

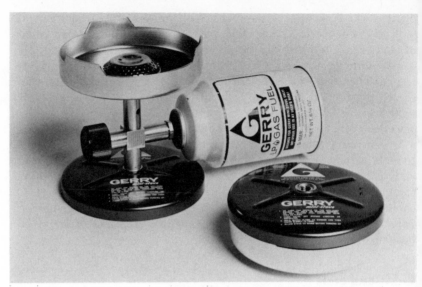

Gerry Ministove folds into a yo-yo shape only 1½ inches tall, will burn more than three hours on one can of butane gas.

This model converts butane flame into flameless infrared rays for either cooking or heating. It costs more than $25.

Here are handy accessories if you don't mind the weight. They include an aluminum kettle set with pot lifter; Sven folding saw; poly water bags (under saw); aluminum bottles; Teflon fry pan; windscreen with grill around a Ministove; poly squeeze tube to hold your peanut butter unmessy; adjustable steel grill; plastic mug; Mautz Fire Ribbon for igniting wet wood; snow seal for boots; flashlight; and a tourist cooking set that includes pots, windscreen, pot lifter and lid.

The gas cartridges hold two to three days' worth of cooking gas, and are compact and light enough so that carrying a few spares is no problem. If you're planning to tour Europe, the Bleuet might be a better choice since replacement cartridges are easier to find there. Also, Gerry makes a special camp stove that converts butane to infrared heat, but it costs about $25.

Cooking gear for the cycle chef

NOW THAT YOU HAVE something to cook *on* you'll need something to cook *with*. If food is just something that you stick in your mouth as far as you're concerned, your needs will be simple. But if you're Julia Child on two wheels, or if you're traveling with friends, things can get a little complicated. Here then are two sample lists, one for simple grubbers and another for those with more sophisticated culinary needs. First the simple list:

1 knife-fork-spoon stainless steel interlocking set. Costs about $1
1 pocket knife such as the Swiss Army Camper model with knife blade, bottle and can-opener, and corkscrew
1 compact aluminum mess kit. They usually include cup, frying pan, plate and 24-ounce pot with lid
1 camp stove
1 Sierra Club cup. If you've ever tried to drink hot coffee out of a metal mess kit cup you know how easy it is to burn your lips. Miraculously this eight-ounce cup won't do that

1 nylon scouring pad
1 dish towel (light cotton)
1 plastic bottle of dishwashing liquid (Remember the one you packed to wash clothes? Yup, the same.)
1 plastic bag to hold all this stuff

And for the pantry:

1 combination salt and pepper shaker with cap
1 leakproof container for cooking oil

Now for you cooks with wilder ambitions:

1 two-man cook set. What this consists of depends on how much cooking you will do, how much you want to bring and how many pans you want to clean. L. L. Bean sells a cookset that goes with the Svea stove. It consists of two pots, a deep skillet, a pot lifter and a base and windscreen for the stove. Recreational Equipment has a Rover aluminum set that consists of one pot with lid, one sauce pan, one plate and one pot-lifter. Whatever you settle on, your basic cook unit should have at least:

2 sets of the knife-fork-spoon units
2 cups, preferably the Sierra Club type
2 aluminum plates
1 large pot with lid (1½ quarts)
1 smaller pot (about one quart)
1 pot lifter (unless you want to test your limits of pain)
1 collapsible water bag (rolls up easily when empty)

After two weeks of traveling, someone else's boiled weiners always taste better than your own boiled weiners

Of course, you'll also need all the applicable stuff (scouring pad, camper knife, etc.) from the first list as well. Cooking always makes two-person (or more) travel appealing since it's nice to have someone with you to share the cooking and the load. For some reason, after two weeks of traveling, someone else's boiled weiners always taste better than your own boiled weiners.

Planning your meals

EARLIER I TALKED ABOUT eating small bits of food while riding. But of course you're going to eat some regular meals too, especially in the morning before riding and at night when you're through for the day.

Frankly, I'm against cooking all your major meals, especially if you're touring through European countries known for their food, such as France. In Europe it seems that in even the smallest towns, fresh bread still warm from the oven, fresh chemical-free fruit, good cheese and cold sausage-type meats are commonly and cheaply available. Even those on a tight budget can buy an inexpensive and uncommonly good meal. And if you're going to France, take pains to save enough money so you can blow yourself to a full-fledged feast in one of her famous restaurants. It seems a shame to make it all the way to France and eat nothing but camper's food.

In America, of course, there are so many roadside stands and eateries that you can probably make it coast to coast without cooking a meal. U.S. food is rarely high-class, but available on a 24-hour basis. In other countries the roadside neon plague has not yet struck in its full ferocity, so quick meals are not so readily available.

Another consideration in planning your meals is local eating customs. In France, for example, the noon to two o'clock lunch break is religiously observed; trying to find an open bakery, grocery store or wine shop during those hours can be a real exercise in futility.

As far as cooking your own meals goes, you'll find no recipes here. You need a whole book to cover camp cooking with the justice it deserves. Fortunately there are quite a few. One is *Food for Knapsackers*, a handy pack-size everything-you-wanted-to-know-about-packing-and-cooking-your-own-food kind of book written by Hasse Bunnelle and published by the Sierra. You can get it at L. L. Bean or write to the Sierra Club, 250 West 57th Street, New York, N.Y. 10019. Price is $1.95. Another Sierra Club publication is *Cooking for Camp and Trail* by Hasse Bunnelle with Shirley Sarris. Also $1.95.

Another good book for bike-trippers is *Backpack Cookery* by Ruth Dyer Mendenhall, LeSiesta Press, for only a buck. Like the Sierra book, it tells how to cook outdoor meals and how to package your own prepared foods for the road, thereby saving money over buying those expensive dehydrated meal-units prepared for backpackers.

As long as we're on the subject, food is where the backpacker and the bicyclist part company. The dehydrated and freeze-dried foods are light, convenient—and expensive. For the wilderness walker who will be miles away from the nearest food supply for weeks (or at least days) at a time, dehydrated foods are a godsend. For the cyclist they're an expensive and not very tasty luxury. On the road, you'll never be far from civilization, so the need to carry *all* your meals is not a pressing one. You might want to tuck away a spare meal or two just in case, but planning a whole trip with prepackaged meals in mind isn't necessary.

Dehydrated foods do offer weight savings and convenience; if that's where your mind is, you can get these foods at most camp suppliers or directly from the manufacturers themselves (see addresses). You can expect a TV-dinner quality from them once they are revived with heat and water. One last distinction: *Dehydrated* foods are basically air-dried foods without special additives, while *freeze-dried* food is dehydrated frozen food usually jazzed up with the usual overkill of chemical additives, preservatives, etc. Both come packaged as individual food items or assembled into packages of entire meals or even as a

If you can afford to do it, you can bike coast to coast in the U.S. without cooking a meal. Eat in the roadside stands. But have enough money left over to pay your hospital bill

189

week of meals. At any rate, they're nice if you can afford them, but certainly not crucial.

Planning the trip itself

GO WHERE YOU WANT TO GO, but on the way you'll have to fight four chief enemies: traffic, wind, hills and dogs. The first three you can plan for to some degree. The last one is mostly a matter of luck, though there are a few things you can do to battle the canine threat.

Oil-company maps are worth zilch to cyclists. A biker measures distance not only from here to there, but up and down

Before we get into the specifics on these four horrors, there's one thing you're going to need—maps. This isn't as simple as it sounds. For U.S. touring, the maps most commonly available are those distributed by oil companies through service stations. These are fairly complete, up-to-date, relatively easy-to-use travel guides—for motorists. For bicyclists they're worth zilch. As a bicyclist your concerns about planning your route will extend far beyond what is the most direct route to any given destination. Your travel time will depend not only on how many miles you travel but also on whether those miles are nice and level or straight up and down.

The best maps for this purpose are those put out by the U.S. Geological Survey. They are generally recent road and contour maps of each state drawn on the somewhat gross scale of 1:500,000 feet or 1:1,000,000 feet. The "index" maps are free from the USGS. For more specific information, get index maps of any states you're interested in. These index maps are marked off with a grid, with the various squares marked with numbers. The numbers correspond to maps of those specific areas, maps which are drawn on a bigger scale with contour intervals of 10 feet—as specific as any cyclist will need. The index maps are free but the local maps cost 50 cents or 75 cents. You can get these and a booklet explaining how to use and read the maps from:

	U.S. Geological Survey
East of	Washington Distribution Section
Mississippi	1200 South Eads Street
	Arlington, Virginia 22202
	or
	U.S. Geological Survey
West of	Distribution Section
Mississippi	Federal Center
	Denver, Colorado 80225

Maps of U.S. National Forests and Parks are available from:
Forest Service
Department of Agriculture
Washington, D.C. 20250

and for Canada:

Map Distribution Office
Department of Mining and Technical
Surveys
615 Booth Street
Ottawa, Ontario, Canada

You can also get detailed road maps of a state from that state's highway department or, more specifically, you can usually get county road maps by writing to the County Engineer at the county courthouse.

Not as good as topographical maps, but better than road maps, are those supplied by the American Automobile Association (AAA). If you're not a member, either sign up or try to find a friend who is. Other handy publications are the AAA camping guides which list and describe both public and private campgrounds in the U.S. in two compact-sized books: *Principal Camping Areas in the Eastern U.S.*, and *Principal Camping Areas in the Western U.S.* Each costs about $3.

Other campground guides that may prove useful are (for some unknown reason) printed in the unhandy size and format of telephone directories, making them distinctly cumbersome as carry-along reference books. They are:

Rand McNally Guide to Campgrounds ($4.95)
Rand McNally National Park Guide ($3.95)
Woodall's Trailer Parks and Campgrounds ($5.95)—a monster in size that makes a good desk reference, but no takealong book
Guide to Outdoors U.S.A. by Ben Cameron ($5.95)—This comes in two editions, one for the Northeast and one for the Southeast. Published by Quadrangle Press

Rand McNally and Mobil both publish travel guides for various parts of the country which are geared to motorists, but they do contain some information on local sights as well as describing hotels and restaurants that might be of interest to the bicycle tourist. You can scout them up at your local book store or library. And don't overlook freebie information available from the tourist bureaus in each state.

The car is the foremost symbol of our civilization. Avoid it at all costs with some extra map study

The most dangerous enemy—traffic

COMMON SENSE is your best guide. One of the benefits of bicycle touring is getting away from it all, so by all means don't travel main thoroughfares and expose yourself to carbon monoxide, noise and possible death or dismemberment by that foremost symbol of civilization, the car. Use your maps. Locate scenic, secondary roads and then ride them. Map out cross-country routes that take you around cities, not through them. Of course, this means getting from here to there might take twice as long as it would using major routes. But then you don't usually travel by bike to save time. In a pinch I have ridden on super-highways (which is technically illegal), but it was always a drag, what with trucks whizzing by every 10 seconds.

Here's a tip for finding fairly direct but uncrowded routes. Look on your map for one of those monster superhighways that would take you exactly where you wanted to go if you were driving a car. These roads are usually federal or state highways, and are drawn with big red or blue lines. Now look for a small black line *very near* the big red or blue line. That's the road to take. It's probably a local highway that served as the main route before the big super-highway was built. Probably it's now used only sparingly by motorists. The only draw-back is that speed limits are usually lower on these roads, so you'll have to keep your pedaling under 50 mph. Sorry about that. . . .

Your invisible enemy—the wind

THIS IS THE MOST underestimated (or even forgotten) factor in trip planning. Wind is probably the most frustrating and demoralizing obstacle you'll run into. Worse than hills, even. At least after climbing a long hill, you have the other side to coast down. Not so with wind. Any energy you expend to buck the wind is lost forever. You never get it back.

So concern yourself with *when* and *where* the prevailing winds blow. An example: A friend of mine pedaled from New York to Jacksonville, Florida, in early summer and then took the train back to New York. He could have gone either way but he chose the north-to-south route for bicycling. What he didn't know was that at that time of year the prevailing winds were southwesterly, meaning that they were blowing *toward* the northeast *against* his route of travel. Even though he is an exceptionally strong cyclist, he spent much of his time fighting the wind. On a bad day he covered only about 50 miles (his average mileage was about 80 miles per day). One day when the wind was *with* him he covered 120 miles.

Find out about local prevailing winds by reading the weather fore-casts in the paper—some have weather maps that can be helpful too. Call the local weather telephone number if there is one, and call the weather number of the locality you're heading for also. If you're going to be traveling along the shore, call the Coast Guard. If you can't avoid bucking the winds, remember that as a general rule winds blow hard-est in early afternoon and are mildest in the early morning and eve-ning. Plan to cover as much ground as possible in the morning, and time your rest stops for the afternoon. Also, if you're just taking a one-day circle trip (start from home in the morning and return there at night), plan your route so you ride against a mild wind in the morning and return in the afternoon with a strong wind at your back.

For those who plan to bike it from coast-to-coast, remember that in the summer most prevailing winds come out of the west so that bikers

Weather is always a big factor. Get all the information you can from every source you can find

Take a tip from racers when you tour: Bunch up so only the leaders must break the wind, while others have a much easier ride.

pedaling from, say, Los Angeles to Boston get a better deal than those going the other direction. If you're planning to bicycle only one way and return by plane, train or bus, try doing it the other way around if you live on the East Coast. In other words, take public transport out to the West Coast and then cycle back home to take advantage of the prevailing westerlies. On the other hand, if you live someplace like Philadelphia and you can't wait to get started on your bike, go ahead and strike out for San Francisco (or wherever). The wind is a factor to consider, but don't let it make you give up your plans entirely.

One final tip: Ride with friends and take turns breaking the wind for each other.

Those vertical enemies—hills and mountains

YOU CAN DO just so much about avoiding steep climbs in your trip plans. Absolutely essential are the topographical maps from the U.S. Geological Survey for those biking in the U.S.; and for riders going to Europe, European road maps such as the Michelin maps have elevation indicators, giving you an idea of the steepness of the grade of the hillier stretches of road. Only with topographical maps can you find

When choosing a route, remember that roads which follow rivers or a coastline will almost always be leveler than other routes.

the roads that go through valleys and mountain passes rather than taking elevations head-on.

Another tip: Pick out roads that follow rivers or streams. They almost always have gentler grades.

Your most sporting enemy—the dog

TO TELL YOU THE TRUTH, dogs love me. I have never had any trouble with my canine friends (nor do they have any complaints about me). When I bicycle into a new town, the local dogs turn out to greet me with a friendly lick on the leg or just a simple, respectful tip of the collar. Yet many of my cycling friends purport to have had negative experiences with these lovable, furry creatures. I therefore feel compelled to speak a few words on this subject, but I must stress that all information and advice has been gleaned from interviews with other riders, since I refuse to bad-mouth man's best friend.

For those with doggy problems, here goes:

Some dogs seem genetically programmed to chase anything that travels less than 15 mph. The antidote is to travel more than 15 mph. In other words, outrun the beast. This is only possible, however, if the dog is coming at you from the side or rear and there is a level or downhill road ahead. Most dogs that chase seem to do it out of some territorial protective urge, or because you are the most exciting thing that has crossed their path that day. Most of these will give a little token chase and drop off after a while.

Those of you who are more aggressive dog-haters can counterattack with a mixture of lemon juice and water loaded in a squirt gun or with a freon-powered boat horn that will scare the poor creature to death. Also on the market is a dog repellent called Halt, originally made for

Dogs can be problems. Even breeds like this English sheep dog can be hazardous—they have been known to lick bicyclists to death.

mailmen, that sprays an irritant at the dog. And then there's always your tire pump which can deliver a stinging blow to a wet nose.

The trouble with all these weapons is that they are never handy when you need them, and if they are handy you can sometimes lose control of the bike while you're trying to shake off the dog by blasting him, hitting him or whatever. You also run the risk of infuriating rather than scaring off the animal.

The best method if you're at all in doubt of your ability to outrun the dog is to forget your pride and get off the bike, always remembering to keep the bike between you and the animal. Belt it with the machine if you have to, but never let go of that bicycle. Try talking to the dog in a soothing voice to calm it down. Try all the usual dog commands to see if you can make it respond (though chances are that if it were a well-trained dog it wouldn't be out there in the middle of the street snarling at you). Eventually you'll bore the dog to tears (dogs have higher standards of conversation than humans) and it will leave.

One biker I know keeps an empty soda or beer can attached to the rear of his carrier with a sandow or elastic band so he can nudge it off onto the pavement whenever he wants. Then when a hungry dog attacks he knocks the can off and he claims the clank and rattle it makes rolling down the road distracts the dog long enough so he can open up a big lead over the beast. Sure, it litters, but it also beats having your leg used as a chewie.

I have also heard of many other counterattacks too diabolical and just plain nasty to mention here. Before you turn all your resources to finding the ultimate anti-dog weapon, take note of the fact that dogs are not the root problem. Ron Testa, the photographer I mentioned earlier, says that one of his most common experiences cycling through the South was that of being chased by tenacious dogs—and as he pedaled furiously away he could always hear their masters yelling, "Git 'em, boy, git 'em!" Vicious dogs are usually created by people who mistreat them or train them to be vicious. If you harbor any thoughts about knocking off the country's dog population on your next trip, forget them. The people who trained the dogs you eliminate will still be around to raise more.

Organizations you can tour with

Sharing common problems make them a bit easier to take, which is one of the reasons for touring with a group

ALL THESE HAZARDS are minimized when you tour in a group. Sharing common problems makes them a little easier to take. With the bicycling fever upon us, a lot of social groups are incorporating bike tours into their regular activities, so if you're not fussy you can always join up with one of these tours.

If you want to tour with a bunch of hard-core bicyclists in the United States or Europe, there are two main organizations: The International Bicycle Touring Society, and American Youth Hostels (AYH). Both organize tours for their members in America and abroad. Very generally speaking, the International Society caters to older, more affluent riders, while AYH appeals to younger and therefore less affluent cyclists. (Is that a *non sequitur?* I think not.) Let's take a look at the International Bicycle Touring Society first.

Touring with people who know how to live

THE INTERNATIONAL SOCIETY minimizes the discomforts of its "huff-and-puff" tours with the addition of a sag wagon. This is a vehicle, usually a station wagon or microbus, that carries most of the group's luggage as well as extra bike parts and tools. The cyclists stay at moderately-priced motels or hotels along the way. The tour structure is free and easy. Anyone can join or leave the tour at any prearranged point. While with the tour, the only demand placed on a tour member is that he reach the next overnight stop at the end of the day. There is no lock-step regimentation of two-wheelers.

The non-profit organization was begun purely for the pleasure of bicycle touring in 1964 by Dr. Clifford Graves, a well-known bicycle writer and authority on touring. Dr. Graves is also famous for inspiring sumptuous bicycle trips through France in which the sampling of fine wines and fine foods and the general social pace many times outranked the physical cycling pace. Obviously, you needn't be a gung-ho spartan type to participate in an IBTS tour.

Everything in the Society is handled on a volunteer basis—from answering mail to organizing and leading the tours—by members of the organization. The group sponsors several tours in various parts of the U.S. and one each year in Europe. Anyone 21 or over with a bike and $3 can join for a calendar year. With membership you get a mem-

The welcome mat is out at this typical American Youth Hostel, the "Little America" at Truro, Mass., the Cape Cod National Seashore.

bership list, a schedule of tours, three to four mailings of literature per year, plus you can send for free bulletins on packing a bike for touring, touring in the U.S. and Europe, itineraries in Europe and information on custom-built touring bicycles. The address:

> International Bicycle Touring Society
> 846 Prospect Street
> La Jolla, California 92037

The champion bike organization—AYH

FOR THOSE who are either under 21, or are older types who still don't mind roughing it a bit, there is the American Youth Hostels Inc. This is the American cousin of the International Youth Hostel Federation, a world-wide organization set up to offer inexpensive (cheap) travel and accommodations for people who travel under their own power. The national headquarters plans over 50 hosteling tours, here and in Europe, each summer. Local councils or branches of the AYH also plan one-day or weekend trips. Costs can run from $30 for a weekend jaunt to $1100 or so for a summer spectacular (still a cheap price for two months in Europe). For instance, one trip offered in recent years included 56 days of cycle camping through Belgium, the Netherlands, Switzerland, Austria, Northern Italy and France; it cost just over $1000.

> **Costs of an AYH trip run from about $30 for a weekend jaunt to $1100 for a spectacular two months in Europe**

Trips are rated according to difficulty: A, B or C. "A" trips are described by AYH as "rugged, designed for those who relish a challenge." Trips designated "B" are less strenuous (presumably for people not so crazy about challenges) but may still contain a few 50+ mile days and some tough terrain. "C" trips are moderate but AYH warns that they're not easy. *The Hosteler*, national magazine of AYH emphasizes that "an AYH trip is not a 'lie-in-the-sun' vacation."

197

Many hostels, such as this Bantam Lake Hostel at Lakeside, Conn., are older homes converted to accommodate young tourists.

Routes are usually planned between hostels or campgrounds. Lump sums charged for the larger tours cover food, lodging and an experienced tour leader.

The advantages of AYH tours are that they are safe, relatively cheap and give you access as a group to special transportation advantages such as special bike trains and bike-carrying buses that an individual would never have. And never have I heard AYH or any of its group leaders criticized for dishonest dealings with members, or irresponsibility when it comes to taking care of younger members on extended trips.

AYH also maintains a system of over 100 hostels throughout the United States for use by its members. Overnight accommodations usually cost no more than $2. You'll be sharing the hostels with more than just fellow cyclists, though. AYH is also involved with backpacking, hiking, canoeing, sailing and skiing trips. And it stipulates that only members traveling *under their own power* are permitted to use the hostels. This includes cyclists, backpackers, hikers and horseback riders. Excluded are motorists, motorcyclists and hitchhikers. (Now, I've never understood why hitchhikers, who spend a good deal of time walking, should be banned while horseback riders, who are carried to their destination by the sweat of a captive animal, are welcomed with open arms. But those are the rules. In all fairness though, I think horses should be allowed to bunk down at hostels while their riders should be forced to seek accommodations elsewhere.)

To become an AYH member for a year, the fee is $10 for anyone 18 or over, $5 for those under 18, and $12 for family membership (good only in U.S. and Canada). Membership makes you eligible to sign up for AYH tours, gives you the right to stay in any hostel, and along with your membership card, you also receive a monthly newsletter from your local council (if there is one) and a handy little booklet called the *Hostel Guide and Handbook* that provides a listing and vital information on all hostels in the U.S. The handbook carries an amazing amount of information about each hostel, and supplies useful maps for many of them. They're obviously designed by people who know how to give directions and point out landmarks for cyclists.

Your membership card also admits you to youth hostels in other countries: 4500 hostels in 47 countries. For further information write:

> AYH Inc.
> National Campus
> Delaplane, Virginia 22025

Here's a typical entry from the AYH Guide *showing the amount of detailed information packed into a small space.*

DISTRICT OF COLUMBIA

Potomac Area Council, 1501 - 16th St., N.W., Washington, D.C. 20036. (202) 462-5780.

---

51. Washington, D.C.
Washington International Youth Hostel.
   1501 16th St., N.W. (Corner of 16th and P Streets) 20036. 8 blks. N. of White House.

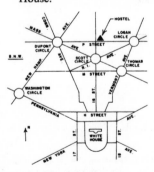

⚐ Capt. & Mrs. Herman Voogel.
☎ (202) 387-3169.
🏠 Year round.
👥&👤 65 in double deck ▬ maximum 5 persons in a room.

🏠 All modern.
🍴 Small kitchen available, modern. Inexpensive restaurant within easy walking distance.
🛒 Stores within 4 blocks.
🚌 City bus for all parts of the city stop at the intersection of 16th and P Streets. Washington can be reached by automobile, train, bus, and plane, as well as by bicycle.
†&✝&✡ Within a few blocks.
⚓ Seneca 25 mi. N.W.
✳ Capitol Building, White House, Library of Congress, Smithsonian Institute, Lincoln Memorial, Jefferson Memorial, Washington Monument, Arlington Cemetery, and many other famous sights of our Nation's Capital.
Ⓗ $2.10.

On the comfort scale, hosteling falls somewhere between camping and the grand hotel tour. For your two bucks at a hostel (in the U.S.) you get at least a roof over your head, a bed to sleep on, a place to wash and take care of other vital bodily functions, and a stove to cook your food on. Some hostels are fairly luxurious and offer even more than this, but you can expect at least this minimum. It's a good idea to bring some change with you, as many hostels have a system affectionately known to members as "cost-you-a-quarter." Extra services such as use of showers or washing machines invariably cost you a quarter. Still, it's a good deal.

There are also specific requirements expected of the hosteler. Each

Table of symbols from the AYH Guide *indicates the tremendous variety of information given for each of the hostels.*

Explanation of Symbols and Abbreviations

△   Houseparent (and/or Sponsor)

☏   Telephone

♧   Opening dates

♧   Advance reservations required˙

★   Accommodations for families and/or married hostelers

⚹   Number of beds for men

⚺   Number of beds for women

!   Accommodations for individual hostelers

(*/*)   Facilities for large groups (30 – 30); suitable for org. use

🛌   Beds

⏣   Bunks

⛱   Toilet, bath and clothes washing facilities

⚊   Kitchen facilities

◢   Meals provided at moderate rates

♪   Nearest food supplies

♔   Nearest railroad

🚌   Nearest bus

†   Nearest Protestant Church

✡   Nearest Catholic Church

☯   Nearest Jewish Synagogue

▲   Nearest hostel

✱   Special attractions nearby

▴   Camping allowed on hostel grounds

⏕   Overnight charge

□   Nearest bicycle repair

     Holiday Hostel: 40 beds & up; modern facilities; may serve meals; may allow longer than three day stay; may charge higher rate for overnight.

F Rate—Family Rate

[SA]—Supplemental Accommodations (see page 10)

S.N.—Special Note

hosteler must provide his own food, eating utensils, sheets and pillow-cases (pillowcases?) or a substitute such as a sleeping bag or an AYH sleeping sack (a specially sewed-together sheet that you can either make yourself or buy from AYH). You must arrive at the hostel be-tween 4 and 7 pm. Lights out is at 10 pm and rising time is usually around 7 am. During peak touring times—weekends and summers (most hostels close in the fall)—call or write ahead for reservations to be on the safe side. It's not so much that individual cyclists are going to flock to any one hostel, but oftentimes a tour group will check in and take up all the bunks.

Touring with the milk and cookie set

A WARNING: While an AYH membership is a handy safeguard for any cyclist, and it's cheap – AYH tours and the youth hostel way of life and touring may not be for everybody. First of all, while AYH stresses that youth hostels are not just for youths and that adults may join, in reality it is a very youngish-oriented association. The organized tours are usually dominated by kids, and even at the hostels most of the independent cyclists wheeling in are high-school or college-fresh-man age.

The puritannical rules of a hostel may throw a monkey wrench into your life style

Another point is that AYH promotes a rather puritannical view of life that could possibly throw a monkey wrench into your life style whether you're an adult or only 16. AYH enforces a rigid set of rules: no smoking, no drinking, etc. Hostels in France and Italy are a little more liberal, allowing wine with meals.

Still another point: Bicyclists are segregated in hostels by sex. If you're traveling with someone of the opposite sex (even your husband or wife) be prepared to sleep in separate quarters. Legally married couples may stay together in hostels that have special family quarters, but these hostels are rare.

This is not to belittle AYH or minimize the importance youth hostels have had in promoting bicycle touring throughout the world. But some cyclists I've talked to have become disillusioned with AYH when they found that the hostel view of life encompassed many more atti-tudes than just a love of cycling—attitudes that they just couldn't conform to.

If you're a teen-ager and you're thinking of going on an AYH or-ganized tour, try if at all possible to meet the tour leader before you commit yourself. Group leaders are always over 21, and if they're leading a national-headquarters-sponsored trip, they have completed a one-week training course. Your compatibility with the tour leader is probably the single most important factor determining whether or not you're going to have a good time.

Also, don't expect hostels to meet all your shelter needs. Hostels are quite common throughout the East, but in the South, Midwest and West they are few and far between. So it's impossible to make long

Bicycling through big cities is rarely much fun, but there are a few treats. Here a cyclist pedals across the Brooklyn Bridge.

rips in these areas and expect to stay in a hostel every night. Pack
camping gear or motel money for those nights in between. Also,
hostels allow you no more than a three-nights' stay. So if you're
planning to cycle to one area and then set up one base of operations
out of which to explore that area, a youth hostel is not the place to
stay—not for more than three days anyhow.

One more organization to consider

ONE GROUP not previously mentioned in regard to touring is LAW,
the League of American Wheelmen. Though primarily an organization
geared to promoting bicycling and to lobbying in its behalf, and not a
touring organization as such, it does offer some assistance. When you
join you get a nationwide list of LAW's members, something that can
come in handy should you plan a trip to an unfamiliar area. Most
members or officers in LAW will cooperate in giving you up-to-date
information on local road, weather and wind conditions. And they
probably know where the good bike repair shops are located. Write to:

> League of American Wheelmen
> 19 S. Bothwell
> Palatine, Illinois 60067

Where to go—some personal prejudices

THE NICEST PART of preparing for a long trip is thinking of great
places to go. There are plenty of them in the U.S. However, some are
greater than others. In general, I'd avoid deserts, glaciers, cities like
Gary, Indiana, and Death Valley. The Rocky Mountains are impressive, but if you're in anything but Olympic shape you'll be too busy
hurting to notice the view. In fact, even approaching the Rocky Mountains is a mental ordeal—imagine pedaling along the same road looking
at the same mountain for days on end with little visual indication that
you're getting any closer to it. It's like riding an Exercycle while facing
a giant life-like backdrop.

Planning your own personal tour is part of the whole gypsy spirit of bike touring

Of course, no section of the country can be ruled out for touring as
long as it has passable roads and it's where you want to go.

Planning your own personal tour unlike anyone else's is part of the
whole gypsy spirit of bike touring, but if you find you need help, a
few guides are on the market that might be useful. One of the best is
AYH's North American Bike Atlas by Warren Asa (about $2). It in-
cludes a map of each suggested tour, rates it for difficulty, states the
total mileage and marks the hostels along the route. The atlas can be
ordered through the AYH council nearest you or from the national
headquarters.

If you live in the northeastern part of the U.S. or plan to bicycle
there, another book worth looking at is *Northeast Bicycle Tours* by
Eric Tobey and Richard Wolkenberg for about $4. Published by Tobey
Publishing Inc., Box 428, New Canaan, Conn. 06840, it offers a good
selection of 130 tours devised by the authors who traveled the routes
themselves. Each tour is rated for difficulty, gives the total mileage, a

map, and a general description of what's to see along the way. There are other guides available, of course, but these are two of the better ones.

Another thing to keep in mind when planning a tour is bike trails. Many federal and state parks and forests already have them, and some states, notably Wisconsin, Kentucky, Ohio, Indiana and California, have developed them in a serious fashion. Keep these states in mind, as their bike trails allow you a pleasant alternative to fighting cars for your rightful share of the road.

How-to on the road

I HATE TO MENTION IT, but things often go wrong, so you'd better pack some tools. I tackle this subject last because it's the most unpleasant. Before you set off on a long haul, check out the bike. Repair or replace anything questionable: stretched or frayed cables, worn tires, squeaky chain, etc. My philosophy is that you can't prepare for every eventuality, so don't bother. Busted frames, smashed rims and exploded derailleurs require professional help anyway. Tool up for the common, minor problems. The major ones are going to do you in anyway, so there's no use burdening yourself with complicated tools.

Here's a suggested list of what tools to take:

You can't prepare for every problem so don't try. Here are the tools to take along for the common problems

- six or eight-inch crescent wrench
- small screwdriver with about a $\frac{3}{16}$-inch blade
- combination wirecutters and pliers (for cutting or tightening cables—not necessary if your bike has no cables)
- two tire irons (for changing clincher tires)
- pressure gauge for sew-up tires (optional if you can check by feel)
- 2 spare tubes for clincher tires and patch kit. Take new tubes on long trips, not patched ones;
    or
- 2 tubular tire spares and tube of tire cement or tape. The same goes here for using new tires as spares. You never know how a patched tire is going to hold up until you ride on it. Find out on short rides, not long ones
- 2 handbrake cables (if you have two handbrakes)
- 1 long derailleur cable (if you have a derailleur)
- 1 three-speed shifter cable (if you have a three-speed)
- small can light oil
- tube bicycle grease such as Lubriplate (handy after pedaling through rainstorms)
- multiple spanner wrench (optional)
- freewheel remover (very optional—especially if you've never used one before)
- tire pump

Want to cut anything out of this list and take a chance you won't need it? Go ahead. The worst thing that could happen is that you'll have to walk the bike somewhere to get it fixed. Best things to eliminate are the extra cables.

For on-the-road how-to advice, take along the Xyzxyx Corporation manuals, one for coaster-brake bikes and three-speeds and another for derailleur bikes. These manuals are lightweight and good for the road.

When you have problems you can't fix yourself, you'll have to find a bike shop with a good mechanic. Look for a shop advertising top components (Campagnolo, Zeus, etc.). If you're lucky enough to have your problem near a city with several shops and don't know which to trust, look in the phone book for bicycle racing clubs. These clubs usually know where the good mechanics are. If you can't find one in the phone directory, start calling bike shops and ask them if they know the numbers of any of the local clubs or racers. If they do, there's no need to take the number from them—just take your bike to that shop.

The worst things that can happen

NASTY LITTLE THOUGHTS about disasters are always lurking in the backs of our minds. One way of dispelling them is to know ahead of time what you can do—and can't do.

Bent frame. Forget it. Your trip is over. Put the bike in a box (or a plastic bag, depending on the shape it's in) and take the bus home.

Bent fork. If your fork is bent backwards, your steering ability will be greatly diminished. Here's what you can do in a pinch until you get it to a shop: Remove the wheel and turn the fork completely backwards. Now loop a rope (how about that clothesline you brought?) around the fork and back around the bottom bracket (the strongest part of the bike). Twist the rope with your wrench or with a stick. This of course shortens the rope, pulling the fork back towards the bottom bracket, thus straightening it (since the fork has been turned backwards). Be sure to pull both fork ends back equally so the drop-outs will align and you can put the wheel back in them.

Broken derailleur cable. Not so bad. You will still have high gear. If you have no replacement cable with you, you can screw in the high-gear adjustment screw all the way. This just might give you the next lower gear. And if not, pedaling all the way home in high gear does one thing for you—it makes you appreciate low gear.

Broken three-speed cable. Again, you still have high gear. Unpleasant but at least the bike still goes.

Broken chain. Well, you can still coast. And if you have pliers, a skinny wire or paper clip, the eyes of a hawk, and the skill of a brain surgeon, you might be able to reconnect it. If you have that kind of talent, go to work for a hospital, make lots of money and buy yourself a better chain next time.

In any case, don't occupy your head with all this bad stuff that probably won't happen. There will always be people who can help you. Especially if you belong to AYH, LAW or some other organization. Cyclists still feel a kind of kinship for one another and are prone to helping each other. After all, we're all victimized by cars, trucks, pollution and shattered Coke bottles. Believe me, there's help if you ask for it. Car drivers pass each other with silent indifference; bicyclists always wave.

Just be sure you give touring a big try. Don't let anybody—including me—give you a rough time about what gear you buy, what bike you drive or what kind of trip you plan—camping in the rough or the grand tour. There's no one right way to do it; the only requirement is to have fun. Long-distance touring and the sense of freedom it gives you is probably the best single reason for having a bicycle.

BICYCLE TOURING EQUIPMENT

(Write the following firms/organizations for additional information)

American Youth Hostels, Inc. (AYH Store)
132 Spring Street
New York, N.Y. 10012

Bellwether
1161 Mission Street
San Francisco, California 94103

Big Wheel Ltd.
340 Holly St.
Denver, Colorado 80220

Cannondale Corporation
35 Pulaski Street
Stamford, Connecticut 06902

Gerry
5450 North Valley Highway
Denver, Colorado 80216

Karrimor Weathertite Products Ltd.
Avenue Parade
Accrington, Lancashire
England

The Touring Cyclist Shop
P.O. Box 4009
Boulder, Colorado 80302

CATALOGS THAT COST

Cyclo-Pedia
311 North Mitchell
Cadillac, Michigan 49601
($2 buys you a catalog of bicycles, accessories and touring equipment)

Wheel Goods Corporation
2737 Hennepin Avenue
Minneapolis, Minnesota 55408
(Again, $2 brings you a catalog with a complete listing of bicycles, parts and accessories for touring, plus a repair manual)

CAMPING EQUIPMENT

L. L. Bean, Inc.
Freeport, Maine 04032
(A dependable all-around source of camping gear and outdoor clothing —and a favorite of Ernest Hemingway)

Bishop's Ultimate Outdoor Equipment
6804 Millwood Road
Bethesda, Maryland 20034
(Exotically expensive but excellently-made tents)

Eastern Mountain Sports
1041 Commonwealth Avenue
Boston, Massachusetts 02215
(Their selection of lightweight camping gear is among the best in the East)

Gerry
5450 North Valley Highway
Denver, Colorado 80216

Holubar Mountaineering
Box 7
1975 30th Street
Boulder Colorado 80302
(Beautiful sleeping bags and a catalog that's a real primer on sleeping gear)

The North Face
308 Columbus Avenue
San Francisco, California 94133

Recreational Equipment Inc.
1525 11 Avenue
Seattle, Washington 98122
(You pay $1 and you join this cooperative for life. They offer a wide listing of camping gear at reasonable prices)

Sierra Designs
Fourth and Addison Streets
Berkeley, California 94071

Ski Hut
1615 University Avenue
Berkeley, California 94703
(Somewhat expensive but worth the money if you can spare it)

LIGHTWEIGHT FOOD MANUFACTURERS

Camplite
40 East 2430 South
Salt Lake City, Utah 84115

Chuck Wagon Foods
175 Oak Street
Newtown, Massachusetts 02164

Dri-Lite Foods
11333 Atlantic Avenue
Lunwood, California 90264

S. Gumpert Co.
812 Jersey Avenue
Jersey City, New Jersey 07302

Kamp Pack
Bernard Foods, Inc.
1125 Harley Avenue
Box 1497
Evanston, Illinois 60204

Kisky Foods
1829 Northeast Alberta Street
Portland, Oregon 97211

Richmoor Corporation
Box 2728
Van Nuys, California 91404

Stow Away Products
103 Ripley Road
Cohasset, Massachusetts 02025

Trail Chef
1109 South Wall Street
Los Angeles, California 90015

Chapter 10

Guide to European touring

**The bicycle is still king abroad, and American cyclists often feel
more welcome in Europe than they do at home. Here are some specific tips for
the prospective European cycle-tourer plus a country-by-country
guide to the nations with the greatest cycleability.**

IN AMSTERDAM a few years ago, two men in a small car came
weaving through a crowded intersection. The driver, in his rush to
move through traffic, grazed the handlebars of a bicyclist. The impact
was enough to flip the bicycle sideways several feet and send its rider
sprawling to the pavement. Several concerned onlookers helped the
man to his feet. He was only slightly bruised. The men in the car were
less fortunate. Within seconds they were surrounded by an angry mob
which prevented their escape and hurled curses at them for dumping
the cyclist. Fortunately, a policeman came along to disperse the
crowd.

Similar incidents often occur in this country—only in reverse.
Under the same circumstances the wounded cyclist is surrounded
by an angry crowd and harangued for scratching the finish on the
driver's car. A cop arrives on the scene and tickets the cyclist for
littering the street with his damaged bike. And the next day an
editorial in the local paper complains about how bicyclists are a
safety hazard because the blood they spill on the road makes the
pavement slippery.

Exaggerated? Perhaps. But it illustrates the far different attitudes
toward cyclists in this country and in Europe.

This is just one reason for cycling Europe. Cyclists are accepted on
the roads, not treated as second-class citizens. While Europeans
slaughter each other on the highways with the same skill as Americans, they have a greater awareness of cyclists and are used to sharing
the roads with them.

There are several reasons for this: One, the standard of living
historically has been lower in Europe, which means that a large percentage of the population has depended on the bicycle for transporta-

tion. There are a lot of cyclists and they command respect by sheer numbers. Two, the distance between neighboring towns is often shorter than in the U.S., making the bike feasible for transportation. Three, bicycle racers often become national heroes in Europe, thereby raising the status of all cyclists.

But no matter what the reasons, the bicycle is considered more than a toy abroad.

On city streets in Europe you can ride in the main traffic stream rather than at the side of the road without harassment from police or motorists—provided of course that you can maintain the traffic speed. In the country you'll have to stick to the side of the road, but many European countries offer networks of fine secondary roads that make cycling a pleasure and also take you into territory that the If-

Even for the Europeans themselves, one of the most popular ways to spend a holiday is on wheels, either alone or in a tour group.

Danish Tourist Board photo

Lufthansa photo

These aren't exactly youngsters (at least some of them) but they're having a great time cycling out from a German health spa.

it's-Tuesday-this-must-be-Belgium tourist crowd will never see. Countries with really phenomenal cycling roads are France, England and Holland; but more about specific countries later.

Of course, when you go to Europe you go as more than a cyclist—you go as a tourist, ready to sample all the pleasures normally enjoyed by any other tourist: the food, historic landmarks, scenery, new people, etc. These should rightfully be considered in planning a trip, but this chapter is mostly concerned with cycling in Europe.

Groups that soften European culture shock

WHETHER YOU TOUR Europe, as part of a group or by yourself, is a matter of preference. But for that first expedition, a group trip eliminates the hassles of planning a tour through a country you most likely have never seen. It eliminates any concern over where you are going to sack down every night. And as part of a group you may get a break on a charter airplane flight.

As mentioned in the chapter on touring, both American Youth Hostels and the International Bicycle Touring Society conduct group tours to Europe. If you're a member of AYH, make sure you have an international stamp, issued for each calendar year.

But there's another valuable cycling organization, the Cyclist's Touring Club. Its address:

> 69 Meadrow
> Godalming, Surrey
> England

The organization conducts tours of England and the Continent, and the tours, as you might guess, are made up mostly of Britishers who enjoy a *vigorous* trip. Tour members stay at inexpensive hotels, guesthouses and hostels. The trips may be anything from a tour of the French Alps to a romp through Czechoslovakia. Only members can go on the tours; if you want to join, the membership fee is two pounds, which is somewhere around $5 depending on whatever the chaotic international money market is doing when you decide to sign up.

Don't forget tour options offered as part of travel packages by the various airlines. These are discussed in greater detail in the following chapter. National tourist bureaus of various countries are also getting on the bike tour bandwagon. So check around.

Traveling with a tour group limits your freedom, and you may go places you don't want to go. The alternative is very careful planning on your own

Of course, traveling with groups limits your freedom and often takes you to places you have no particular hankering to visit. To avoid these drawbacks you (or you and your friends) can plan your own route and make all your own arrangements. But this takes careful planning.

Where to get information for planning your trip

DON'T THINK of trip planning as a chore. Planning can be an integral and enjoyable part of the trip itself. It's a good way to get some feel of the country or countries you plan to visit as well as straightening out the logistics of getting from one point to another.

For general information your first stop should be the national tourist offices of the countries on your itinerary (their addresses are listed later on). Write if you can't stop in. They usually have reams

This tourist family didn't want to do the complete bike bit, so they simply rented bikes for a day's outing in Germany.

KLM photo

Another option (unstrenuous) open to a touring couple is to rent bikes in each city. You'll see much more than you can by car!

of free or inexpensive booklets, brochures, pamphlets and folders on the costs and locations of hotels, hostels and campgrounds, sights to see, handy facts for travelers, and in some cases information on roads, bicycle tours and even where to rent bicycles if you go without yours. One caution: I've found that tourist bureaus are often geared to more affluent, non-cycling travelers, and that much of the literature on display is not applicable to bikers. But cycling info is available if you ask for it. It may be stuffed in a musty old drawer, but it's usually there.

Tourist bureaus are geared to more affluent travelers, but they usually have special info for bikers stuffed in a musty drawer

There are also countless guide books available which are not geared especially to bikers but offer advice on everything from the culture and history of countries to what the weather and food is like. One complete book series is the somewhat ponderous but informative *Fodor's* line that covers 18 European countries in separate books with one general book on Europe. And there are the sketchier but more portable *Holiday* paperbacks that give you a vest-pocket rundown of nine European countries and capitol cities.

The Michelin tire company offers a great series of guidebooks on France, its provinces and other countries as well. Its *Red Guide* is a classic listing of good to fantastic hotels and restaurants in France and its *Green Guides* list the sights. In fact, the Michelin restaurant guide is considered *the* gourmet's guide to French cooking and its top-of-the-line three-star rating is coveted by restaurateurs.

Can't find the Michelin guide in your local book shop? Write:

French & European Publications Inc.
Rockefeller Center Promenade
610 Fifth Avenue
New York, N.Y. 10020

Who ever heard of a guide to the best truckstop eateries in France? Here it is—and invaluable

Another valuable restaurant guide is the *Guide des Relais Routiers* ($6.95) available from the Libraire de France, 610 Fifth Avenue, New York, N.Y. 10019. Basically this is a guide to all the best truckstops, so to speak, in France. For the cyclist interested in cheaper eateries, this is a better book than the vaunted Michelin.

European guides for cyclists, campers and other superior travelers

FOR LITERATURE specifically for bikers, try AYH. It puts out two books in particular that will come in handy: the *AYH International Handbook Volume I*, which has a complete listing of all hostels (locations and fees) in the Mediterranean area and Europe ($2.25), and the *Youth Hosteler's Guide to Europe* ($2.95), which is a combination guide book, tour listing and hostel directory. Both are available from the national AYH office.

Hostels in Europe are more numerous than in the U.S. and fairly evenly distributed throughout most of western Europe, so that planning routes from hostel to hostel is easier than it is in America.

Here's a common sight in Southern Ireland (and throughout Europe for that matter)—a cross-country bike race. Many secondary roads are well paved but carry little auto traffic.

Irish Tourist Board photo

The rules and requiréments for staying at hostels are basically the same as in the U.S.: You must be a hosteling member, provide your own food and eating utensils, sleeping bag or sack, and there usually are specific check-in and check-out times. Costs run from 50 cents a night for the more basic places to a whopping $1.30 a night for the more luxurious ones. Some even serve meals for a small charge. And in France and Italy you are allowed to pour down some wine with your meals.

Cycle campers can get campground information through national tourist offices, but other guides are more useful. The *Youth Hosteler's Guide* mentioned above has a partial listing of campgrounds. A more comprehensive guide is *Europe Camping and Caravanning*, which you should find in bookstores, but if not, try the publisher, Recreational Equipment Incorporated. There is the *AA Camping and Caravanning Handbook* ($2.95) from Harper & Row covering England and Ireland, and for France there's the *Michelin Guide to Camping and Caravanning in France* ($3). You can send away for the latter at French and European Publications, Inc. (address given above).

Campgrounds in Europe are luxurious even by American standards, and many major cities have campgrounds close to the downtown area

Campgrounds are fairly luxurious even by American standards, offering in some places hot showers and restaurants on the premises. Campground camping is very big in Europe and camps can be found everywhere. Many major cities even have campgrounds very close to the downtown area. The costs are hardly extravagant, ranging from 35 cents to 90 cents per person per night. The nice thing about campgrounds is that real Europeans use them, not just American tourists; they offer an opportunity to meet people with far different backgrounds.

If you visit the very few countries where campgrounds are somewhat scarce, don't rule camping out. As a general rule, countries with **few** campgrounds have more open land to camp informally on. In Ireland, for example, most people are very friendly and you can often set up camp on a farmer's land. Be sure you ask permission first.

215

Hotels and other more comfortable sleeping places

EXCEPT FOR THE LARGER cities, hotels can also be a fairly inexpensive (by American standards) alternative. For example, in the
village of Arnay le Duc in France, there's a little inn where two people
can get a room for under $4 a night. Typical of many small hotels in
European villages, the shower and toilet are down the hall and the
rooms are spartan—bed, washbasin and a couple of chairs—but clean
and comfortable. Even cheaper alternatives are pensions which usually
require a minimum stay of two or three days, and a requirement that
you take your meals there.

Also found in some countries are guesthouses, which are govern-
ment-approved lodgings, often private homes, that let out rooms.
Here you eat meals with the family and get an inside look at European
life besides. National tourist offices usually have available a listing
of hotels, pensions and guesthouses along with their rates and a
luxury rating.

Other services tailored to the bicyclist

FOR INFORMATION designed specially for bikers, try the Cyclist's
Touring Club of England (address given earlier). The club, besides

Left, what's he looking at, when he could enjoy the close-up scenery?

KLM photo / German Tourist Information office photo

planning group tours, also offers pre-planned tours for individuals in the form of a marked map of the Continent and the British Isles. Included is touring information such as mileage, elevation changes and sights en route. The club will also plan specific tours for members in the British Isles and has a great selection of road maps that show those little back roads that make cycling so enjoyable. Membership includes a year's subscription to the club magazine *Cycletouring* and third-party insurance. The club will also arrange reservations for trains, boats, planes and hotels.

Another British organization worth joining just for the information they offer is:

> The British Cycling Federation
> 26 Park Crescent
> London, England

They offer services similar to the Cyclist Touring Club: an invaluable handbook of bike dealers and accommodations in Great Britain, third-party insurance, over 50 pre-planned tours of England and over 45 tours of the Continent, all with vital statistics such as mileage, routes and points of interest. The Federation also sells a full supply of inexpensive maps particularly suited to the bicyclist. Membership costs 1.65 pounds per year (a little more than $4) and includes free legal aid and subscription to Federation publications. The organization has a

Right, German Federated Railroad offers cyclists special rates.

wealth of information free for the asking. It also sells travel insurance as complete (bike, baggage and you) as you could want.

The lowdown on European maps

YOU STILL AIN'T going nowhere without maps. Unlike the U.S., maps in Europe are not gas station give-aways; they have to be bought. When you get there you can pick them up at book and stationery stores. But, depending on the country you want to visit, you can usually order the maps you need before you leave through outlets in the U.S. or through European cycling organizations. Relevant maps usually cost from 25 to 75 cents apiece and are always well worth the investment.

One of the most inclusive series of maps is published by Michelin, the same company that puts out those great tour guides. Their maps are drawn to different scales, but the ones to look for are the regional maps on a 1:200,000 scale. These not only give a thorough and clear layout of location and types of roads but as an extra boon to the cyclist also indicate hill gradations with chevron symbols. One chevron is a slight grade, two is a pretty tough hill and three means you hit your lowest gear, stand up in the stirrups and grunt. The Michelin series covers all of France, Belgium, Holland, Switzerland, Portugal and the northern part of Spain, western Germany and northern Italy. If you're lucky you can find them in a local book store or you can order them from French & European Publications Inc. (address given earlier), or Simon & Schuster, Rockefeller Center, New York, N.Y. 10020; or Michelin Tire Corp. 2500 Marcus Avenue, Lake Success, N.Y. 10040.

Another series is published by John Bartholomew & Sons Ltd. Bartholomew maps cover England and Ireland. For the kind of detail you need for bicycling (terrain gradations as well as roads), you'll want the ½-inch series. There can be ordered from the British Cycling Federation or the Cyclist Touring Club if you're a member. Or you can get a free catalog of the maps available and the maps themselves from:

> The Marketing Department
> John Bartholomew & Sons Ltd.
> Duncan Street, Edinburgh EH9 ITA
> Scotland

If you plan to do some biking in Scandinavia you can get maps of those countries from the British Cycling Federation, and for touring in the Netherlands you can order maps from:

> Royal Dutch Touring Club
> A N W B   Stichting Fiets
> Wassenaarsewg 220   or   Europaplein 8
> Den Haag, Holland   Amsterdam, Holland

Above: Often the bicycles supplied with package tours offered by airlines are the small-wheel folding variety. While these are less than perfect for long distances, they couldn't be better for bopping through the inner city areas, left.

A final caution about finding your way

ASSUMING YOU STICK to maps like those listed above, finding the levelest routes should be easy. Most of the maps listed indicate terrain gradations with different colors or, in the case of Michelin, with the chevron system. There is one thing you should be aware of, however. As a general rule, roads in Europe are marked a little differently than they are here in the U.S. Europe seems to be town-oriented rather than road-oriented. That is, while routes are numbered, when you arrive at an intersection the signs will indicate the next towns rather than route numbers. So it's not enough to know that Route 17 will take you to your destination. Study your map and write down what towns Route 17 takes you through. It is the names of these towns that will appear on the signs.

Friendly public transportation awaits you

FOR THOSE LONGER TRIPS or as an alternative to getting around a hilly stretch of country or to avoid pedaling in the rain, don't forget about Europe's public transportation. In general, buses and trains abroad take more kindly to the bicycle than here in the States. You can often load your bike on the top of a bus for a short hop or take advantage of fast, comfortable trains which have accommodations designed specially for bikes.

The procedure for loading your bike on a train is simple. On short jaunts you need only arrive at the station half an hour before departure. But give yourself more lead time, perhaps two to three hours, if you are making a trip of more than 100 miles or one on a train between two major cities or two countries. Buy your ticket first, then strip your bike of luggage (weight counts as well as distance in determining the charge), and bring it to the baggage counter. There it will be weighed and you'll pay the shipping charge. In France the cost is seldom more than $1.50 but in England it will cost you half your train fare in second class. Make sure there's an I.D. tag on the bike giving your name and home address. The bike is loaded onto the baggage car and you pick it up at the baggage counter at your destination. Storage is free at baggage counters for the first 24 hours and a small charge is tacked on for each extra day. The only hitch arises if you take a fast train in which case you may have to wait a while for a later train to bring up your wheels. Tender care is normally taken with bikes, and in Holland many of the trains are equipped with special bike racks that are wheeled on and off baggage cars.

Chances are your bike will have very tender care on the train. In Holland it may travel in its own ritzy rack

Buying a bike in Europe

MOST CYCLISTS prefer to take a bicycle to Europe that they have grown to love and trust over a period of time. While this approach is highly logical, perhaps even advisable, there's something irresistibly appealing about going bikeless and buying your wheels once you arrive in Europe.

If your taste runs to European machines, you'll find a far greater selection abroad, obviously, with many exotic brands readily available that are hard to come by here in America. For example, Motobecanes are hard to get in many parts of the U.S., while Peugeots are all over the place. No wonder American cyclists view Peugeot as *the* French bike. However, in France Motobecanes outclass Peugeots in popularity. Many other brands are also either impossible to buy here or must be ordered through an importer. It's a lot more fun to see the bike in the flesh before buying it. The pure fun of shopping for a bike in Europe is reason enough for many cyclists not to bring their wheels on the plane with them. Another advantage is that you'll save the hassle of shipping a bike abroad with the possible companion problem of uncrating the bike at the Paris or Rome airport only to find it has been bashed by the airlines.

There are problems; however. First of all, if you don't know French, Italian or whatever, you will have to find a dealer who speaks English well if you're going to get exactly what you want. Second, the savings in money isn't all that much. It's true that you save five to ten percent over U.S. prices, but then you get hit with a 15-percent duty at customs bringing the bike back into the U.S. Everyone gets a $100 exemption, so a $200 bike will theoretically cost you $15 at customs (15 percent of the second $100, assuming you have bought nothing else abroad). Since you will have ridden the bike all over Europe, however, the customs appraiser will usually only apply the 15-percent duty to an estimated 40 to 65 percent of the original purchase price (make sure you have the receipt to back up the declared value).

If you don't speak their language, you'll have to find a dealer who speaks yours. And you don't really save a lot of money

This means you'll have to do a little arithmetic to figure out whether you'll be saving money, losing money or breaking even by purchasing a bike on the trip. Roughly speaking, if you plan to buy a bike for $200 or less, you're assured of saving some money.

Let's look at some rough figures. Say you've got your eye on that nifty new Spumoni Special from Italy. Here in America it costs $220. But you buy it in Milan for $200. Okay, you are now $20 ahead of the game. But then you bring it through customs where it is appraised as used with a 65-percent value of $130. You get a $100 exemption, so you pay the 15-percent duty on only $30 which comes out to $4.50. Your net savings are $15.50. But let's say you also brought back over $100 of other Italian goodies: souvenirs, clothes, ravioli, etc. You then have to pay a duty on the entire appraised $130 value of the bike or $19.50—which means you have saved a whopping 50 cents by buying the bike abroad.

In short, the more expensive the bike, the lousier your chance of saving money. An alternative is to sell the bike before leaving for home, thus avoiding customs and the hassle of getting the bike on your plane.

If you're going to France and you want a new bike waiting for you, Peugeot offers a convenient deal whereby you can order the bike ahead of time and they will deliver it to almost any town in France, where it will await you fully assembled at European prices. Write:

Cycles Peugeot
72 Avenue de la Grand-Armee
Paris, France

This is for people who like to be sure they'll have a bike and who are partial to Peugeots. But there are plenty of bike shops in major cities, so you should be able to pick up something decent even if you go unprepared.

A European trip is also the time to get that custom-built bicycle you've always dreamed of. You'll get socked at least $500 to start with plus that hefty duty at customs. But if you've always lusted after a bike made by one of the great European craftsmen especially tailored to your body—arms, legs and torso—you can't expect to pinch pennies. Such a bike will also cost you time. Expect to order a bike *at least six months in advance*. In fact, getting a bike out of the great Faliero Masi of Italy can take up to 18 months depending on how busy he is.

If you lust after a great European custom-made bike, you may have to order at least six months in advance

I'd. therefore suggest writing to several builders, depending on where in Europe you're going, and ask each how much time he needs to make you a bike. You may be forced to settle on a second or third choice simply for time considerations. Here are the names and addresses of several top frame makers in various countries:

Austria: Franz Drusika,
Fasangasse 26
A-1030
Vienna, Austria

Belgium: Cycle Plume Sport
Van Genck
Rue de la Rossee
Brussels, Belgium

Denmark: O. F. Olsens Cyclefabrik
Godthaabsveji 8
Copenhagen, Denmark

England: W. F. Holdsworth Ltd.
132 Lower Richmond Road
Putney, S.W. 15
England

or

Bob Jackson
148 Harehills Lane
Leeds, LS8 5BD
England

France: Rene Herse
12 Rue de President Wilson
Levaillois Perret
Paris, France
or
Alex Singer
53 Rue Victor Hugo
Levaillois Perret
Paris, France
or
Urago & Ce
Nice, France
Italy: Faliero Masi
Via Arona 19
20149
Milano, Italy
Norway: Jonas Oegland
Sandnes, Norway
Switzerland: Arnold Grandjean S.A.
Allegro-2002
Neuemberg, Switzerland

If you're not the possessive type you can always rent . . . and eliminate the problem of transporting your bike back and forth on planes, boats, etc. It's fairly easy to rent in most countries. Probably the best example is Ireland where the Raleigh Company has a chain of over 60 rental offices scattered throughout the land. Rental costs, at the time this is written, are about $7 per week with a slight extra charge for picking a bike up in one location and leaving it in another. Rental bikes are usually three-speeds, however, so if you yearn for ten gears, better bring your own or expect to buy one.

Rental rates for three-speeds are low. If you're quirky enough to absolutely require a ten-speed, then you'll have to buy one or bring one across the ocean

Nation-by-nation biker's guide to Europe

THE COUNTRIES you tour will probably be chosen for reasons that have nothing to do with cycling: Spain for climate, Italy for art, France for food, Sweden for women, England for language, etc. But a nation's cycle-ability might help you decide between countries if you're in doubt. England, France and Holland head the list of most rideable countries. The features that distinguish them are well-paved secondary roads with little motor traffic (such as offered by France and England) or widespread systems of bike paths (such as Holland). Well-spaced villages and towns also make for pleasant touring in these countries; food and shelter are rarely very far away.

No reason for cyclists to restrict themselves to the Big Three, however. All of Europe offers pleasures to the cycle tourist. Let's take the countries one at a time. They are listed here in alphabetical order. However, England, Scotland and Wales are all included under Great Britain; Ireland (both northern and southern) is listed separately; Denmark, Norway and Sweden are all included under Scandinavia. For each country we've picked a favorite month weatherwise for cycle touring. Except in a few cases, we've restricted these choices to summer months (when most people travel) with the main criteria being moderate temperatures and lack of rain.

AUSTRIA. Much of the country is anti-bike in its terrain, pimpled with mountains, and you will have to share the roads with cars and trucks, as secondary roads are not that common. What secondary roads exist are often ill-paved and winding. The Danube Valley and the territory around Innsbruck are probably the most rewarding areas to tour because of the scenery and the ease of pedaling. Hotels are everywhere; hostels are concentrated southeast of Salzburg, along the lake district of Carinthia and just south of Vienna.

The climate is warm and dry during the day and cool at night. August and September are the best months weather-wise for cycling, offering the least amount of rain.

Hallwag brand maps, which can be bought in Austria, are best for the cyclist. To get one before you leave the U.S. you can try writing:

Rizzoli International Book Store
712 5th Avenue
New York, N.Y. 10019

Austrian tourist offices are located at:

444 Madison Avenue
New York, N.Y. 10022

and

3440 Wilshire Boulevard
Los Angeles, Calif. 90010

Aim for Belgium in June, and head for the southeast corner of the country where you'll find challenging hills and the best accommodations for bikers

BELGIUM. The home of cycle champ Eddie Merckx, Belgium is a heavily industrialized country, especially in the west where the two places that warrant a stop are the cities of Antwerp and Ghent. The real scenery is in the southeast corner of the country where you'll find the Ardennes forest and challenging rolling hills. Hostels, campgrounds and hotels are concentrated in this territory where the secondary roads are fair.

Maps: Michelin.

Climate: Cool and showery in the summer with chilly nights. June is probably the best month.

Tourist office:

589 Fifth Avenue
New York, N.Y. 10017

FRANCE. It has everything for everybody in both the variety of terrain and cultural experiences. The people are friendly (despite what you may have heard to the contrary), and the countryside is still amazingly unspoiled and interlaced with excellent well-marked secondary roads. Most of the rugged terrain is on the fringes of the

International Youth Hostel Federation photo

Hostelers join up at the new 300-bed hostel in Luxembourg City.

country—the Vosges in the east, the Pyrenees in the southwest and the Alps in the southeast. Well worth a visit are areas like Britanny on the Atlantic coast, the picturesque farmlands and quaint villages in Burgundy and the wine-producing regions of Bordeaux (though Burgundy and Bordeaux have their share of hills). Winds in the Rhone valley make cycling difficult and the crush of summer vacationers takes some of the pleasure out of visiting the Mediterranean coast. But you can always visit the fantastic chateaux along the Loire River valley instead. Campgrounds and reasonably-priced hotels outnumber the scattered settling of hostels in the country, but accommodations in the countryside are seldom a problem.

Weather: Cool and comfortable in the north; warm and dry in the south. June is the best month for cycling.

Maps: Michelin.

National tourist office:

> 610 Fifth Avenue
> New York, N.Y. 10020

and

> 9418 Wilshire Boulevard
> Beverly Hills, Calif. 90212

and

> 323 Geary Street
> San Francisco, Calif. 94102

GERMANY. (West Germany—known as the Federal Republic of Germany). The really interesting places to see are located in the central and southern regions where cycling can get a little rugged. In the central area you can visit the Black Forest or Bavaria with its Disneyland-style castles. If you keep going down country you will eventually run into the Alps where you can fork off into either Switzerland or

German Tourist Information Office photo

Austria. Germany is full of historic and picturesque towns and cities such as Heidelburg and Munich. All roads are good but are crowded, especially the primary routes, so travel secondary roads at every opportunity. Hostels and campgrounds are evenly distributed throughout the country as well as hotels. Camping in areas not designated as such is discouraged.

Climate: Damp and chilly German summers dictate some weatherproofing and waterproofing for your body. May is a little drier than other touring months.

Maps: Michelin and the British Cycling Federation supply good maps and in the country you can pick up maps at Shell stations.

National tourist office:

>500 Fifth Avenue
>New York, N.Y. 10036

and

>11 South La Salle Street
>Chicago, Illinois 60603

and

>323 Geary Street
>San Francisco, Calif. 94102

GREAT BRITAIN (England, Wales, Scotland).

England: A comfortable place to tour for a number of reasons: the roads are excellent, the countryside is lush, the people are friendly *and* they speak English (sort of) besides.

Tremendously attractive and almost Switzerland-like in its scenery is the northwestern corner of the country—better known as the Lake District. It is endowed liberally with both lakes and mountains. The

British Tourist Authority photo

northeast offers the history of its ancient abbeys and draws a crowd of seacoast-seeking tourists as well—if you want the chance to meet Englishmen at their leisure. Another popular touring area is the center of England which features Shakespeare country, Stratford-on-Avon and all that. In the south you'll find Stonehenge, seaside resorts, fishing villages on the coast and generally easy bicycling across the Salisbury Plain. In the west and east is the flat and relatively untouristed English countryside.

Though the roads are in excellent condition for cyclists, they were originally built for cars which in the more popular tourist areas may crowd you off the roads at times. The English take the time out to enjoy their country, too, so during the summer make reservations at hotels everywhere you can.

Campgrounds are generally scarce but hostels are fortunately numerous. All have cooking facilities and most serve meals. Guesthouses are also common, found almost everywhere without much difficulty.

Climate: Mild and a little moist, sometimes with chilly evenings, so bring a sweater. The best month is June.

Maps: Bartholomew.

Wales: The north and west of Wales are the places to go. The cycling varies from easy to rugged along the northern coast because of a stretch of mountains; but farther inland the terrain becomes more merciful where it turns into moors. You'll have to stick to the main roads unless you are a real adventurer because what you'll find is unpaved secondary roads. Campgrounds and hostels are common in the north of Wales but thin out below that. Hotels and guesthouses, common all over Wales, take up the slack.

Climate: A little wetter and chillier than the rest of Britain, so keep

227

that sweater handy in the evenings. Best month to travel—June.
Maps: Bartholomew.

Scotland: Hilly, lush and crammed full of lakes, mountains and moors with primary roads but lousy secondary routes. The gorgeous countryside and the historic castles located throughout, especially in the northern highlands, are its prime attractions. Hostels are common and you can also pitch your tent almost anywhere without much problem by getting the land-owner's permission. Hostels and guest-houses are also common.

Climate: Cool and wet. June is best month.
Maps: Bartholomew ½-inch series
National tourist office for all three areas and Northern Ireland:

> British Tourist Authority
> 43 West 61st Street
> New York, N.Y. 10023

and

> 612 South Flower
> Los Angeles, Calif. 90017

When writing, ask for the BTA information sheet, "Cycling in Britain," which lists camping equipment rental agencies, includes all sorts of information on public transportation and, most important, lists shops throughout Britain which rent bicycles to tourists. The list even indicates the few shops which rent 10-speeds. The pamphlet also describes tours conducted by the English youth hostel organization.

GREECE. Rough pedaling is part of the price you pay for touring Greece. You have a choice of two kinds of roads, both undesirable: busily traveled primary roads and wide dirt paths. The latter choice is too bumpy for most people which means you'll be riding amidst cars and trucks most of the time. There are rewards, however. In the summer when Greece really heats up in the inland areas you can enjoy the Mediterranean luxury of its coastline with tropical waters and cool offshore breezes. Visit the major islands by ferry.

Greece is a country for the cycle camper who can settle down almost anywhere. Hostels and campgrounds are distributed only spottily, and not all of the small villages and towns have hotels or inns to accommodate you.

Climate: Bring your suntan lotion because it gets warm, especially inland. Breezes along the coast help though. May is the best month.

Maps: Hallwag (available through Rizzoli bookstore—address in Austria section).

National tourist offices:

601 Fifth Avenue   and   627 West Sixth Street
New York, N.Y. 10017   Los Angeles, Calif. 90017

Left, student tourists wait for a train pick-up in England. Right, a cyclist pedals up a brick street in The Netherlands. Holland is a paradise for bikers—no hills, and miles and miles of cycle paths running right along beside the main highways.

HOLLAND (The Netherlands). Holland is the Valhalla of the European bicycle tourist. It's got it all: terrain flat as a tabletop; almost as many bicycle paths as roads (only a slight exaggeration); it is impeccably charming, inexpensive to travel and English is spoken practically everywhere. The bike paths make touring almost anywhere in the country a real pleasure and in your travels you'll see businessmen, grandmothers, students, practically everyone on bicycles. The bicycle has status as a legitimate vehicle.

The traditional sights of Holland are concentrated in the west with its tulip fields and such cities as Amsterdam, Utrecht and The Hague, but if you get bored and want to see what a hill looks like again, they've preserved a few in the eastern countryside area. Hotels even in the larger cities are reasonable, and campgrounds and hostels are common throughout most of the country. You'll have to try hard to get lost as the Dutch Tourist Office (initials VVV) has offices everywhere that provide you with local maps and guides for cyclists. They will also tell you where you can rent a bike.

Climate: Very cool mornings and evenings, and brief showers may punctuate your travels, so go prepared. If you plan to bicycle westward, there is a prevailing westerly wind that sweeps across the flat Dutch landscape so you might want to schedule the bulk of daily bicycling for the morning. June is the best month.

Maps. Local maps available at VVV offices. Michelin has maps as well as the Royal Dutch Touring Club (address given earlier) which also offers pre-planned tour routes. Stichting Fiets (address given earlier) publishes a series of maps under the title, "Discover Holland by Bicycle."

Netherlands national tourist offices:

576 Fifth Avenue
New York, N.Y. 10036

and

681 Market Street
San Francisco, Calif. 94105

NORTHERN IRELAND. It has had a lot of bad press in recent years but if you crave green rolling countryside it's still worth a visit. The countryside is the prime attraction, so you won't have to spend much time in the notorious city of Belfast, a no-nonsense-looking shipbuilding center. There are few secondary roads but that should be no problem as the primary roads are not heavily traveled. And though few campgrounds and hostels exist, clean inexpensive guesthouses are a recommended alternative.

Visit Northern Ireland in May, and avoid the trouble spots. The guesthouses are clean and inexpensive

Climate: Rainy, cool in the summer. Try to make your visit in May.
Maps: Bartholomew.
National tourist office: same as for Great Britain.

SOUTHERN IRELAND. It's hard to believe any country could be so consistently lush and green until you hang around and see how wet it gets a large part of the time. Most of the sights, both historically and geographically, are along the coast. Areas to see are immediately to the north and south of Dublin, southwest coast of the country with its gem of scenery at Dingle Bay, and north of that the rugged Aran Islands off Galway Bay. Castles and history are everywhere and so are the comfortable and inexpensive guesthouses. Hostels are

Thatched homes in Country Limerick, Ireland—a typical sight.

Trans World Airlines photo

evenly scattered throughout the country but no campgrounds as such exist. However, you can usually get permission from a farmer to pitch your tent on his land. The legendary friendliness of the Irish is no myth.

Secondary roads are well paved, numerous, and only lightly traveled by automobiles.

Climate: like Northern Ireland, it is cool and showery, and May is the best month.

Maps: Bartholomew.

National tourist office (Republic of Ireland):

> 590 Fifth Avenue
> New York, N.Y. 10036

and

> 224 North Michigan Avenue
> Chicago, Illinois 60601

and

> 681 Market Street
> San Francisco, Calif. 94105

ITALY. Italy for the cyclist is really two countries: north and south—with the north winning out easily on many counts. It has better roads, is less searing in the summer and a little less rugged (although by no means is it another Holland). It's also a little more picturesque as it shares the Alps and Riviera with France. The Italian Lake Country in the north, a popular tourist haven, is especially worth a visit.

Hostels are few but campgrounds are common and hotels can be found in most towns.

Climate: Dry and temperate in the north and scorching in the south. Best month is July.

Maps: Michelin. Maps also available in larger BP gas stations.

National tourist offices:

> 630 Fifth Avenue
> New York, N.Y. 10020

and

> 500 North Michigan Avenue
> Chicago, Illinois 60611

and

> St. Francis Hotel
> Post Street
> San Francisco, Calif. 94101

To be on the safe side, specify that you would prefer your travel information written in English, not Italian.

It's a long jump from Northern Ireland, but plan your route so you'll arrive in northern Italy in July. Don't miss the lake country, and you may even want to pedal up an Alp

PORTUGAL. Not a tourist country with the same drawing power as Spain, Portugal is much less traveled during the peak seasons which makes it less-than-perfect primary roads reasonably easy to navigate. Cycling on these main thoroughfares (don't look for any other roads) is easy along the coast but tends to get a little harder in the hilly

Denmark is an entire nation of cyclists, including very pretty girls.

interior. Pedaling is especially easy along the flat southern coast, while the western coast consists mostly of rolling hills. Many of the towns you'll be cycling through are really tiny and not geared to tourist business. In fact, you may have trouble finding a restaurant. It's not that they're not there—it's just that in the smaller villages they're usually not marked and look like a private home. A clue: look for an open door. Hostels are almost non-existent, but there are quite a few campgrounds and hotels along the coast.

Climate: Except for its torrid southernmost province, the Algarve, Portugal enjoys a comfortably warm climate. June is the best month. However, for those who can only vacation in the winter, Portugal is a good bet with temperatures often in the 60's and 70's in February and March.

Maps: Michelin.

National tourist office:

570 Fifth Avenue
New York, N.Y. 10036

One final note: If you plan to wait until you get over there to buy a bike, be forewarned that in Portugal bicycles are not sold with normal three-speed gear hubs. You'll have to find a dealer who will install one for you if a three-speed is what you want.

SCANDINAVIA (Denmark, Norway, Sweden).

Denmark: Denmark, largely a country of islands, is similar to Holland in that it welcomes the cycleperson (See? Our unprejudice is showing.) and makes life for him (her) as easy as possible. First of all, the terrain is level and generally physically untaxing. The countryside is dotted with ancient Viking castles, rolling hills, picture-postcard farms and villages. For island hopping there is an extremely efficient ferry service. The national tourist office offers special bicycle tours that include the rental of a bike if you need one. The railway system also rents bikes, and you can rent one at one train station and turn it in at another.

Special Danish tours include bikes, meals, overnights in cozy inns.

Hostels are plentiful and there are over 500 approved camping sites. These government-run campgrounds require an I.D. card called an International Camping Carnet to register at their facilities. Anyone can get one when he joins:

The National Campers and Hikers Association
7172 Transit Road
Buffalo, N.Y. 14221

The price for membership and the carnet is $11. Reasonably-priced hotels are also plentiful all over the land.

Climate: Cool in the summer with June being the driest of the three months while July is the warmest.

Maps: Hallwag (address listed under Austria or can be bought in book stores) and Ravenstein, also available in book stores, but if not, write:

Ravenstein
Geographische Verlagsanstalt und Druckerei GMBH
Frankfurt/Main
Wielandstrasse 31/35

Norway: Norway seems to be the "in" country for tourists these days, as more and more cyclists are discovering this land of fjords (narrow inlets along the country's coastline that sometimes extend a hundred miles inland). The countryside created by these great shoreline intrusions is rugged but extremely beautiful in both the western and eastern areas of the coast. In the south the scenery is less dramatic (no fjords), but rolling tree-covered hills and many resort and beach areas make it worth the trip.

Any part of Norway is worth a tour in itself. Promise yourself now that you'll see a fjord someday

Any part of the country is worth a tour in itself. For example, you could spend your entire trip exploring the five great valleys running off the Oslo fjord in the east—or you might confine your vacation to just one single grand fjord. Now is a good time to visit Norway as you'll find a comfortable number of American tourists to trade notes with, but not so many that you'll feel like you're back home in East Orange, N.J.

Road conditions are uneven, especially in the north, and sometimes road surfaces change from paved to gravel or dirt without notice. Hostel and campgrounds (requiring carnets) are all concentrated along the coast and hotels are plentiful everywhere.

Norway also presents a unique opportunity to the younger cyclist on a budget who doesn't mind working during his (or her) summer vacation. Work in Europe is usually difficult for American tourists to find, but Norway features three working vacation plans. First, the Norwegian Committee for International Information (NIU) arranges farm work for anyone between 18 and 30 years old. You need no previous experience and you live and work as part of the farmer's family, which usually speaks English and German. You and the farmer fix the number of hours per week you'll work (maximum of 40). You get free room and board and some pocket money. You must stay at least four weeks but no more than three months. Write:

> NIU
> P.O. Box 8260 Hammersborg
> Oslo 1, Norway

Second, Norwegian Youth Hostels in conjunction with the Norwegian State Railways runs a camp in the summer months (mid-July to September) at Fagernut, an area of wild mountain scenery. Campers must help clear the railway line for six hours per day in exchange for food and lodging. Frankly, this is a great deal for the railroad while being a labor camp for tourists. But if you're really broke or you'd just like to see how life must have been for Chinese railroad workers in the early American West, write:

Wanna pick strawberries in Norway for money? Here's the place to do it

> Norwegian Youth Hostels Association
> NUH
> 26 Dronningens gate
> Oslo 1, Norway

A third alternative is picking strawberries at Valldal. The age limit is 18 to 25 and the earnings are piecework. Write:

> Mr. Aimar Myklebust
> 6210 Valldal
> Norway

Climate: It's a cool country even in the summer and sudden rains are not uncommon. June is probably the driest month. Winter cycling is for creeps who have an affinity for cold and darkness.

Maps: Hallwag, Ravenstein.

Sweden: Like Norway, Sweden is best enjoyed piecemeal, concentrating on just one or two points of the multifaceted country: the canals and waterways in central Sweden, the fishing villages and farmlands in the west or the mountainous north if you are in good shape (and if you want a glimpse of some real wilderness). Somewhat difficult to travel is the western section, where hilly terrain makes for slow going, and the north, where there is a paucity of paved secondary roads. In the south around Stockholm the roads are much better and there are some bicycle lanes. If you need a guiding hand as to where to go, some pre-planned tours are offered by the Scandinavian Tourist Office.

Hotels are common,. but rather expensive; fortunately a healthy number of hostels and hostel-like accommodations are run by the Swedish Touring Club and there are over 500 campgrounds throughout the country. Swedish laws are liberal, permitting you to pitch your tent almost anywhere as long as it is not too near a house or fenced land.

Climate: Summers are warm with chilly evenings. Weatherwise June is probably the best month to chance it.

Maps: Hallwag, Ravenstein.

Tourist office for all three Scandinavian countries:

> 505 Fifth Avenue
> New York, N.Y. 10017

and

> 612 S. Flower
> Los Angeles, Calif. 90017

Also, an excellent pamphlet called "Young Scandinavia" is published by Scandinavian Airlines (SAS). Designed mostly for tourists 26-years-old and younger, the pamphlet is full of budget travel ideas: places to stay and eat, cheap entertainment, etc. It also includes complete addresses (sometimes phone numbers) of student centers, sailboat and canoeing charters, pony stables, even discotheques and amusement parks.

Here's our nomination for a good pamphlet for the young (or the young at heart). It will help you find anything from a bed to a discotheque

Also, SAS and the Crescent bicycle company offer a deal whereby you can reserve a bike along with your airplane flight to Scandinavia. SAS claims you can save up to 45 percent over U.S. prices. Collapsible, two-speed and 10-speed bikes are available. One advantage of this deal is that it simplifies transporting your bike back to the U.S. You can pick up free shipping cartons at Crescent outlets in Copenhagen or Stockholm (SAS departure cities) where Crescent experts will help you disassemble and package your machine. Reservations should be made two weeks before departure, and bikes can be picked up in five cities: four in Sweden plus Copenhagen. For more info write:

> Scandinavian Airlines
> 638 Fifth Avenue
> New York, N.Y. 10020

Maps: If you're not satisfied with the maps previously listed for each Scandinavian country, you can try the British Cycling Federation for further maps of all three nations.

SPAIN. If you're looking for challenging variety in terrain, Spain has it. Hemingway once wrote that the Spanish do not know how to pedal. Maybe it's because there's not much incentive. Many of the interesting sections of the country—the mountain-riddled central plateau, the Andalusian basin in the south and the Pyrenees in the east—severely limit cyclists by their lack of decent secondary roads or, in some cases, even primary ones.

For an easy, pleasant tour, try cycling along the coast in the northern part of the country, and if you are determined to see the interior go in early spring when the weather is kind. Traffic and sizzling heat are the two biggest enemies of the two-wheeled Spanish tourist. Spain is really not a paradise for the beginning cyclist, as it's a long haul between towns; the roads are badly surfaced with gigantic holes; and trucks rumble along the narrow roadways scaring hell out of bikers.

Another reason for sticking to the coast is that that's where most of the available accommodations are—hostels, campgrounds, hotels.

Climate: Blazing in summer. Go in early spring if you can.

National tourist office:

> 589 Fifth Avenue
> New York, N.Y. 10017

and

> 209 Post
> San Francisco, Calif. 94108

SWITZERLAND. The first thing that comes to mind when anyone mentions Switzerland is mountains. But don't let that discourage you. Switzerland is actually good cycling territory, especially if you stick to the long valleys bounded by the Jura Mountains in the west and the Alps in the south and east. The scenery is phenomenal. The country looks as though it were designed by a postcard artist, what with its mountains and the beautiful midland regions which are sprinkled liberally with lakes, immaculate towns and villages. You'll be treated to a cross section of three cultures: French, German and Italian. About 100 hostels are clustered around the lake areas, but they enforce a maximum age limit, 25. Don't worry if you're too old; there are plenty of campgrounds and hotels.

Not too many secondary roads exist, but the ones that do are well-paved and easy to ride even though you must share them with cars.

Climate varies with location. The mountains generally are cool, but can be warm, wet or temperate depending on where you are. Bring a sweater just in case. On the whole, July might be best.

Maps: Michelin.

National tourist office:

> 608 Fifth Avenue
> New York, N.Y. 10020

It's a great way to spend a honeymoon—exploring parts of Europe on bikes. You can camp as you go, or rent bikes in each city stopover.

Some other international touring organizations that might help

WE'VE COVERED the major touring groups already. Here are others that might appeal to you:

World on Wheels
P.O. Box 212
San Rafael, Calif. 94902
(Yearly membership is $6 a year; each additional family member costs $1. Brings you info on Europe tour planning plus news on new equipment and cycling events.)

In France:
Federation Francaise de Cyclotourisme
66 rue Rene Boulanger
75-Paris, France
(Sponsors tours and other bicycling events.)

In Italy:
Italian Touring Club
Corso Italia 10
Milano, Italy
(Good for maps of Italy. Must join for services.)

In Switzerland:
Alliance Internationale du Turisme (AIT)
9 rue Pierre Fatio
Geneva, Switzerland
(Another source of International Camping Carnet.)

Chapter 11

Take your wheels with you

It's a drag to talk about other modes of transportation in a bicycle book—but it's a fact of life that we often depend on cars, planes, trains, buses and boats. Here's how to transport your bike on each of these. It includes a rundown on car racks, details on how to take your bike on each of 45 airlines, foreign and domestic, plus bike-carting regulations on the most popular train, bus and steamship lines.

WE HARD-CORE CYCLISTS like to think we can go anywhere we want on just two wheels. It's a pipe dream. We can't do it. Things get in the way. Like oceans. Ugly cities that are dangerous and unpleasant, if not impossible, to bike through. And perhaps worst of all, short vacations that don't give us time enough to bicycle all the way to where we want to go.

Because of such obstacles, we must often depend on our arch enemy, the car, or on public transportation to get us to our take-off point. Fortunately we're in luck. Today, more than ever before, it's easy to take your bicycle with you on car or public transportation. You have your choice of a wide range of car racks, and public transportation is opening up its luggage compartments to your wheels.

Let's start with automobiles.

Finding the right carrier for your car

BASICALLY, THERE ARE three types: rear bumper racks, roof racks and rear deck racks.

Right off I'll make a very subjective and biased statement: the *roof racks* are the best ones to own. By and large they hold bicycles more securely, hold more bikes than other racks, don't obscure the driver's vision and don't obstruct entrance to the trunk (or engine). Also, with the bikes on the roof, there's no danger of some clown in another vehicle crushing them from behind.

There's another psychological advantage: With a bumper rack I often found myself studying the bikes in the rearview mirror,

looking to see if they were shaking loose or banging up against each other when I was driving at high speed. This is dangerous—but hard to avoid. With the bikes out of sight on the roof, it's impossible for them to distract you.

Nevertheless, the *rear bumper rack* is by far the most popular type. This is mainly because it's cheaper and more readily available than the roof rack, and doesn't require you to hoist a bicycle over your head when loading. (Roof carriers start at over $30 and can cost up to $80 while bumper racks start at slightly over $10.)

The *rear deck carrier* is a compromise between the two but can only be installed on cars with sizeable trunk lids; this eliminates many small foreign cars.

Before we get down to specific models, there are several questions you should ask yourself in selecting a carrier:

1. How much do you care about your bike? Maybe you can just disassemble it and throw it in the trunk, or tie it to a luggage rack—if it's nothing but a clunker.

2. How many bikes must the carrier hold?

3. What types and sizes of bikes must it carry?

4. How is it installed?

5. Will the rack fit your car?

6. How much road clearance does the rack allow with *your* bike on it?

7. How secure is the rack? Will it hold your bike steady at high speeds?

8. Will the rack affect your car's performance?

9. Can the rack be transferred easily from car to car? (In case you rely on rent-a-cars.)

10. Can it be used to carry things other than bikes?

11. Finally, how much does it cost?

Another thing to consider when shopping is a rack's weather resistance. Usually the metal is plastic-, chrome- or zinc-plated. The first two afford the best protection. I've seen (and owned) some zinc models that turned rusty pretty fast; but this is mostly a matter of aesthetics.

Also, most racks come with incomplete equipment for holding the bikes in place: usually ineffectual straps or belts. No matter what the instructions in the kit tell you about how rock-solid secure the rack holds the bikes, don't believe it. Go out and get yourself some sandows (or rope) and tie down those bikes until they won't move. You want the bikes as tight as possible so they don't bash against each other (especially critical on rear racks) and so they don't swing in the wind and loosen the rack's fittings. There's nothing like having two bikes and a rack go flying off your car at 60 mph.

Roof-top bicycle carriers

ROOF RACKS usually attach to the car's rain gutters, using a clamping system or belts which have clips that fit over the gutter. Some models also employ large suction cups but the main holding power is applied to the gutters. This means roof carriers require a car with rain gutters, which includes almost all automobiles except for a few exotic sports models.

I consider the roof rack superior on several counts; besides the points already mentioned, you don't have to worry about road clearance.

But there are three drawbacks:

• You must lift the bikes over your head onto the rack. No sweat if you ride a 20-pound racer; somewhat of a sweat if you ride a 35-pound three-speed and are a midget.

• Cars with small engines and high profiles may experience handling or power problems with several bicycles sticking up above the roof. The problems are minimal and not at all dangerous; bikes will slip lengthwise through a head wind and don't have much area of resistance should you get hit by a cross wind. However, some cyclist/ drivers report speed losses up to ten mph with bikes on the roof. As a rough rule of thumb, if your car is powered by an engine less than 1600cc in displacement and is built high off the ground, you can expect some speed loss or drop in gas mileage. I once installed a roof rack on a car boasting only 1300cc of power, however, and still preferred the safety of bikes on the roof despite the drop in gas mileage.

• Roof carriers are the most expensive racks available. Because they run from $30 to $80, the casual cyclist who has but $60 invested in his bike would probably not want to invest an equal amount in the rack to carry it.

While we can't list every rack on the market, here are a few representative carriers to give you an idea of what's currently available:

Bike-Porter. The Bike-Porter holds bicycles in an upright position. A V-shaped channel supports each bike by its tires, and a clamp on a vertical post secures the bike by its seat tube. The standard Bike-Porter carries two bicycles and an add-on kit lets you stack on two more. The carrier attaches to the car via gutter hooks and tightening straps along with large suction cups. The manufacturer claims the

Below top, Bike-Porter holds bikes right side-up. Wheels fit in V-channel, and a clamp holds the seat tube. Bottom, the same carrier also mounts on a trunk deck.

Bike-Porter has been road tested at speeds up to 100 mph. This is good to know should you decide to enter the Daytona 500 next year with bicycles on your roof. The Bike-Porter also mounts on large trunk decks. So if you buy two of them with add-on kits, you could theoretically carry up to eight bicycles. The Bike-Porter costs about $40 with the extra kit for two more bikes running about an extra $20. Made by:

Atkins-Graber, Inc.
5252 Verona Road
Madison, Wisconsin 53711

JCI 2+2. This carrier comes with fittings to transport two bikes, but you can buy extra fittings to handle up to four bicycles. The 2+2

Below top, JCI 2 + 2 holds bikes upside down in special fittings.
The unit includes a special chain for protection, but you provide
the padlock. Bottom, you use the same unit for two bikes.

can be attached to any car with standard rain gutters having outer lips. It cannot be used on cars with no rain gutters, flat rain gutters, or plastic- or sheet-metal-covered gutters. The JCI has been road-tested at maximum highway speeds.

The bikes are carried upside down, and by juggling the various seat fittings on the support bars you can accommodate different sizes of bicycles at the same time. This takes some pretty careful arranging, however.

The 2+2 is incredibly easy to remove from a car—no tools needed. You just hand-twist two large rings on the rain gutter clamps and the carrier pops free. The carrier also adjusts fairly quickly to fit different cars. The support bars and clamps are zinc-plated and the seat and handlebar fittings are plastic-coated to prevent scratching the bikes. The rack is widely available throughout the U.S., including Hawaii, and Canada. Like most roof racks, it can be used to carry items other than bikes: canoes, lumber, etc.

The JCI 2+2 has one idiosyncrasy. Because of its hollow support tubes which are perforated with a series of holes (to allow for various settings of the seat and handlebar fittings), the rack "hums" after a rain. Somehow the water gets in the tubing and the wind blowing through it causes a high-pitched tone. Not only that, the rack can't carry much of a tune. Any rack with this type of construction could create this effect. There's no real danger to it, but it's a bit disconcerting if you don't know what it is, or if you don't like the song it's humming. I was highway-testing a rack when I first noticed this hum. I spent an anxious 20 minutes at the side of the road trying to find out what was wrong with my car before I finally figured out it was my operatic bike rack.

If you can't find the 2+2 in your town, write:

JCI
904 South Nogales Street
City of Industry, California 91744

Wil-Go. The Wil-Go is the *creme de la creme* of bicycle racks. It's called a "professional bicycle carrier" and with good reason; it is the favorite rack of European racers. One heck of a sturdy rack, it is hand-made, hand-brazed, all steel and weighs 37 pounds. The makers say it will fit all cars.

The bikes attach to the carrier upside down. The handlebar fittings are easily hand-adjusted using wingnuts so that different size bikes can be fitted without trouble. (It should be noted that few bikes are exactly the same size. On any carrier which secures the bikes upside down, the important measurement is from the seat to the handlebars, and this distance will vary even among bikes with identical frame sizes. Adjusting the fittings to handle different bikes is normally a big pain on most roof carriers, which makes the Wil-Go adjustment feature such an important one.)

All contact points on the rack are plastic-coated. You pay a pile for all these nice features, however. Over $70. The rack has only recently

Some racks hum as you drive. There's no real danger, but you can be a bit uncomfortable if you don't like the tune your rack is playing

244

been imported from France, so you may have trouble finding it. Write:

> Wil-Go Corporation
> 365 Reed Street
> Santa Clara, California 95050

The story on bumper racks

THIS TYPE OF RACK is the simplest and cheapest. It also has many drawbacks which makes buying the right one more of a challenge than buying the right roof rack. Here are the dangers:

• *Low road clearance.* Many of the racks on the market dangle the bicycle dangerously close to the ground. If your car's shocks are in bad shape you could damage your bike when hitting a hard bump or a deep pothole. To be absolutely safe, your rims should not extend below the bottom of your car's bumper (or body—whichever is lowest). Many carriers have uprights with several holes in them. Insert the attacher bolts through the lowest holes to keep the carrier high. A friend of mine once ignored this advice and flattened an expensive new pair of Mavic rims.

Your bike may develop square wheels unless you mount it high on a bumper rack

• *Weakness.* This can stem from two factors—wimpy rack unrights or a malnourished bumper. If your bumper is chintzy you can tighten up the carrier bolts until you're blue in the face and all you'll do is bend the bumper. The carrier will continue to wiggle under the weight of a bicycle.

To remedy this problem somewhat, install some blocks of wood behind the bumper and replace the hook-bolts with U-bolts that will slip around both the wood and your bumper and back through the holes in the carrier uprights.

Hook-bolts on this carrier are inserted through lowest holes in the uprights to keep the bike safely off the pavement. The bike is tied with twine around the seat tube; this supplements the holding straps supplied with the rack, which rarely are adequate.

Here's the proper way to load two bikes on a bumper rack. The first bike goes on with the derailleur facing inward toward the car. The second bike goes on in the opposite direction. And both bikes are mounted high to prevent damage if car hits a hole.

Another problem occurs when you load the carrier with more than one heavy bike and the whole affair begins leaning away from the car. Most racks have belts to solve this problem; they run from the top of the carrier to the top edge of the trunk. If your rack doesn't include these straps, make your own. All you need is two ropes and a couple of hooks. Even so, I wouldn't trust any rear rack with more than two bikes unless it was some super-special design.

• *Vulnerability.* Your bikes can be creamed from behind. Conceivably you could just be nudged by another vehicle and lose several hundred dollars worth of bicycles without a scratch to either vehicle. The cops may not be interested in writing it up as a motor vehicle accident and your insurance company then might balk at handling your claim against the other driver. No matter what happens, it's a drag.

• *Fitability.* Most rear racks attach to the bumper with two sets of hook-bolts. One hook clamps on the top rear edge of the bumper and the other clamps on the bottom rear edge. If your car's bumper is built as an integral part of the car, you may not be able to find an edge to clamp the hook-bolts around. Check this out before you buy.

Despite all these badmouthings, the rear rack is a good carrier for the money—a good buy for the cyclist who's not overly sensitive about his bike. Chances are heavily against any harm befalling a rear-carried bicycle if you don't spend too much time in traffic, so it's only the cyclist with an expensive and hard-to-replace bike who should rule out this type of rack. Also, positioning the bikes in the rear keeps them out of the airstream on most cars and thus they exert little drag on the car. And if you drive a truck with a high front end, a bumper rack is perfect up front where it will be better protected than in the rear.

Most bumper carriers come with inadequate gear, however, for protecting the bikes from damaging themselves by bumping up against each other or the rack. First of all, you'll want to pad the uprights where the bike contacts them. Old clincher bike tires are good for this. Cut the tire in lengths and clinch them around the uprights. When carrying two machines, stuff rags between the bikes wherever they touch. Also, make sure you stretch sandows or something around the bikes to keep them steady. Here are a few rear-rack models now on the market:

The wealthy cyclist with an expensive hard-to-replace bike should rule out a bumper rack. One very small accident would be too many

Allen Universal Bike Rack. The R.A. Allen Co. claims this rack will fit all cars, station wagons and vans, both foreign and domestic, except the Opel GT. Once you've assembled it you need no tools to fit it to your car—it is secured through a system of belts and hooks. The maker claims it will hold three bikes normally and four if loaded carefully. It can be transferred easily from car to car, requires no bumper (a big point) and is well-covered with vinyl at bike-contact points. The rack can be hung on the wall to serve as a storage or repair rack and turns into a ski rack for two or four pairs of skis with company-made attachments. The rack is widely available for under $25.

R.A. Allen Co.
Bowles Terrace
Lincoln, Massachusetts 01733

Allen Universal rack, left, attaches easily to the car, requiring no tools. The rack, right, will carry four bikes as shown here, but the author doesn't recommend trusting it with that heavy a load, nor should derailleur bikes be stacked against each other.

Mijon Imperial has mounting posts that stay permanently attached while the upper structure can be removed to get at the trunk or the tailgate.

There are four "Cycle Caddy" models varying in the size of their uprights and the quality of their weather coatings. This one has long uprights for road clearance.

JCI. The same company that makes the 2+2 roof rack also makes seven different rear racks. Four are conventional racks of various quality and size, one is a low-profile model and two are loop racks (instead of two uprights, the rack uses one curved section of tubing to support the bikes). The four conventional models are called Cycle Caddies. The uprights vary from 29 to 36 inches. The finishes are zinc, chrome or vinyl. Some models include stabilizer bars and one uses wingnuts rather than regular nuts for quicker installation.

The low-profile model is called a Mini-Caddy and has only 20-inch uprights so that the bikes sit low and do not obstruct rear vision. The lower profile also means easier access to the trunk and greater rigidity. Drawback: poor road clearance.

The loop racks are named the Circle Caddy and the JCI Loop Rack (thankfully, JCI is better at building racks than naming them). The major feature of these racks is that their mounting posts can remain permanently in place while the loop is removable. No need to disassemble the whole thing to get at the trunk. Prices on all JCI rear racks range from about $13 to about $20. All carry a maximum of two bicycles (JCI address given earlier).

Mijon Secure and Imperial. Mijon makes two different racks, each handling two bicycles. The Secure costs under $20 while the Imperial costs about $7 more. Both racks are low-profile models and hold the bike, not by the top tube but by the V-frame (see photo), thus reducing the tendency of the bike to sway while underway. The Secure also features a stabilizing bolt which exerts a third pressure point against the bumper for extra firmness.

The Imperial is a deluxe model that works like a loop rack. The bumper posts are permanently attached while the frame of the carrier quickly slips on or off. It also features hinged hangers (the things the bikes hang on) that fold out of the way when not in use. The company says this is a handy feature because it eliminates the potential of another car running into the hangers and getting damaged. I suppose this is a real plus if you're the kind of person who worries about the welfare of tailgaters. Both racks include belts which strap around the bike's wheels. Both handle two machines. The Secure is anodized aluminum; the Imperial is heavy-duty steel and chrome-plated.

> Mijon Co. Inc.
> 1105 Redondo Boulevard
> Inglewood, California 90302

Nate Scorcher's Hot Rack. The Nate Scorcher is the most unusual on the market, the brainchild of Bob Saffold, a cyclist who became dissatisfied with existing racks. There is no *one* Scorcher rack; there are several, each made for specific models of cars. Safford has made racks for about every kind of Volkswagen (whose owners have trouble getting at their engines with conventional carriers) plus exotic imports whose bumpers reject normal racks (such as the Datsun 240Z).

All Scorcher racks work on the same general principle, however. They hold the bike in an unusual manner, using two J-bars with

Nate Scorcher Hot Racks are individually fitted to your car, no matter what type or model you own. There are even special racks for Volkswagens that attach to the bumper bracket.

fingers at the tops (see photo). You slip the wheels of your bike into the bottom curved part of the J-bars and the fingers at the top slip between the frame and the hubs. This, of course, carries only one bicycle. But you can tote a second bike with a two-part attachment. A rod attaches between the car and the first bike's frame to give extra rigidity, and then a rack attaches to the first bike and provides a pair of arms to hold a second bike. All parts of the rack are covered with vinyl.

At this writing, the Hot Rack is not widely available through normal retailers. The company plans eventually to sell the carrier through catalog houses and even car dealers. But at present your best bet is to write the manufacturer directly to place your order for your specific model of car. Prices vary from about $15 for a basic VW rack to around $30 for a model to fit a more exotic type of car. The attachments for holding a second bike will cost about another $10. For a price quotation, write:

If you write the manufacturer, be sure you tell him your specific car model. In effect, every rack is made specifically for a particular car

> Nate Scorcher's Pedalry
> P.O. Box 3332
> Santa Barbara, California 93105

A sensible compromise—the trunk rack

FOR THE DRIVER who owns a car which cannot easily be fitted with a rear rack or has a flimsy bumper, but who does not want to spend the money for either a customized bumper carrier or a roof rack, the *trunk rack* makes sense. It can be fitted to almost any car with a sizeable rear deck. It won't sway with the bumper because it isn't supported by the rear bumper. The drawback, of course, is that this type of carrier blocks the trunk more than any other. Here are two representative models:

AMF. The AMF trunk carrier attaches to your car with suction cups and four straps and hooks. Two hook to the top edge of the trunk, two to the bottom. Two conventional carrier arms hold the bikes (a maximum of two) behind the car, leaving the top of the rack free to carry luggage.

AMF has dealers most everywhere, but if you have trouble finding one, write:

> Wheel Goods Division
> AMF Incorporated
> Olney, Illinois 62450

JCI Cycle Lugger. This trunk carrier attaches either temporarily or permanently. Temporary installation is similar to the AMF rack, using straps and suction cups. But a hardware kit is included to attach the carrier permanently if you choose. Luggage can also be carried on this rack but only when empty of bicycles, which are carried upside down in seat and handlebar fittings identical to those used on the JCI 2+2 roof rack. In effect, it's a roof rack that sits on your trunk, but will tote only a maximum of two machines. The Cycle Lugger is made of chrome-plated steel tubing, with a price tag close to $40. (JCI address given earlier.)

Make your own carrier

STRANGE BUT TRUE, the easiest rack to make yourself is the best kind—the roof type. This is because hardware for attaching the rack to the car is freely available. The point in making your own is not so much to save money, since after buying the appropriate hardware you're not that many dollars ahead, but to build a sturdier rack than any on the market. Plus you can customize the rack precisely to your bikes. Also, the investment in time on your part is not that significant. The ready-made racks we've tested have all come in kit form. By the time you sort out all the parts and muddle through the directions, you've wasted an hour or so and you haven't even started putting the rack together yet.

In the same amount of time you could convert a conventional auto-top carrier to a bike rack simply by adding bicycle fittings. You can make these out of two grooved wood blocks to accept the handlebars of each bike (with the seat just tied to the other crossbar—which can be padded if you wish to protect the leather). Or you can buy special fittings from JCI; $7 buys two handlebar hooks and a seat plate.

If you don't have a top carrier already, you can buy an excellent one made of aluminum alloy with steel tube crossbars from L. L. Bean (Freeport, Maine 04032) for about $26. Bean also sells rain-gutter

You can customize your own rack from a standard roof rack, like the one from L. L. Bean below (about $26). Bean will also sell you just the brackets (right), which clamp to rain gutters, cost $14 for set of four.

You can tailor-make your own rack with a set of crossbars and clamps. You can even buy handlebar hooks and seat plates

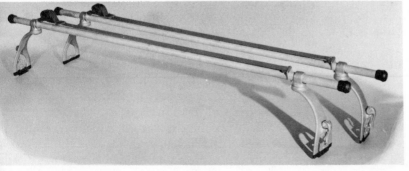

Okay, so there are no bikes in this picture. Except that there really are. Several are buried in the cargo section of that flying machine. Which proves that you can take your bicycle with you, wherever you go, anywhere in the world. Check with your travel agent or the airline, though.

clamps that are superior to most offered on bike racks for about $14 for a set of four. They come with carriage bolts which will attach to wood crossbars.

Driving with bikes on the car

WITH THE BIKES on the roof it's easy to forget about them entirely. Don't. Watch out for low overheads such as garages, overhanging tree boughs, ultra-low bridges and low-flying planes.

If you pack a rear rack, you'll have to reform into a park-by-sight driver if you're presently a park-by-ear driver. In other words, look behind you when backing up. Avoid potholes and take it easy when entering steep driveways if the wheels on your bike extend below your bumper. Or be prepared to buy new rims after every trip.

Another danger often overlooked is side overhang. On many skinny foreign cars a bike will extend almost a full foot on either side. And drivers of skinny foreign cars often take great pleasure in snaking through tight places where domestic behemoths fear to tread. If you're one of these devils, don't forget you're going to need a couple more feet of clearance than usual.

On some skinny foreign cars, a bike will extend almost a foot beyond the side. Don't try to snake through traffic

A final warning: Keep your concern over your bike secondary to your own physical welfare when cruising the highway. Don't get distracted by your cargo, no matter how valuable it may be. I know how rough it is to keep from darting an anxious eye backward to see how your new Mercier or Falcon is faring on the rack. Resist that urge. Watch the traffic, buddy. We want you back safe so you'll read the next chapter.

What about crooks?

DON'T LEAVE BIKES unattended on a rack for any length of time. Even if chained to the rack, most bikes will still be vulnerable since a rack can be disassembled to get around this obstacle.

As for the safety of the rack itself, it's kind of a pain to remove it and re-install it constantly. You'll have to judge for yourself how safe it is to leave yours attached in your neighborhood.

But even in some of the worst neighborhoods in New York City I see loads of cars with their racks intact. And if nobody's interested in swiping the racks in the Big Apple, I guess they're safe anywhere.

Dealing with the airlines

TO PUT IT BLUNTLY, there is no form of public transportation in this country—plane, train, bus or boat—that welcomes cyclists or bicycles with open arms. But the airlines seem to be coming around to our side more than the others. They are at least making a token gesture at getting the cyclist business. United Airlines in particular has widely advertised free bicycle cartons. And several international carriers are pushing their European cycling package tours.

Don't take these overtures too seriously, though; there's still a big gap between the friendliness shown toward bikers in the ads and the reality of dealing with airline personnel in the flesh.

There's a good reason for this. Airlines don't make their living by carrying luggage. They make their money off freight, mail and passengers—with luggage flown along just as a favor to the passengers. Bicycles are awkward pieces of luggage to fit into a hold, especially if they're uncrated. So no matter how favorably airline executives and their advertising agencies view bicycles, this loving feeling toward cyclists may not filter down to the clerk who actually has to stick your Schwinn on the plane. You have to remember that the bike is probably just a big pain in the neck to him.

I don't tell you this to discourage you from flying your bike. Far from it. I only tell you this so you'll be prepared for the reception you'll probably get when you hit the terminal. After interviewing personnel at 45 airlines, we found the general feeling toward bicycles something less than enthusiastic (with some notable exceptions). The chart that follows lists each airline's policies toward bicycles *as luggage*, except where noted. In other words, we're concerned here with whether an airline *lets you take your bike along with you on the same flight*, just as you might take a suitcase, and how that airline specifies it must be packaged, if at all.

Most of the lines we contacted urged that cyclists send their machines *as cargo*. While at times this is cheaper, it is definitely an inconvenience, especially if you're depending on your bike to get you to and from the airport. You will have to crate your bike and take it to the freight terminal·days in advance of your real departure. Don't get sucked into this unless absolutely necessary. If the chart says an airline accepts bikes as baggage but a clerk urges you over the phone to

There's still a gap between the friendliness toward bikers shown in the airline ads and the attitude of airline personnel in the flesh

253

ship it as cargo, stick to your guns. It's possible they've changed their policy, but more likely you're being given the runaround. Act authoritative. Let them know that *you know* official policy allows bicycles on their planes. Sometimes employees, through no fault of their own, aren't aware of the policy.

If you still meet resistance (and you might), be tough. Act like you're going to ride your bike right down their throats. Most of us don't like to come on strong, but the airlines are starting to make firm offers about flying bikes and we should hold them to these claims before they're withdrawn due to lack of interest on our part.

Even so, phone the airline ahead of time to re-affirm its bike arrangements. Then it's not a bad idea to show up with your bike in the proper form 30 minutes earlier than you normally would to allow for any snags, arguments, etc.

Now, on to the chart. The two crucial columns are "Take Bike?"

United provides a "bike box" to enable passengers to take along their wheels. Handlebars are fixed sideways and pedals removed.

and "In What Form?" An airline merits a "Yes" to the first question only if it accepts bikes as take-it-right-along-with-you-on-the-same-plane baggage. In most cases, the answers given to the second question are straightforward. But after some airlines you may see the words "IATA regulations." IATA stands for the International Air Transport Authority. Strangely enough, when we contacted the IATA, we found that it stipulates no definite rules on bicycles as baggage, leaving all arrangements to the individual airlines. But there are evidently unofficial IATA guidelines that these airlines comply with. This is not easy to comprehend—you just have to accept it on faith, sort of like those religious mysteries you learned about in Sunday school.

In any event, when you see "IATA regulations" it *really* means: The front wheel must be removed and wired to the frame; the handlebars fixed sideways; and the pedals removed.

All the information listed in the chart refers to single-seat bikes only, not tandems. For the latter you'll have to throw yourself and both your seats on the mercy of the airlines and hope they'll take your two-seater.

"Extra Charge?" is another hairy question. Only United has specific rates for bikes, ranging from $2 to $8 depending on the distance traveled. Most of the others simply apply either a "regular baggage" charge or an "excess baggage" rate. Here's the difference:

Airlines which treat bikes as *regular* baggage lump your bike together with the rest of your luggage to determine if there's any extra charge. Airlines which treat bikes as *excess* baggage will always make you cough up some extra dough.

For instance, on international flights you are allowed 44 pounds of baggage with any excess charged at a rate of one percent of the first-class one-way fare per kilogram (2.2 pounds). So, if an airline considers a bike *regular* baggage it is simply weighed along in one lump sum with the rest of your stuff. That means if your bike weighs 30 pounds and you can keep the rest of your baggage down to 14 pounds, you will incur no extra charge. If the rest of your baggage comes to, say, 24 pounds you will be charged the standard rate for the extra ten pounds, and so on.

However, if the airline regards bicycles as *excess* baggage, you will automatically be charged the overweight rate for the entire 30 pounds of the bicycle no matter how light the rest of your luggage is. Don't try to get your total weight to come out under 44 pounds because it won't do you any good. They're going to stick you for the entire 30-pound bike weight.

By "Special Plans?" we mean any deals the airlines offer that somehow include a bike or bicycling. More about those later. First, here's the chart. We want to point out that the airline with the most liberal policy toward bicycles is, of all people, Alaska Airlines. It accepts bikes "as is." No dismantling, no crates, no nothing. Just roll it in. Bravo!

AIRLINE	FLIES TO	TAKE BIKE?	IN WHAT FORM?	EXTRA CHARGE?	SPECIAL PLANS?
Aeroflot	Moscow Paris from New York	Yes	Wrap up in some way or charge is higher.	Regular baggage.	No
Aeronaves de Mexico	Mexico	Yes	Take both wheels off, tie to frame. No box required.	Regular baggage.	No
Air Afrique	Africa	Yes	Put in own crate or box. Airline takes no responsibility for damage.	Regular baggage.	No
Air Canada	Canada Russia Caribbean	Yes	Remove front wheel, handlebars, pedals, tie together.	Regular baggage.	No
Air France	Mexico Caribbean Europe	Yes	No specifications.	Regular baggage.	Yes
Air India	30 countries	No	Freight only.		No
Air New England	New England	No	Freight only.		No
Air New Zealand	New Zealand from Los Angeles	Yes	Take handlebars, front wheel, pedals off.	$1.55-a-lb. baggage.	No
Air West	Western USA	No	Freight only.		
Alaska Airlines	Seattle to Alaska	Yes	As is.	Regular baggage.	No
Alitalia	Europe	Yes	No specifications.	Regular baggage.	No
Allegheny	Pennsylvania, Northeast, New York	Yes	Turn handlebars, remove pedals.	Excess baggage.	No
American	USA Caribbean Pacific	Yes	Turn handlebars, remove pedals. Bag supplied for $2.	Excess baggage.	No

AIRLINE	FLIES TO	TAKE BIKE?	IN WHAT FORM?	EXTRA CHARGE?	SPECIAL PLANS?
Braniff	USA Caribbean S. America	No	Cargo only.		No
BOAC	Europe Asia Bermuda Caribbean Pacific	Yes	Prefer crated. You supply crate.	Regular baggage.	Yes
BWIA	Caribbean Miami	Yes	IATA regulations.	Regular baggage.	No
Canadian Pacific	World from Canadian cities	No	Freight only.		No
Continental	Chicago West USA Hawaii Pacific	Yes	IATA regulations.	No information.	No
Czechoslovak Airlines	Prague Europe from New York Montreal	Yes	IATA regulations.	Regular baggage.	No
Delta Airlines	USA Canada Caribbean	Yes	Turn handlebars. Crate provided.	Regular baggage.	
Eastern Airlines	USA Bermuda Caribbean	Yes	Turn handlebars, remove pedals.	Regular baggage.	No
El Al	Europe Mid East	Yes	Will accept in any form but suggest turning handlebars and removing pedals.	Regular baggage.	No
Finnair	Helsinki from New York	Yes	IATA regulations.	Regular baggage.	No
Iberia	Spain Europe from New York	Yes	Crated. You supply crate.	Regular baggage.	No
Icelandic	Europe from New York	Yes	Turn handlebars, remove pedals. Recommend crate.	Regular baggage.	No

AIRLINE	FLIES TO	TAKE BIKE?	IN WHAT FORM?	EXTRA CHARGE?	SPECIAL PLANS?
Irish International	Ireland from New York Boston and Chicago	Yes	IATA regulations.	Regular baggage.	
Japan Airlines	Orient from New York San Fran. L.A.	Yes	IATA regulations.	Regular baggage.	No
KLM	Europe	Yes	IATA regulations.	Regular baggage.	No
Lufthansa	Europe	Yes	Crated. You supply crate.	Regular baggage.	No
National Airlines	East Coast Southwest USA	Yes	Remove handle bars, pedals and tie to frame.	One piece of sporting equipment free.	No
North Central	North-central USA	Yes	Turn handle-bars, remove pedals, tie to frame.	Check with airline.	No
Northwest Orient	Northwest USA Alaska Orient	Yes	Turn handle-bars, remove pedals, tie to frame.	Regular baggage.	No
Ozark	Mid-western USA	Yes	Remove handlebars, pedals, front wheel, tie to frame. Crate recommended, not supplied.	Regular baggage.	No
Pan Am	Europe Caribbean Pacific S. America	Yes	Wrap up in some way or charge is higher.	Regular baggage.	Yes
Piedmont	South-eastern USA	Yes	Crate recommended. Not supplied.	Regular baggage.	No
Qantas	Australia London	No	Freight only.		

AIRLINE	FLIES TO	TAKE BIKE?	IN WHAT FORM?	EXTRA CHARGE?	SPECIAL PLANS?
Sabena	Belgium Europe	Yes	IATA regulations. Crate recommended, not supplied.	Regular baggage.	Yes
SAS	Scandinavia	Yes	IATA regulations. Crate recommended, not supplied.	Regular baggage.	Yes
Southern Airways	Southeastern USA	Yes	Bike carton only. Not supplied.	Excess baggage.	No
Swissair	Switzerland Europe	Yes	Remove wheels, pedals, tie to frame.	Regular baggage.	Yes
TAP	Portugal Europe	Yes	IATA regulations.	Regular baggage.	No
TWA	Europe Caribbean USA	Yes	Take apart and tie together or place in sealed bag in one piece.	Regular baggage.	No
United Airlines	USA Hawaii Canada	Yes	Turn handlebars, remove pedals. Crate supplied but call ahead.	Special rate from $2 to $8.	No
Varig	S. America Japan	Yes	IATA regulations.	Excess baggage.	No
Western Airlines	Western USA Hawaii	Yes	Turn handlebars, remove pedals. Crate recommended.	Excess baggage.	No

Letting the airlines plan your bike tour

WE'VE GIVEN no details under the last column in the chart ("Special Plans?") but simply indicated whether or not the airline offers them because these plans have a way of changing from year to year or even month to month. But just to give you an idea of what these tours are like, we'll run through a few of the major offerings.

Swissair is the airline to contact for cycle tours through Switzerland and Austria. At last count they offered three tours. One is based

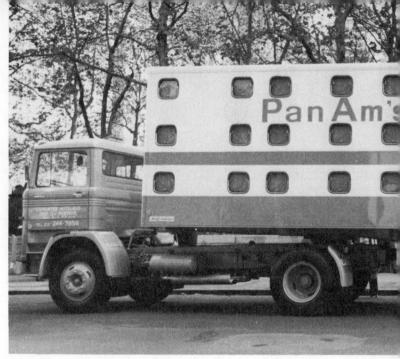

Hotelbus includes bunks, closets, bathroom and storage space, follow

around the city of Graz, Austria, and explores the gentle Styrian countryside in southern Austria. Unlike many airline-sponsored tours, this one is aimed at somewhat experienced cyclists, who can cover up to 50 miles per day. A second tour strikes far into the northeast of Austria, and a third explores Switzerland north of the Alps.

All Swissair tours are planned in one-day steps so you can take off on your own, knowing full well where everyone else will be the next day. A sag wagon (a bus, really) follows the pack to pick up stragglers. Every tour takes 15 days and prices vary according to season but average around $700.

As mentioned in the previous chapter on Europe, Scandinavian airlines (SAS) offers a deal whereby you can order a Crescent bicycle before you leave the U.S. and it will be waiting for you when you reach your desination. (Look under the *Scandinavia* heading in the previous chapter for details.)

Sabena offers three tours, ranging from 15 to 22 days. All tours include a 10-speed Belgian-made bike (which you take home with you) and cost between $300 and $600 *not* including air fare.

One tour takes you through Belgium's west coast while the other two take you through Belgium, France, Luxembourg, Germany and Holland. Sabena follows the pack with a sag wagon, supplies break-

You can pedal off on your own if you wish, knowing where the rest of the gang will be the following day

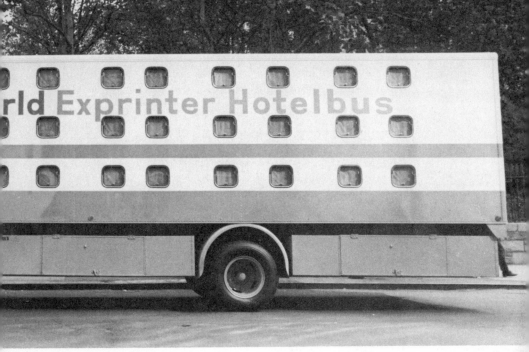

cycling groups across Europe.

fast, dinner and accommodations. Sabena specializes in youth and group fares with their tours aimed mostly at students on a budget. Sabena also offers a fourth package deal called "The Wanderer" which is a do-it-yourself special for those who like to travel alone. The airline hands you a 10-speed at the Brussels airport complete with customs documents, gives you one night's bed and breakfast at a student-type hotel, a packet of bicycle maps, and puts you on your own.

KLM offers some simple, basic (and cheap) bike tours of Holland, either one week or two weeks long. The airline offers a rented bike and a place to stay at the end of each day's ride. Pan Am sponsors rather luxurious tours of four countries: England, the Netherlands, Denmark and France.

A tour-planning agency called Exprinter adds a unique twist to airline bicycle tours—the Hotelbus. This is not just an ordinary sag wagon, but a tractor-trailer that's really a hotel on wheels. In the past, Exprinter's Hotelbus has followed all Pan Am bike tours. At this writing the company was planning to arrange tours for KLM. In any case, if you pick a trip featuring the Exprinter Hotelbus, you will get your own bunk, closet, locker space, individual window and reading lamp. The Hotelbus also has its own self-contained bathroom facilities.

Most nights are spent in real hotels, not in the Hotelbus, but it meets the tour group each day at its designated destination so that cyclists can leave their luggage in the vehicle all day, thus allowing them to pedal with no extra weight.

Easing that big pain—customs

WHEN YOU TAKE your own bicycle out of the country, you have to get it back in without paying duty on it. This may be difficult unless you're driving a Schwinn, Huffy or other domestic brand. Bikes like Peugeot, Raleigh, Atala and Gitane may now seem American as apple pie because they're all over U.S. roads, but don't forget that they're foreign and you may be forced to pay duty on a foreign-made bike if you can't prove you bought it at home. So take some proof of purchase with you.

Better yet, U.S. Customs recommends that you get in touch with them before leaving the country so they can mark the bike for you. In most cases, the person to ask for is the Staff Officer, U.S. Customs, at an international airport. If you buy abroad, get some sort of receipt for your bike so you can prove its precise value when new. By the way, don't even consider smuggling dope, stolen diamonds or other contraband in your handlebars. They all know that trick by now.

If you take your bike out of the country, take along some proof that you bought it at home. Otherwise you may find yourself paying duty on it

Handling the Casey Jones Syndrome—trains

I SHOULD ADMIT right off that I'm fond of trains. I've always had good vibes riding them and this may color what I have to say about them as far as cycling goes. Certainly, trains lose to airplanes on several counts: they are much slower; their cars are often antiquated, dirty and in disrepair; they are often poorly and erratically heated in winter; and trainmen are often insensitive to passengers' needs, if not downright insulting.

On the other hand, trains do not share with planes that annoying habit of occasionally falling out of the sky. This means that people you meet over a drink on a train are probably drinking out of congeniality rather than stark terror. Also, while conductors and stewards may sometimes be rude, for many of us it is a welcome relief from the frozen grins of airline stewardesses.

Plus, riding the train for eight hours or more is a great way to relax between cycling legs of a long trip. If you're alone you can meet new people by hanging out in the club car or just walking around. And if you're cycling with a group, you can usually find a place to talk, drink, play cards together or whatever, something difficult to do on a plane or bus.

In this country, riding a train usually means riding Amtrak. It's debatable whether train service has improved since Amtrak has taken over, but some definite changes have been made. Among them are movies and closed circuit television on some trains. Frankly though, these gimmicks will never outclass the scenery.

There is one more advantage to the train that a cyclist can appreciate. Train stations are usually located near the center of cities, near normal streets and roads. Airports, on the other hand, are usually located outside the cities they serve, and force cyclists to pedal into town on superhighways.

Amtrak's policy toward bicycles is extremely liberal. You can ride your bike to the station and check it through on the baggage car *as is*. For this Amtrak charges a $2 handling fee for as far as you are ticketed. This means the price is the same whether you're going three miles or three thousand. The bicycle is accepted in lieu of one of three pieces of baggage totaling 150 pounds allowed each Amtrak passenger.

This sounds simple and convenient enough in theory. But remember this is only Amtrak's *advertised* policy. In actual practice, we found dealing with train personnel more frustrating than dealing with any other kind of transportation personnel. At one station we were shuffled from person to person before we could find one who would re-confirm this policy. Most just pleaded ignorance, saying they didn't know anything about shipping bicycles. Others were downright nasty. But if you stick with it, you will eventually get your bike on the baggage car. And as time goes on, perhaps the bigwigs who set company policy will take the time to tell their employees about it.

Another negative point is the risk of damage. While the convenience of shipping a bike *as is* has been something for which cyclists have lobbied for years, it can be a jaded convenience. Amtrak seems to be serious about servicing cyclists, but at present they haven't developed an adequate system for handling bikes. Oftentimes bikes are harshly treated and packed too close to one another. Cyclists complain of retrieving scarred machines at their destinations. This, of course, varies from station to station and train to train depending on the baggage people. Hopefully the man who lugs your bike to the baggage car will be a Belgian immigrant who once raced in the Tour de France rather than a former vice president of the Ford Motor Co. who was thrown out of work by the bike boom. In any case, you might wrap the vulnerable parts of your bike (derailleur, cranks, brakes, cables) with furniture padding or other protection just to play it safe.

Amtrak seems to be serious about welcoming cyclists, but it doesn't have an adequate system for handling bikes

At this writing five Amtrak cities (New York, Washington, D.C., Minneapolis, Los Angeles and Chicago) have a limited supply of free cardboard cartons. You must pack your own bike, which is easy enough: remove pedals, loosen the handlebars and push them down and turn them sideways. Cartoning is especially advisable if you're ticketed on a long run that requires transferring the bike from one train to another.

No need to lock your bike since baggage cars are adequately

guarded. Amtrak automatically insures your bike for a lousy $25 but you can buy more insurance for 30 cents per $100 value.

Collapsible bicycles may be carried right into the passenger car of any Amtrak car and stowed in a vestibule or on an overhead luggage rack.

If you plan a trip, check out the two great Canadian railways, Canadian National and Canadian Pacific. Both offer continuous trans-continental routes (coast-to-coast on a single train) and charge you nothing extra for your bike. Among other comforts, the Canadian trains serve meals superior to most of the food you'll be offered on American trains.

The following is an easy-reference chart for American and Canadian trains along with some of the major European lines. While most of them charge only a nominal amount, one Mexican railroad employee pointed out that tipping the baggage master won't hurt you any. It's something to keep in mind should you meet any resistance to your bicycle. As you can see, only the Swiss railways offer any special plans for cyclists. The Swiss will rent you a three-speed bike for about $2.35 a day for the first day, $3 for each additional day.

Packing it on the bus

BY BUS, WE MEAN long-distance haulers, not intercity buses. As a general rule, you can't legally take a bike on any form of urban mass transit—buses, subways, streetcars, etc.—except under special circumstances.

But the two main U.S. interstate bus companies, Greyhound and Trailways, will accept bikes if they are cartoned. Trailways is the more liberal of the two. You need make no advance reservations or arrangements and there is no extra charge.

Greyhound has a more complicated policy. While your bike can ride the same bus you do, it does not go as your personal baggage, but rather as an express package. It must be checked separately, and charges vary according to weight and distance. Greyhound suggests you show up an hour before departure. The drawback is that the bike can be shipped only to a city with a terminal that handles package express.

Greyhound does make one exception. The company sells folding bikes for under $100 that it will let you stow as personal luggage in the bus's luggage compartment. For further information write:

Department NR
Greyhound Lines
Greyhound Tower
Phoenix, Ariz. 85077

RAIL	ACCEPT BIKES?	IN WHAT FORM?	ARRANGE-MENTS & COSTS	SPECIAL PLANS?
Amtrak	Yes	As is. Will be carried in baggage car.	$2.00	None
BRITRAIL (British railroad)	Yes	As is. Will be carried in baggage car.	Cost is ½ fare up to maximum of 3 pounds (roughly $7.50).	None
Canadian National	Yes	As is. Will be carried in baggage car.	No extra charge.	None
Canadian Pacific	Yes	As is. Will be carried in baggage car.	No extra charge.	None
French National Railroads	Yes	As is. Will be carried in baggage car.	Nominal charge.	None
German Federal Railroad	Yes	As is. Will be accepted only on trains with baggage cars.	Cost is 2 D. Marks (roughly 70 cents) regardless of length of trip.	None
Mexican Government Railroad	Yes	As is. Will be carried in baggage car.	No charge or nominal.	None
Scandinavian Railways	Yes	As is. Will be carried in baggage car.	About $1 per 500 km. (310 mi.) Bikes must be checked 72 to 24 hours ahead (48 hours in the summer).	None
Swiss Federal Railroad	Yes	As is. Will be carried in baggage car.	Nominal charge—$1.	Yes

No, we haven't forgotten about ships

OCEAN LINERS are still the most luxurious way to travel. It's too bad they don't let you keep your bike in your cabin since most liners have so much room you could sneak out for a midnight ride around the deck.

Cyclists are evidently a new phenomenon to the ship lines because the only major one with a definite policy is Cunard, which requires you to pack your machine in a carton and informs us they will take no responsibility for its safety. Cunard charges $10 per one-way voyage. While other lines have no definite policy, most allow passengers upward of 600 pounds in luggage, so you should be able to slip your bike in under this limit. If your two-wheeler runs over 600 pounds, I'd say your chances for an enjoyable cycle trip were slim anyhow. . . .

Most steamship lines allow 600 pounds in luggage, including a bike.

Schwinn photo

Chapter 12

Section 4: Fun on a bike

Racing . . . and lesser cycle sports

The man who had a matter of two minutes' lead in the race had an attack
of boils, which were very painful. He sat on the small of his back. . . .
The other riders joked him about his boils. He tapped on the table with
his fork. "Listen," he said, "tomorrow my nose is so tight on the handlebars that
the only thing touches those boils is a lovely breeze."

—From *The Sun Also Rises* by Ernest Hemingway
Reprinted with permission of Charles Scribner's Sons

BICYCLE RACING is pretty rough stuff. As in any other serious sport,
bike racers make tremendous sacrifices and suffer agonies to win. In
fact, most suffer a lot of pain just to lose. There's the pain of pushing
your body to its limits and then there are the medical hazards—boils
on the behind, broken collarbones from bad spills and other injuries.
This is why racing may not be for you (and if it isn't, there are some
less serious games described at the end of the chapter).

Anyone who has pedaled his 10-speed down an open stretch of road
past slower-moving cyclists has wondered in the back of his mind how
he would do in a real race. If you're willing to put in the time required
and you have no physical disability, there's no reason why you
shouldn't find out. Mind you, you probably won't become a champion.
Few do, but with work you can get yourself into good enough condition to ride with the pack—the minimum required before you can say
you were "in the race."

Be forewarned that cycle racing is not the same as touring at high
speed. Except for the bicycle, racing shares little in common with
touring. You're not there to enjoy the scenery, but to beat the other
guy.

If you join a racing club, you're unlikely to find warm camaradarie;
at least not while training or racing. Your fellow racers will likely be
grim individuals, more dedicated and fanatic than most other athletes.
I don't mean to exalt bike racers, but the obstacles placed in their path
often make it necessary for them to be more self-motivated than most
other sports competitors.

Dale Vergauwen, left, of Detroit, battles Jeff Spencer of Pasadena in a sprint race during the national championships.

Sandwiched between Demolition Derby and Evel Knieval

FIRST OF ALL, cycling as a sport is not encouraged in the U.S. It's not taught in the schools and gets little coverage in the press. So the man-in-the-street lumps the bicycle racer in the same category of curious sportsmen as members of the Olympic walking team and curling champions. His only chance to see the sport is on a TV sports show, where five-minute filler items on bike racing are sandwiched between more important events like Demolition Derby and guys who jump over trucks on motorcycles.

In Europe, bicycle racers are not considered freaks. Just about every country has bike races on local, national and international levels, and bicycle fans follow the careers of such racing stars as Eddy Merckx, Felice Gimondi and Luis Ocana with a fervor that would put to shame any bloodthirsty Monday-night football freak.

If we were somehow able to combine the World Series, the Superbowl, and the NBA and Stanley Cup playoffs into one sporting event (throwing in the St. Valentine's Day Massacre for good measure), we *might* approximate the excitement generated by the Tour de France, a three-week, 2000- to 3000-mile road race of the world's best cyclists. During the Tour, even one racer's boils and another's hemorrhoids become the subjects of in-depth newspaper features.

European racing money is strictly big-time. Merckx, for example, averages $400,000 per year just for his racing efforts. He makes even more for endorsing products. And not just bicycle products, but chewing gum, razor blades, etc., just like football stars in the U.S.

In Europe, cycling is a big-money sport. A champ can make $400,000 a year—and that doesn't even include endorsements

Cyclists race en masse toward St. Etienne on the 17th lap of the 1968 Tour de France. Rolf Wolfshol of Germany (second from right, wearing the Bic hat) leads the race at this point. The leader of the race traditionally wears the maillot jaune—*a yellow jersey. Winning just one stage of the Tour can mean fame and fortune for a rider because of the resulting product endorsements. The Tour lasts three weeks and attracts the world's greatest cyclists.*

Wide World Photo

*Jackie Simes of Closter, New Jersey, has been America's foremost
track racer in recent years, and one of this country's few real
professionals. In 1968 he placed second in the kilometer time
trials during the world championships in Uruguay, and thus became
the only American to win a medal in world championship competition
during the 1960s. He has also raced extensively in Europe, and
in the 1968 Olympics in Mexico City. His victories in Europe
have made his name familiar to sports fans abroad. Contrast that
with this country, where few sports fans have ever heard of him
because of the lack of press coverage of cycling. Today Simes
spends most of his time running his bike store in Nanuet, New
York, though he occasionally still races professionally. In 1973
he coached the American track team in the world championships
in Spain, where the U.S. won its first gold medal in 50 years.*

American cyclists receive no such adulation—or money. So the
people you meet racing are bound to be a no-nonsense group. They're
into racing, not because they seek the roar of the crowd or because it's
the thing to do, but because they believe in it.

Second, the American motorist's attitude toward cyclists in general
militates against racing. If you live in a large city you'll find it nearly
impossible to find a good road where you can practice freely at high
speed without interference from traffic. Because of this, dedicated urban
racers often arise at four or five in the morning to practice before the
roads are polluted with cars and the air is polluted with their exhaust.

In Europe, a motorist pulls out of the way for a cyclist; in America, bike racing is a kind of underground subculture

Jim Huetter of Buffalo, New York, leads two other racers through a tight turn in an Allentown, Pennsylvania, criterium. Note shift levers mounted on the tips of his handlebars.

And official races themselves are often somewhat spoiled by the angry American traffic, which seems reluctant to give up even a small portion of the road to a group of cyclists. Compare this to France, where even teen-age events merit a police escort that warns automobiles of the racers' approach.

Whereas European racing stars' names are household words and motrists pull out of the way for cyclists, the American racing world is a kind of underground subculture, whose stars glide silently about in the early hours of the morning, unknown and unappreciated by the general public.

Yet once you enter that subculture, you'll find a potent vitality. Bike people have their own standards, vocabulary and—though they rarely make the headlines—their own heroes: such people as pro track racers Jackie Simes and John VandeVelde, roadmen John Howard, John Allis, Wayne Stetina, and the brother-sister team of Roger and Sheila Young. Roger is a national sprint champion, Sheila the women's world sprint champion. (By the way, unlike Eddie Merckx, Sheila does not make a million dollars a year. In 1973, when she became world champion, she had to fight to get an extra $100 food money so she could make the trip to Spain to win the title.)

Sorting out types of races

IF YOU'RE STILL interested, let's take a look at *some* of the types of races that are run for cyclists. We can't cover them all because there are zillions—indoor races, outdoor races, pitting one team against another, one man against another or one man against no one but a clock. But we'll talk about the main events, and the rest are usually variations in length of these same races (for example, the half-mile sprint is a variation of the more popular 1000-meter sprint).

In general, there are two main types of racing: road and track.

Road racing comes in two shapes—called massed-start and time trial. The *massed start* is the basic race, a group of hyper-adrenalined racers hunkered up to a starting line, each determined to be the first across the finish line that can be almost any distance away: 10, 25, 40, 100 or 3000 miles—or any distance in between. Massed-start road races include: the *long road race, criteriums, stage races* and the *cyclo-cross*.

The *long road race* is the most popular and has the most ambiguous title, in that *long* can mean anything. In the U.S., these races vary from 25 to 140 miles. The U.S. road-racing championship, for instance, is run over a 120-mile course. The winner of this event will cover the distance in about 4¾ hours for an average speed of 26 mph.

Much less grueling than the long road race is the *criterium*, a much shorter race held over a course about a mile long which includes a variety of tight curves. The racers are required to make several laps around the course (usually for about 25 miles). Though the race doesn't demand the superstamina of a longer road race, it does require the riders to demonstrate superior cornering and handling skills. Normally, a rider will choose a lighter bicycle for a criterium, since it needn't stand up for a hundred miles, and one with steeper tube angles and a shorter wheelbase for faster cornering.

Both criteriums and the longer road races can be handicapped, using a staggered start in which weaker or less experienced riders start first with the faster riders given a later separate start.

The *stage race* is a superlong road race that proceeds in stages—say 100 or more miles per day. Stage races are rare in the U.S. but common in Europe, the most famous being the Tour de France. By the way, the length and course of this greatest of all tours varies from year to year, being laid out annually by *L'Equipe*, France's leading sports journal. The 1972 race, for example, ran 2400 miles in 20 uneven stages. And while many have been longer (some around the 3000-mile mark), difficulty is not always determined sheerly by length. In fact, the shorter Tours may be rougher in that they may include more mountains. The '72 Tour ran over half of its stages in the mountains, and of the 139 who started the race, only 88 sprinted into Paris on the final day, the rest having been eliminated by broken collarbones, exhaustion, fear of the 55-mph descents down the mountains or the sudden realization that it just wasn't worth it to them personally.

The Tour de France ran over 2400 miles, many through mountains. Of 139 who started the race, 88 sprinted into Paris the last day

272

Wayne Stetina leads a muscular pack in a Canadian stage race.

Another kind of mongrel massed-start race is the *cyclo-cross*. This is
a combination of cross-country running and cycling that attracts a
select group of self-flagellants. The course consists of part road, part
field, part valley, part hill and part stream. In short, it's a mix of natural
obstacles that guarantees the cyclist will have to dismount and run
with his bike over his shoulder more than once. Because of the varied
terrain, a cyclo-cross race is not very long, about 2 to 15 miles at
most, and it may demand as much running as pedaling. The winner is
the first one across the finish line with his bike. The bicycle normally
used is a five- or six-speed (only one chainwheel) rather than the road
racer's standard 10-speed.

The second type of road racing is the *time trial*. Time trials can be
held over varied terrain and varied distances, and are distinguished
from massed-start races in that participants are started at one-minute
intervals. The cyclists therefore never really race directly against each
other, but against the clock, the best time winning. Time trials are won
by pure speed unlike massed-start races in which strategy plays a big
part.

While some cyclists do well in both massed-starts and time trials,
the two different types require different temperaments. A time trial is
very close to being a purely physical event, with the racer trying to
squeeze everything out of his body that he can without regard to the
other cyclists, whom he probably never sees during the race. The
massed-start is more of a total human involvement, requiring speed, of

Robert F. George photo

273

course, but also cunning, nerve, composure and also a little acting ability with which to psyche an opponent.

Sometimes time trials are team events. On a two-man team, time is taken on the first rider to cross the line; with three or four men, it is taken on the second to last man to cross the line; and on five and above, time is stopped on the third to last man across the line.

A *hill climb* is just what its name implies—a grueling time trial up a monster hill. This is really a specialty event; if you think about it, the idea of riding nowhere but uphill doesn't make much sense. Bicycles are based on the machine called the wheel, which increases the effi-

Sue Novara leads Sue Gurney through a turn in a national championship track race. She must stay between the parallel lines during the final 200 meters because she is leading. Ms. Novara was the 1974 national sprint champ and 1974 world silver medalist.

Robert F. George photo

ciency of the human body by converting its momentum into a smooth and continuous forward motion. Unfortunately this only works well on level ground or going downhill. Going uphill, a bicycle is extremely inefficient, especially since the wheels want to convert the force of gravity of your body into a smooth, *backward* motion. That is why during a recent bicycle hill-climb assault on Mt. Washington, a jogger easily beat the winning cyclist up the mountain (the cyclist, by the way, was no slouch—he set a cycling record for Mt. Washington).

Bicycling in a bowl—track racing

ROAD RACES ARE more common in the United States simply because they're easier to run. All that's required is a bunch of racers and a road. Less common is the *track race*. Tracks, indoor or outdoor, are rare because they're so expensive to build ($75,000 or so). For that reason only a few can be found in this country. They are located in New York City; Encino, California; San Jose, California; Kenosha and Milwaukee, Wisconsin; Northbrook, Illinois; Portland, Oregon; Detroit, Michigan; and St. Louis, Missouri.

Like road racing, track racing comes in different shapes and sizes, but probably the most exciting event is the *match sprint*. The most common distance is the 1000-meter sprint for single riders and the 2000-meter sprint for tandem riders. This race is probably the most difficult for the casual spectator to understand, since for most of the 1000 meters (in the case of single riders), the cyclists seem to be trying to lose rather than win. Here's the scoop:

While the race is run over 1000 meters, only the last 200 meters is timed since no one can really sprint all-out for the entire distance. So the first 800 meters usually finds the racers crawling along jockeying for position until they make their mad dash that last 200 meters from the line. The times recorded over this final sprint distance are usually in the 11- or 12-second category, but the entire race sometimes lasts 30 minutes or more.

A simple case of riding against the clock is the *kilometer time trial*. It obviously is also 1000 meters long, but in this race the cyclist turns it on from the start, since the entire ride is timed. The racer is put on the track all by himself and goes as fast as he can. And he must do it from a standing start. This is a grueling race, similar to the 440 in track, since it is not really a sprint and not really a distance event. It is also one of the few events which has seen an American triumph in world competition. Jackie Simes III of Closter, New Jersey, in 1968 placed second at the world championships in Uruguay. Times in the kilometer run about one minute 11 seconds or so (for the winners).

Another track race, in which both individuals and teams participate, is the *pursuit*. Two evenly matched individuals or teams start out on opposite ends of the track and try to catch each other over a distance of 4000 meters (usually). Since it rarely happens that one opponent catches the other, the winners are those who complete the course in the shortest time.

When pursuit teams race each other, however, time is usually taken on the second to last rider to cross the finish line. As in the case of the four-man teams which participate in the Olympics, time is taken on the third man across.

A pursuit team is a beautiful thing to watch. Each rider takes his turn leading the team, setting the pace and breaking the wind for the rest of the team. The four riders follow right on each other's wheels to take advantage of the wind-break. The changing of the lead is most impressive if done right. The lead rider speeds up, then suddenly swings a few feet up toward the top of the track, lets his teammates pass him, and drops down smoothly behind the third rider just behind his rear wheel. When executed perfectly this maneuver looks like one smooth motion. If done awkwardly the new leader will have to slow down to avoid hitting the departing leader or the latter may drop back too far behind the third rider and have to pedal hard to catch up with his team. Don't underestimate the effect that changing leads like this has on the final time. A four-man team can cover the 4000 meters about 25 seconds faster than a single racer.

Another pursuit race is the *Australian pursuit*. Two teams, eight men each, are spaced out evenly on the track. Any team member passed by someone on the other team is automatically out of the race. And if you like your races even more complicated, there's the *Italian pursuit*, which uses two or more teams each with three to five riders. After each lap, a man from each team drops out until the last lap when one rider from each team finishes the race. The fastest time wins.

The individuality of tracks

EXCEPT FOR THE last two kinds of pursuit races, each of the track races described are Olympic events. There are specific rules governing all these races. But ironically, with the regulations in track racing, there are no uniform standards regarding the construction of the track itself. So before we get into the more exotic kinds of track races, let's take a look at the surface all these cyclists race on.

Despite the lack of standards, there are some similarities from track to track. The shape is usually oval, with curves and straightaways. Two parallel lines serve as the start and finish lines. Another line 200 meters before the finish indicates the sprint distance. On opposite sides of the track are lines which mark starting points for pursuit races. Ringing the inside diameter of the track are two parallel lines about a meter apart. Once the leader of a sprint race drops into position at the bottom of the track's bowl to make his sprint, he must stay between these lines (so that his opponent has room to get around him). Finally, there is one more line marking the upper limits of the track called the stayer's rope (this named after the motor-paced racer, or

Robert F. George photo

Clara Teyssier whirls through a pursuit race. It's virtually impossible for her to see her opponent since pursuit racers start at opposite sides of the track and try to catch each other.

stayer, whose high speed behind a motorcycle keeps him higher on the oval).

All these elements are common to tracks everywhere. There the resemblance ends, however. Any material, including wood, asphalt, concrete or even packed earth can be used for the surface of the track. Tracks can vary between 100 and 1000 meters in length and can be banked between 25 and 50 degrees. Even their width can vary from five to nine meters.

Other track events

THERE ARE A FEW other types of track races worth mentioning. In *handicap* races each rider is placed on the starting line according to his ability. The course is a short one, a quarter or half mile. For those who like surprises there is the *mystery* race where the number of laps is chosen secretly and at random just before the race starts. Only the officials know what the number is—and they ain't telling until the leading rider completes the next to last lap. Those who bargained on a short race may have played themselves out by the time the gun lap is sounded and those who hung back in the pack expecting a longer run may not be able to sprint to the front in time. It's a bad race for a cyclist with ulcers.

Another weirdie is an event known as *le Madison* to the French. It's named after the sadistic six-day bicycle race that used to be held in the old Madison Square Garden in post-depression days. For six days cyclists were required to spend most of the time pedaling. As riders became drowsy a lot of messy accidents occurred.

Today a version of this race is still run, only it's now just called a *six-day race*. In fact, the six-day race is one of the few *professional* track races you'll find in the United States. In recent years such races have been staged in Los Angeles and Detroit.

The format is intriguing. First of all, the riders do race for six days, but not continuously, the time ridden each day varying from race to race. Each team has two men, but only one races at a time. What's unique is the method of changing riders. The non-racing partner will circle the oval on the outside or top of the track, and on a prearranged turn he speeds up, drops into the race lanes and is flung into the competition by his teammate who grabs him by the hand or by a handle sewn into his racing pants. This can make for an exciting race, especially if one rider is wearing cheap shorts which occasionally are ripped off by an over-zealous partner. America's most successful professional six-day racers in recent years have been the team of Jackie Simes and John VandeVeld.

For indoor types there are also *roller* races. Pedaling his bike while perched atop rollers usually used for exercising, the rider goes nowhere, like someone walking on a moving belt. These are very big in Japan where an odometer is hooked up to the rollers and the cyclists "ride" to see who can crank up the most mileage in a set amount of time. This has to be one of the most boring of bike events and I only mention it here as a curiosity item.

Finally, the most dangerous of all weird events is not strictly a track or a road event, and isn't even purely a bicycle race. This is *motor-paced* racing and requires a motorized vehicle of some sort (motorcycle, car, train) for the cyclists to pedal behind. The car or motorcycle plows through the air for the cyclist who follows in its wake. Racers sometimes compete directly against each other on a track, but the event is really made to order for breaking speed records. The bicycle used usually has a smaller front wheel and a huge chainwheel for a high gear ratio. The pacing vehicle has a special roller protruding from the back so that if the front wheel of the bicycle hits it the cyclist won't go down from the impact. Motor-paced racers routinely hit speeds of

In a roller race (very large in Japan) you cycle indoors and don't go anywhere. You pedal like fury, perched atop rollers

50 to 60 mph. In Europe these cyclists are also called *stayers*, and the event *demi-fond*.

Cyclists who go after speed records in this fashion are genuine daredevils. Jose Meiffret of France set a record in 1962 that remained unbroken for over a decade. He hit a speed at that time of 127.243 mph! Then in 1973 an American finally broke the record by pedaling 138.674 mph on the Bonneville salt flats (Allan Abbott, a physician from San Bernardino, California).

Both set their records behind racing cars. Abbott's bike was built on a frame very similar to a motorcycle and weighed 35 pounds. The wheels were only 18 inches in diameter and the chainwheel had 230 teeth, connected to a rear sprocket of 13 teeth.

Motorpaced racing is the zaniest of all events. The world's record is 138.674 mph pedaled across the Bonneville salt flats

One danger of this kind of bicycling is the jeopardy of falling too far behind the pace car, in which case you can be caught in the tremendous air turbulence that converges just a few feet behind the vehicle.

Ideally, you should have two bicycles

MOST CYCLISTS who have a yen to race will choose road racing rather than track. Road races are more common than track events and, for most people, they also come closer to real life (riding on a road from one point to another rather than circling around a specially surfaced track).

Therefore, you say, the guy who plans to work only the road needs only his road bike. Right? Wrong. Ideally, he also should have a fixed-gear track bike. When getting into shape during the late winter or early spring, the fixed-wheel will hone your pedaling form faster than your freewheeling 10-speed. It keeps your legs moving constantly and works you harder. Its quick handling can also boost your agility. Now, it's not absolutely necessary that you purchase two bicycles, but having that fixed wheel can definitely help. It will also introduce you to track bikes and perhaps you'll find track racing is more your style than road racing.

To save on money, don't get a competition-grade track bike. Buy a straight-gauge standard machine if you'll just use it for conditioning. You should be able to get by for about $150 for a 23- or 24-pound bike. If you're spending the money for a special-order bike, I'd suggest one with road-length cranks and a road drive (chainwheel, rear sprocket and chain). Most track racers prefer cranks 165 mm long. Road cranks are usually 170 mm. The extra length provides a little more leverage for hills. Road cranks also have a lip that will accept two chainwheels. You need only one chainwheel, so track cranks are in order, but get them in the 170 mm length. This will better prepare you for your road bike.

A track powertrain usually includes a chainwheel and rear sprocket that are slightly thicker than road gears, along with a thicker chain to fit them. This gives sprinters a little extra grab when they really turn it on. If you're a beginner in this sport, get the thinner road gears and chain. And try to get the same brand chainwheel that you have on your road bike (or one that attaches to the cranks in an identical way). The reason for this is that it makes it easier to use the chainwheels from your road bike on the track bike and thereby have three different gear ratios readily available. For instance, if your 10-speed has chainwheels of 47 and 52 teeth, get a 49-tooth road chainwheel with your track bike. If you're a real stickler for accuracy, you'll have to change the chain length every time you bolt on a new gear, but there's no need to do this if you're not going to race the bike. Just adjust the rear wheel in the rear drop-outs to compensate for different chainwheels.

If you ever decide really to race the bike on a track, you may want to switch to shorter cranks. However, you should be able to leave the road drive on, since many riders are switching to this set-up for track use anyway—especially on the longer events.

Stick also to road rims. Fiamme, for instances, makes special Yellow Label track rims which weigh only 270 grams apiece. They won't hold on the road, so don't use them. Get the lightest-weight road rims instead.

Now for the bike you'll actually be racing on. Too much is made of the superiority of one kind of equipment over another since races are usually won by riders, not bikes. But there's no use handicapping yourself with a bike not really built for high speed. I therefore suggest that you don't try to race on your medium-priced or economy touring bike, even though it may have gotten you across North America, South America and Asia in great style. By this I mean a bike weighing over 25 pounds with clincher tires and a wide range of gears. You'll want close-ratio gears, sew-up tires, and rims and a frame made of Reynolds 531, Columbus, Super Vitus, Titanium or similar tubing. This generally means a minimum of $250.

Don't try to race on your touring bike, even though it may have carried you around the world

If you're into track racing, you'll only need a track bike. But if you're this far along you've probably also got a road bike anyway. Most track racers prefer a frame that's a little smaller than their road bike, by about an inch or so. This gives them a shorter profile against the wind, though it forces them to pedal in a rather uncomfortable position.

There are different designs for different track events. Sprint machines, for example, generally are stiffer, with more upright seat and head tubes and a straighter front fork. Pursuit and other longer events require a slightly "softer" bicycle. However, it's obviously too costly for most prospective racers to go out and buy a bike for each event. Luckily, most of the production bikes now on the market are of the all-purpose type. The Schwinn Paramount is just one example of an all-purpose track bike and serves many racers well in a variety of events. If you're definite you will be either a sprinter or a six-day racer, the Raleigh track model is a good example of a stiff, upright machine.

Most production track models are made with Reynolds 531, certainly adequate tubing. But if you're going to put in a special order for a bike, you might consider specifying one of the heavier types of Columbus tubing, especially if you feel your major interests in track will be sprinting or six-day racing. This will result in a heavier bike, but don't let this dissuade you. Never get hung up on weight in a racing bike, since stiffness is always more important than light weight when it comes to sprinting. In the six-day events you need the extra durability. Some excellent track bikes weigh 20 pounds and more, and there are also some real losers in the 15-pound range. The savings in weight is no good if the frame soaks up all your energy with its flexibility.

The titanium-frame track bike is making a name in world competition. This model from Teledyne, ridden by Ron Skarin, weighs only 11½ pounds. Most track bikes are made of conventional steel tubing and weigh around 18 pounds, still considerably less than road bikes because they have no brakes or derailleurs.

Robert F. George photo

Wide World photo

Wow! Cyclo-cross races involve both cycling and running. This racer took a spill in the Netherlands national championship when he tried to ride down a muddy hill.

Teledyne Linair Engineering has built an 11½-pound titanium track bike, but it's not available to just anybody right now. At this writing, models of this bicycle are being built for professional Jackie Simes and for world sprint champion Sheila Young. If you're in that class, maybe you can persuade Teledyne to build one for you too.

Other specialty events that definitely require special bikes are cyclo-cross and motor-pacing. Lightness *is* essential for a cyclo-cross bike since you spend a good deal of time carrying the damn thing. The frame should be the opposite of a track frame—you want a flexible design that will have plenty of give to absorb the brutality of off-road pedaling. The frame should also have a high bottom bracket for ground clearance and you'll want a chainwheel guard to help keep mud off (sort of). The tires used have special knobby treads.

The rider sits low on the bike so he can use his feet for skid control. Normally five- or six-speeds are used, but not always. A multi-speed bike is not such a great advantage once you leave the road, so some riders use a single-speed freewheel bike with a fairly low gear instead.

What the well-dressed racer wears

BICYCLE RACERS aren't the type you find pouring over the latest issue of *Gentleman's Quarterly,* but they do take some care selecting their clothes. What the well-dressed bicyclist wears often depends on the kind of racing he does and what the weather is like if he's racing outdoors. His basic wardrobe includes special shoes, shorts, shirts, gloves and helmet.

Racing shoes are useless for anything but pedaling. They are usually narrow black leather shoes with holes for ventilation in the uppers and soles to let your rank feet breathe. Their snug fit lets the foot slip easily into the toeclips and straps. Some models have a stiff fiberglass sole, but most have a stiff leather sole, sometimes with a piece of metal sandwiched in to give you a responsive feel to pedaling.

Attached to the bottom of the shoe is a metal cleat with grooves running horizontally to fit neatly over the raised edges of the rattrap pedal. In the case of the cyclo-cross cyclist these may also have two spikes, one on each side, to give traction when he's running with his bike on his back.

For colder climates you can get fur-lined, high-cut shoes that are waterproof. These are worn by the fanatic amateurs who want to race in crummy weather and the professional cyclist who sometimes must. Unless you anticipate a lot of winter pedaling the low-cut style should be adequate both for racing and long touring trips if that's where your interest leads you. A snug but comfortable fit is essential in buying bike shoes to minimize foot problems and to keep your pedaling efficiency at its peak.

You feel like you are sitting on a wet sponge with two razors inside. But there are good solutions to the problem of protecting your vital parts

Saving your tender parts

ANYONE WHO'S pedaled any distance on a hot or even a not-so-hot day knows that one of the areas of greatest discomfort will be that part of you which covers the bicycle seat. Even if the saddle is comfortable and well broken in, there are still problems that can plague you. Perspiration builds up, and the seams in your underpants and pants are at first a little irritating, then annoying and ultimately downright painful. You feel like you're sitting on a wet sponge with two razors inside it.

Fortunately a solution exists. There are special tight-fitting cycling shorts made of wool or cotton with a reinforcement patch of soft chamois in the crotch. They prevent any direct rubbing on the inside of the rider's legs. They soak up moisture while at the same time giving ventilation and comfort to the crotch area. No underwear is ever worn with them because none is needed for maximum comfort. They're the best solution yet devised for you and your tender spot. You can get a pair of wool racing shorts from the American Youth Hostel store, 132 Spring Street, New York, N.Y. 10012 for about $19 and a pair of

Rider wears both a helmet and a Fuji racing cap. The pack on the front of the bike is not normal gear for a racer, but this cyclist is participating in a 24-hour marathon.

Pepsi-Cola photo

cotton shorts for $11. Or you can probably get them through a local racing club (to which you should belong if you're going to race seriously).

If a good pair of shorts is temporarily beyond your means, a workable substitute is a pair of cut-off sweat pants. Although they're not as comfortable as the genuine article, they're a hundred percent improvement over a pair of cut off jeans or any old pair of shorts. If you plan to get involved in racing though, the more expensive shorts are a must.

Another part of the racer's uniform is the racing jersey. These are short-sleeved and usually made of wool for the same reason as the shorts—ventilation and sweat absorption. They soak up the rider's sweat without that wet-rag feeling you get wearing a cotton T-shirt or sweatshirt. Like the shorts these are close-fitting and not cheap. Prices run from $12 to $20 depending on the brand and where they are bought. Again one place that carries them is the AYH store.

For the rider's convenience jerseys usually have three pockets in the front and two in the back for carrying such items on road races as food, maps, spare tires, pictures of the family cat, anything the rider wants close at hand. In a big race they are emblazoned with the name of the rider's club or sponsor.

Not all jerseys are made of absorbent material. The one worn by track and time trial riders is usually made of a silk or nylon material which absorbs almost no perspiration. Its chief value lies in the fact that it is so low in wind resistance. Since these racers are not usually pedaling for any great length of time, the discomfort of wearing this kind of jersey is minimal.

If your heart or budget is not quite up to buying the ultimate jersey, you probably can make do with a good sweatshirt and a light nylon jacket that breathes a little. With this combination you can cut down on the chilling effect of the wind while letting moisture escape from your body. It's not as comfortable as *the* jersey, but it ain't bad.

For pedaling around in cooler weather, a little better protection is in order. For practicing or even racing in cold weather, there are long-sleeved versions of the bicycling jersey made of wool and special tight-fitting leg warmers that take the place of shorts. They give the rider that warm-all-over feeling, and for extra warmth you might even wear a pair of cycling shorts over the longies.

Or, if you haven't yet cut off those sweat pants, you can make them do by tucking the legs into a pair of knee socks so they don't get torn to shreds in your chainwheel.

If you're insane enough to take a try at cyclo-cross, you might include in your wardrobe long-legged pants and racing jerseys to protect yourself against brambles and other hostile vegetables. Things will be rough enough without having to worry about getting clawed to death by a wall of thorns.

Although sometimes considered optional, headgear—the racing helmet and the cycling cap—can be worth their weight in titanium. The helmet hardly looks like what it claims to be. It reminds me of those animals people used to make by twisting together a group of long skinny balloons. It consists of a padded leather tube that goes around the head horizontally with three tubes crossing the top of the head from front to back. The whole thing is held to the rider's skull by a chin strap. It is required in all Amateur Bicycle League of America races.

The advantage of this design is that it offers the cyclist some head protection while giving his head ventilation and keeping the sweat out of his eyes—and all for very little weight.

A newer, less common style is a lightweight, plastic bowl-shaped model that fits over the head and gives a little more protection—for the safety conscious rider who wants to remain conscious. Cyclists who participate in official races outside their clubs are usually required to wear some style of helmet according to the laws of the governing racing organization.

Another handy and more or less optional piece of headgear is the cycling cap, usually made of lightweight cotton with a short stiff brim and an elastic head band.

Most people would think the last thing an overheated rider would want is a hat on his head. But it does come in handy. It absorbs sweat and the brim can be popped down to shield the rider's eyes from the sun, wind, rain and the grit other riders may splash up in his face.

One other item of clothing that deserves mention is a pair of bicycling gloves. These are usually designed with half-fingers, a leather palm and a fabric back. They give the rider a good grip on the handlebars, absorb sweat (more sweat around here!), and on long rides prevent chafing and blisters from developing. They also give some protection against skinning a hand in the event of a crackup.

For track racers with their fixed gears (remember, no brakes) there are gloves with an extra thickness of leather on the palms. The reason for this is that a track racer may slow down his bike by holding his gloved hand against the front wheel.

More merciless cold weather will dictate thicker gloves such as ski gloves for protection; or, if the weather also warrants it, goggles.

A contest of spartans

GETTING THE RIGHT bike and the right clothes is the easy part. Now—race!

Anyway you look at it, racing is a competitive, not a social, pastime. When racers go out for even an unofficial club race, they're not out there to have a leisurely good time joshing, coasting, poking along the road with their buddies. They're out there trying to grow stronger, faster, more agile, generally more skilled on two wheels than anyone else in the field. In short, it takes a killer mentality. If you're the type of person who likes to beat other people, racing is for you.

If you just like to bicycle, though, it may not be for you. Even if you've had a lot of experience as a tourist and are looking for a change of pace, racing may be too radical a change. Commenting on would-be racers who were avid bike trippers, Louis Maltese of the Century Road Club in New York (who has over 40 years of experience in both professional and club racing) remarked: "We get some people who maybe traveled across country or took a long trip of a couple thousand miles. They come here and expect to do well racing, maybe muscle out the race. The fact is, they don't do well at all. The speed kills them. Some get the hang of it. But most eventually drop out."

So if you've worried about embarrassing yourself with a racing club and wonder what standards you'll be competing against, give yourself a taste of what it's like before joining up. First, go watch a few races. Watching the cyclists will give you a rough visual idea of the speeds and the physical abilities of the riders. Visit a local club that you might join and take a look at the times recorded at their time trials. This will give you something to aim for.

Give yourself a test, and if the feeling of pushing your body to the maximum turned you on, you are halfway home

Then give yourself a couple of weeks of moderate road training. Try riding at least 20 miles a day (or night) for one week (six days out of the seven). If you can do this without much trouble, push it up to 30 miles per day the second week.

Now give yourself a test. Map out a 40-mile course (over roads you're familiar with) and see if you can ride it in under two hours. That's 20 mph (and a bit slow for a racer) but a helluva good start for a beginner. More important than your time, however, is whether you liked it or not. If you were slow, but the feeling of pushing your body to the maximum turned you on, you've got it half made.

Cycling organizations to look into

ONCE YOU'VE DECIDED to take the plunge, it will behoove you to join a racing club of some sort. You can develop the physical stamina and speed you need on your own, but for tactics, tricks and other skills required for riding in a group, you'll have to ride with other racers who know what they're doing.

The racing organization in the U.S. is the Amateur Bicycle League of America (ABLA). At this writing, a membership costs $3 for anyone under 18 and $5 for those 18 and over. You get the paper *Cyclenews* free with your membership. For information on joining you can write to the ABLA national headquarters at P.O. Box 669, Wall Street Station, New York, N.Y. 10005, or better yet, write to your state representative listed at the end of this chapter. (If you want *Cyclenews* but don't want to join the ABLA, write the monthly racing journal at 12 Cherry Street, Brattleboro, Vermont 05301. At this writing, a yearly subscription costs $2.50.)

Members of the ABLA participate in the national bicycle championships, Pan American Games and the Olympics. The top riders from every state compete in the national championships, and the ABLA also chooses and trains riders for the Pan Am Games and the Olympics. The state representative can put you in contact with clubs in your area.

Sponsored vs. unsponsored clubs

ONCE YOU have your ABLA license, as they call it, sign up for a club *muy fasto*. There are two kinds, sponsored and, logically enough, unsponsored. A club with a sponsor usually doesn't have to worry about financing transportation for its riders or entry fees, and usually has a more elaborate training and racing program. Members of clubs without sponsors usually pay their own entry fees for races, pay their own transportation, etc.

Because of the extra advantages they offer, sponsored clubs usually attract the more dedicated and skillful riders. If you don't feel you're up to this club's intense kind of competition right away in spite of the advantages, then you may opt for the unsponsored club where the competition may be a little less intense. This assumes, of course, that

Racing is not a social pastime. As a matter of fact, it takes a killer mentality

you are offered a choice. You may have no alternative to riding with an unsponsored group.

There are those who say that the high level of competition in sponsored clubs will give you much more of a challenge. But the fact is that

Not all unsponsored clubs belong in the now-it's-time-for-cookies group

not all unsponsored clubs are of the once-around-the-block-and-go-for-cookies category and are certainly a good place to start for someone unsure of his racing seriousness. After all, if you find yourself hankering after more of a challenge (and those free goodies), you can always switch to another club later on. Most unsponsored clubs encourage their more talented and ambitious riders to do this, and watch them move on with some pride.

A prejudiced vote against sponsored-club domination

THERE IS A CURRENT movement toward sponsored clubs. This is both good and bad. Good because it points the way toward more professional races, which means more interest in racing, which means top riders coming in from Europe and Japan, and just a higher level of excitement all around.

However, some racing spokesmen have made a push to limit ABLA races to sponsored clubs. I think a de-emphasis of purely amateur, shoestring-budget competition is a mistake. Granted, its demise is not a current problem. The top concern, as seen by many promoters and cyclists, is that high-class American racers can't afford to get themselves here and there for races, and have to beg for food money so they can bop off to Spain to win world championships.

What American racing enthusiasts would like to see is a European-type racing scene in this country. While this is fine for professionals, it's not the ideal scene for every racer to aspire to. Many cyclists have an idealized view of racing, especially road racing. It means going cross-country over normal, everyday roads at a high rate of speed with no help from an engine. There's a purity and a beauty to a race of this sort. And if it's just an amateur race with no spectators, held in the early morning hours to avoid the traffic, so much the better. It's rider against rider in the solitude of the morning, not money against money. One of the appeals of bicycling is that the cyclist relies purely on his body, with help from a very simple machine which he can instantly repair himself should it break down. And pure amateur club racing maintains this ideal. Professional (and sponsored amateur) racing is a far cry from it.

A parade of macaroni and beer

A CYCLIST'S FIRST VIEW of a professional road race can be a supreme disappointment. The riders are beautiful to watch to be sure. But the sponsors really detract from the spectacle.

First of all, the racers look like walking (or rather, pedaling) billboards, with brand names plastered all over their jerseys, shorts, caps and bikes. Perhaps you've seen photos of Eddy Merckx with the word "Molteni" written all over his body. Molteni is an Italian brand of macaroni. Other racers and their teams are sponsored by beer companies, bubble gum, coffee, all the usual crap. Secondly, the racers are followed through the course by their sponsors' cars, sometimes done up in the shape of their products: beer bottles, cigarette packs and other insanities.

Finally, the whole idea of a cyclist's self-sufficiency is destroyed. When a racer ruins a tire, a wheel or a bike, one of his mechanics in a trailing car tosses him a whole new part—usually this means a wheel, but sometimes a whole new bicycle. Remember that sew-up tires were invented so racers could change flats in a hurry. Well, even in American amateur events a racer who changed his own tires would definitely lose, since most of his competition have lackeys to toss them whole new wheels.

The point is this: All-professionalism is great for professionals— guys who make their living at it. But it's not all that beautiful for the amateur. So don't put yourself down or bewail your station in life if

World champ Eddy Merckx of Belgium and teammate Joseph Bruyere ride to victory in a two-man-team time trial, prologue to the 1974 Paris-Nice road race. Note team car with replacement bikes.

all you can hook up with is an unsponsored club. Many cyclists who have turned into successful pros, says Louis Maltese, return later in life to their original unsponsored clubs. In many ways it is the most pleasant way to race.

And you don't have to advertise macaroni on your jersey.

The secret to racing success revealed!

YOU HAVE TO RIDE a lot. That's it. Ride as much as you can and you'll learn everything you need to know on your own. Training regimens vary, but all racers recommend that you ride, ride, ride.

There are some other things you can do, however, and some methods of training that can help you make the most of your riding. Now, let's make it clear that if these suggestions don't work for you, drop them immediately.

Sheila Young, for example, world sprint champion, ignores the standard advice of starting out on low gears. She's a world-class speed skater and the skate season cuts into her training time so she cuts corners by starting out in high gears. It works for her. However, if you're new to the sport, stick to orthodox training methods at first. Let's start at the beginning of the year, which for most of us means (yech) winter.

Professional racers ride in all sorts of lousy weather. Here the pack labors through snow and slush in the 1973 Paris-Nice race.

How do you train in the snow?

YOU DON'T. Road experience is best, but with snow on the ground or the temperature under 20 degrees, you'll have to do some alternate exercises. There are two areas a cyclist must worry about: his wind (cardio-vascular development) and his legs. Choose activities that develop both. Jumping rope, running, skating, basketball, and cross-country skiing are all excellent. If you have to choose between doing an exercise intensely for a short period of time or leisurely for a lengthy period, choose the latter, especially if you want to race longer road events. Ideally, do both. For instance, if your thing is running, do a sprint-jog, sprint-jog routine.

If you can stand the boredom, bicycle rollers are a good idea. They're expensive, though, close to $100, and work best with a track bike. Pedal with low gear values (about 60 inches) and try to wind up those rpms.

One sport to stay away from is swimming. It's great for wind but it will ruin your legs for cycling. It stretches out those big muscles the wrong way.

In your training, try jogging, calisthentics—anything that will develop wind and legs. But stay away from swimming

Calisthenics can help. Some cyclists do deep knee bends with a maximum of 100 pounds of barbell on their shoulders. Stay away from this exercise, however, if you have any doubts about your knees. It's not worth the risk. I half-ruined mine several years ago. Instead, do half knee bends to work your thighs, then do toe raises to develop the calf muscles. Stay away from the really heavy weights. Too much muscle before you know how to pedal can make you sluggish. Don't be over-concerned with growing Charles Atlas legs.

The rest of the body needs strength, too, for cycling and it's best to develop this in the winter. Because of the arched position of the body over the handlebars, you need muscle tone in your trunk. If you have strong legs, you'll need upper body strength to offset their thrusts. For stomach and back, do sit-ups, maybe 50 per day. Leg raises are also good. Raise your legs six inches off the floor (you're on your back), spread them to make a Y, bring them back together and drop them to the floor; 50 times, tops.

For chest and arms you can do arm curls with a barbell, maximum weight 40 pounds, four sets of 10. Or do a full press with 50 pounds for four sets of 10 repetitions. To give your body time to recover, limit weight exercises to about three times each week. You need a little upper body development, but not a whole lot. As for your wind exercises—running, skating, etc.—do them as much as you want. At least four days per week and preferably five or six.

For breathing control, you can try yoga, hypnosis or whatever turns you on. Take deep breaths while lifting weights and try to get the most out of each intake. The average person's rate of respiration is about 16 in-outs per minute; the racer in condition does about 10. Yup, six less.

Get out on that road and rattle them chains and gears

COME THE SPRING THAW, stash the barbells and hop on your bike. The more miles you ride the better. Some experts recommend a minimum of 200 to 250 miles per week, but these guys obviously either don't have jobs, wives, kids, and friends or don't care about them. You may not be able to do that much riding, so do the best you can and don't worry about it. Some amateurs get in under 100 miles per week; they aren't world-beaters but they do race, and enjoy it.

Keep a record of the miles you cover during each practice session and the time it took you. Keep track of your weight and pulse, also. A weekly check on your weight will help you spot drastic drops in pounds which may indicate that you are overdoing it. Find out what your pulse is at rest (the easiest way is by pressing your thumb to the carotid artery at the side of the neck). Then check it after a practice session and see how long it takes for your heartbeat to return to normal.

If possible, start your training on a track bike and use a low gear; somewhere between 62 and 67 is right for most people. Your primary concern is not to work yourself into the heavier gears, but to perfect your pedaling motion. That means cranking out the revolutions per minute; a cadence of 100 or more is not too high. Foot speed is all important. There are plenty of tourists who have stamina and strength, who can ride all day long and tackle the tallest mountains, but foot speed is where they fall down, and why so many fail at racing.

The high speed of a racing cadence will feel unnatural at first and the low gear may feel awkward, as though your feet are just floating through the air. You may even feel that you're not training, that you should be using bone-crushing gears to gain strength. Don't worry about it. A high cadence is probably *the* most important thing a new racer can learn. Don't think you're not doing any work. Keep up those high rpms, and your legs will ache plenty at the end of the run. This is where a fixed-wheel bike comes in handy because the pedals rotate smoothly and *force* your legs to learn proper pedaling. Freewheel bikes often feel sloppy in the cranks at high revs.

A high cadence is the single most important thing a new racer can develop

After you're satisfied with your new cadence, try pulling up against the toeclips and straps. This is rough to master because it's an unusual strain for most people's legs.

Find a couple of other beginning racers and practice with them. Keep the group small, three or four riders, so you don't get in each other's way. Practice riding on someone's wheel—that is, follow closely on one another's bikes so you break the wind for each other. Change leads frequently so one poor guy doesn't have to take the brunt of the work. Riding on another's wheel is one of the basic tactics of road racing. Theoretically the lead rider breaks the wind for you, thereby tiring himself, and you can sprint past him at the opportune moment.

While we're on the subject of sprinting, one thing that should be made clear is that every racer must be able to put on a burst of speed. You can develop your sprinting by running *intervals;* these are long periods of moderate pedaling broken by death-defying bursts of speed. Take it easy on intervals during your first week of training because your body may not be ready for it, and in cold weather you may sprint yourself into a cramp. As spring wears on, sprint as much as you want, trying to sustain each burst for 400 or 500 feet. As you really get into intervals, you'll want to switch to your road bike (if you're a road racer) so you can find the right gear for your sprints.

Practice "intervals" —death-defying bursts of speed during long periods of slower pedaling

Also, should you have the opportunity, practice on a track, even if you plan to work the road, because some road races finish on tracks.

A suggested schedule—three stages

WHAT WE'VE just discussed is a general format for your training. Now here's an idealized (and suggested) schedule for planning your mileage.

Divide your training period into three stages.

In the first, which may be two to three weeks long, set a daily goal of 25 miles using a moderately low gear—again, between 62 and 67 inches. *Ride* every day you can and *train* every other day of riding. In other words, if you can ride Monday through Saturday, spend Monday, Wednesday and Friday putting in your miles but not really pushing yourself. But on Tuesday, Thursday and Saturday you're going to go all out. If you can practice on the weekends, take advantage by doing 50 casual miles one day and 25 rough ones the next.

Follow the same procedure in the second stage of practice, only this time up the mileage to 40 and switch to a higher gear (for example, if you were in a 62, go to a 66). Push yourself on alternate days and build up the miles.

In the third stage take it very easy on your easy days, say 20 miles, then really reach on your power days, 40 or 50 miles of hard riding. This can be a plateau of conditioning to maintain. Work on moving into bigger gears, say around 80 or 84, to build up power and endurance. Remember, the gears you turn are a matter of taste and strength—my specific suggestions here are only to give you an idea of the gears normally used. Also, the length of each of the first two stages can vary according to your progress. You should be able to *feel* when it's time to move on.

Sprinters, pacers and climbers

A RACER MUST FIND his own particular talent or talents and then capitalize on them during a race. Even the professional stars of Europe have failings, and compete only in those races which they stand a chance of winning. In general there are three main types of riders. The ideal rider has the abilities of all three, but more commonly an unusually good racer will boast two of the dominant abilities.

The first and most glamorous is the *sprinter*. Physically he may be small, but stocky and solidly built. His talent is that fierce burst of speed that annihilates competition in the track races or lets him blur past opponents in the final 50 meters of a road race.

He may not have the continuous but more moderate speed needed for time trials, and he's probably too heavy for hill climbs or long road races up hilly terrain. Between sprints on the road he takes it as easy as possible, always hanging behind the pack, never leading, and makes up for lost ground by spurting to the front when he has to. Tall, long-legged cyclists usually have the power and the leverage for sprinting but present too big a profile for supersprinting. Short cyclists have the right profile but often lack the strength. That's why the ideal sprinter is moderately short for wind resistance, but packed with muscle for power.

Secondly, there is the kind of racer who cannot turn on those killing bursts of speed, but can maintain a higher than average rate for long stretches, thus wearing out the *pelethon*, or the main body of racers. He wins or loses his race long before the finish line by forcing the pace to the point where most of the riders can no longer compete, and depleting his archenemy's (the sprinter's) reservoirs of energy so he is no threat down the stretch.

The *pacer*, as he is called, must win the race at least 500 meters from the finish line. That is, he must either be alone or surrounded only by fellow pacers at that point whose *rush* (the final sprint) is weaker than his own. Often a group of several pacers will conspire with each other to wipe out the sprinters. But if even one good sprinter survives until that final few hundred meters amidst a bunch of, say, 10 pacers, he will most likely take them all.

> Sometimes a group of several pacers will conspire to wipe out all of the sprinters

Finally, there is the real specialist, the *hill climber*. The ideal physique for a climber is a tall, lightweight body with long muscles. Obviously, lighter cyclists have an advantage going uphill and being tall isn't much of a disadvantage since speeds are low anyway and wind resistance isn't that much of a factor. How well the climber does in a race is directly related to the geography and also how far the finish line is from the last hill. The closer the better. The racer who possesses only this specialty is at a disadvantage to cyclists who are either just pacers or just sprinters because climbing is so specialized and tied into the terrain.

No good racer, of course, is strong in only one area and totally void of talent in the others. The master of them all, Eddy Merckx became world road champion and winner of four consecutive Tours de France by having no weaknesses. As one cyclist said of him: "He is not a real climber, but he climbs. He is not the strongest in the sprint, but he is very strong." Plus he has developed one ability that racers often neglect. He is an incredible descender, having been timed downhill at close to 60 mph. Now, not many people can be like Merckx. So if you find you have even one dominant strength, consider yourself lucky.

Which of the three talents is the best to develop? Well, this is highly debatable. As said earlier, probably not hill climbing because you *must* have either a purely vertical course or one that finishes on a hill. Yet if you're light in weight and wiry, you'd be foolish not to practice this ability. But you'll have to develop something else, too.

So it's a toss-up between sprinting and pacing. Louis Maltese claims sprinting is most important and that a race is basically a series of sprints, including the start, finish and breakaways in the middle. Sprinters are also capable of taking advantage of unusual circumstances: accidents, a group of pacers wearing each other out, etc. When something like a crash occurs, the sprinter is best equipped to burst ahead in the confusion before the rest of the pack knows what is happening. And in a mass finish he will take all the pacers despite the fact they've led the whole race.

The sprinter's vulnerability is that he is extremely dependent on the rest of the pack; that is, they must inadvertently set the pace that is right for him. Too fast and he will fall behind or burn up. His tack is to stick with the pelethon and benefit from their wind-break, so he has no choice but to go with the pack. Pacers in the race are well aware of this and will do their best to break him, or box him in so that he can't sprint the finish no matter how much wind he has left. In effect then, a pure sprinter rarely gets to run his own race, being forced to follow the leaders; his strong point is his ability to capitalize on circumstances.

> The pure sprinter rarely gets to run his own race, but his advantage is his ability to capitalize on circumstances

The pacers are the guys who determine how the race is run. As mentioned earlier, they must win it early or lose to the sprinters, but they do have the opportunity of planning the race ahead of time. A pacer, with no dependence on the pack, can decide in advance what his tactics will be: set a high pace, make a breakaway from the pack, etc. Pacers lose more often because they can't live up to their own plans than because a sprinter or a climber beats them. The pacer's ultimate weapon is the breakaway. The pacer simply takes off from the main pack and goes it alone. He will often gain several minutes on the pack in the early part of the race and then begin losing this advantage as the race draws to a close and the pack speeds up.

Because the breakaway cyclist must break the wind all by himself, he expends much more energy than a rider who sticks with the pack. Therefore, two pacers will often get together and attempt a double breakaway. This way they can exchange the lead and share the wind burden. The breakaway rider often fails because he is caught and has no sprint left for the finish, having been done in by the brutal pace he has set for himself. But the breakaway is still one of the most exciting tactics in road racing and is symbolic of the independent approach of a pure type of rider.

The breakaway also puts quite a scare into the rest of the pack. A lead of several minutes means the breakaway artist is out of sight of the pelethon and the other riders have little idea of how fast he is going. They must depend on his weakness. In effect, they rely on him to lose the race rather than their own ability to win it.

Despite all the kudos given Merckx for his sprinting and climbing talents, he is essentially a superpacer. This shows up in the fact that he owns the world record for the longest distance traveled in a one-hour run—slightly over 30 miles! (Time trials are almost the sole domain of pacers.) He likes to run by himself, setting his own pace and often winning through breakaways. He frequently wins not by just a few seconds, but by five or six minutes. While he also has a great sprint and a good climb, you don't win a race by five minutes by either of those methods.

Road racing tactics

YOU WON'T LEARN much about road racing tactics practicing by yourself. You'll have to race with a club to develop these skills. But after you've acquired the conditioning and the speed, learning tactics is actually a lot of fun and the reason many people race. A topnotch race can be like a high-speed chess match. Here's what you can look forward to:

First, before you ever take the starting line, find out as much as you can about the general layout and topography of the course, what its surface is like (so you can choose the proper tires and inflation), and take note of the weather and prevailing winds. Find out who the top riders are, what their strengths are, and *their* favorite tactics. All this information will minimize the surprises you may face and help you plan your strategy of gearing, pacing and sprinting. (If you plan a breakaway, for example, you'll want to do it at a point in the course where the wind is negligible or at your back.)

When the race begins, the last place you want to be is within the mass of riders that leaves the starting line, especially if it's a huge field —such as 100 riders. For this reason it's a good idea to incorporate in your daily practice a fast jump from an almost dead start. For the sake of your own mobility you want to be at the leading edge of the pack— maybe not right up in *the* front where you buck the wind, but close to it. You may have to suffer a few uncomfortable jabs of the other riders' elbows as you make your way toward the front. Just keep your cool and concentrate on getting where you want to go. (I should mention that tactics described here are simply things you will try to do, with the understanding that other riders are going to be doing their damnest to stop you from doing them.)

Once you get rolling be sure to avoid the far edges of the road, as these tend to be unpredictable in their surface and littered with tire-threatening debris. Unless you're a Merckxian pacer, it will be to your advantage to hang back slightly and ride the wheel of a cyclist you think approximates your style and speed. Often your success will depend upon choosing the right wheel to follow, and this is often a matter of luck.

Developing your tactics is a real challenge; a top-notch race can be like a high-speed chess match

Above, the pack advances through heavy rain during Tour de France.
Below, racers in Quebec's Tour de L'Estrie find similar weather.

No road race is complete without a few good hills. This is just what the hill climber prays for. For everyone else hills are murder. If you're a pacer, stay as close to your pace as you can. If you're a shortwinded but powerful sprinter, by all means don't try to get on a climber's wheel going up the hills. His pace will kill you. Follow the slower pacer and he'll get you up at a respectable rate.

Coming down the other side of the hill, most riders have a tendency to gasp for breath, and to check their heart to make sure it hasn't exploded. This slackens their pace, and they tend to coast. Avoid this. To make the most of the downhill slope, give yourself the boost of a few strong thrusts of the pedals to get going.

Position is most important while going downhill—both in terms of winning and in staying in one piece. You ideally want to be toward the

Five riders go down in a spectacular (and painful) crash during a Mexican road race. Crashes are especially likely during the final rush, when racers go all-out while jockeying for position.

Wide World photo

front of the pack, but not leading. The reason is speed. Experienced cyclists are going to be approaching 50 mph down steep grades, and if you're in the middle of the pack and someone ahead crumples, you have a good chance of hitting the pavement. A fall at such a speed means more than a skinned knee. At the same time you don't really want to be the lead rider because he must explore the road and its hazards. So let someone else take the lead (assuming you have the choice) so he can help you anticipate changes in the road surface, pot-holes, loose gravel, etc.

When it's finish-line time there should be no surprises. In your survey of the course, pay special attention to the final stretch. Note whether it finishes on a hill, after a sharp curve, and whether you'll have to fight the wind. As you get ready to make your move, your straps should be tight. Your sprint gear should be as low as possible to benefit from fast pedal action. Again, the right gear is an individual thing, but common sprint gears are in the 90s. Some riders are inordinately strong, however, and one prominent national champion, John Howard, has been known to sprint a 108-inch gear. You don't need that much power, though, and can make up for lack of strength with high pedal speed.

If it should happen that the race finishes on a track, be sure to make your move before you reach it. There is limited room to do any maneuvering on a track (at least not with a bunched finish with all the racers riding less agile road bikes), so how well you do before the track is reached likely will determine where you finish.

Before you reach your sprint point, stay on the wheel of the rider in front of you but don't let your front wheel creep up on either his right or left—that gives him the opportunity to hedge you against the side of the road or another rider while he makes his sprint. By the time you wobble free and recover, you have lost valuable seconds.

When you do make your final rush, get over to one side of the road so you can watch your competition creeping up by looking over only one shoulder. Concentrate on that finish line. Keep your arms in and watch every move in front of you.

One common move is to fake a sprint, forcing other sprinters to start their rush before they're ready

As riders approach the finish line they begin revealing their final tactics. One common move is to fake a sprint, thereby forcing some of the shorter-winded sprinters to start their rush before they're ready. Many riders telegraph the beginning of their real sprint when they shift gears in the final stretch. Keep your eye on the others you feel are threats; when they make their move, shift into your rush gear instantly.

Where different members of the same team are riding in a race, the tactics are even more complicated. In unsponsored racing clubs, the members are pretty much allowed to run as they wish, each man trying to win for himself in open events (races where more than one club competes). But professional teams and even some amateur teams dictate that some members will *not* try to win. They are only in the race to help the team's stars. In Europe the riders who must perform this service are sometimes degradingly called "domestics" and this points out another reason why the purely amateur scene is sometimes more attractive than the pro scene.

For instance, one man may be chosen as the guy to finish while the other team members spread out on the road and hold back the pack. By the time the other riders realize the leader is making a sprint, they may be too late to get around his cohorts.

Another tactic is for a couple of riders to begin their sprint early on one side of the road and move diagonally across the pack, disrupting everyone's rhythm and creating havoc as they move. Sometimes a pacer will be instructed to "tow" a sprinter. That is, the pacer must set a pace most comfortable for his teammate and let him sit on his wheel for most of the race. Toward the finish he will then tow his charge to the front of the pack and let him loose for the final 500 meters or so. The pacer thus totally sacrifices his chances, having finished himself off at the same point that the sprinter is just beginning his race.

Eating on the run and before the run

ON THE LONGER RUNS you'll have to learn to eat in the saddle. But even if you restrict your racing to shorter events you'll have to learn to eat in a specialized manner. If you plan to eat a meal the day of a road race, make sure you get it down at least three hours before you start. Avoid the toxins of coffee and hard liquor in your diet as well as junk foods, synthetic anything, and fatty, fried foods.

This doesn't mean you don't eat well. The racer in training burns up 5000 calories a day and more. This has to be replaced, and a lot of those calories should come in the form of protein. Do it with the best food available: fresh meat, fresh vegetables, milk—all the things that used to be on those funny meal charts they showed you back in fourth grade.

There are varying opinions about the correct diet. Anyway, avoid all the junk, and fatty or fried foods

Once again, the correct diet is open to debate. A popular eating technique that has cropped up in recent years is called carbohydrate loading. Basically it involves eating a lot of protein early in the week and then loading up on carbohydrates the last couple of days before the race (assuming you will be racing once per week on the weekends). The theory behind this is that protein is a good long-range building material, but not much good for short-term energy. The racer satisfies his long-range needs at the beginning of the week while preparing for a specific event toward the end of the week. If you don't yet have much experience, I'd suggest sticking to a more conventional diet.

When you eat those masses of food is also important. The reason for the three-hour-before-the-race time limit on a big meal is simply so you won't start off with a huge lump of undigested food in your stomach. Besides burdening your body, you might regurgitate during the race, thus causing mass skidding.

Most of the races you run will probably be short, so don't worry about carrying food. In races that don't go over an hour, all you'll need is some sweetened tea or sugar water in your feeder bottle. Liquids are always preferable to solids in short races because the body assimilates them more quickly.

On longer races, say over 50 miles, you may get pretty hungry so you'll have to bring some snacks. A carry-along lunch is generally called a "food packet" and what goes in it is up to you. If it's a really long race you might want to carry three sandwiches, pieces of apple, orange slices and maybe a few sugar cubes or M&Ms (seriously!). Oranges are especially good, but make sure you peel them before packing them. You can stuff all this in the special pockets of your neato racing jersey, though you may do mayhem to the sandwiches. Even if you bring food, be sure to fill the feeder bottle with sweet tea or what-ever. In hot weather carry a little salt to help keep your body chemistry in order. Throw it on your food (but not on your jelly sandwich) or mix it with a little water.

If you've done your homework, you know the layout of the course, which will help you plan your eating schedule. All you really have to remember is never to eat just before you are about to make any kind of strenuous effort, whether it's climbing a hill, making a sprint or rushing for the finish.

The time to eat is when you are relatively free from stress, physical or psychological. A good time, for instance, is after the first 20 miles or so when you've established your position in the race. Remember, just like a tourist, you must eat before you're really hungry because of the time lag built into your digestive system. Eat in little bits so you don't draw the blood away from your limbs and into your stomach, and take only small sips of liquid. After you've burned up a lot of energy on a big hill, eat as soon as you've finished the downhill plunge and are back to normal speed so you can prepare your body for the next chal-lenge. Finally, save as much of your liquid as possible to drink in preparation for the final rush.

As far as eating after a grueling race goes, keep it light. You can always eat more later. Concentrate on getting liquid back into your body first.

Special training for the trackie

The track racer not only must have endurance, but en-durance at high speeds

BOTH ROAD AND TRACK racing are much alike in that both de-mand incredible stamina and speed and the ability to balance a two-wheeler without training wheels. They differ in that a rider who is not particularly fast but skillful and powerful can put in a respectable showing in a road race, while in a track event he would be left in the dust. Endurance is only one of the requirements for a good track rider. Endurance at high speeds is the key.

A desirable quality in all road racers and a necessary one in track racers, especially those who plan to race in sprint events, is a certain suppleness or agility in reaching high rpms. Pedaling at high rpms gives you a ready power source to tap when those spurts of speed are needed. It is simply much easier to go from a fast rate of pedaling to a faster one than from a medium or slow rate to a very fast one.

It will take you a while to find your true event. If there is no track available for you to practice or race on, then your potential as a great track racer will remain one of life's mysteries. If you do get a taste of the track and feel you want to make a strong effort at track racing, you will have to adjust your training to suit it.

Assuming you've already got some miles in your legs with the pre-season warm-up series of practice runs described earlier, your next goal will be to tune your body to track racing. Practice surging forward from an almost standing start. Whether you end up in track or road racing this is bound to come in handy.

Obviously, you'll need a track bike. Start with a fairly low gear, about 59 inches or so, and pick a straight stretch of road 12 to 15 miles long. Work on those rpms, practice intervals, and work on your style. Your position on the bicycle will be somewhat uncomfortable; extremely low-profile with your knees pumping up close to your chest. Fortunately you don't have to hold this very long, but get your body into shape by assuming the racer's crouch.

There's no way any rider is going to learn how to ride in track races from a book. What you need is the advice and criticism of more experienced riders and the club coach. Basically your apprenticeship will depend on your natural abilities and how fast you learn. Figure on roughly a month on the average for special track warm-up. Ride about four times a week, each time increasing the number of intervals and, when you feel ready, move from a 59 to a gear in the mid-sixties and ultimately to your final gear, which can be anywhere from 70 to 100 depending on the event you choose.

You won't learn from this book—or any other book—how to ride in track races. You need the help of a club

As a track racer, most likely you'll be competing either in sprint or pursuit races individually. As you get more experienced and sophisticated you may move onto pursuit teams. If sprinting is what you aim for, you'll find you'll be doing fewer miles in practice but more work per racing foot.

The sprinter is usually an explosive kind of rider who routinely cranks out speeds of 45 mph or more in that last murderous 200 meters, all the while making sure his opponent isn't doing any better. To get ready for something like this, divide your four training rides equally between the road and the track. How you work out on the track is a matter of personal preference, your training needs and your experience or lack of it.

To get an idea of what can be involved, one U.S. professional racer, Skip Cutting of California, described his regimen in *Cyclenews*. In preparation for the world championship sprint races he would begin training about three months before the event. He mixed road work with three sessions at the track each week. At each track session, he did three sprints, resting in between. After about six weeks of this, he would begin tapering off, eventually eliminating road practice altogether, doing about two practice sprints on the track each training session.

A sprint in a training session should be as close to the real race as possible, but with much more effort. Get someone to train with you, and work on repetitions of sprints that are going to be longer than that 200-meter run you will have to face. For example, in one session try a series of 300-meter rushes with rest periods in between. If you feel up to it, on another session extend these to 500 meters. Remember, the harder you train the easier the real thing will be.

Since the track should be a lot easier to ride on, work yourself up to a higher gear than you use on the road, around 88 inches. If you're

*Four South African riders pile up in a spectacular crash during
a six-lap scratch race. Crashes occur frequently in such races
because of high speeds, frequent blow-outs, limited track area.*

a more powerful rider you may go even higher, so experiment. And
since few people end up as naturals as sprinters, you may discover as
you train or early in your races that your riding is not everything it
could be. The three most common problems of the new racer are an
inability to get those rpms cranked up fast enough, the speed of a
tortoise in beginning that spurt for the finish, and short wind in the
sprint.

For the first problem, low foot speed, find a very, very steep hill.
Make sure your fixed-wheel bike has a fairly low gear on it (about 58
inches), walk the bike to the top of that hill, get on it, strap your feet
in, say your prayers and go ripping down the hill. You will be forced
to move your feet fast, and hopefully you will retain control of the
bike without hitting your chin with your flying knees. After a series of
runs like this you will have either improved the speed and agility of
your pedaling or totally dislocated your body from your waist down.

If you have problems getting that sprint going, concentrate on
spurting from dead starts over stretches of about 150 meters. And for
those who start to peter out before the finish line, incorporate longer
sprint lengths in your training, practiced both from standing and running starts.

As simple as it may look, sprint racing is not just a matter of speed. It can be a dangerous and tricky event and deserves a little respect for these reasons. Danger on a bicycle track? The hazards are a little less evident than in the roller derby but no less real. For example, Danish sprinter Neels Fredborg fell during a sprint match in Europe and as a result of his fall ended up in the hospital with a fractured skull and broken collarbone. For some reason, track racers have cornered the market on broken collarbones. The first thing you can do to avoid meeting this fate is to make sure your tires are solidly shellaced to the rims.

Track racing tactics—clean and dirty

AT FIRST GLANCE it may not seem that the sprinter uses any strategy. But how a rider handles himself in a race depends on his strong points, those of his opponent, the length and banking of the track, wind direction if it is an outdoor track, and whether he rides second or first.

In a two-man sprint race, some riders favor being the front runner because it suits their particular skills or because they get stuck with the position. (In match sprints one rider is required to take the lead from the starting line. Usually this is determined by a drawing, and since the winner must take two out of three races, the riders take turns leading each race. The rules do not require the leader to lead the entire distance, however. He may roll a few inches and stop dead.)

Your strategy during the race must depend upon a clear understanding of your own talents

A common mistake made by the inexperienced rider who becomes a front runner is to move out at top pace from the line in hopes of tiring out his competition before he gets to the 200-meter sprint line. What happens more often than not is that the other rider gets on his wheel and then jumps to the lead at the sprint mark.

Your strategy will depend upon your personal talents. If you're good at long distance and your opponent does better from a start closer to the 200-meter mark, you can force him to start with you. Ride high on the bank, pinning him between you and the upper boundaries of the track by letting your back wheel overlap his front wheel. Keep your right elbow out (your outside elbow since you are riding counterclockwise) so he can't sneak by you. In this way you keep him boxed in and you can pick your time to begin that final long rush you do so well.

You can use the high bank of the track to build up speed by diving down it. Stay high for most of the race, then as you approach the straightaway opposite the finish line start to build up speed. On the last bend before the finish, dive down for the final sprint. Of course, once you hit the 200-meter line you have to stay between the sprint lines (assuming you are in the lead) and your only defensive tactic against the other rider is speed or if he gets too close, a bony elbow.

Elbow tactics are not all that uncommon, and though illegal, officials either can't detect these goings on or prefer not to call them. Sheila

Young was knocked off her bike in the world sprint finals and had to run the next two races with clamps holding together an ugly gash in her head. Another tactic short of elbowing is mere intimidation. A leading sprinter who keeps close to the pole line will suddenly swing up the banked track as the other rider tries to get by. He doesn't necessarily hit the other racer, but perhaps frightens him to swing upward, forcing him into a longer line to the finish.

If you are a short-term sprinter in the lead, you'll be better off keeping a long-winded opponent trapped in the bottom of the bowl, using the same wheel trapping technique described earlier. Because your strong point is a quick burst of speed, you can move more quickly to the top of the bank on the last curve and make more of that dive downward in the rush for the finish.

If both riders are evenly matched, there's probably more psychological than physical maneuvering involved. One tactic used quite often is to fake the start of a spurt to get the other rider sprinting before he's ready. By throwing him off balance mentally this way, you can take advantage of his confused state of mind, and make your dive from the top, zipping on by him.

Many riders prefer to be in second place for a number of very good reasons. While the front runner wishes he had two heads so he can see where he's going while watching what his opponent is doing, the second man can keep his eye on the other rider with little trouble. In fact, just by tagging along behind, the second rider takes advantage of the hole the first one has funneled through the air. In short, this is one case where number two doesn't have to try harder.

Now if it should happen that you do get pinned between the lead rider and the top or bottom of the track, obviously you can slow yourself down drastically by about two bike lengths, and surge up or down the bank to give yourself maneuvering distance to bypass the leader on the upper or lower track. Just make sure he doesn't see you coming.

When both riders refuse to lead—racing by going nowhere

IF BOTH RIDERS are determined to go second, a war of nerves and a balancing act begins. If you are required to go first and do not wish to do it, you'll have to learn how to stop dead on the track and stand there without falling over and embarrassing yourself, your team, your coach, your parents and the bike manufacturer. There are certain speeds at which you can easily stop yourself on a fixed gear bike but only practice will tell you which ones.

Once you've figured this out without throwing yourself over the handlebars with your feet still in the pedals, time it so you stop just before a bend in the track. This way if you lose the stand-off you can surge ahead into the sweep of the curve to spurt ahead.

Basically this stopped position, sometimes called *surplace*, requires that the frame of the bike be angled slightly toward the inside of the track with the front wheel turned toward the outside of the track.

Sheila Young of Detroit, on the right, defeats Iva Zajickova of Czechoslovakia to win 1973 world 1000-meter sprint championship.

Since most people are right-footed, they keep the right pedal position somewhere between nine o'clock and 12 o'clock to balance the bike and give them a good pedal position to sprint from.

Finally, make sure in picking the spot for this kind of tactic that you don't come out on the dirty end of the cranks. You most likely will not use a tactic like this in your early racing days because it does take a good deal of control and experience. And you shouldn't use it just because you want to prove you know how. You should have some plan in mind—some goal that the *surplace* will help you achieve. If you do intend to practice this maneuver, or non-maneuver as the case may be, don't overdo it. It causes terrific tension in the muscles which should be loosened by a few turns around the track between balancing sessions.

Coping with the three-man sprint

IT MAY HAPPEN that the sprint event you ride in has *two* other riders and not just one. The most favorable spot you can be in is the number two position because you only have to worry about one rider sneaking behind you while being in a much better position to burst by the first rider and win the sprint. The one thing you have to be careful of while riding as number two is that number three doesn't zoom by, boxing you in behind the first rider or sandwiching you between him and number one.

In racing, the younger you start the better. This kid is especially adventuresome; he's cutting his racing teeth on a track bike.

If you have a faster than average spurt, then you may prefer the third position because you can shock the other two riders in a surprise sprint. The third rider also has the advantage of being able to watch the other two with much more ease.

Another third-rider tactic is to begin the rush early, pinning the number two man against the first and reducing it to a number one vs. number three sprint race.

Pedaling your guts out—the pursuit race

NO ONE IS AS FAST as a speeding bullet, so for the slower bullets there is the pursuit race. These normally take place over a course about 4000 meters long and require a tremendous amount of stamina and pedaling at high speeds for five minutes or more. The qualities of the pursuit cyclist are basically that he be quick off the starting line and be able to maintain high speeds for long periods. He is longer-winded than the sprinter but not always as fast.

Unlike the sprinter, the pursuit cyclist never fully relinquishes the road for the track. After breaking himself in with the fixed gear in general preparation, he should then tackle some long hills with a fairly low gear (about a 58 incher) on a freewheel road bike to build up both power and agility in pedaling. The goal should be to develop power at a moderately high gear, about 80 or 90 inches, a skill which also makes the pursuit racer a valuable road racer.

The pursuit race itself is an intense physical effort, one which can easily cause cramps in a rider not limbered up sufficiently. It is best if you do about 10 road miles on the morning of a race just to warm up those leg muscles and get your body in tune. In the race situation you have two basic strategy alternatives. One is to pedal like hell and actually catch up with the other rider—pretty hard to do. The other, if you are not that fast, is to save most of your energy for the last kilometer, or 1000 meters, after the other racer has burned himself out.

As with the sprinter, *when* you make your strategic moves will depend on the length of the track, wind direction and the strong or weak points of the other rider. Strategically the pursuit is a simpler race than the two-man sprint, but physically it can take a greater toll because it is an almost constant, total effort.

There are zillions of other kinds of track races. The best thing is to get out on the track and give them a try. No matter what event you choose, the basic training rule will prepare you for the race: ride, ride, ride.

Other bicycle games not quite so painful

BY NOW YOU'RE either convinced the racing life is for you or you're trying to figure out what would drive some people to get up at four in the morning to go through pain and suffering . . . and then probably lose anyway.

If racing sounds too painful for you, there are plenty of other ways to enjoy yourself on a bike without collapsing across some finish line. Here are some less serious-minded races and games you can enjoy with your friends. They can be held anywhere from a vacant football field to a deserted parking lot—anyplace where there's room for a group of crazy cyclists to move around. Many of these games were designed originally for kids. But what the hell, don't let that bother you. If it sounds fun, try it. These games also are ideal for youth-group meetings. Tire out those Cub Scouts and the little devils won't give you much trouble later.

Probably the best organized of bicycle games is *bicycle polo*. There are two ways you can play, the official way or your own. If special teams, regularly scheduled games, uniforms and the shallow camaraderie of total strangers getting together once a week excite you, then you'll probably want to do things officially.

For starters you'll need a field up to 80 by 100 yards; a football field is perfect. The goalposts can serve as the goals (makes sense) or you can stick in your own, spaced the regulation distance of 12 feet apart. Use the field's boundaries and center lines and then find eight individuals willing to take part in this insanity. The length of play is divided into six 15-minute periods, or chukkars, with one-minute rest periods between.

Some bicycle polo players saw off the right half of their handlebars (if they are right-handed) to give them swinging room

Official players wear things like uniforms, buy special balls and mallets from the U.S. Bicycle Polo Association, and use small bikes, usually those fold-up kinds with small wheels, coaster brakes and high handlebars because they are so maneuverable. Some players saw off the right half of the handlebars (if they're right-handed) to give them swinging room.

A player is allowed to hit the ball only three times in succession and then only when no part of his body is touching the ground. Each goal counts as two points unless it's the result of a free drive after a foul is committed, in which case it counts as one point.

In official games there is a referee who watches for rule violations such as catching or kicking the ball, or body checking—which can get pretty messy on a bicycle. He also rolls out the first ball of the game unless the President happens to be in town. Balls that go out of bounds are returned back to play by a backward, over-the-shoulder throw by a player.

These are the rules, in brief, which should give you some idea of how to play. Obviously your custom-designed rules will relate to the number of people available and no doubt you may wish to make a few creative innovations of your own, accommodating not only the size of the field but the equipment as well. A workable compromise for the official balls and mallets are croquet balls and mallet heads on the end of broomsticks. If your courage is up to it, almost any bike will do in a pinch although the smaller version is probably a safer and saner bet. Even though it may not be an official game, some rules do help the game move along more smoothly. For example, equally divide the players (if you have even numbers) between forwards and defense. And if you can get some brave, well-meaning friend to act as referee, so much the better.

Other team bike games require nothing more than a little imagination. Everyone likes to race and so the *bike relay race* can be a fun way to pretend you're Eddy Merckx. In all racing situations, for the sake of fair play, each team should have bicycles and riders that are approximately the equal to the other's.

For a good relay race all you need is two or more teams with the same number of evenly matched players and about 100 feet or more of open space. At the starter's signal, the number one man on each team takes off, "baton" in hand, around a marker about 100 feet or so away, returns to his starting line and hands off to the number two man. As in any relay, the team which completes the course first wins.

One variation of the relay is the *pony express run*. The course is run the same way as the relay, the only difference being that when number one hands off to number two, he hops off his bike and turns it over to number two. As in the relay race, the first team whose men complete their pony express run are the winners. In this race it is especially important that the bicycles be as evenly matched as possible to keep the race fair.

Even a plain old *potato race* takes on added drama when it's on two wheels. As in the relay, everyone breaks up into the same numbered teams. It makes the race more interesting if the teams are spread out more with a small number of individuals on each team.

All the equipment you'll need is your bicycle, something to use as potatoes (rocks, wooden blocks, bricks, old hamburgers—anything that can be held easily in one hand) and a course laid out with a starting line and a spot marked to place the potatoes. If you're using a course about 100 feet long you could use four potatoes and mark the drop-off and pick-up points at 100-, 80-, 60- and 40-foot points from the starting line.

The race proceeds as any potato race only this time the participants are two-wheeled. At the starting signal, the first man dashes out, picks up one potato at a time and pedals back until finally all have been removed and dropped into a receptacle at the starting line. When they are all picked up he tags the second man who has the job of replacing them in any order. This cycle continues until one team has completed its potato duties.

One game that needs lots of roaming room is a two-wheeled version of *Ring-A-Lievio*. Two teams are chosen, one as the captors and the other, the prisoners. For a prison a (chalk) circle about 50 feet in diameter is drawn and two or three of the captors' team are designated as guards.

The game begins when all the captors close their eyes while one of them counts to 100. During the count the prisoners scramble to hide— on their bicycles. At the end of the count, the captors open their eyes and set out looking for their prey. A capture is made when a prisoner is tagged by a captor. The tagged prisoner has to turn himself in to prison until freed or the game is over. Any prisoner can be freed by one of his own who rides over any part of the circle and shouts "Ring-A-Lievio." The game is over when all the prisoners have been captured or a pre-arranged time period has elapsed. For a new game the captors and prisoners just exchange roles.

The hare that harries the hounds

IF INDIVIDUAL COMPETITION is more your style there are also a number of other ways you can have fun with your bike. One of the more elaborate games is called *Hare and Hounds*. Any number can play and the cast of characters consists of one person, who is usually a speedy cyclist, that plays the hare and everyone else, who are the hounds. The game starts when the hare hops on his bike, and after having given him a 20-minute head-start, the hounds take off after him. The first one to tag, or catch, the hare is the winner. Sounds simple, eh?

Well, a lot you know. The distance and difficulty of the chase is limited only by the hare's speed and imagination. The only requirement he has to fulfill besides trying to keep from getting caught is to chalk all the changes in course he makes with an arrow.

The chase can be anything from a pleasant ride along quiet streets to something that may closely resemble a cyclo-cross event. Usually the hare will plan his escape well in advance to make his pursuers work to catch him.

Those with sportier inclinations can work out a two-wheeled version of the *sports car rally*. What you need for this is a number of interested people, a preplanned route and a group of people willing to man **Why not run your** check points at different legs of the route. As in sports car events, the **own two-wheeled** object of the competition is to cover the course in a specified amount **version of the** of time. Those coming closest to or matching the official course time or **sports car rally?** the official time for different segments of the course win. Individuals can compete but it's more fun to have teams of two or three.

There are a number of ways you can set it up. For guidance you can go to any sports car fanatic or devise your own route. One way to do it is to first map out a not too heavily trafficked route with a few tricky turns or challenging hills and ride over it at a brisk pace, keeping careful track of your time between predetermined points. Draw up a map of the route or a series of maps, one for each section of the stretch.

At the start of the race each participant or group of participants is issued a map of the whole route, or one of the first leg, and a time card. Participants leave at 15-minute intervals with their starting time marked on the card. As each team gets to the end of its first leg, they find a check point with officials who mark their arrival time on the card. If a series of maps are used, the team then picks up a new map for the next section of the race.

For bicycle moto-cross racing, kids use the ever-popular banana-seat, high-rise type of bike, sometimes called a "Sting Ray" or a "Chopper."

This procedure is followed throughout the race with the time cards collected at the finish line. Winners are selected on the basis of the best overall time and the best time for each section of the race. It's a good excuse to get out and do a little bicycling and is certainly a more leisurely kind of competition than a grueling road race.

Another copycat sport cyclists can indulge in, especially the younger racers who are too young to get their driver's licenses, is a bicycle version of *motocross*, or dirt track motorcycle racing with jumps and hairpin turns. The pedaling version is a miniature of this run on a shorter course. The object is the same. The first rider across the finish line is the winner.

How it is done may not be so simple. In California where this sport is very big, there are even mini-dirt tracks for bicycle motocross. Lacking this, most racers will have to make do with a vacant lot or any fairly even open space with one good "jump" hill. Equipment is basic: crash helmets for a rough course, and a bicycle, usually the sporty kid's model "Stingray type" with the high seat and handlebars and small wheels. It should have a coaster brake and one good low gear. Some riders adapt their bikes with special studded tires and handlebars with a special padded brace across the "Y".

If you just want to race up the hills without the dirt then have a *hill* race. All that's needed is a good steep neighborhood street and some competition. Get two bikes about equally matched and see who can get up the hill the fastest or, if it's a real pistol, who can get furthest up it.

Skiing on your cycle

FOR AN EVENT demanding a little more skill than strength, have a bicycle *slalom race*. Like the skiing event, you are required to zig-zag in and out of obstacles lined up between you and the finish line. The rider who does this in the shortest time wins.

This kind of course is fairly easy to set up. On a paved surface such as a parking lot or freeway, use something lightweight such as plastic wastepaper baskets as markers that will move if bumped by the rider. On grassy surfaces such as a football field you can use stakes, each five or six feet high, as markers. Anyone who hits the markers while running through them can either be disqualified or penalized by having extra seconds added to his time.

To make it challenging there should be at least four markers, about 10 feet apart, the last one about 15 feet from the finish line. If you have a group of riders who enjoy challenges you can always increase the number of markers or move the ones you have closer together.

A different kind of control is needed for the *tightrope race*. You need a stretch of ground about 100 feet or so and some kind of marker

State representatives of the Amateur Bicycle League of America:

ALABAMA (see Ga.)
ALASKA (see Wash.)
ARIZONA
  David Mann
  6th W. Santa Fe
  Flagstaff, AR 86001
ARKANSAS (see Miss.)
CALIFORNIA–
NEVADA:NORTH
  William Harrison
  539 Cashmere Court
  Sunnyvale, CA 94087
CALIFORNIA–
NEVADA:SOUTH
  Robert Enright
  4079 Abourne Rd.
  Los Angeles, CA 90008
COLORADO–WYOMING
  Don Stankovsky
  ,1018 West 30th Street
  Loveland, CO 80537
CONNECTICUT
  Joe Tosi, Sr.
  Prospect Park
  Warehouse Point, CT
  06088
DELAWARE (see Md.)

FLORIDA
  James Spatafora
  6780 Charlston Street
  Hollywood, FL 33024
GEORGIA–ALABAMA
  Nestor Gernay
  10603 White Bluff Rd.
  Savannah, GA 31406
IDAHO (see Oregon)
ILLINOIS
  Alfred Herreweyers
  4836 N. Melvina St.
  Chicago, IL 60630
INDIANA
  Donald Elliot
  P.O. Box 304
  Marion, IN 46952
IOWA–NEBRASKA
  J. E. Nachod III
  P.O. Box 171
  Marshalltown, IA 50159
LOUISIANA
  Bob Perrin
  5245 Coliseum
  New Orleans, LA 70115
KANSAS (see Oklahoma)
KENTUCKY
  Joe R. Gluck
  P.O. Box 295
  Cumberland, KY 48023

MAINE
  Larry Poulin
  558 Riverside Drive
  Augusta, ME 04330
MARYLAND–DELAWARE
  George Sandruck
  1779 Pin Oak Road
  Baltimore, MD 21234
MASSACHUSETTS–
RHODE ISLAND
  Herbert O'Neil, Jr.
  21 Lunenburg Street
  Fitchburg, MA 01420
MICHIGAN
  Douglas G. Croft
  15 Elm Park Boulevard
  Pleasant Ridge, MI
  48069
MINNESOTA
  James E. Wilbur
  2001 Sumter Avenue
  North
  Golden Valley, MN 54427
MISSOURI
  Howard Althoff
  3809 Castleman Avenue
  St. Louis, MO 63110

tape to delineate two lanes each about six inches wide. A racer in each of the two lanes takes off at the starting signal and the first one to finish wins if he has not touched the tape during the run. A steady hand on the handlebars can count more than speed in this event. If both riders touch the tape before the finish, the race can be run over, or the one who went the farthest without touching it can be declared the winner. You may need a sharp-eyed judge for this. To make it a little more interesting you may want to move the tapes closer together or add a few zigs and zags.

Everyone knows a moving target is hard to hit and the same holds true if the shooter is moving and the target isn't. This is the challenge of the *shooting gallery game.* You'll need: a number of cardboard cartons or baskets all the same size, a bicycle with a basket on it and some balls all the same size. Set the boxes up in a line about 10 feet apart and parallel with the "riding" line.

Each rider takes a bike, his ration of balls in the basket, rides down the line and tries to land a ball in each container. The winner, of course, is the one who makes the most baskets. You can vary the setup or the rules, moving the boxes further out or by putting score numbers

MISSISSIPPI–ARKANSAS
Larry Savell
205 Virginia Street
Indianola, MS 38751
MONTANA (see Wash.)
NEBRASKA (see Iowa)
NEW HAMPSHIRE (see Vt.)
NEW JERSEY
Dick Swann
c/o Elm Field,
Cherry Valley Rd.
Princeton, NJ 08540
NEW MEXICO
George Gamble
11444 Freeway Place
Albuquerque, NM 87112
NEW YORK:NORTH
Tom Pares
230 Cresent Avenue
Buffalo, NY 14214
NEW YORK:SOUTH
Peter Senia, Sr.
418 Grant Avenue
Brooklyn, NY 11208
NEVADA:NORTH
(see Calif.)
NEVADA:SOUTH
(see Calif.)
NORTH CAROLINA
William Long
P.O. Box 947
Brevard, NC 28712

NORTH & SOUTH DAKOTA
Dr. Earl Scholz
1128 North 7th Street
Fargo, ND 58102
OHIO–WEST VIRGINIA
Pete DiSalvo
117-B McClure Street
Dayton, OH 45403
OKLAHOMA–KANSAS
Kenneth Driessel
P.O. Box 591
Tulsa, OK 74101
OREGON–IDAHO
Ernest Drapela
1320 Corum Avenue
Eugene, OR 97401
PENNSYLVANIA
E. James Harper, Jr.
921 Delmont Dr.
Wynnewood, PA 19096
RHODE ISLAND
(see Mass.)
SOUTH CAROLINA
Ray Guest
1994 Forrest Drive
Sumter, SC 29150
S. DAKOTA (see N.D.)
TENNESSEE
James L. Mugler
Route 1
Brentwood, TN 37027

TEXAS
Edward Fries
1224 Cloverdale Drive
Richardson, TX 75080
UTAH
Charles Stewart
Box 792
Provo, UT 84601
VERMONT–
NEW HAMPSHIRE
Robert Anderson
R.D. No. 2, Box 185
Brattleboro, VT 05301
VIRGINIA–
WASHINGTON, D.C.
Gerald Teeuwen
946 Schillelach
Chesapeake, VA 23230
WASHINGTON–ALASKA–
MONTANA
Terry McLellan
Route 1, Box 141-S
Ravendale, WA 98051
WASHINGTON, D.C.
(see Va.)
WEST VA. (see Ohio)
WISCONSIN
Virgil Pearce
1109 West Birch Avenue
Milwaukee, WI 53209
WYOMING (see Colo.)

Bike marathon in New York's Central Park attracted 7000 entrants!

on them, making some hits count more than others. It's great practice if you occasionally have to deliver your little brother's papers.

If you prefer things easy, then have a *snail* race. Mark off some lanes about four feet wide with tape or chalk over a distance of 50 feet or more. In this race the rider who comes in last is the winner. The rules are that no rider's foot can touch the ground and his wheels can't stray outside his lane or he is disqualified. At the word "go," or "gentlemen start your engines," each rider hops on his wheels and proceeds to move as slow as he can along the course. This is one race where size, strength, speed or the kind of bike you have (as long as it isn't a fixed gear) means little. It's a lot of fun and a lot of laughs. If you don't get giddy and fall over you have as good a chance of winning as the next man. No tricycles.

Not for the nervous is the *race to the unknown*. This is a race where the number of laps is unknown to all but the race official. After the race has started he reaches into a hat containing numbered slips, two to 20 for example, and chooses one of the slips. If the number is seven, that's the number of laps the race will go. But he doesn't tell the racers this until the lead rider finishes the sixth lap. That's when the scramble starts. Those who banked on a longer race may be faked out of their toeclips while those who paced themselves for a shorter one may be too tired to finish. If nothing else, this will keep you on your toes. To keep it more of a game than a grueling event keep the maximum number of possible laps small and it will be more enjoyable.

Finally, a cross between a bicycle game and an out-and-out race is the bicycle marathon or *bikathon*. This is a race (sort of) among people who don't normally race and is run more for distance than speed. Pepsi-Cola, for instance, sponsors marathons in several cities on Memorial Day weekend. Cyclists pedal over a safe course continuously for 24 hours (if they can), with prizes going to those completing the most miles. Awards are broken down into several interesting categories: oldest man finishing high, youngest girl, etc. Many charitable organizations also hold bikathons to raise money. The beauty of these events is that they're half-social, half-competitive. And while it's difficult to win one of them because of the large number of entrants involved, you have the pleasure of passing hundreds of other riders.

Chapter 13

Section 5: Taking care of your bike

Basic maintenance and repair for riders, not mechanics

An unpretentious approach to various bike repairs for those who think riding a bike is more fun than fixing one. Also, various painless instructions and detailed drawings to help you keep your bike off the rack and on the road.

MAYBE YOU'VE HAD this sad experience: Your bicycle (or some other machine) breaks down, so you take it to a professional mechanic. He graciously agrees to fix it, but succeeds in intimidating you for your ignorance, and your total neglect of the machine. "My, my," he intones, "you haven't oiled your framus in years."

Properly filled with guilt for your mechanical shortcomings, you repent by buying a how-to book on maintenance and repair. With self-righteous fervor, the book sets down hundreds of rules for you: "Lubricate your framus every six minutes. Adjust your glotz during heavy winds. Overhaul your gazornimplatz when the moon is full. Or else!"

Overwhelmed with the complexity and amount of everything you *should* do, you give up on the how-to idea entirely, feeling you're not man enough to enter the ultra-masculine world of mechanics (or if you're female, you conclude you're too much of a woman).

So, before we get into the details of bike maintenance and repair, let's get one thing straight: it is the honest belief of this author that *how you take care of your bicycle is strictly your own business.* In the following pages you'll find loads of instructions—orders, if you will— telling you what to do to your bike and when to do it. You may follow some to the letter; other chores you may do less frequently than recommended. Some you may assign to a professional; others you may skip altogether.

Do what you can do, and don't get in a sweat about the tasks you haven't done. Luckily, the bicycle is a forgiving beast and will continue to function with almost no care. And how to care for it is mostly a matter of personal preference anyway.

Let's take a case in point. Recently a friend asked me how often he should overhaul his bottom bracket. Frankly, I don't know for sure. One popular manual categorically states that a bottom bracket *must* be overhauled every six months. What happens if you don't? Probably nothing. It's just another silly rule that sounds mechanically virtuous. Consider that, as this is written, there are an estimated 60 million bicycles in use in the U.S. I doubt that more than five percent of them (if that) get their bottom brackets overhauled every six months. What happens to the other 95 percent? Do they explode on the bike paths? Dismantle under their riders in the middle of intersections? Not many. Most are still in faithful service.

This is not to undermine the value of bike maintenance and repair. Indeed, there is even a section on overhauling bottom brackets in this very chapter. And I encourage you, if you are so inclined, to follow its advice when the time comes. But if you don't want to do this chore, stick around. Keep in mind that the repair and maintenance advice detailed in the following pages represents the *ideal*—the work you should do to keep your bike in perfect running condition. You may choose to do less, but the information is here if you want it.

Most shops are interested in selling bikes, not in fixing them. So try being your own repairman

On the other side of the coin, knowing a little bike repair is almost always necessary considering the lack of really good professional bike mechanics in this country. Most shops are interested in selling bikes, not fixing them, so you can often do a better repair job yourself, and if you're on a long country tour, you may be forced to do your own repairs.

Don't fret if you're mechanically inexperienced. You can do it. To make things as simple as possible, we've enlisted the aid of the Xyzyx Information Corporation, which has supplied technical illustrations for this chapter. Xyzyx believes that if you read instructions or look at a drawing and don't understand what to do, the instructions are at fault, not you. Xyzyx also publishes two handbooks, one a repair manual for derailleur bicycles and the other for coaster-brake and 3-speed models. Both are perfect for throwing in a saddlebag for quick on-the-road repair reference.

Okay, let's get to work:

First, a few suggestions to work by

HOT TO GET started reading? Well don't. First go get your bike. Wheel it into the livingroom or the bathroom or wherever you do your reading. Look at each part as it's referred to. You'll understand better, faster, and retain the information longer.

• For each operation, read the appropriate section *all the way through* before beginning work. It's no fun to have a hub's innards scattered all over the garage floor and then discover in the next step that you're missing the proper lubricant.

- There's no need to read the chapter from beginning to end. *Read each section* as you need it.
- Keep in mind that the instructions given here may not fit every bicycle. It's impossible to cover every model in the world in one volume, so don't get upset if the directions or diagrams on these pages don't match your bike precisely. Just follow the directions that best apply. Where necessary, separate instructions are given for derailleur bikes (5-, 6-, 10-, 12-, or 15-speed), 3-speeds (and other interal-hub-geared bikes), and coaster-brake bicycles.

Now you're going to need some tools

I WON'T BOTHER giving you a complete tool list. It could go on forever, since there are special tools to do almost everything. If you want to go all the way, buy a professional Campagnolo tool set. You can pick one up for a few hundred dollars. Of course, you may have to sell your bike to buy one.

Buy your four basic tools first. They are very inexpensive. Then add others to meet your needs

A better idea is just to buy some basic tools, then add others as you need them. Here are four items that will give you a good start:

- Crescent wrench (adjustable). There's always a temptation to get a cheap one. Don't. The jaws will wear away fast. This tool is your workhorse.
- Screwdriver. Get one with a ¼-inch blade.
- Tire irons. There are special ones for bicycles. You need these to change standard clincher tires (you sew-up tire owners don't need these).
- Portable tool kit. I mean the kind that straps under the saddle. You'll need one anyway for touring. Mafac is one brand available. These kits come with an assortment of cheap wrenches that cover

Your basic—and essential—tool is an adjustable crescent wrench. Buy a good one; a cheap one will ruin your bike.

The biggest enemy of your chain is dirt—and grease picks up dirt. Keep your chain clean and lightly oiled.

many repairs. Make sure they're the right size for your bike. A bike made in the U.S. needs wrenches sized in fractions of inches. European and Japanese bikes require metric wrenches (sized in mm). American 5-, 10- and 15-speeds will also need metric tools for their derailleurs. Another wrench size is called Whitworth—used on some older British bikes. If confused, try the wrenches on your bike before buying them. *Don't use a wrench on a bolt or nut unless it fits exactly.* Some portable tool kits also include a small cable cutter and a set of Allen wrenches.

Basic maintenance even an all-thumbs guy or gal can do

LET'S START WITH some real easy stuff that will make life easier for your bike while demanding very little from you.

- **Keep the chain clean.** After every ride, wipe road grime off the chain with a rag or paper towel. This is probably the single most important thing you can do (see *Chain* section for further details) and one of the easiest.
- **Keep other parts clean, too.** Wipe them off when they need it: derailleurs, derailleur rollers, rear and front sprockets. Try to work out dirt from around the hub cones and that tiny bit of crank spindle that's exposed where it sticks out of the bottom bracket. Don't go bananas on cleaning, though. Clean the rest of the bike if the spirit moves you, but don't use metal polish or any other strong stuff. Use kerosene on metal parts if you have to, but then wipe dry.

Arrows show the points requiring lubrication. Use a light oil, and use it very lightly. Don't over-oil your bike!

Drawing courtesy Raleigh Industries of America

• **Oil it.** How often? The best rule is only when the bike needs it—but it takes some experience before you know when that is. For the new owner, every other month is a rough rule-of-thumb. I recommend lubricating your bike regularly with great trepidation. Some people turn into maniacs when they get an oil can in their hands. *Do not over-lubricate.* Better you should leave the bike alone. That extra oil will pick up dirt and cause extra friction. *If you have any doubt as to whether a part needs oil, don't oil it.* When you do oil, wipe off the excess. Use a lightweight motor oil or bicycle oil. Places to hit are brake-cable pivot points, inside the brake lever ends, the chain (go sparingly here—only lubricate if it feels dry or sounds squeaky), the freewheel, derailleur rollers and the stem where it fits into the head tube. (See the drawing.) Also oil 3-speed hubs or any other hubs with oil fittings.

Some parts on your bike are lubricated with grease, and should not be oiled. Examples are headsets, wheel hubs, bottom bracket and pedals. This varies from bike to bike. Some pedals and hubs, for instance, *are* packed with oil. If there's any doubt, spare the oil can. Grease-packed parts get overhauled, not oiled.

Some parts need grease, not oil. And these parts vary from brand to brand and model to model

• **Tighten loose nuts, bolts and screws.** Grab the bike by the saddle and shake. Any loose parts? Tighten them. Fenders are especially prone to coming loose and rubbing on your tires.

Things better left to others

THERE ARE A few things you shouldn't try to do yourself unless you're a professional or you're trying to become one and don't mind ruining a few bikes in the process. Take the following jobs to a good mechanic:

• **Frame repairs.** Don't attempt to fix a broken joint or a crushed tube or an out-of-alignment frame. In fact, probably no one can handle these problems. Tubes can be replaced on very superior frames, but they're the exception. You'll probably have to get a new frame.

• **Bent cranks or fork.** Take these to a mechanic with the right equipment.

• **Paint job.** Painting a bike doesn't make it run any better and is one hell of a job. Why? First, you have to strip the frame of all its parts. Then you have to put them all back correctly.

• **Overhauling internal hub gear changer.** A good job for masochists. Inside that innocuous 3-speed hub lurk a zillion parts ready to roll all over the floor. Better you should pay a guy to handle this headache.

• **Wheel truing** (and especially rear-wheel truing). This is the one job every amateur wants to try, and almost every one of them fails. It's appealing because a spoke wrench only costs about a buck, and it's fun to fiddle with the thing. But don't do it. Your wheel should be trued if it wobbles noticeably. It must be done on a truing jig by a mechanic with a real feel for this art. He tightens or loosens the spokes until each has exactly the right tension.

Okay, let's get down to specifics.

The chain

YOUR CHAIN, in my opinion, deserves more attention than any other component on your bike. It's the heart of the power train and has over 500 parts—500 parts that, if left uncared for, can build up a lot of needless friction. Luckily, maintenance is simple.

First of all, keep it clean. Make a habit of wiping dirt and grime off the chain after every day's ride. Don't worry about the fact that you're also wiping off oil. You won't be destroying the chain's lubrication. Oil on the outside of the chain doesn't do any good—it just collects dirt. The oil that's doing all the work is inside among the rivets, plates and rollers.

Even following this routine though, chains usually get hopelessly crudded up once in a while. If your chain is really dirty, corroded or rusty, clean it with a cloth dampened with solvent or kerosene. Wrap the cloth around the chain and turn a pedal backwards to run the chain through it. Dry the chain, and again while turning a pedal, lightly apply Lubriplate (a special brand-name chain lubricant) or lightweight oil (no heavier than 20 weight). *Do not over-lubricate.* You only need one tiny drop per chain roller. Run the chain through a rag again to spread the oil. Now clean all excess oil off the chain. Rub it hard with a clean cloth. This is most important. If you over-lubricate

After every day's ride, wipe the dirt off the chain. Don't worry about wiping off the oil, too. Enough will remain for good lubrication.

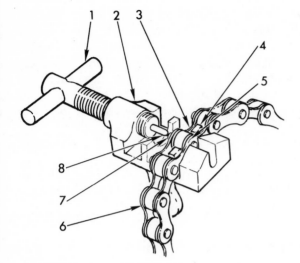

Figure 1

Typical chain tool costs only two or three bucks, is used to connect and disconnect chains and loosen tight links. Ask your bike dealer for the correct size for your chain.

you end up with exactly what you set out to eliminate in the first place: excess friction. The oil will pick up even more sand and grit, and you would have been better off leaving the chain alone. (Chains which feel dry to the touch or which squeak should also be lubricated no matter how clean they are.)

Often the grime is too packed in the chain to clean it on the bike. That means you'll have to take it off the bike. If you have a coaster-brake or 3-speed bike, you're in luck. The chains on most of these bikes have a master link, which has a U-shaped or oversized plate on one side that you can pry off. Chains on derailleur bikes don't have master links. Such links are so thick they would catch in the shifter mechanism and between the sprockets on the freewheel cluster. This means you'll have to take your 10-speed chain apart with a chain tool (Figure 1) available in bike shops for two or three bucks. *Chain removal* is as follows:

1. Place one link of the chain (3, in drawing) over the tab (4) of the chain tool. Turn the handle (1) clockwise until the point (8) touches the rivet (7). Line up the rivet with the point.

2. Now turn the handle clockwise until the rivet is free of the link, but *do not push the rivet all the way out of the sideplate* (5). If you do you'll regret it. You may not be able to get the rivet back in again when it's time to reconnect the chain. Now back the tool off until it's free of the chain.

3. If you've left some of the rivet in, you might have to finish the job by twisting the chain away from the rivet or prying it apart with a screwdriver.

Now that your chain is disconnected, take it off the bike and soak it overnight in kerosene or some other cleaning solvent. If it's really a mess, you might have to work it over with an old toothbrush. Let it drip dry for a couple of hours and then relubricate with oil or Lubriplate. Wipe dry. Put the chain back on the bike. You master-link people just go ahead and snap the chain back on and you're finished.

If you're re-installing the chain on a 10-speed, you may be a bit confused—especially if you never studied how the chain was threaded through. Thread the roller end of the disconnected chain first; then, with your rear derailleur in high gear, place the end of the chain on the smallest sprocket of the cluster. Now thread the chain over your derailleur's jockey pulley and around the idler pulley. Pull the chain around the small chainwheel and through the front derailleur. Confused? If you're worried you haven't got it right, take a good look at Figure 2.

Okay, once you have the chain properly threaded, use the chain tool to drive the rivet back into the sideplates. Make sure the rivet extends the same distance from both sideplates.

Here are some other kinky chain problems

LOOSE CHAIN. You should have about ½ inch of play in your chain (track bikes should have less). That is, you should be able to pull the chain only ½ inch away from its normal straight line from the top of

If your 10-speed chain sags, you'll be in luck if you have rear fork ends with adjustable stops. Just screw in bolt, turn in the nut, and pull wheel back in slots. Other parts are front fork ends.

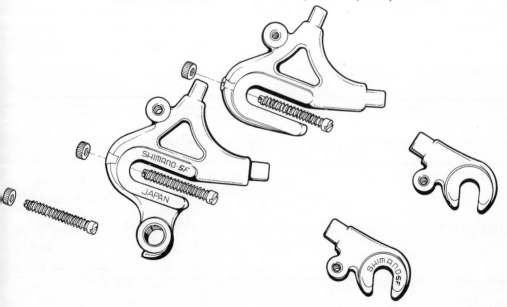

the front sprocket to the rear sprocket. If it sags more than this, you can do one of two things:

1. On coaster-brake and 3-speed bikes, loosen the rear axle nuts and pull the axle back in the frame to take up improper slack. Align the wheel and re-tighten. You can also do this on some 10-speed bikes which have adjustable stops in the rear drop-outs. Screw the stops back farther and move back your rear wheel.

2. Another solution is to remove one or two links with your chain tool, and then reconnect the loose ends. If you have to take out more than two or three links, your chain is in tough shape. Replace it.

Tight link. This is a link that doesn't swivel smoothly around its rivets. Perhaps it's not oiled enough, or one or both of its sideplates is bent, or it's hung up on the rivets. The result is a chain that kinks when it goes around, making a clunking sound as it jumps off the sprocket. There are four ways to deal with it:

1. Find the tight link and work some fine oil into it. Twist the link back and forth with your fingers. Hopefully that will solve the problem.

2. If not, you'll have to use a chain tool to move the offending rivet slightly to break the kinking. (Check first, though, to see if the sideplates are bent. If they are, go on to Step 3 below.) Use the chain tool as in *"Chain removal,"* but this time don't push the rivet through the sideplate. Just turn the tool handle about ¼ inch clockwise, then back it off. Try swiveling the link. Looser? Then try some more oil to get it completely free. If it's not any looser after the first ¼ turn with the tool, try another ¼ turn. After you get it loose, check to make sure equal amounts of rivet are sticking from both sides of the link. If not, even it up by pushing the rivet back from the other side with the tool. Check again to make sure the link is still loose.

3. If this process doesn't work, you may have bent sideplates or some other nameless problem. In any case, the link is no good and must be replaced. Installing a new link is just like disconnecting and reconnecting the chain with the special tool explained earlier. Only this time, you have to push in both rivets of the bad link. Perhaps, though, after removing the bad link you may not have to buy a new one. Is the chain too loose on the bike as described in *loose chain?* If so, maybe you're better off just removing the bad link and reconnecting the chain.

Senile chain. Your chain is worn out and must be replaced. Lots of tight links? Replace it. Chains can die after just a couple years. Other signs of chain death throes are side-to-side deflection of more than an inch, or stretchiness. To test for the latter, pull the chain tight around the large chainwheel. With the other hand try to pull the chain away from the chainwheel where the chain is tightest. If you can pull it away, the chain should be replaced.

Chains come in different sizes. Be sure you get the exact size of your old chain as they are not interchangeable. Coaster-brake and 3-speed models generally come with ⅛-inch chains while derailleur bikes use a thinner ³⁄₃₂-inch chain. Also, make sure the chain is the right length. Compare it to the old chain (assuming *it* was the correct length). You may have to knock off a few links with the old chain tool. Oil and wipe the chain before installing it. Of course, if you have a derailleur bike you'll have to use the chain tool to install the chain. On others you can use the master link.

Wheels and tires

DON'T GET PSYCHED OUT by your wheels. The more you stare at a bike wheel the more you're convinced it isn't really round. It probably isn't. No bike has perfectly round wheels. The goal is to have a wheel that's round enough to spin smoothly.

Stop looking at the wheel and spin it. Does it wobble noticeably from side to side? The wheel must be trued; that is, the tension on the spokes must be adjusted. Take it to an expert. If you have a wobble, you might also have a rim blip, or a bump on the rim (in fact, you can have blips even without a wobble). Blips and wobbles are often caused by hitting pot-holes or other rough spots, and sometimes by blowouts that suddenly leave you riding on your rims. Blips can foul up your braking if you have hand brakes. If you're brave you can carefully squeeze out these bumps with a vise-grip, but I'd recommend having it done by a mechanic. It's fairly cheap.

Watch your wheels for blips, bumps and wobbles. They can foul up your braking

That still leaves a lot you can do yourself. In this section we'll cover: removing and replacing wheels; removing, repairing and replacing tires; adjusting and overhauling hubs.

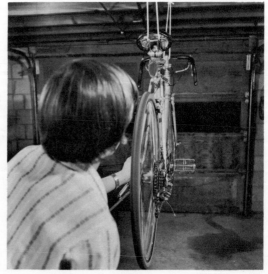

Suspend bike from ceiling or a tree, spin the wheels, and watch from either end. If the wheel wobbles noticeably you'll have to have it straightened.

Easiest way to work on your bike is to suspend it. This gives you instant access to either side, and prevents damage to the bike.

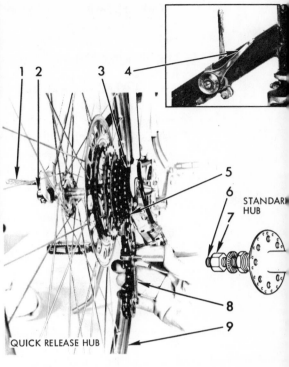

Figure 2
Here's a typical 10-speed rear—→ wheel. Parts are: 1) quick-release lever. 2) quick-release unit. 3) smallest sprocket. 4) proper high gear position of right gear-selector lever. 5) chain. 6) axle. 7) axle nut. 8) derailleur. 9) wheel.

Figure 3 ——→
Here are the parts of the front wheel: 1) quick-release brake lever. 2) quick-release wheel lever. 3) quick-release wheel unit. 4) wheel. 5) wingnuts for a standard wheel. 6) standard axle nuts.

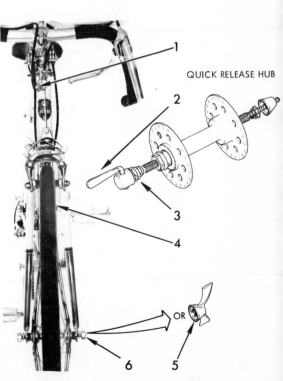

Let's start with wheel removal and replacement. You need to know this so you can repair tires, strip down the bike for stowing in a car trunk, and many other tasks, including that fateful day when you blindly ride into a curb and have to take the wheel to the shop to get it trued.

Front wheel removal (all bikes). The first thing is to get the bike off the ground, though this is admittedly more important for rear-wheel removal than for front. Ideally, clamp the bike in a rack. If you have a rear car rack, it will work nicely. Another idea is to screw an eye-hook into your ceiling and suspend the bike from a cable or twine. Out in the woods a rope over a tree limb will suffice. If none of these is possible, lay the bike gently on its left (non-chain) side. But try to suspend it—it makes everything easier and the wheels slip out better.

1. If the bike has hand brakes, you have to make sure the wheel and tire will clear the brake pads. If you have quick-release brakes, you've got it made. Just flip the quick-release lever which you'll usually find right above the brake on the cable hanger (see 1, Figure 3). On most bikes without quick-release brakes your wheel will clear the shoes if you just deflate the tire. If not, and your brakes are center-pulls, find the transverse cable that goes from the carrier to the brake arms. There are barrels that fit into loops on the arms. While squeezing the brake shoes against the rim, pull one of the barrel ends out of its loop and the brake will be released. If the brake is a side-pull, loosen the cable anchor bolt. (Confused? See *Brakes* section.)

2. If your wheel has a quick-release unit (3 in Figure 3), simply loosen it by holding the wheel tight and pulling the quick-release lever (2, Figure 3) away from the wheel. Remove the wheel by pulling it down and forward.

If you have a standard (non quick-release) wheel, loosen the two nuts (6, Figure 3) or wingnuts (5, Figure 3). Turn both the nuts or wingnuts simultaneously using two wrenches or two hands. Again, remove the wheel by pulling it down and forward.

Rear-wheel removal (derailleur bikes). When removing a 10-speed rear wheel it is even more important to have the bike off the ground, as the chain and derailleur make removal a little more difficult. First, release the brake if necessary, as detailed in *front-wheel removal*. Then, make sure the chain is on the smallest rear sprocket. Remember that to shift the chain you must be turning the pedals. Now, while holding the wheel, pull your quick-release lever (1, Figure 2) away from the wheel. If you have a standard hub, loosen the two axle nuts (7, Figure 2).

While your wheel is now technically loose, you'll find it doesn't slip right out of the drop-outs like the front wheel did. Stand behind the bike and while pulling the derailleur back with your right hand, gently push the wheel down and forward with your left. This will get the wheel past the derailleur and you can then disentangle the chain from the small sprocket by hand.

Rear-wheel removal (3-speed internal hub bikes). First, shift the bike into high gear. Get the bike on a rack or somehow off the ground. Loosen the shifter's locknut (9, Figure 4) and remove the sleeve (10, Figure 4) from the chain (8) by turning the sleeve counterclockwise. Loosen the barrel (5) and then your two axle nuts (7). Pull the wheel from the drop-outs, free the chain from the sprocket and remove the wheel.

Rear-wheel removal (coaster-brake bikes). Get the bike off the ground. You must first disconnect the coaster-brake bracket from the frame. The bracket is held to the chain stay by a clamp held by a bolt and nut. Remove the clamp. Now remove the two axle nuts and washers. Free the wheel from the chain stay clips. Lift the chain from the rear sprocket and remove the wheel.

Okay, sooner or later you'll have to put wheels back on again

Front-wheel replacement (all bikes with standard, non-quick-release wheels). Ideally, put the bike back on a rack or suspend it somehow, though this is not crucial for a front wheel. Place the axle tightly against the front drop-outs. Hold the axle against the drop-outs with one hand while tightening one nut or wingnut with the other. If tightening one nut turns the axle, you'll have to tighten both at once. Make sure the wheel is centered between the fork arms. Do not attempt to center the wheel by centering it between the shoes of your caliper brakes if that's what you have—your brake shoes may not be precisely equidistant from the wheel (this is nothing to worry about).

Now reset your brakes (if any) if you had previously released them. When you start riding again your brakes may screech at you when ap-

Figure 4. The parts of a 3-speed rear wheel: 1) wheel. 2) sprocket. 3) chain. 4) drop-out. 5) barrel. 6) axle. 7) axle nut. 8) selector chain. 9) locknut. 10) sleeve. 11) chain stay.

Right, adjust brakes for even touch.

plied just as they did when brand new. This is because you have replaced the wheel in a slightly different position, and either a new part of the brake-shoe rubber is hitting the rim or one shoe is hitting before the other one. This can mean one of two things: One, you've replaced your wheel off-center; or two, the wheel was originally misaligned and you've replaced it correctly, thus upsetting the brakes which had developed a cozy arrangement with the old off-center wheel. Strangely enough, this latter possibility is the more likely one, as the shop that sold you the bike is more likely to have slapped the machine together than that you have made a mistake. In any case, re-center the wheel if it's misaligned. If it's centered okay, either adjust the brakes to center the shoes over the wheel or forget about it—the squealing will stop after the brake shoes wear in, and adjust to the new wheel position.

Front-wheel replacement (quick-release wheels.) Place your axle against the drop-outs, centering it between the fork arms. Make sure the quick-release lever is open (pointing straight out). Spin both the lever and the cone on the other side of the axle so they are snug against the fork clips. Now tighten the quick-release lever by pulling it toward the frame. It should be difficult to push. If not, pull the lever out again and screw the cone in farther. Now try locking it again. The average guy should be able to close the lever with one hand: a thumb on the lever and four fingers around the fork arm for leverage. If you're of average strength and you need two hands, it may be too tight and you could snap off the mechanism. Also, the lever will close in any position, but it's safest to point it upwards, lined up with the fork arm at about a one o'clock position as shown below. Reset your brakes if necessary and you're ready to go. The same advice given above for squealing brakes applies to quick-release bikes as well, and is applicable to rear wheels, too.

When tightening up a quick-release wheel, line up the lever with the fork arm. It is much less likely to snag on any obstacle in this position.

Rear-wheel replacement (derailleur bikes). Get the bike on a rack or somehow off the ground. Make sure the rear derailleur is shifted into high gear. Slip the axle into the rear drop-outs, maneuvering the chain over the smallest sprocket. If you have a quick-release, screw the lever and cone hand-tight against the frame. If you have a standard wheel, hand-tighten the nuts or wingnuts. Now pull the wheel back until the axle seats against the stops in the drop-outs. Keeping the right end of the axle seated, move the left end until the wheel is centered between the fork arms. This is more difficult than lining up the front wheel as you have more play in the rear drop-outs. Wheel centered? Okay, quick-release owners: Push up your levers. You others tighten your nuts or wingnuts. Reset the brakes if necessary.

Rear-wheel replacement (3-speed internal hub bikes). Get the bike off the ground and throw the shift lever into high gear. Spin axle nuts to the ends of the axle. Slip the chain on the sprocket and pull the axle into the drop-outs. Pull it in to approximately the position you had it before (the nut marks on the frame should tell you this). The chain should flex only half an inch up or down in this position. Center the wheel between the fork arms and tighten the nuts. If the axle turns while you tighten one nut, tighten both simultaneously. You may need somebody to hold the wheel while you do this. Tighten the barrel (see 5, Figure 4) and connect the indicator sleeve (10, Figure 4) to the chain (8, Figure 4). Tighten the locknut (9, Figure 4). Reset brakes if necessary.

Rear-wheel replacement (coaster-brake). Same as above, only instead of reconnecting gear shifter, re-attach the brake clamp with its bolt and nut.

Fixing a flat—what to do when the tire goes blam or pssst

THE MOST COMMON repair problem is the flat tire. Nothing is more discouraging than that rough sound of metal against road surface that means your tire has gone flat and you're basically riding on a rim. Occasionally you'll hit a big nail and the tire will go blam. More often, flats sneak up on you because of a bad valve or a slow leak. In any case, if the tire can't hold its proper pressure, *stop riding and get off the bike.* You can ruin the tire by continuing to ride or, worse, you can bend the rim. If you can't fix the flat on the spot, and you're a purist, carry the confounded machine by slipping your head through the diamond so the top tube rests on your left shoulder while you support the bike with your right hand on the bottom of the seat tube (vice versa if you're left-handed). The object of this is to avoid damaging the tire tube or the rim. But frankly, you can usually get away with pushing the bike home.

As mentioned in an earlier chapter, there are two types of tires: clinchers, which have separate inner tubes, and sew-ups, which do not.

Clincher tires. You'll need tire irons or a reasonable substitute, a patch kit and a tire pump. Clincher tubes are easy to patch with any of the commercial patch kits available, but you might want to carry an extra tube on the road in case you get a really bad tear. The trick is taking the tire off and putting it back on. Here goes:

1. Check the valve stem first. Pump up the tire and put some spit (you perhaps expected expectorate?) on the end of the valve. If bubbles come up, the stem is loose. You'll have to get a metal valve cap with two prongs on top. Stick the prongs into the valve and rotate the cap until you catch hold of the stem. Now tighten the stem.

2. If the valve is okay, you have a bona fide flat. Remove the wheel. Make a quick check on the outside of the tire for the cause of the flat. Tacks and nails are easy to spot. If you find one, pry it out of the tire. If you can't find the problem, don't labor over it; go onto the next step.

3. Pry one side of the tire off the rim making sure the tire is entirely deflated first. Ideally, use a pair of tire irons. However, other *blunt* instruments will do, such as a spoon handle. Some skilled mechanics use a screwdriver, but this is a lousy technique for beginners; you can easily puncture the tube. Insert one iron between the tire bead and the rim. Get just one bead with the iron. If you get both you'll squeeze the tube in between. Pry the iron down and hook the handle on a spoke for convenience. With a second iron, pry out some more of the bead about two inches away from the first iron. At this point the bead probably will not tend to snap back into the rim, but if necessary, make a third pry. Now run your finger around inside the rim to loosen the bead all the way around. Do not pry the other bead out—one is all you have to do. You leave the tire on the rim.

Don't take the tire all the way off the rim. Just pry one bead loose, and leave the tire in place

If your tire leaks, check the valve first. Put spit on end of stem and watch for bubbles.

Pry one side of tire off rim with a pair of tire irons or old spoon handles.

Reach inside the tire opposite the valve and carefully pull out the tube. Now pump it up and feel around for the leak.

4. Pull the tube out of the tire, starting opposite the valve, but don't pull the valve out. Not yet anyway. Pump the tire way up, about 50 percent more than usual. This will help you find the leak if you haven't located it yet. If you can't pump it up, the puncture must be gargantuan, so replace the tube. If you can pump it up, feel around the tube to see where the air is escaping. If you can't find it, you'll have to take

Leave the valve in place. When you find the leak this will help you spot the cause, in the tire itself.

Mark the leak with chalk, then line up tube with tire. Look there for glass, a nail or anything sharp.

the tube all the way out of the tire and run it through some water to watch for bubbles.

Now if you didn't have to remove the tube completely, and if you found the leak—mark it. Then place the tube next to the tire. You haven't pulled the valve out yet, right? So the tube will line up with the tire just the way it was when you got the flat. This is to help you find the culprit that made the flat. Look for glass, tacks or thorns on the tread, a sharp burr on the rim, or a sharp spoke-end sticking through the rim strip. Remove the glass, file down the spoke or whatever.

5. Now you take the tube completely out of the tire. Deflate it, push the valve inside and pull it free (your valve may have a holding ring which you'll have to unscrew first).

6. Apply the patch. Directions vary from kit to kit but generally you must:

    a. Clean the puncture area and rough up the surface. Usually the latter can be done with the special roughing cap that comes with most patch kits.

    b. Spread on some glue and let it dry for a few seconds.

    c. Take the backing material off a patch, making sure you don't touch the sticky surface beneath.

    d. Press on the patch as hard as you can.

7. Now put the tube back in the tire. Sometimes it helps to inflate the tube slightly first. Poke the valve in its hole and stuff the tube around inside the tire, using only your hands. Once you've got it neatly in the tire, put the bead back into the rim. Work in both directions and try to do it with just your hands. You risk pinching the tube using a tire iron or other pry, but of course, if your hands are too weak you'll have to risk it. The last couple of inches will be especially tough. One trick is to push the bead on the opposite side of the wheel more deeply into the rim by pushing the wheel into the ground. While doing this, pull that troublesome couple of inches of bead on top up and into the rim with your hands.

If you are wealthy enough to have sew-up tires, you can afford a lousy two bucks to have them patched

8. Check that the valve is straight and that the bead is securely and uniformly in the rim all the way around the wheel. Inflate the tire to the proper pressure.

Sew-up tires are easy to remove, difficult to patch

SEW-UPS. My advice to people who get flats in their tubular tires is to forget about them. That is, don't try to patch the tire yourself. Take it to a good bike shop, where they know how to fix such things. For the novice, patching sew-ups is extremely time-consuming and most shops will do it for about $2 or less (if they do such repairs). Sew-ups usually come only on expensive bikes, so if you have sew-ups you should be able to afford a lousy two bucks. However, if you *do* want to do your own patch jobs, sew-up patch kits come with adequate instructions.

In any case, whether you patch your own tubular tires or not, you do have to know how to take the tires off and put them back on. This requires no tools and is quite simple. That's one of the beauties of sew-up tires:

1. Remove the wheel. Deflate the flat tire if there's any air left. Then gently peel the tire off the rim, working from the part of the wheel that's opposite the valve.

2. Inspect the rim to see that no spoke heads are protruding. If any are, file them down flush with the spoke nipple so they won't damage the new or repaired tire.

3. You'll need some tire cement or tape to hold the tire to the rim. Tire cement (or glue) comes in a tube, and most brands include instructions helpfully written in Italian. You Americanos will have to suffer in ignorance. You can also use tape. The most popular brand of tape sold is made by Jantex. The tape is touted to be easier to use, but I've always found the glue less cumbersome than the tape, although it does have a tendency to smear up your hands and your rim. If you buy the glue, clean excess glue from the tube nozzle before you screw the cap back on or you'll never get it off again. That's potent stuff. Also make sure you pack it near the top of your saddle bags when camping, or it'll get squashed and you'll have one hell of a mess. If you buy tape, keep it in the refrigerator. No kidding. The tape tends to melt and fuse in the heat, making it difficult to unwind. Both tape and cement are super sticky so it's always nice to have some solvent around to unglue yourself from your bike.

Anyway, if you go the cement route, spread some of the stuff on the rim with your finger or a brush, trying not to get any on the braking edges of the rim. Let the cement dry until it gets tacky. For extra sticking power, also spread some glue on the base tape of the tire. Inflate the tire slightly and it'll turn inside out making the base tape more available. This is not absolutely necessary, however, and may be omitted—especially if you tend to be sloppy, as you'll just gum up the tire with the glue.

If you get caught with a flat without any cement, you can get by with what's left of the old cement. This is one advantage of using cement rather than tape. If you use only the old cement, be sure you inflate the tire to the maximum normal riding pressure; the heavy pressure helps keep the tire on the rim. You can re-install the tire with fresh cement when you get the chance.

One disadvantage of glue is that you should remove the old cement from the rim to prevent build-up. This can lessen sticking power and cause bulges that will make the tires fit unevenly. Any good solvent or even turpentine will do this, but keep such stuff away from the paint (if you care about looks) and away from the tire rubber.

If you have opted for tape, just stick one strip of it around the rim. Stay away from any sort of dirt as the tape will snatch up everything in sight. Also, you'll have to stick a pencil or something through the tape at the valve hole to permit passage of the valve. A good idea is to spin the rim through some water as the tape will be quite sticky and

That glue is potent stuff; if it gets squashed, you'll have one hell of a mess. And keep that sticky tape in the refrigerator

hard to handle and this will take some of the stickiness out of it temporarily. Later, when the tire is on, the water will evaporate and the sticking power will be restored.

4. Now you're ready to put the tire on. First stretch the deflated tire by hooking it around your neck (don't get glue in your hair) or over your knee, and firmly and evenly pulling on it. Rotate the tire around your knee or whatever so the whole tire gets stretched. Now insert the valve through the valve hole. Push the tire onto the rim with both hands, working away from the valve. This really takes some muscle, especially if you're installing a brand new tire (as opposed to a used but repaired tire). The best bet is to set the wheel on a soft surface (such as grass) to give you something to push against. Once you start pushing the tire on, don't stop—don't release the tension. And when you get to the bottom, flip the wheel up to horizontal to finish the job.

Make sure the valve is straight; if it's not, tension is uneven near the valve and should be corrected. Now inflate the tire slightly, just enough to make it take shape, and check for tread trueness. Just roll the tire in the proper direction with your hands to line the tread up (out-of-true tread makes for excessive wear). Check for high or low spots. Stretch the tire to get rid of highs and push to correct for lows. Inflate the tire to the proper pressure. If you've used tire cement, it's advisable to wait eight to twelve hours before riding on the tire to allow the cement to set fully. Just between us, there will be times you won't want to wait that long, so don't worry about it. The high air pressure should keep the tire on the rim—just don't take sharp curves at flat-out speeds right away. Also, before putting the wheel back on the bike, remove with solvent any cement you smeared on the braking surface of the rim.

In replacing the tire, be sure the valve is straight; if it's not, you're in trouble

To install a sew-up tire, set rim on soft ground. Insert valve and start pushing tire on. Apply tension evenly. When you have only a few inches of tire to go, tip rim off ground (keep pressure constantly on) and roll last bit of tire on rim.

Adjust those hubs and eliminate loose wheels

YOU ADJUST A HUB simply by tightening or loosening its cones (see 4, Figure 5). A hub needs adjustment if the wheel wiggles (cones are too loose) or if the axle binds, keeping the wheel from spinning smoothly (cones are too tight). The latter is rare and usually only happens if you have tightened the cones too much to correct a wiggle. A wiggle is not the same as a wobble, which is what your wheel does when it's out of true. To test for looseness, grab your wheel by the tire and try to move it from side to side. If the wheel does wiggle, check first to see if your axle or quick-release unit is properly tightened. If that's not the problem, your hub needs adjustment.

Look at Figure 5, or better yet, look at your bike. Starting from the left side of a standard wheel, you should find an axle nut or wingnut, the fork drop-out, a washer, a locknut, another washer and then a cylindrical object which is the cone. If you look closely you can see that there is a cone-shaped part of it which presses against the bearings. Some bikes skip one or two of the washers and some have no locknut. In this case the axle nut serves as the locknut and the drop-out serves as a washer. If your bike is like this, make all adjustments with the wheel on the bike.

The cone is the vital part. It has two slots that a spanner fits into. A spanner is a tool that looks like a super-thin open-end wrench, and is essential for working on your hubs. You'll need two. Campagnolo makes a good set. Some bikes have slots on only one of the cones, usually the one on the left side. If that's the case, just work on the slotted cone. Usually you only have to adjust one of the cones anyway.

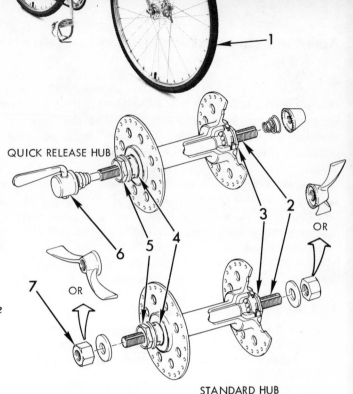

QUICK RELEASE HUB

Figure 5

Hub adjustment: 1)
wheel should not
move from side to
side when properly
adjusted. 2) axle. 3)
locknut. 4) adjust-
able cone. 5) lock-
nut. 6) quick-release
unit. 7) axle nut.

OR

OR

STANDARD HUB

Standard hub adjustment (all bikes). For once you guys with cheaper standard hubs have it easier than your richer quick-release friends. You can do the job with the wheel on the bike:

1. Loosen the axle nut or wingnut on the left side. Leave the right one tight (if you have only one slotted cone and it's on the right, reverse the process).

2. With a spanner, loosen the locknut slightly (5, Figure 5). Get the spanner in the cone slots and tighten the cone against the bearings, then back it off just slightly. Now tighten the locknut against the cone. Test the wheel. If it wiggles you'll have to repeat the process, tightening the cone and then locknut. If the wheel won't spin freely, back the locknut off the cone, and then the cone off the bearings, and then tighten the locknut against the cone again. Watch that when you're tightening the locknut you aren't tightening the cone also, pushing it too tight against the bearings. Hold the cone steady with one spanner as you tighten the locknut with the other. Re-test. If everything's okay, tighten the axle nut. If you can't get the wheel to spin freely without wiggling no matter how much you adjust, the hub must be overhauled.

Quick-release hub adjustment. Remove the wheel from the bike. Now remove the quick-release unit by unscrewing the adjusting nut and then grabbing the lever end and pulling out the shaft. Screw the nut back on the shaft so you don't lose the little springs in the unit.

It's easiest to work on the hub by clamping the wheel in a soft-jawed vise, if possible. Now you can follow the same directions given above for standard hub adjustment. *Except for one thing.* Standard hub owners have their tight right-side axle nut to keep the right-side locknut-washer-cone assembly in place. This facilitates adjusting the left-side assembly. With the wheel out of the drop-outs, you'll have to work on both ends at once. In other words, you'll probably have to put a spanner on the right-side locknut in order to work on the left-side locknut and cone (and vice versa). Work on both cones to get precise adjustment. Again, if you can't get the wheel to spin freely without wiggling, the hub should be overhauled. If you get the hub adjusted, slide the quick-release shaft back in the axle and screw on the spring and adjusting nut on the other side. Replace the wheel on the bike.

Why you overhaul a hub and how to do it

OVERHAUL YOUR HUBS when your wheels aren't rolling right. Some experts recommend an overhaul twice a year. My philosophy is to leave the hubs alone if they're working right. If the wheel wiggles or binds and you can't correct the problem through simple adjustment, then overhaul the hub. When you become an experienced biker, cycling more than a couple of thousand miles per year, you should be able to *feel* when you're getting too much friction in the hub, and not rely on any expert's time table.

When you finally get that hub apart, here's what you're going to be concerned with:

The hub has four basic elements that can go wrong—an axle, two sets of bearings, two cones and a lubricant (grease usually, but sometimes oil). The axle spins around inside the bearings. If the bearings get worn and out-of-round, there will be more friction on the axle. The axle sometimes gets bent or stripped. The cones also can become worn. And lubricant should always be replaced. The hub casing (the main body of the hub) usually holds up pretty well. In short, you're looking for worn parts, and cleaning everything up.

You're going to need two hub spanners, solvent, and grease or oil. Most of you will restrict overhauls to the front wheel only. If you have a coaster-brake or internal-hub-geared bike, take the back wheel to a good shop (or a bad shop if you're a masochist). These hubs are too complicated to mess with. If you don't believe me, go ahead and take one apart. But don't call me for help putting it back together.

If you have a derailleur bike, you can remove the freewheel and treat the rear hub just like a front hub. However, you'll need a special freewheel-remover tool. These can cost $6 or more (and I'd recommend a good one so you won't mar the freewheel body). So unless you plan to have further use for this tool, it may be cheaper to have a shop do the overhaul.

The following operation appears long and complicated. Actually, you're just taking the hub apart—the amount of detail in the instructions is mainly to help you avoid spilling the bearings.

How to avoid runaway bearings

YOU CAN WORK on the hub with the wheel loose on the floor or you can clamp it in a soft-jawed vise. With a vise you can lock up one side of the hub while you disassemble the other. However, on most bikes the ball bearings are loose (as opposed to being held in a cage, see 10, Figure 6) and slippery, which is how they should be. If the wheel is held vertically in a vise the bearings can and will fall to the floor. So clamp the hub as close to horizontal as you can even though this is more awkward. The following directions assume you have no vise and will do the overhaul with the wheel on the floor with a large rag underneath to catch errant bearings:

1. Remove the wheel from the bike. Remove axle nuts and washers from standard wheels and quick-release units from quick-release wheels. To do the latter, release the lever, unscrew the adjusting nut and remove it and its accompanying spring(s). Pull the rest of the unit from the hub and then put the nut and its spring(s) back on the unit to help keep all parts together.

2. Place the wheel on the floor on the right end of the axle (the right side of the bike is the chainwheel side). Unscrew and remove the left locknut (4, Figure 6) with a spanner while holding another spanner on the right cone (12, Figure 6). Now unscrew and remove the left cone (5). Be careful. Once the cone is removed only gravity is holding the bearing in the hub.

3. If the bearings are protected by a dust cap (6, 11), pry it off with a screwdriver, working around its circumference easily so as not to crimp it. Now you should be looking at your left-side bearings (7). The balls should be touching all the way around. If there are any gaps you're short a bearing or two. Whether you have enough or not, record the number of bearings to help when putting the hub back together. That's right, actually write the number down somewhere. It can save you a headache later.

4. Remove the bearings. You have to be careful not to accidentally dump the right-side bearings while doing this. So hold the right end of the hub and the axle tightly and turn the wheel over to dump the left-side bearings (7) into your hand or into an old pie tin (anything to catch and hold them). It's possible the grease may hold the bearings in the hub. If so, keep the wheel on its left side and slowly pull out the axle from the other side of the hub—you must do this eventually anyway. If that doesn't work, pry the bearings out with a screwdriver, taking care not to mar them. When removing bearings held in a retainer, note how the retainer goes into the hub so you can replace it exactly. If the retainer has a solid side and an open side, the solid side usually faces outward.

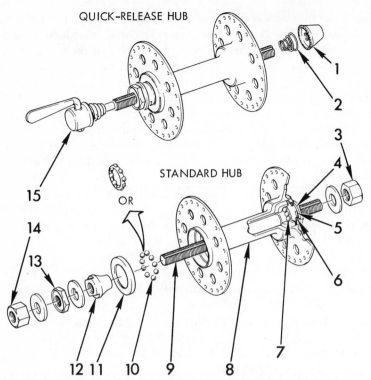

QUICK-RELEASE HUB

STANDARD HUB

OR

15 14 13 12 11 10 9 8 7 6 5 4 3 2 1

Figure 6. Hub: 1) adjusting nut. 2) spring. 3) axle nuts. 4) left locknut. 5) left cone. 6) left dust cap. 7) left ball bearings. 8) hub casing. 9) axle. 10) right bearings. 11) right dust cap. 12) right cone. 13) right locknut. 14) axle nut. 15) lever end of quick-release unit. You are viewing hub from front of bike.

5. Now pull out the axle if you haven't already done so (with the wheel still on its left side) and remove the right-side dust cap (11) if there is one. Inspect the bearings for gaps and write down the number of balls. Is it the same as the left side? I hope so. If not, one side is running short. Dump out the bearings.

6. The hub is now disassembled and you're ready to do the gut work. First, clean all parts with kerosene or some other solvent and wipe thoroughly. Then conduct a thorough medical examination:

a. What's the health of the bearings? Are they discolored, pitted or otherwise damaged? If so, replace them. Don't skimp—you'll throw away all the work you've already done. Take a bearing with you to the bike shop so you can replace the damaged or missing bearings with identical parts. The same goes for other hub parts.

b. In the hub cups (where you found the ball bearings) and on the cones you should find rings in which the bearings roll. These are called races. If pitted, replace the cones. If the cups are badly damaged you'll have to replace the whole hub casing, but this is rare.

c. If the axle has stripped threads, replace it. If you have disassembled the hub as suggested, the axle will still hold the right-side locknut-washer-cone combination intact. To check the axle for straightness, it's best to remove these parts and roll the axle on a smooth surface to discern any bends. Before you do this, carefully measure the distance from the end of the axle to the cone, as you'll want to reinstall the axle exactly. Do this also if you must replace the axle. However, you can get away without removing the cone and locknut by placing the axle on a table with the cone-locknut hanging over the edge so that most of the axle can be rolled over the surface. You can check the straightness of the other end of the axle by eye. This will suffice if you're lazy.

7. Now set the wheel on its left side and repack the right side of the hub with bike grease. Spread it around inside the cup. Again, don't go crazy with the grease—it'll just attract dirt. If you have expensive hubs that were packed with oil, repack them, of course, with oil.

8. Put the bearings back into the hub. Check the number you wrote down earlier so you get the right number of balls back in (assuming you had the correct number to begin with). Make sure the bearings are blotted dry of any solvent before replacement. If the bearings are held in a cage or retainer, replace the cage the way you found it.

9. Slide the right dust cap (11) onto the axle and down around the right cone. Stick the axle into the hub so the cone hits the bearings. Push the dust cap into position.

10. Holding the axle, turn the wheel over and repeat the process for the left side: grease the hub, replace the bearings (do you have the right number?) and dust cap. Now screw the left cone on down to the bearings, then screw on the washer and locknut.

11. Spin the wheel to check if the bearings are seated properly. If the wheel wobbles, shake it until the bearings get in the groove. Now go back to *hub adjustment* directions to get the wheel spinning right. Since your wheel is off the bike, you must follow the adjustment directions given for quick-release hubs even if your hubs are standard.

12. Replace quick-release units, or standard axle nuts, or wingnuts; replace the wheel on the bike.

Brakes

DON'T FRET CONSTANTLY about your brakes. When something goes wrong the problem is easily remedied. And if it can't be remedied, replacement parts are cheap. The most common problem you'll run into is weak brakes: the brake pads are too far from the wheel rims, and you must squeeze the brake levers until they almost press against the handlebar to apply stopping power (lever travel should be no more than about two inches). This might be caused by worn-out brake shoes or by a misadjusted or stretched cable. And occasionally the cable breaks.

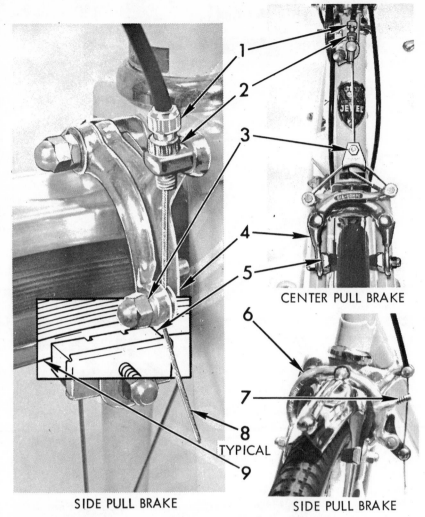

CENTER PULL BRAKE

TYPICAL

SIDE PULL BRAKE

SIDE PULL BRAKE

Figure 7. Brake assembly: 1) cable barrel; 2) lockring; 3) nut;
4) brake arms; 5) brake pads; 6) screw-in side-pull model;
7) adjusting screw; 8) cable end; 9) rim.

Replace brake shoes. If your problem is worn pads, you can buy whole
new shoes or just the rubber pads. Both are fairly cheap. Install new
shoes (5) so they will strike the rim, not the tire. They should be about
⅛ inch from the rim when the brakes are open. If you are putting new
rubber in a shoe, make sure the closed end of the shoe is facing forward when you re-install them. Otherwise the rubber will fly out when
you apply the brakes. On some brakes the pads toe-in slightly—the
front of the pad is closer and strikes the rim before the rear does. This
is fine; some riders even prefer this design. But if the pads are equidistant all the way, fine too. Just so the rear isn't closer than the front. If
it is, try bending the brake arms very carefully with a vise grip to
rectify the situation.

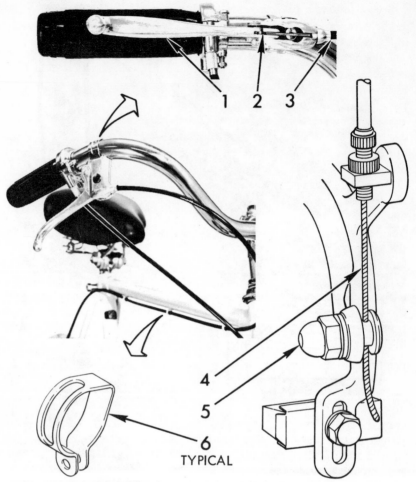

Cable removal and installation: 1) lever; 2) upper cable end;
3) housing; 4) lower cable end; 5) retaining nut; 6) housing clamp.

Misadjusted or stretched cable. Another easy problem. First, try
futzing with the cable barrel (1). Note different placement of barrel on
side-pull and center-pull brakes (Figure 7). Loosen the lockring (2)
about four turns. Unscrew the cable barrel and see if that brings the
pads within ⅛ inch of the rim. If that doesn't work, you'll have to pull
the cable through. Tie the brake arms (4) closed with twine or use a
special third-hand tool. Loosen the nut (3). Pull the cable end down
with pliers to remove the slack. Tighten the nut when the cable is
taut. On side-pulls the cable end (8) is down near the brake shoe. On
center-pulls it's right under the cable carrier. Side-pulls are a breeze,
but it's tough holding up the center-pull carrier while you pull down
on the cable. Maybe you can get a friend to help. If not, maybe you can
get a small socket wrench to fit the nut (3). This makes it relatively
easy to hold the carrier up and then tighten that nut in a hurry when
the cable is taut.

Some side-pulls (6) have an adjusting screw (7). Turn this screw to get brake shoes the proper distance from the rim. If that doesn't work, pull the cable through as explained above.

Cable replacement. Sometimes adjusting just won't solve your problem. Brake cables don't last forever. Sometimes they stretch into uselessness; sometimes they just plain break. If it hasn't broken outright, try a little oil before replacing—a drop in each end of the housing. Now squeeze the lever several times. Okay? If not, pull the cable out. First, disconnect the cable end (4, opposite page) by loosening the retaining nut (5). Note that the diagram shows a side-pull brake. On center-pull brakes you remove the cable from the nut on the crossover carrier. Depress the hand lever (1) and disconnect the upper cable end (2). Pull the cable from the housing (3). If you also need a new housing, you'll have to remove the housing clamps (6).

Take your old cable to a bike store for replacement so you get one of the same type that will fit your lever housing. Don't worry if it's too long (just so it isn't too short), as you can cut it to size with cable cutters after you've installed it. Before installing, coat the cable lightly with oil. Stick the cable in the housing (3) at the lever end. Push it all the way through. Now depress the lever (1) and connect the cable end (2) to the lever. At the other end, thread the cable through the holder in the retaining nut (5). Tighten the retaining nut. Adjust the cable as explained earlier if necessary.

Other problems. Sometimes you'll find the brake pads unequal distances from the rim. Maybe your problem is a poorly installed brake assembly. Find the big bolt that holds the brake to the frame, loosen it, align the brake correctly and retighten. Sometimes brakes don't release properly after you take your hand off the lever. One pad sticks to the rim. On side-pulls, try tapping the spring with a hammer and pin. On either side-pulls or center-pulls, try oiling the pivot points (wipe away any excess lubricant though). Also, you can try loosening *slightly* the mounting bolt on side-pulls since this bolt holds the two arms together and may be binding them. Finally, new brake pads will usually squeak a lot. This is perfectly okay from a mechanical standpoint. Some people don't like it though, and if you're one, try sanding them slightly.

Handlebars and stem

IT'S WISE TO GET acquainted with your handlebars (Howdy, handlebars!). Besides wanting to be able to adjust their height from time to time, you will also want to be able to lower them completely and turn them sideways to conform with airline regulations and to save room when stuffing your bike in the trunk of your car. These adjustments, however, are not done directly to the handlebars, but to the stem. There are only a couple of things you can do to a handlebar, so let's get them out of the way before we talk about the more important stem.

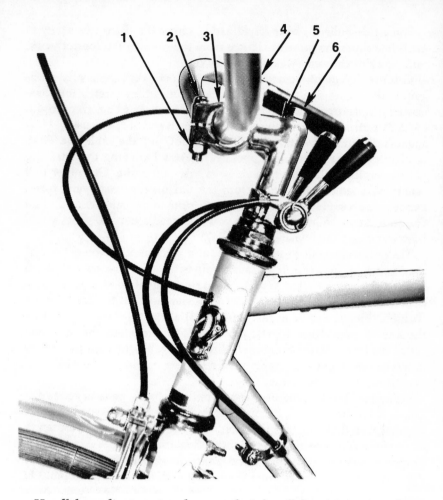

Handlebar adjustment and removal. A handlebar (4) is just a bent tube with no parts, so anything you do with it will be done to the stem (5), which holds it, or to the brakes, tape or end plugs that adorn it. When you buy your bike, the position of the bars is usually adequate. If, however, you have the mad urge to tilt them a little, all you need do is loosen the nut (1) or bolt (2) or whatever you find on your bike's stem. If you want to remove the bar entirely you will have to strip one side of the bar of its brake and handlebar tape and then pull it through the clamp (3). Should you want to replace your handlebars, be sure you get the same size diameter so the new model will fit the stem's handlebar clamp.

Some stem clamps have a keyed binder bolt so all you need do is turn the nut, the bolt being automatically held in place. If turning the nut just spins the bolt ineffectually, the key has been sheared off. Get that nut off somehow (maybe you can grab the bolt with needle-nose pliers while you get a wrench on the nut) and remove the bolt. Your best bet is to replace it with a bolt of the same size, of course, but one which has a head on it like the one shown (see 2, photo).

346

Stem adjustment and replacement. Right at the top of the stem you will find an expander bolt. This bolt extends down into the stem and culminates in a wedge nut. The stem goes into the head tube, of course, but is not really connected to it. If you looked inside the steering head, what you'd find instead is a fork tube (which is connected to the fork crown) that extends up the head tube from the bottom. The stem fits into this fork tube. The wedge nut expands the bottom of the stem against the fork tube and thus lets you steer the bicycle.

To loosen the expander, first turn the bolt a couple turns (on some bikes you'll need an Allen key). In most cases this will not loosen the stem. So you must bop the bolt lightly with a hammer or the side of your wrench or something. This will spring the expander and you will be able to raise or lower the stem. You will also be able to turn the stem sideways.

To tighten, you just turn the bolt back again, making sure the stem is aligned with the front wheel. The best way to get leverage on the bolt while lining everything up is to straddle the front wheel so you can hold the fork between your legs, and hold the handlebar with one hand while you turn the bolt with the other. Get this thing really right as it takes more stress than you might imagine. While riding a friend's bike I once had the strange experience of having the bars turn sideways in my hands while pulling hard up a hill. It's not a pleasant surprise.

When raising your handlebars, don't go too far. You should have at least two inches of stem inside that head tube. If you need to extend it farther than that, your frame is too small for you.

You may want to replace your stem if it's cracked, broken or it's the wrong size (extension too long or short). First, remove the handlebars. Then loosen the stem in the normal way and pull it out of the head tube. Take the old stem to a dealer so you can get a new one with the right size handlebar clamp. Many stems are slotted; make sure this slot at the bottom lines up with the lug on the wedge nut. Stick it into the head tube; tighten up in normal fashion.

Headset

THE HEADSET, sometimes called the steering head, holds the fork tube in the head tube. The headset has two sets of bearings, at top and bottom, so the fork can move and you can steer, a valuable arrangement if you're interested in going around corners.

What goes wrong with a headset? Well, it can work loose. It may rattle when you ride over rough roads. To fix it, all you have to do is adjust the top cup (5). If, however, the headset gets stiff and it's hard to steer the bike, or if you hear crunchy noises coming out of that head tube when you swivel the fork, any number of things can be wrong: damaged bearings, races, cones, etc. You need an overhaul. And I say don't try it. This is one of the trickier assemblies on the bike, with lots of things to go wrong. Take it to a good shop. For the inexperienced it's a long, hard job. It's not something you really need to learn, like a hub overhaul, because it should only have to be done on rare occasions. Some experts recommend overhaul once per year, but that's ridiculous and unrealistic (many racers who ride daily aren't that meticulous). Get it overhauled only when something goes wrong. If it steers okay, leave it alone. Adjustment is something else; you may have to do that from time to time (it's impossible to say exactly how often).

Headset adjustment. To tighten the headset you must tighten the cup (5) against the bearings. But first, loosen the top locknut (2). You'll need a big crescent or a small pipe wrench to do this. Now tighten the cup snugly against the bearings. Not too tight, though. Make sure the fork (9) still swivels smoothly; if not, back the cup off slightly. To check if your headset is now tight, lift the front wheel off the ground a couple of inches and drop it to simulate hitting a bump. It shouldn't rattle. You may or may not have a keyed washer (3). If you do, bring it down tight against the adjustable cup. Ditto the brake cable hanger (4). Now tighten the top locknut down on the whole thing. If you don't have wrenches big enough to do this job comfortably, I suggest taking the bike to a shop. They probably will make the adjustment while you wait.

Headset overhaul. If you really want to try this, okay. Just do it like any overhaul, checking all parts for damage, cleaning with solvent and regreasing the races and bearings. The thing to remember is that loosening the cup (5) will loosen the fork and it could fall right out of the head tube. Lay the bike down and hold the fork while disassembling to avoid damaging it. Your headset may not be assembled *exactly* like the one shown in the drawing. Headsets vary. Just remember how yours is put together while you're taking it apart. Remove the stem before starting.

Saddle

THERE'S NOT MUCH you have to fix on a saddle: You can change the height of the seat post, the angle and position of the saddle on its bracket, and on most seats you can also increase or decrease the tension on the leather or plastic.

Seat post adjustment. If your saddle twists side to side while you ride or you find yourself sinking closer and closer to the ground and have to lift your knees up to your chest to pedal, your post is slowly disappearing inside the seat tube. To rectify this condition or to change the height of your saddle, all you must do is put a wrench to the binder bolt. Get the saddle to the height you want (keep 2½ inches of post in the tube) and try to find a box wrench that will fit over that nut (5), or set your crescent wrench carefully to fit it. Tightening the nut on most bikes takes considerable effort to make it stick, and you don't

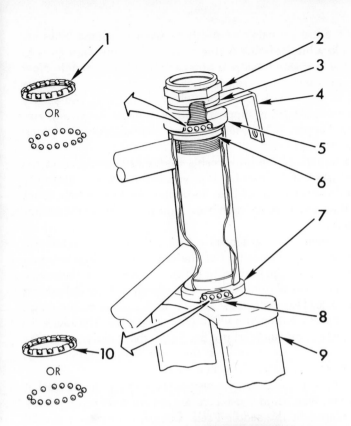

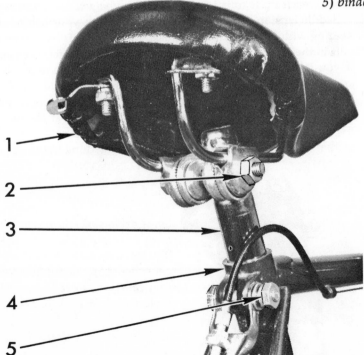

Headset:
1) *bearings;*
2) *locknut;*
3) *keyed washer;* 4) *cable hanger;*
5) *adjusting cup;* 6) *cone;*
7) *bottom cup;* 8) *cone;*
9) *fork;*
10) *bearings.*

Saddle:
1) *seat;*
2) *nut;*
3) *seat post;*
4) *seat tube;*
5) *binder nut.*

want to strip the nut by using an ill-fitting wrench. (Some bikes require an Allen key binder bolt.) A clue to when it's tight enough is to try to swivel the seat side to side. If you can't, it's tight enough. Now mark the seat post with a grease pencil or a spot of paint right above the seat tube so you will always know where to set it. If you simply can't prevent the post from slipping, you may have the wrong size post. This can happen if a dealer has been haphazardly switching saddles. Go get the right size.

Note: Usually part of the brake cable assembly is attached to the binder bolt (5). As you tighten the bolt you will move this assembly about ¼ inch downward out of line. So tighten the binder bolt about ¼ turn more than you need to, then back it off to put the cable assembly back in place.

Bracket adjustment. To tighten up a seat that tilts backwards and forwards or to change the position of the saddle on its bracket, you simply tighten or loosen the bracket nuts (2). You can move the saddle backward or forward, and point the nose up, down or level depending on your preference. However, most saddles aren't made well enough that you can get *any* position you want. (An exception is the Ideale 90 which has a super-adjustable clip.) So jiggle the saddle as you're tightening the bracket to make sure the teeth are meshing firmly. Tighten the nuts evenly, each a little at a time.

You can do something about a saddle that's too hard for your behind. There's an adjusting bolt, with a nut. Just find either one

If you have one of those expensive seat posts with a built-in bracket (see drawing) you won't find those nice convenient nuts on the sides. They're up underneath the saddle itself. Campagnolo sells a special tool to reach these nuts for about $5. Maybe you can borrow one.

Saddle tension. If your saddle is too hard for your behind, or if it is sagging with old age, you can loosen it or tighten it by means of a long bolt in the nose of the saddle. You'll find a nut, which is easier to turn if you take the saddle off its bracket. You don't have much room to work with, so use an open-end wrench. Some saddles have their leather (or plastic) cut away up front to make adjustment easier, but on others you just have to bend the material to get at the nut.

New saddle break-in. Neat's foot oil will help soften a brutal new leather saddle, but lots of saddle soap is something better. Besides, the

Some expensive seat posts, such as this Campagnolo, have an integral bracket, with nuts at the top which get covered by the saddle when it is installed. You need a special tool to work on such a post.

dye in some new saddles can stain your pants, and oil just compounds this problem. Try the soap and save your clothes.

Derailleurs

THESE ARE THE GADGETS 10-speeders ooh and ah at in the shop when they're new and swear at when they break down. But you can tame them. First, it always helps to know how they work, so go back to the chapter, "The 10-speed primer," if you don't understand derailleur principle. This helps de-mystify the gadgets and gives you a clue as to how to fix them. Oftentimes you will think something is terribly wrong with your shifter when actually only a small adjustment is required. Here are the two most common problems and their simple remedies:

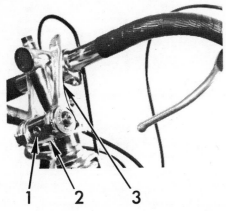

Not all shift levers are on the down tube. Stem lever at top includes a loosening screw (1) that holds a clamp (2) and the levers themselves (3). Handlebar levers, bottom, include: selector body (4), screw (5), nut (6), trim nut (7) and the lever (8).

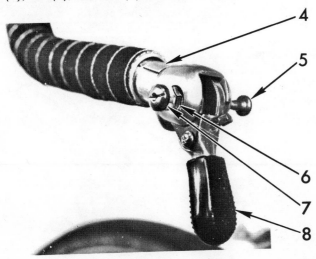

Uncontrolled shifting. The chain shifts when you don't want it to. Don't get upset. Your control levers are just too loose, letting out slack and throwing the chain onto smaller sprockets. Tighten up the wing bolt or whatever you find on the side of the lever.

Shifting difficult. If you haven't figured it out yet, this means your levers are too tight. Maybe you can fix the problem just by loosening the wing bolt or whatever, but this is unlikely since parts have a tendency to loosen rather than tighten by themselves. Probably the mechanism is crudded up with dirt. Take the unit apart by unscrewing the wing bolt, but record the order of parts so you can put them back together.

High-gear adjustment: High-gear travel screw (5) is shown on five major brands of derailleur. Keep shift lever in high-gear position (1) while adjusting, and get chain (2) to stay on smallest sprocket (3). When you think you have it, shift chain to second smallest gear (4) and then back again, or shift into biggest gear and back out again.

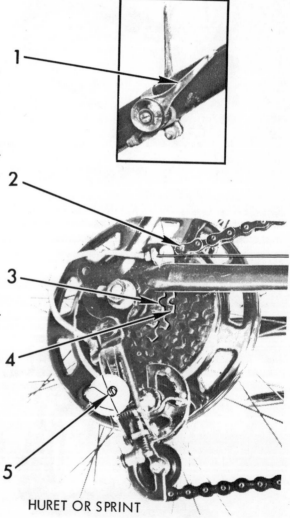

HURET OR SPRINT

Hairier problems—derailleur adjustment

MANY MEDIOCRE derailleurs get out of adjustment after rough, or even normal, use. When this happens you have one of two problems: Either you are unable to get the chain on the highest or lowest gears, or you throw the chain right off the sprockets. The easiest way to take care of this is to get the bike on a rack or off the ground so you can spin the cranks. It's always helpful to have a friend turn the pedals while you fool with the adjustment screws. Let's look at rear derailleur adjustment first.

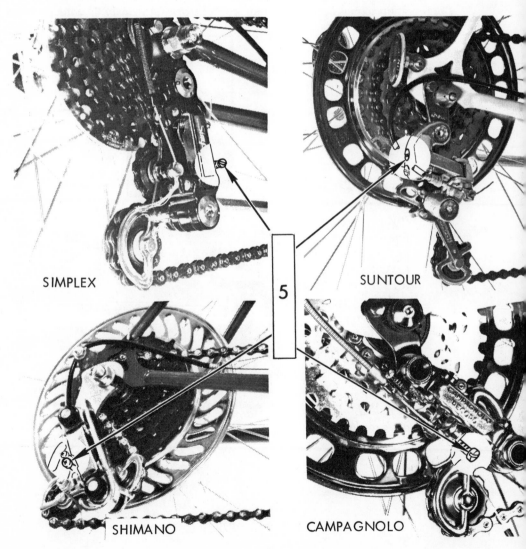

SIMPLEX

SUNTOUR

5

SHIMANO

CAMPAGNOLO

Rear derailleur. You'll need a screwdriver. What you have here are two throw-adjusting screws which determine how far the derailleur can throw the chain. One screw governs outward throw toward the small sprocket; the other governs inward throw toward the big sprocket. See diagram to determine which is which for your brand of shifter. The rear derailleur should be adjusted with the chain on the smaller chainwheel up front.

Okay, let's say your problem is that the derailleur throws the chain too far outward, thus knocking the chain between the cluster and chain stay. Put the chain back on the smallest sprocket and screw the high gear adjustment either clockwise or counterclockwise (usually clockwise) until it no longer throws as you turn the pedals. Turn the screw in ¼-revolution increments during this adjustment. When you think you've got it, shift the chain all the way inward, then all the way out again to make sure the chain won't throw. Obviously, if your problem

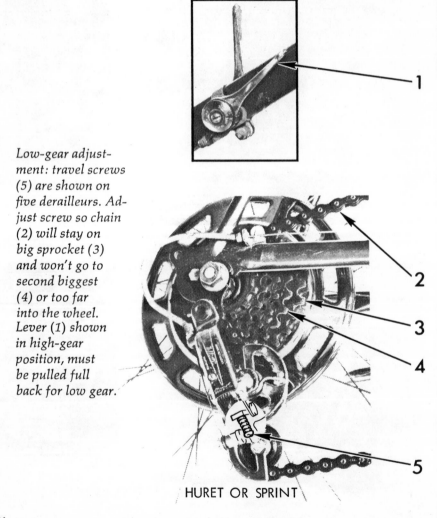

Low-gear adjustment: travel screws (5) are shown on five derailleurs. Adjust screw so chain (2) will stay on big sprocket (3) and won't go to second biggest (4) or too far into the wheel. Lever (1) shown in high-gear position, must be pulled full back for low gear.

HURET OR SPRINT

is an inability to get into high gear, you'll have to loosen that high-gear screw.

If the derailleur throws the chain past the largest sprocket, you must fix it immediately before you end up ruining your wheel, derailleur, chain or all three. Put the chain back on the sprocket and follow the same procedure as above. If your problem is not getting the chain far enough inward to mount that big sprocket, it could be a matter of adjustment (so turn the screw) or it could be a loose cable. We'll get to that in a while. But first . . .

Front derailleur adjustment. On most European shifters, the inside adjusting screw is for inward throw, the outer one for outward throw. This is not the case with all shifters, so you may have to experiment. (If there is but one screw, it's for outward throw and you have my condolences. To adjust inward throw, you must move the front cage on its shaft and tighten the cage locking screw.)

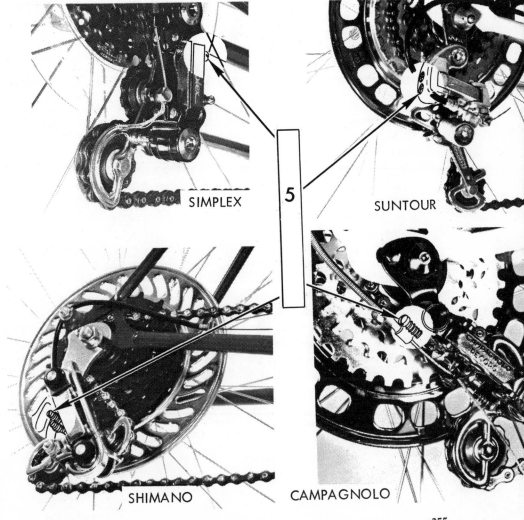

SIMPLEX

5

SUNTOUR

SHIMANO

CAMPAGNOLO

To adjust for inward throw, get the chain on the largest sprocket in the rear. Adjustment is a little more difficult than rear adjustment because you want to adjust the throw to allow a slight clearance between the chain and the inside plate of that front derailleur cage (so it won't rub). Then shift the chain in the rear to high gear and adjust for outward throw. Again, you must make sure the chain will not rub, so get some clearance between the chain and the outside plate of the cage. Okay, now try it out a few times by shifting back and forth. Don't be satisfied with the front derailleur just being able to bop the chain from chainring to chainring. Adjust the derailleur lever after each shift to get the cage so it won't rub the chain, just as you would do if riding.

All together now. Okay, shift the bike into all ten gears. Frankly, I wouldn't expect too much. That is, in those extreme gears (large chainring to large rear sprocket and vice versa) you might still get some front-cage rubbing. If everything else works smoothly, I'd forget about it and just not use those gears. They're not efficient anyway. But you should be able to eliminate any front cage rubbing in the other gears. If not, re-adjust that front changer.

Of course, your problem may not be adjustment at all. Check that front derailleur cage. Is it bent? Are the plates parallel to each other, straight up and down? If the cage is screwed up in any way, perhaps you can bend it back into alignment very carefully with pliers.

Cables and other problems. Sometimes your problem is neither the derailleur nor the levers but a loose or overly taut cable. Too much slack or a stretched cable, and you won't be able to pull the derailleur into the bigger sprockets. If the cable is too tight, the derailleur can't return to the small sprocket position. (Remember that the Sun Tour front shifter works just the opposite—its spring returns it to the large gear position.) Anyway, to tighten most cables, shift the derailleur to the smallest (in size) gear, loosen the anchor bolt on the derailleur and pull the cable taut with pliers. Tighten the anchor bolt and try shifting again. If you have trouble getting the derailleur into the small sprocket, let out just a slight amount of cable at the anchor bolt with the shift lever in the far forward position.

Sometimes a derailleur shifts slowly because it's dirty or isn't lubricated. Clean those jockey and tensioner rollers and spritz some light oil on the derailleur's pivot points; these are two bolts—one that holds the derailleur to the frame and the other that holds the cage to the derailleur body. Shifting problems can also be caused by a loose or dry chain.

A crooked frame, misalignment between your chainwheels and cluster, and a broken derailleur spring can also foul up shifting. The first problem you're stuck with; the latter two you'd better take to a dealer.

Hub shifter

THE ONLY THING you should do with a hub shifter is oil it. You'll find a fitting on the rear hub; just put a few drops in every month or so. If something goes haywire inside (which doesn't happen often), take the wheel off and bring it to a mechanic you trust or a reasonable facsimile.

But wait! Your problem may not be in the hub at all. If your bike won't stay in the selected gear or the shift lever (or twist grip) doesn't move smoothly, the problem may be in the shift lever mechanism, in the cable or in the indicator (the device that connects the cable with the hub, see diagram).

Two types of 3-speed shift indicators: standard (top) and bellcrank (below). Bottom: two speed selectors. You may not have cable pulley (7). Parts: 1) indicator; 2) locknut; 3) double locknuts for bellcrank type; 4) sleeve; 5) cable; 6) housing; 7) pulley; 8) selectors; 9) chain rod; 10) axle; 11) "N" marker; 12) nut groove.

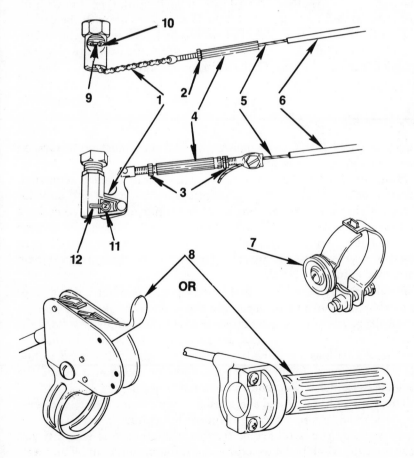

When shifting trouble hits, first make sure the cable (5) is okay. If broken, get it replaced. Check also that the cable is threaded through any pulleys (7) on the frame. If the cable is okay, your problem is in the shift mechanism on the handlebars or in the indicators. Back pedal the bike slowly (with the bike on a rack) and shift the bike. If the lever (or twist grip) is hard to move or won't stay in place after shifting, replace it. Let's say you're not sure whether it's the indicator or the shift lever mechanism. The thing to do is to disconnect the indicator from the shift mechanism to find out. Loosen the locknut (2) or locknuts (3) and disconnect the sleeve (4). Now work the gear selector. If it is still hard or impossible to move into any of the gears or overly slippery, it is definitely your problem, and must be replaced. However, if it works fine, your problem is the indicator. This calls for adjustment.

Indicator adjustment. Shift the bike to direct drive, usually designated N (for normal) or 2 (second gear). Now go to the back wheel and look at the indicator. You should find either a standard mechanism (top in diagram) or a bellcrank type ((bottom). If you find the standard type, loosen up the locknut (2) and turn the sleeve (4) until the end of the chain rod (9) is even with the end of the axle (10). Now tighten the locknut against the sleeve. If you have the bellcrank type, loosen both locknuts (3) and turn sleeve until the N (11) lines up with the groove (12) in the housing nut. Now tighten the locknuts against the sleeve.

If that doesn't do it, and the shift lever gizmo and cable are okay, the problem is inside the hub. That's a job for an expert.

Pedals

PEDALS DON'T REQUIRE much care. All they must do is turn on their spindles so you can pedal properly.

However, there are three things you can do with a pedal: remove it, adjust it or overhaul it. The last project is a drastic one and only for those with expensive pedals. Some pedals are nonadjustable (they have no bearings) and you can't work on them even if you want to (except for removing them). Surprisingly, many of these cheapie models work fine. But if yours give you trouble, don't try to fix them; replace them with good adjustable pedals.

You should know how to remove your pedals in case you want to take your bike on an airplane

Pedal removal. No matter what kind of pedals you have, you'll want to be able to remove them, especially if you want to take your bike on an airplane. All you have to do is unscrew the spindle (5) from the crank. Check to see if you can get an adjustable wrench around the spindle. Sometimes a thin pedal spanner is required. It's good to find out what you need, for instance, before you get to the airport and the baggage clerk insists you remove those nasty pedals.

There is a right pedal and a left pedal. They are not interchangeable. So mark them before you take them off the cranks if they aren't already marked. You will have no trouble telling which is which if you have toe clips. Each pedal unscrews in a different direction. The right-

side (chain-side) pedal unscrews counterclockwise; the left pedal unscrews clockwise. An easier way to think of it is that both pedals
unscrew toward the back of the bike, screw in toward the front.

Pedal adjustment. If your adjustable pedal—adjustable models can
be spotted by their dust caps (1)— won't spin smoothly, your bearings
are too tight; if the pedal moves side to side when pedaling, the
bearings don't have the proper pressure against them.

First, remove the dust cap. Some have wrench surfaces; others must
be pried off with a screwdriver. Inside you'll see a locknut (2), a keyed
washer (3) and a cone (4). Let's say your problem is that the pedal is
too loose and moves side to side. Loosen the locknut and hand tighten
the cone (clockwise). Now back the cone off about a quarter turn. Hold
the cone and tighten the locknut against it. Spin the pedal. If it binds,
you have to loosen the cone. Replace the dust cap and you're set.

If you can't get the pedal to spin smoothly without side play, try to
get a drop of oil into the bearings on both sides of the pedal; note that

Rattrap pedal: 1) dust cap; 2) locknut; 3) keyed washer; 4) cone;
5) spindle; 6) crank-side bearings; 7) outside bearings; 8) pedal.

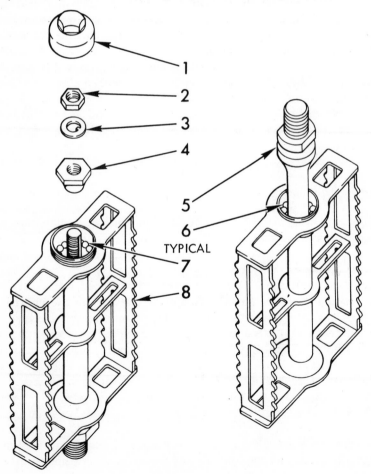

TYPICAL

there are bearings (6) around the spindle on the crank side as well (these have no adjustable cone).

Pedal overhaul. If that doesn't work, an overhaul might help, though there's a good chance it won't. If your pedals are cheap, it may be best just to replace them. If you have something like Campagnolo or Lyotard pedals, you'll want to try an overhaul before replacing them. Some Campi pedals cost close to $40.

Overhauling a pedal is like overhauling a hub or anything else. You take it apart, and clean all parts; check for missing or damaged bearings, replacing them. The same goes for pitted cones. However, if you find pitted races (the surface in the pedal the bearings roll around in), the pedal will never work right. You'll have to replace it. If you find the spindle threads damaged, you'll have to find a replacement spindle, which may be difficult. This probably means replacement, too.

See the drawing for aid in disassembling and re-assembling your pedal. Keep in mind that when you remove the cone (4), the bearings will be loose, so be ready to catch them. The next step is to pull the spindle out of the pedal in which case the crank-side bearings (6) will fall out. After you've cleaned all parts and replaced any that are damaged, reconstruct the pedal, first coating the bearing races with grease. Stick the spindle (5) only about two inches into the pedal. Holding it in place there, replace the crank-side bearings. Tweezers always help. Now apply a little grease over the bearings and slip the spindle all the way into the pedal. Holding the pedal and spindle, turn the pedal over and place the outside bearings (7) in their race. Apply grease over these bearings. Install cone, washer and locknut. Adjust the pedal as described earlier and re-install the dust cap; re-install pedal on the crank.

Don't forget that when you remove the cone from the pedal, the bearings will drop out. Be ready to catch them

Cranks

CRANKS SOMETIMES WORK LOOSE, in which case they must be tightened. Or they sometimes break, in which case they must be replaced. Bent cranks can be reshaped, but this must be done by a shop with the proper equipment.

There are three kinds of cranks: cottered, the expensive cotterless kind and one-piece (or American) cranks. The last are the cheapest, but they have the fewest problems, which is one reason I refuse to sneer at them. One-piece cranks can't come loose on their axle (or spindle) because cranks and axle are all one unit. All they can do is break, in which case you must replace the whole thing. Take the bike to the shop where you bought it. Hopefully the warranty will cover it. Cottered cranks have the most problems and are the hardest to work on. Most 10-speed cranks are (you guessed it) cottered. Let's start with the hardest.

Cottered cranks (tightening). If your cottered cranks are slipping, fix them as quickly as possible to avoid damaging them (though this is less critical than with cotterless cranks). You'll feel a loose crank easily when pedaling. To determine which crank is slipping, hold one crank at a time and try to move the other one. You can try to tighten up the offending crank by tightening the nut (4) on the cotter. If that doesn't work, and it probably won't, either the cotter must be tapped in tighter or the cotter is bent or broken and must be replaced. In either case, I'd suggest you find a shop with the special tools for tapping in or tapping out the pin. But if this is not convenient, you can use a light hammer to try it yourself. To tap in, rest the crank firmly on a wooden block and hit the cotter lightly on its head (5). Don't clobber it hard, or you could wreck bearings in the bottom bracket. After tapping in, tighten the nut again.

Here is a typical cottered crank set. Yours may not look exactly like this, but the parts will be similar: 1) chainwheel; 2) the chainwheel bolt; 3) crank; 4) cotter-pin nut; 5) the cotter-pin head; 6) spindle.

1   2   3   4   5   6

Cottered cranks (removal). You must remove the crank if tapping in will not tighten it (usually the sign of a damaged cotter) or if the crank is bent or broken and must be replaced. To remove, you'll have to drive out the pin. If convenient, take the bike to a shop. But if you want to try it yourself, remove the nut and washer (4) and support the crank on a wooden block. Now you must loosen the cotter by striking the threaded end. If you have a drift punch, this is the best weapon for this chore. Otherwise bash it with a hammer. Hit the cotter sharply; this is actually safer than tapping it lightly, which can bend the cotter. Remove the pin and take the crank (3) off the spindle (6). Get a new pin, new crank, whatever you need. If you're replacing a right-side crank, you'll have to remove the chainwheels (1) by removing their bolts (2). If the chainwheel and crank are one piece, you'll have to get a whole new unit.

A drift punch is the best weapon to use to loosen the cotter, but next best thing to do is just to bash it with a hammer.

Cottered cranks (installation). Replacing a cottered crank with a new pin or installing a brand new crank is fairly simple. Stick the crank on the spindle so it's pointing the opposite direction of the other crank. Press the cotter through its hole finger tight. You should have threads extending ¼ inch or more on the other side. If you don't, pull out the cotter and file down its flat side. Now try it again. Support the crank on a wooden block and tap the cotter in gently until it's properly seated. Install washer and nut.

Cotterless cranks (tightening). As soon as you suspect your cotterless cranks are loose, stop pedaling and tighten them. Cotterless cranks are invariably made of soft alloy and their axle holes can be distorted if they're loose. Tightening is easy, but you'll need a special two-part tool: a socket, sometimes called an installer (5 on page 363) and an extractor (4). Different crank brands require their own brand of crank tool.

You should find a dust cap (1) on the crank. The one shown can be removed with a large screwdriver; other brands require a 5mm Allen wrench. After the cap is off, look inside and you'll find a bolt (3). Stick the crank socket tool on the bolt and tighten it hard. Check the crank by trying to move it while holding the opposite crank firm. Everything okay? Then replace the dust cap and you're set.

Cotterless cranks (removal). If the crank just won't tighten up, the axle hole is probably reamed out of shape. You'll have to replace the crank. And, of course, if your crank is broken you must remove and replace it. Remove the dust cap and put the socket tool on the bolt. Turn it counterclockwise to remove it. Remove the washer. This, however, will not take the crank off. Take your extractor tool in hand. Note that it consists of a post (7) that screws in and out of a threaded cup (4). Screw the post all the way out. Now thread the extractor cup into the dust cap threads finger-tight. Grab hold of the crank with one hand and put the socket tool over the head of the extractor post. Screw in the extractor post until it pushes against the axle, thus loosening the crank. If this doesn't loosen the crank, take the socket off the post and tap the post lightly with a hammer or the side of a wrench. When

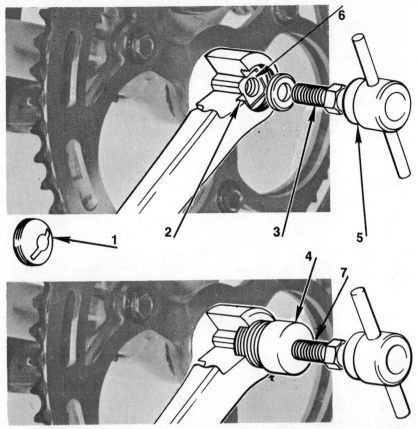

the crank feels loose, take it off the axle. Replace it with the exact size and brand. If replacing the right-side crank, remove the chainwheels.

Cotterless cranks (installation). First, with a clean rag clean the end of the spindle (6), the crank threads (2) and the crank bolt (3). Lightly apply oil to the latter two. Slip the crank on the spindle (pointing in the opposite direction of the other crank). Put the washer on the bolt which you thread into the axle. Thread it as far as possible with your fingers. Now put the socket tool on the bolt and tighten it. As you tighten up, keep checking the crank to make sure it's seated solidly on the spindle. Screw the bolt in hard. Install the dust cap.

Bottom bracket

THE BOTTOM BRACKET is the assembly of bearings, cups, lock-rings and an axle that connects your cranks and let's them rotate smoothly. (On one-piece cranks there is no separate axle because it's an integral part of the cranks.) What can go wrong? Sometimes the assembly works loose so the axle slides sideways. Less common, the bottom bracket is too tight and it's hard to turn the cranks. Either of these problems can be cured with adjustment. In the second case, tight axle, check also for more serious problems. Take the chain off the front sprocket and rotate the cranks. If you hear crunching noises your hanger assembly is full of dirt or your bearings, cups, etc. are damaged. This calls for overhaul.

How often should you mess around with the bottom bracket? One expert says he overhauls his about every 20 years.

Hopefully you will be plagued by none of these problems. Don't mess with the bottom bracket unless you have a specific problem. I asked one rider, who also happens to be president of a large European bike company, how often he overhauls the bottom bracket. "Every twenty years" was his reply.

Working on the bottom bracket (even making a simple adjustment) is best done with the special tools for the job. You can improvise, but if in doubt take the bike to a shop.

Bottom bracket adjustment. On bikes with cottered and cotterless cranks, the bottom bracket consists of an axle with a set of bearings on either side. The chainwheel side has a fixed cup (1); the left side has an adjustable cup (6). Obviously, you must adjust from the left side. First, loosen the lockring (5). Note that it has slots in it which can be hooked by a special spanner (or hook wrench). If you have this tool, fine, but

Cottered, cotterless bottom bracket: 1) fixed cup; 2) axle; 3) caged bearings or 4) loose; 5) lockring; 6) adjustable cup; 7) right-side loose bearings or 8) caged right-side bearings.

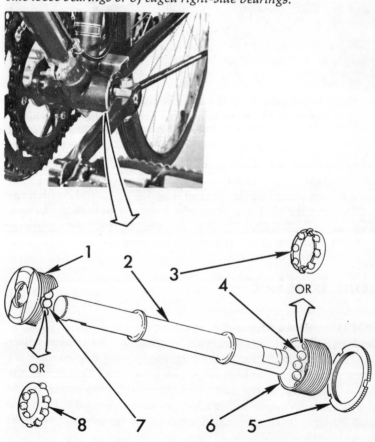

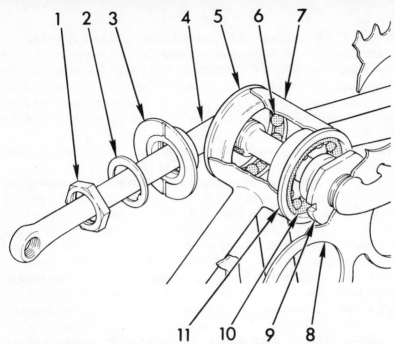

*One-piece bottom bracket: 1) locknut; 2) washer; 3) adjustable cone;
4) crank arm; 5) cup; 6) bearings; 7) bracket shell; 8) chainwheel;
9) cone; 10) bearings; 11) cup.*

who does? So stick a screwdriver in one slot and carefully tap it with
a hammer to drive the lockring open. If your problem is a loose axle
(usually the case) you must tighten the adjustable cup (6). Again, a
nice special tool is called for (a pin wrench), but you can get by with a
small Phillips screwdriver. Note there are a bunch of holes in the cup.
Fit the screwdriver in at an angle and drive the cup tight with a hammer. Like any other bearing adjustment, when the cup is tight, back it
off slightly. Check the cranks to see if they rotate properly, re-adjust if
necessary, and tighten up the lockring.

One-piece adjustment. Adjusting a one-piece bracket is really no
different except that you'll find a locknut instead of a lockring, and you
loosen it by turning it clockwise instead of counterclockwise, the case
with most lockrings. See the one-piece diagram. The cone (3 in one-
piece drawing) under the locknut is loosened counterclockwise, tightened clockwise. Note it has slots to accept a screwdriver.

Overhaul (cottered and cotterless). While I don't agree with those
who want to pull everything out of the bracket at the drop of a wrench,
the thing can get dirty because it's so close to the ground. First, you
have to get the cranks off. Now take off the lockring (5) on the left
side of the bike. Remove the adjustable cup (6). Get the bearings out
which may be loose (4) or caged (3). The stationary cup (1) on the
other side of the bike will come off if you have the right tool and plenty
of strength. But don't bother. It's much better to work on the hanger
shell from one side only. Pull the axle out from the open side. Get out

the right-side bearings (7 or 8). Some bottom brackets (Campagnolo for one) also have a plastic collar around the axle to protect it from dirt coming down from the seat tube. Hook it out with a wire.

Overhaul the assembly as in any other overhaul. Clean everything with solvent. Check for damaged parts, etc. Be sure to check the fixed cup (1) as well, which you left installed. Clean out the inside of the shell, too.

Reconstruction is straightforward if you lay the bike on its right side. But you'll have to reach in the shell to grease the fixed cup. Then place the bearings in before putting back the axle. If you have caged bearings you can slip them over the axle, then stick the axle in. The long end of the axle goes in first. Replace the plastic collar if you have one. Then grease the adjustable cup (6), place the bearings in it, and screw into place. Adjust the cup so the axle spins freely but without side play. Replace the lockring and tighten up. Replace the cranks.

One-piece crank bottom bracket overhaul. Overhaul is the same as above except that you have to pull the left crank (4) right through the hanger shell. Take a good look at the one-piece drawing. To disassemble, remove the locknut (1) and keyed washer (2). Remove the adjustable cone (3) with a screwdriver. Pick out the bearings (6) and you will now be able to pull the crank arm all the way out of the bracket shell. Remove the right-side bearings (10) and overhaul as usual. The cups (5, 11), however, will remain in the shell. If they're damaged and must be removed, drive them out with a hammer and punch.

Chapter 14

Section 6: Where to write for info

Bicycle manufacturers and/or distributors

HAVING TROUBLE FINDING the bike you want? Here's a selected list of manufacturers/distributors who perhaps can give you the name of the store nearest you which handles their brand. Those brands marked with an asterisk (*) include a track model in their line.

AMF: AMF Wheel Goods Division, P.O. Box 344, Olney, Ill. 62450.

*Atala: Stuyvesant Bicycle Distributors, Inc., 8 East 13th St., New York, N.Y. 10003.

Azuki: West Coast Cycle, 1241 E. Watsoncenter Rd., Carson, Calif. 90744.

Bertin: Moretti Imports, Inc., Box 37, Vail, Colo. 81657.

Bianchi: Sentry Products, 884 Mahler Rd., Burlingame, Calif. 94010.

Bottechia: See Atala.

Bugatti: 715 Park Ave., New York, N.Y. 10003.

Caloi: See Azuki.

Cazenave: Benoto, Inc., 360 N. Michigan Ave., Chicago, Ill. 60601.

CCM: CCM, USA, 75 Boxwood La., S. Cheektowago, N.Y. 14227.

Columbia: Columbia Manufacturing Co., Inc., Westfield, Mass. 01085.

Crescent: Don Docksteader Enterprises, 1090 W. Georgia St., Vancouver, B.C., Canada.

Crystal: Beacon Cycle & Supply Co., Inc., 1801 E. Bolivar Ave., Milwaukee, Wis. 53207.

DBS: Intersport, Inc., P.O. Box 1341, Bellevue, Wash. 98009.

*Falcon: Omega Import-Export, 7607-B East Sewells Point Rd., Norfolk, Va. 23513.

Ficelle: Ficelle, Inc., 120 E. 16th St., New York, N.Y. 10003.

*Follis: Euro Imports, 2124 Sepulveda, Los Angeles, Calif. 90025.

*Frejus: European Bicycle Importer, Inc., Robert C. Bentley, 3030 Bridgeway, Sausalito, Calif. 94965. Also, Thomas Avenia, 2191 Third Avenue, New York, N.Y.

*Fuji: Toshoku America, Inc., 551 Fifth Ave. Room 1010, New York, N.Y. 10017.

*Gitane: Mel Pinto Imports, 2860 Annandale, Falls Church, Va. 20042.

Hosteler: Wheel Goods Corp., 2737 Hennepin, Minneapolis, Minn. 55408.

Huffy: Huffman Manufacturing Co., 7701 Byers Rd., P.O. Box 1204, Dayton, Ohio 45401.

Italvega: Lawee, Inc., 531 W. 15th, Long Beach, Calif. 90813.

C. Itoh: C. Itoh & Co. (America) Inc., 270 Park Ave., New York, N.Y. 10017.

Kabuki: See C. Itoh

Legnano: See Frejus.

*LeJeune: Franklin Imports, 106 W. 18th St., New York, N.Y. 10024.

Liberia: Shaker Velo-Sport, 18735 Chagrin Blvd., Shaker Heights, Ohio 44122.

Maserati: Elsco Corp., 1645 Jessie St., Jacksonville, Fla. 32206.

Mercian: See Liberia.

Mercier: Beacon Cycle & Supply Co., Inc., 1801 E. Bolivar Ave., Milwaukee, Wis. 53207.

Mirella: See Mercier.

Mossberg: O. F. Mossberg & Sons, Inc., 7 Grasso Ave., North Haven, Conn. 06473.

Motobecane: See Italvega.

Murray: Murray Ohio Manufacturing Co., 635 Thompson La., Nashville, Tenn. 37204.

Nishiki: West Coast Cycle, 1241 E. Watsoncenter Rd., Carson, Calif. 90744.

Nord-France: Victor Sports, Inc., 184 Main St., Ridgefield Park, N.J. 07660.

Olympia: See Nord-France.

Panasonic: Panasonic, Pam Am Bldg., 200 Park Ave., New York, N.Y. 10017.

Paris Sport: See Nord-France.

*Peugeot: See LeJeune.

Raleigh: Raleigh Industries of America, Inc., 1168 Commonwealth Ave., Boston, Mass. 02134.

Rapido: American Jawa, Ltd., 185 Express St., Plainview, N.Y. 11803.

*Schwinn: Schwinn Bicycle Co., 1856 N. Kostner Ave., Chicago, Ill. 60639.

Sutter: Belleri, Inc., 1700 Avenue 'L', Riviera Beach, Fla. 33404.

*Teledyne: Teledyne Linair, 651 W. Knox St., Gardena, Calif. 90248.

Triumph: See Raleigh.

*Urago: See Cazenave.

Velo-Sport: See Liberia.

Windsor: See Nishiki.

*Zeus: Zeus/USA, 11 Stone St., New York, N.Y. 10004.